Global Human Smuggling

Global Human Smuggling

Comparative Perspectives

Second Edition

Edited by
David Kyle and Rey Koslowski

The Johns Hopkins University Press
Baltimore

© 2001, 2011 The Johns Hopkins University Press
All rights reserved. Published 2011
Printed in the United States of America on acid-free paper
9 8 7 6 5 4 3 2 1

The Johns Hopkins University Press
2715 North Charles Street
Baltimore, Maryland 21218-4363
www.press.jhu.edu

Library of Congress Cataloging-in-Publication Data

Global human smuggling : comparative perspectives / edited by
David Kyle and Rey Koslowski. —2nd ed.
    p. cm.
  Includes bibliographical references and index.
  ISBN-13: 978-1-4214-0198-0 (pbk. : alk. paper)
  ISBN-10: 1-4214-0198-3 (pbk. : alk. paper)
  1. Emigration and immigration. 2. Illegal aliens. 3. Smuggling.
4. Transnational crime. 5. Organized crime. I. Kyle, David. II.
Koslowski, Rey.
  JV6201.G56 2011
  364.15—dc22   2011000462

A catalog record for this book is available from the British
Library.

*Special discounts are available for bulk purchases of this book. For
more information, please contact Special Sales at 410-516-6936 or
specialsales@press.jhu.edu.*

The Johns Hopkins University Press uses environmentally
friendly book materials, including recycled text paper that is
composed of at least 30 percent post-consumer waste, whenever
possible.

Contents

Preface to the Second Edition

Ten years ago the topic of human smuggling and trafficking was relatively new for academic researchers, though smuggling of people as part of a wider migration industry is very old. In the past decade since the first edition of this volume, much has changed globally, directly impacting the phenomenon of human smuggling. Migrant smuggling and human trafficking are now more entrenched than ever in many regions, with efforts to combat both—within a narrow criminal frame—largely unsuccessful and often counterproductive.

As an attempt to understand and broaden our understanding of this phenomenon, the first edition of *Global Human Smuggling* was well received based on the number of citations and positive reviews it received; it even inspired a 2003 PBS documentary, *Dying to Leave* (Wide Angle Series; www.pbs.org/wnet/wideangle/episodes/dying-to-leave/video-full-episode/1126/). However, there is much left to be done in understanding this complex area of global social life. This updated and expanded edition takes into account some of the trends and events of the past several years. Because the contributors have had varied careers and interests on this topic, and because of the requirements of each chapter, some chapters have only minor edits, whereas others are completely revised, including the Introduction. We have also added three new chapters in this edition.

For this edition, David Kyle would like to thank research interns and fellows at the Gifford Center for Population Studies at UC Davis, especially Rachel Ray, Danielle Salas, and Rachel Goldstein. At the Johns Hopkins University Press, he thanks Henry Tom and Suzanne Flinchbaugh for their excellent guidance.

Rey Koslowski thanks Kate E. Tunstall, who asked him to write a comment on former assistant secretary of state Harold Hongju Koh's "The New Global Slave Trade," which appeared together with Koh's essay in *Displacement, Asylum, Migration: Oxford Amnesty Lectures 2004* (Oxford University Press, 2006). The sections of the Introduction to this second edition entitled "Moral Economy of Human Smuggling and Trafficking" and "Asylum and Human Smuggling"

viii   *Preface to the Second Edition*

are based on lines of argument that Koslowski initially developed while writing the piece. Koslowski also thanks the John D. and Catherine T. MacArthur Foundation for grant support during 2006 when he expanded his writings on international cooperation on human smuggling and trafficking, some of which are incorporated into his completely revised chapter "Economic Globalization, Human Smuggling, and Global Governance." Finally, he thanks Laura Gonzalez-Murphy, who assisted with research that contributed to his chapter.

Preface to the First Edition

This project has its roots in our late night discussions of a paper David Kyle presented while we were fellows of a Summer Institute for Young Scholars sponsored by the German American Academic Council (GAAC) and the Social Science Research Council (SSRC), held in New York City in 1996 and in Berlin in 1997. We are very grateful to the GAAC and the SSRC and to the Institute co-conveners, Rainer Munz and Aristide Zolberg, for bringing us together. We also benefited enormously from the provocative and informative discussions we had with the other GAAC Summer Institute fellows and invited speakers. We hope this volume demonstrates the need for ongoing cross-disciplinary discussion and cooperation on the multifaceted topic of international migration and, more specifically, irregular clandestine migration.

This volume is based on a set of papers presented at two meetings that we planned together. The first workshop was held at Rutgers University–Newark, under the auspices of the Center for Global Change and Governance, on May 15, 1998. The second meeting was held at the University of California, Davis, on October 10, 1998, and was sponsored by the University of California's Comparative Immigration and Integration Program, the University of California's Institute on Global Conflict and Cooperation, and the Institute for Governmental Affairs. We are grateful to Phil Martin for co-organizing our meeting at UC Davis. Special thanks go to Richard Langhorne, director of the Rutgers Center for Global Change and Governance, for providing financial support for both meetings. We also thank the Center for Global Change and Governance for cosponsoring a June 2000 meeting in Washington, D.C., which enabled several contributors to this volume to present their findings and arguments to policymakers and other academic researchers from the United States and from several other countries; we also thank the co-organizers of the Transatlantic Workshop on Human Smuggling, at which they were presented, Frederick Heckmann of the European Forum for Migration Studies, and Susan Martin of the Institute for the Study of International Migration at Georgetown University.

David Kyle is very appreciative of a year-long research fellowship and participation in multidisciplinary meetings on the topic of international migration sponsored by the University of California at Davis Humanities Institute. Rey Koslowski also thanks the Center of International Studies at Princeton University for supporting his research and writing as well as his organizational efforts to place the issues raised in the volume before the policy community. Most of all, we wish to extend our heartfelt gratitude to the contributors of this volume for their professional efforts; they made this volume not only possible but a pleasure on which to work. Undoubtedly, we will hear more from them on this important emerging topic.

Global Human Smuggling

Introduction

David Kyle and Rey Koslowski

United by powerful technologies, complex economic systems, and social institutions, the world is globalized for the first time in human history; it also now faces the truly global challenges of a transformative financial recession, the myriad effects of climate change, and the implications of an additional three billion people by midcentury. In sharp contrast, the ability for people to seek opportunities and escape serious problems of scarce resources, distributed unevenly within and among states, by resettling elsewhere is far from globalized. In fact, the earth is now carved up by political boundaries deeply entrenched in the global system of nation-states. This book is about people on every continent with impossible choices crossing international borders; it is also about how attempts by states to thwart, regulate, manage, exploit, and limit human mobility are creating informal and illegal (though not entirely illicit) industries in close partnership with legal institutions of capital production and consumption, especially employers also attempting to survive under "globalization" and now a global recession. Borders are not in themselves a problem for human mobility and resettlement, as they may imply many things, including the frontiers of exploration and ambiguous zones of cooperation and multiculturalism. Today, however, borders are more entrenched than ever in a discourse of state security and distrust of "foreign nationals," whether they are escaping political corruption and conflict, a crushing lack of economic opportunity and freedom, or the devastating impact of too little or too much water.

Like the first edition of *Global Human Smuggling*, this second edition explores the historical context, social organization, and political ramifications of human smuggling across international borders as a global phenomenon, presenting diverse empirical research, conducted in several different regions, that is either explicitly or implicitly comparative. More than a subcategory of international migration, the trade in humans and migrants is a topic that intersects contemporary anxieties concerning the global political economy, ethnic and gender stratification, multiculturalism, population growth, political corruption, transnational crime, the Internet, human rights abuses, climate change, and the (in)ability of states and global agencies to manage any of these effectively. Using social scientific research, this volume examines the regional and organizational diversity of unauthorized migrations, some leading to freedom and safety and others to slavery, in several sending regions. Though our initial vision of a growing body of empirical research has only been partially realized since the first edition, we still believe that it is the combination of grounded regional and policy research and a global comparative vision that will be most fruitful to the development of our understanding of this complex form of human mobility defined, if not instigated, mostly by state policies. We consider in this revised introduction to *Global Human Smuggling* some of the original themes since its publication in the spring of 2001, which have held up surprisingly well during the past ten years. Of course, the events of September 11, 2001, and the creation of the U.S. Department of Homeland Security soon after only deepened the security frame for understanding human smuggling and trafficking that we explored in the first edition. We also reflect on the moral economy of human smuggling and trafficking, the increasing percentage of the world's asylum seekers who escape political violence only by being smuggled, and the implications for human smuggling of a warming world.

If 1993 is the year human smuggling crashed into our living rooms with the *Golden Venture* fiasco (the name of an ill-fated ship carrying undocumented Chinese from Fujian Province), the year 1998 could be viewed as the year that human smuggling became an official "global problem." In that year there were major busts of human smuggling rings, denouncements of undocumented migrant exploitation by national and world leaders, several international conferences, and a popular Hollywood movie (*Lethal Weapon 4*) depicting "evil snakeheads" and their human cargo from China. For example, the U.S. Justice Department created the Worker Exploitation Taskforce primarily because of a specific case involving sixteen individuals who had orchestrated an elaborate scheme to enslave young female Mexican nationals and force them into prostitution. The women, some as young as fourteen, were smuggled into Texas, transported to Florida and South Carolina, and, instead of being given legitimate work as promised, forced to become prostitutes to pay back their smuggling debt. "We must get these modern day slavery cases off the front pages of the newspapers and into the history books," said former attorney general Janet Reno (Justice Department press release, April 23, 1998). As a global phenomenon, human trafficking in slaves from such places as Ukraine, Myanmar (Burma), Laos, Nepal, and the Philippines, mostly for a commercial sex industry, is so profitable that criminal business people invest in involuntary brothels much as they would do so in a mining operation; in step with arms-length capitalism, Kevin Bales asserts that some investors in Asia may not even realize they are profiting from human misery in the form of slaves held in brothels (1999).

Yet these cases of trafficking in humans as commodities signal a wider phenomenon of the increasing smuggling of *migrants* seeking the living standards of developed countries as well as those escaping political persecution and disasters in a world with ever more restrictive asylum policies. Although many human smuggling operations around the world are more analogous to travel agencies than to the infamous slave traders of the past century—some even offering legitimate guarantees of successful entry and work—there is a diverse range of smugglers with differing levels of organization, ability, and trustworthiness; some prove to be just as deadly as the brothels of sex slaves supplied by the human traffickers. Since the late 1990s, nearly every week has brought stories of the deaths of clandestine migrants somewhere in the world, deaths resulting from horrendous acts of violence or simple miscalculations on the part of smugglers or the migrants themselves as they attempt to evade the authorities. One incident that captured world attention involved fifty-eight migrants from Fujian, China, on June 19, 2000; trapped inside a sealed tomato truck in Dover, England, they had already suffocated to death by the time a police officer had it pried opened. Ten years later, reports of migrants dying en route are now relatively common: For example, on April 9, 2008, fifty-four Burmese refugees suffocated to death in a container truck in Ranong Province on the west coast of Thailand while they were attempting to enter the country illegally; similarly, one year later, sixty-two Afghan migrants suffocated to death in a truck packed with one hundred fleeing into Pakistan.

These incidents illustrate not only the complex human rights issues involved in contemporary smuggling—given that some would be considered more properly asylum seekers and, hence, the smugglers are providing an escape route—but also the global nature of the human smuggling of migrants and the trafficking of people tricked into contemporary forms of slavery. Few countries of the world remain untouched by human smuggling, migrant tragedies and victimization, the related corruption of public officials, and the political ramifications of all of these. In fact, it is the long-term political consequences and enforcement strategies that may have a wider effect on all of us. For example, on August 25, 2000, in Washington, the president-elect of Mexico, Vicente Fox, outlined his vision of a completely open border with the United States; as part of the reason, he cited the hundreds of deaths resulting from migrants running the gauntlet of a virtually militarized border with an ostensibly friendly neighbor. Just a year later, and one week after Vicente Fox returned to the United States floating the same idea with President Bush by his side, the events of September 11 not only killed any chance of an open border but also completely transformed cross-border mobility, soon reorganized in the United States under the new Department of Homeland Security. While tens of millions of air travelers from the global north were inconvenienced by new security measures, others from the south have given up hope of a return to a more welcoming period of legal pathways for asylum seekers and migrants that do not entail visa application queues of years or even decades to clear.

Defining Smuggling, Trafficking, and Illegal Migration

Human smuggling is an individual's crossing of a state's international border without that state's authorization and with the assistance of paid smugglers. International human trafficking occurs when an individual who has been smuggled across a border is coerced, especially into forced labor or prostitution.

Human trafficking across international borders is often a subset of human smuggling, which is itself a part of the broader phenomenon of what is variously termed "irregular," "unauthorized," "undocumented," or "illegal" migration. Illegal migration can be the result of individuals entering states though authorized ports of entry by fraud or concealment within conveyances, crossing states' borders without authorization between ports of entry, or entering though ports of entry with appropriate authorization and/or a visa but then overstaying the terms of entry. Trafficked individuals who are forced into prostitution or labor may have initially voluntarily engaged the services of a smuggler to cross international borders illegally but then upon arriving find themselves coerced into labor through violence directed at them and/or their families back home. The key difference between human smuggling and trafficking is coercion, whether through direct application of physical force or the threat of the use of force.

It is very difficult to disentangle the processes of human smuggling from the trafficking of people because these processes are generally handled by networks of intermediaries rather than end to end by the same individual or organization. Consider a typical situation in which a young Moldovan woman is told by an Italian trafficker's Moldovan recruiter that he has friends in Italy who can get her a job working illegally in an Italian restaurant in Germany. The recruiter makes arrangements with a series of smugglers (who may or may not know that he is a recruiter working for an Italian trafficker) in order to transport the woman to Italy. The Moldovan woman might be transported across the Adriatic in an Albanian smuggler's speedboat together with Turkish men seeking to work in the Netherlands and Iraqis fleeing sectarian violence. In the instance of the crossing, all the individuals are being smuggled, as they are simply paying a fee for an illegal border crossing. However, when the Moldovan woman arrives in Italy, has her passport seized, and is forced into prostitution, what on the face of it was an act of human smuggling becomes an act of trafficking for forced prostitution.

Most media coverage, legislation, and past international treaties on human trafficking focus on the trafficking of women and children into forced prostitution. Although such exploitation of women and children is the most reprehensible variant of trafficking, it is only a part of the trafficking of all forms of labor. For example, a study by Free the Slaves and the University of California, Berkeley (2004) that was based on cases of trafficking reported in the American media estimated that at any given time more than ten thousand people, if not tens of thousands, work as forced laborers in the United States; approximately half of the identified cases are of prostitution and child exploitation, but the rest are forced labor in domestic services, agriculture, sweatshops, and food service. Of those forced laborers, the largest group was Chinese, then Mexicans and Vietnamese.

Debt bondage and involuntary servitude are defining features of human trafficking, as opposed to just smuggling people across borders for a fee. Because of very high smuggling fees, migrants who have been smuggled from China are more likely than other smuggled migrants to enter into debt bondage arrangements backed up by threats of violence against them and their families in China. The 260 passengers of the smuggling ship the *Golden Venture*, which washed ashore at a New York beach in 1993, agreed to pay an average fee of $35,000 to be smuggled to the United States. The fee for passage from China to New York City in 2009 was as high as $75,000 (see Chin, this volume, Chap. 7). Typically, customers pay smugglers a down payment (usually $1,000–$1,500), and then family members, relatives, or friends pay the balance of the fee upon arrival and the migrant repays the debt at no or relatively low interest rates. A smaller percentage of migrants become indebted to organized crime groups and loan sharks who charge much higher interest rates and back up debt repayment with enforcers. Generally, the migrants work in garment factories and Chinese restaurants, often up to eighty hours a week, and live in very small spaces where it is not uncommon for them to share beds by sleeping in shifts.

While in the New York City area debts might be primarily held by relatives and friends (whose treatment of the migrant may also vary), in American Samoa and the U.S. Territories of the Northern Mariana Islands, Chinese, Taiwanese, and Korean employment agencies, migrant traffickers, and unscrupulous subcontractors in the territories have exploited migrants through debt bondage arrangements to cheaply produce "made in the USA" garments that can be sold at high profits. It was a case of trafficking of sweatshop labor to these territories that produced the largest antitrafficking case in U.S. history (Jordan, 2007). With fees of up to $75,000 for the promise of work in the United States and Europe, the potential for exploitative debt bondage arrangements among smuggled Chinese migrants is all too great. This is reflected in the increasing number of cases of Chinese workers found working in exploitative and dangerous conditions, whether in U.S. sweatshops, in Italian shoe factories, or along United Kingdom beaches picking cockles.

A definition of human smuggling, including its social organization and political and economic significance, is still very much a work in progress. In part, this is because, while this activity is not new, its global scope, diversity, and complexity are new: professional human smugglers have plied their trade with the educated Indian middle class and impoverished Cubans; North Africans have been smuggled into Spain; Albanians and Kosovar refugees have been ferried to Italy; Chinese have been flown into the European Union via Moscow; and tens of thousands of Russian and Eastern European women have been trafficked throughout Western Europe to work as prostitutes—some unwittingly (International Organization for Migration [IOM], 1996, 1998a; Global Survival Network, 1997). Consequently, both governments and activists socially construct "the problem" in different ways depending on what or for whom they are advocating action. For example, sending countries have a different set of concerns than receiving countries. Because the activity also intersects with other well-known and novel social problems such as unemployment, illegal migration, prostitution, and cybercrime, preexisting advocacy groups and state agencies tend to follow a predictable pattern of either promoting or discounting certain aspects of human smuggling as a global social problem. As the contributors to the first edition of this volume pointed out, simply defining the phenomenon of human smuggling, which was sometimes used synonymously with human trafficking and sometimes contrasted with human trafficking as a more coercive form, was one of the main stumbling points for greater governmental and nongovernmental organization (NGO) cooperation. The definitional issue was taken up by the member states of the United Nations in November 2000, when the UN General Assembly adopted the UN Convention against Transnational Organized Crime, as well as its Protocol to Prevent, Suppress and Punish Trafficking in Persons, Especially Women and Children and the Protocol against the Smuggling of Migrants by Land, Sea and Air (for a detailed discussion, see Koslowski, this volume, Chap. 2). The UN defined the "smuggling of migrants" as "the procurement, in order to obtain, directly or indirectly, a financial or other material benefit, of the illegal entry of a person into a State Party of which the person is not a national or a permanent resident." In contrast, "trafficking in persons" was defined as "the recruitment, transportation, transfer, harbouring or receipt of persons, by means of the threat or use of force or other forms of coercion, of abduction, of fraud, of deception, of the abuse of power or of a position of vulnerability or of the giving or receiving of payments or benefits to achieve the consent of a person having control over another person, for the purpose of exploitation. Exploitation shall include, at a minimum, the exploitation of the prostitution of others or other forms of sexual exploitation, forced labour or services, slavery or practices similar to slavery, servitude or the removal of organs." Over the past decade these UN definitions for smuggling and trafficking have largely become operative in the policy and research communities and have increased the precision of discourses and decreased miscommunication and misunderstandings. Nevertheless, some of the deeper questions we asked in the first edition of this volume have not been fully addressed. For example, to what degree do we build into the definition of human smuggling or trafficking the intentions and knowledge of the person smuggled as opposed to the smuggler? What about cases of coercion to smuggle a third party or join a criminal enterprise, or cases of self-smuggling? Should all cases of trafficking for prostitution be treated as coercive and exploitative regardless of the specific conditions and treatment of the women, or should we conceptualize a separate category for those in which violence, or the implicit threat of violence, was used?

Antismuggling and Antitrafficking Policies

States endeavor to reduce clandestine entries between ports of entry as well as unauthorized entries though concealment in conveyances or through document fraud at ports of entry by increasing the number of border control officers, supplying them with better technology, and changing laws and regulations to enable more aggressive pursuit of clandestine border crossers as well as to turn back those individuals suspected of identity and document fraud. As declining travel costs reduced the geographical barriers to international travel, visa applications and border controls imposed by states became the primary barrier to entry. As increasing numbers of individuals attempted to enter destination countries without authorization in the 1980s and 1990s, these states tightened their visa and border control policies and also increased the staffing, funding, and legal authority of border guards. As unauthorized border crossing became more difficult, those who wanted to cross borders increasingly purchased the assistance of professional smugglers. For example, based on research by the Mexican Migration Project, the United Nations Office on Drugs and Crime (UNODC) has estimated that the share of Mexican illegal migrants using smugglers increased from 73 percent in 1975 to 96 percent in 2005 (2010, 63). As the assistance of smugglers helped individuals to cross despite stepped-up border controls, states responded with policies that specifically targeted human smugglers.

U.S. border control authorities, for example, launched operations such as "Hold the Line," "Gatekeeper," and "Safeguard" during the mid-1990s that increased the number of border guards in the most heavily crossed urban areas of the U.S.-Mexican border. Fences had also been put into place along the border in these areas, and U.S. military troops were enlisted to support the Border Patrol. Legislation passed in 1996 to combat illegal migration increased penalties for those who enter the United States illegally and made human smuggling a federal crime. It also enhanced undercover investigative authority, which includes wiretaps; expanded application of asset forfeiture laws; and enabled sting operations to catch smugglers and counterfeiters in the act. A national antismuggling strategy engaged all enforcement departments in coordinated operations intended to disrupt smuggling organizations (Nardi, 1999). The biggest bust came in November 1998 with "Operation Seek and Keep," which broke up an organization that had smuggled as many as three hundred (mostly) Indian nationals per month for three years (Immigration and Naturalization Service [INS], 1998), and soon thereafter came announcements of arrests of members of an organization that smuggled Chinese nationals into the United States through the Mohawk Indian reservation, which straddles the U.S.-Canadian border (INS, 1999). In 2000, the U.S. Congress passed the Trafficking Victims Protection Act, which authorized an Office to Monitor and Combat Trafficking in Persons to support the President's Interagency Task Force to Monitor and Combat Trafficking in Persons (see Koslowski, this volume, Chap. 2).

There is little evidence that tighter border controls have been successful in stopping the smuggling of people across borders or in reducing the debt bondage and forced prostitution that some of those who are smuggled endure once they get into a target country. Even immigration officials recognize the limitations of this parochial approach: according to a U.S. official, "even with all the manpower available at our disposal, the US remains totally vulnerable to smuggling operations unless they are stopped *at their point of origin*" (quoted in *Far Eastern Economic Review,* April 8, 1993). The Trafficking Victims Protection Act attempts to address this problem by threatening to impose economic sanctions on those sending and transit countries that tolerate traffickers and do not cooperate with U.S. efforts to apprehend them. The Trafficking Victims Protection Act also mandates an annual Trafficking in Persons Report, which assesses the efforts of the world's states in combating trafficking; is the basis for sanctions determinations; and adds a "name and shame" dimension to implementing antitrafficking policies.

Although the United States receives the largest numbers of smuggled people and therefore has perhaps the greatest incentives to do something about it, other major target states have taken similar border control tightening and internal enforcement initiatives. Largely in response to the growth of smuggling in the late 1990s, European Union (EU) member states have increased cooperation to combat smuggling organizations and conduct joint antismuggling operations (see Koslowski, this volume, Chap. 2). In response to the wave of boat people from China and the Middle East washing up on Canadian and Australian shores, policymakers in these target states adopted new antismuggling measures. The Australian government instituted a new visa policy that limits refugee visas to three years, bars refugees from bringing their families, and denies refugee status to boat people who passed a "safe" country without lodging an asylum application. In addition, the government expanded the authority of the coast guard to intercept suspect ships on the high seas, and it opened new detention facilities for the growing numbers of boat people. Similarly, Canada revised rules for the detention of smuggled asylum seekers and increased penalties for human smuggling.

An additional concern fanning the flames of the illegal alien issue is human rights concerns because some human smuggling networks use trickery, physical coercion, and emotional degradation either to exploit migrants economically or to force them into slavery. Typically, contemporary slaves come from the world's politically weakest groups: the impoverished, the handicapped, ethnic minorities, women, and children. However, contrary to the conventions of enforcement agencies and news reporting, which tend to identify "the bad guys" and their victims, much migrant smuggling or trafficking operates in an ambiguous area that is neither purely voluntary nor involuntary from the perspective of the migrant. Many contemporary slaves know that they will be smuggled illegally across borders to work, and they sometimes know the nature of the work—what they often do not know is the terms of the "contract." Similarly, many "voluntary" migrants who choose a clandestine route to work abroad feel compelled to leave their home communities because of economic crises, political conflict, ethnic persecution, and fear of rape at home in the case of many ethnic minority women. The treatment of contemporary migrant trafficking and human slavery among news reporters and activists is reminiscent of the earlier "white slavery" scare, with a similar evolution into a debate regarding the pros and cons of legalizing prostitution as one of the primary activities in which slaves are engaged (Stange, 1998; Scully, this volume, Chap. 4). The trafficking of women and children has become a global moral panic.

Critics contend that immigration has spun out of control and that the unintended economic, social, and political costs will be high, though no one can say with any certitude what those are or will be. What is missing from this parochial political argument, however, is the global economic and sociological context in which some U.S. "natives" compete not so much with those who come here from "Third World" countries as with the vast majority *who stay behind* and work in free-trade zones and export manufacturing enclaves set up by transnational corporations and compliant states. The transformation of the U.S. economy from an industrial base to a postindustrial service and information base, buffeted itself by global capital flows, has been painful but not unsuccessful—thus far anyway. *Globalization* is the term used both to explain and to normalize the ideology of neoliberal free-trade policies. Immigration levels increased precisely during this period of significant restructuring of the U.S. economy and the global economy more generally. As many have observed, we can explain the strong negative reaction to current immigration patterns among some Americans and Europeans as due, in part, to a scapegoating of immigrants during the transformation to postindustrialism and to what many now call the globalization of national economies. While immigrants may be blamed for facilitating the destruction of the old corporate-labor contract under industrial capitalism, they are rarely credited for helping to build the new economy in the United States, whose population has a total fertility rate that is slightly below replacement level. It is perhaps due, in part, to this ambiguity regarding the *economic* impact of immigrants that nearly every "immigration reform" in the past two decades has been accompanied by so many loopholes, back doors, and side doors that they have typically facilitated even greater levels of immigration (Hollifield, 1992; Cornelius, Martin, and Hollifield, 1994; Joppke, 1998).

Of course, there is much more to the contemporary immigration story than invidious comparisons of immigrants using cold economic logic, a point that comes into clearer view when we examine the politically sensitive issue of "illegal aliens" or "undocumented migrants," estimated to be around 11.1 million currently living in the United States (Passel and Cohn, 2010), which is, by definition, partially the outcome of human smuggling operations. Some view the fact that over one in ten Americans is "foreign-born" as a threat to the "social order" and "political culture" of the United States (e.g., Beck, 1996; Camarota, 1998). Owing to the fear of an immigrant minority backlash, a significant segment of the U.S. population believes that foreigners who are here illegally may carry the corrupting seeds of a more generalized lawlessness. The fear is not that they are different culturally per se but rather different in a particularly political way that threatens state stability and constitutional democracy and undercuts labor unionization and fair wage competition. Of course, state officials and representatives, regardless of the economic logic of immigration, are especially sensitive to questions of social order and territorial integrity when so many foreigners seem to be able to cross their borders so easily at will.

The prospect of terrorists being smuggled into target states was considered as a potential threat in some law enforcement circles, but it was not until after the September 11, 2001, attacks in New York and Washington and the March 11, 2003, attacks in Madrid that human smuggling was viewed as a security threat in a qualitatively different way. For example, it became clear that terrorists could take clandestine routes that transnational criminal organizations use to smuggle illegal migrants into the United States. The 9/11 Commission staff detailed linkages between human smugglers and Al-Qaeda and other terrorist groups in need of travel facilitation (9/11 Commission, 2004: 61). Investigations into the Madrid bombing produced reports demonstrating that Ansar al-Islam, an al Qaeda-affiliated group linked to the attack, had been running a human smuggling and document fraud operation to fund terrorist actions as well as to smuggle its own members into countries like Spain and Iraq (Simpson, Crawford, and Johnson, 2004). As intelligence screening and visa security are tightened so as to stop terrorists from entering legally with valid visas, the threat of clandestine entry of terrorists using smuggling organizations increases and, with it, international cooperation to combat terrorist travel. Within weeks of the September 11, 2001, attacks, the UN Security Council, "acting under Chapter VII of the Charter of the United Nations," issued resolution 1373 on threats to international peace and security caused by terrorist acts, which included a provision that "all States shall: . . . Prevent the movement of terrorists or terrorist groups by effective border controls and controls on issuance of identity papers and travel documents, and through measures for preventing counterfeiting, forgery or fraudulent use of identity papers and travel documents" (United Nations [UN], 2001). The actions called for by the Security Council to increase the effectiveness of border controls essentially reiterated the measures outlined in the UN Transnational Crime Convention's Protocol against the Smuggling of Migrants by Land, Sea and Air (see Koslowski, this volume, Chap. 2). Such post-9/11 linkage of terrorism to human smuggling reinforced political support for growing border guard ranks and interior ministry budgets that, in turn, enabled staffing and budgets well beyond levels justified by previous public concerns over illegal migration, human smuggling, and trafficking.

Estimates of Human Smuggling and Trafficking

As we underscored in the first edition, it is very difficult to estimate the extent of human smuggling and trafficking worldwide owing to their clandestine nature. As a starting point, it has been estimated that there are 50 million migrants in an irregular status worldwide (United Nations Development Programme, 2009, 2). Given that a very high percentage of those illegal migrants who have clandestinely entered the United States and the European Union have been smuggled, it is likely that a sizeable percentage, if not the majority, of the world's 50 million illegal migrants have been smuggled. Increasing human smuggling has been reflected in increases in reported cases, which researchers, particularly those associated with the International Organization for Migration (IOM), have been gathering, as well as in regional estimates from around the world (Salt and Stein, 1997). Over ten years ago, the IOM estimated that as many as 4 million people were being smuggled across borders on an annual basis (1997). The UN has estimated total global revenues from smuggling to be $10 billion in 2006 (UN, 2006), up from a 1994 UN estimate of $3.5 billion (IOM, 1996).

As far as the subset of the human smuggling estimate that is composed of those who are trafficked, the 2003 U.S. State Department Trafficking in Persons Report (TIP) estimated that between 600,000 and 800,000 people are trafficked across international borders each year, and this estimate was repeated until the 2007 report, which (based on a 2006 study sponsored by the U.S. government) set the estimated number at 800,000, and this estimate was repeated in 2008. Instead of providing estimates for international trafficking, the 2009 TIP report references International Labor Organization (ILO) estimates that at least 12.3 million adults and children are in forced labor, bonded labor, and commercial sexual servitude at any given time; at least 1.39 million of them are victims of commercial sexual servitude, both transnational and within countries.[1] Some of the early estimates of trafficking did not include trafficked men, and the underlying assumptions and definitions of trafficking (vs. smuggling) were not as clear in earlier estimates as those made after the adoption of the UN definitions of smuggling and trafficking in the Transnational Crime Convention.

All of these smuggling and trafficking estimates must be taken with more than a grain of salt, as such global estimates have historically often been made by officials without any background data and analysis, reported in the media as authoritative, and then read and repeated by other officials.[2] A U.S. Government Accountability Office report (2006) found that statistics provided by the U.S. State Department's annual Trafficking in Persons report were full of inconsistencies, incomplete data, and weak methodologies for estimating trafficking. There is every reason to believe that other estimates have similar problems. Related to the inconsistent definitions and distinctions between migrant smuggling and human trafficking is the assertion that 80 percent of those trafficked across international borders worldwide are women and girls, and over two-thirds of them are forced into the commercial sex industry. Once again there are few systematic data that would allow us to accurately describe the phenomena that precisely; unfortunately, since 2000 both the rhetoric and figures surrounding human smuggling and trafficking have ballooned without any real improvement in the validity and reliability of the underlying data gathered across an extremely diverse set of states.

Information gained from failed smuggling operations does provide an indication of the diversity and growth of such activities, and occasionally a glimpse into the smuggling operation itself, but it also suggests several unanswered questions explored in both editions of the volume: What are the broader historical, political, and sociological foundations of migrant smuggling? Is there a systematic difference between failed smuggling operations and successful ones? Is the trafficking in women to be sold into slavery an outgrowth of migrant smuggling as a service, or should it be considered separately? How much of this phenomenon is inadvertently created by states to meet other economic and security goals?

Academic Research Issues

In the 1990s, as news reports from around the world documented the growing export of people for profit, some criminologists and policymakers began to investigate the linkage of transnational migration and crime from the perspective of the impact on states (Den Boer and Walker, 1993; ISPAC, 1996; Wang, 1996; Kerry, 1997; Smith, 1997; Winer, 1997). However, international migration specialists had largely ignored this phenomenon, with some notable exceptions (Salt and Stein, 1997; Ghosh, 1998). Given the strategic political and intellectual location of illicit labor mobility across international borders, it is somewhat surprising that relatively few social researchers, apart from criminologists of transnational crime, have focused on this topic. During the 1990s, when research on "transnational migration" (and, more generally, "transnationalism") became a social science growth industry, the topic of human smuggling or migrant trafficking was largely left to states, nonprofit organizations, and journalists to define and explain the phenomenon within their own agendas.

While several books by journalists focusing overwhelmingly on the problem of the sex trafficking of women and children have been published over the past decade, empirical social science research of the kind advocated in this volume still remains largely undeveloped. It is still true that much of the discussion and debate surrounding human smuggling and trafficking proceed from either estimated aggregate data using deductive logic (e.g., recent increases in smuggling *must* be due to large criminal enterprises) or emotional testimonies of victims who were trafficked for sex. Although these are valid and important types of information, what is missing is a sustained historical and empirical examination of different smuggling activities using more inductive and comparative reasoning by observers not so directly tied to advocating a priori a specific state policy or political/philosophical position. This volume demonstrates that social science researchers do have a role in helping to understand a complex area of transnational social life precisely because their research and analyses are different from those of a state enforcement agency. It is even more painfully clear that some researchers may understandably wish to avoid areas of research that may link migrants with crime for fear of further stigmatizing immigrant minorities, or they perceive such research to be too risky, if not impossible. The fact is that institutional review boards at major research institutions mix with the often considerable need for in-depth regional knowledge and contacts to make research in this area uniquely challenging; this is especially true for younger scholars not wanting to pursue a risky line of inquiry in a highly competitive professional environment.

The claim that academic researchers are unbiased in their analyses of this area of social life would be naïve—in fact, it is our acute awareness of the ability of bias to color our findings, even when we have corroborating evidence, that leads to some of the seemingly cumbersome approaches and traditions of social scientists. However, there are two features of the claims of the contributors of this volume that make them different from those of state officials or journalists, who have largely shaped public opinion on this topic thus far. First, there is a great deal of diversity within the "academic community" because of our range of disciplinary and methodological approaches. It is the multiplicity of findings and theories and our ongoing debates that contribute to social research; no one researcher claims to have all the answers, but collectively we may begin to understand the different facets of a social activity as complex as contemporary human smuggling. Second, and most important, we have the freedom from organizational policy directives and news posting deadlines to explore more diverse social, political, and historical dimensions; our intellectual goals may evolve in directions very different from, even tangential to, the immediate topic at hand as state officials would formulate it. Many of the contributors to this volume broaden their analytical frame beyond state constructions of human smuggling, thus allowing them to focus on the role of a range of state policies and actors who have both facilitated and hindered human smugglers.

Chapter Overviews

A theme running through these otherwise disparate chapters is how politics, not just economics and criminality, creates professional human smuggling (as opposed to self-smuggling) of the scale we are witnessing today.

In the first chapter, David Kyle and John Dale compare two cases of human smuggling that would normally be viewed as the opposite ends of this phenomenon in terms of coercion and exploitation. By comparing human smuggling out of Ecuador, a country of clandestine labor migration driven mostly by migrant demand, and Myanmar (Burma), a country that has been the site of some of the most horrific forms of trafficking in girls for brothels in Thailand and elsewhere, they explore some of the basic assumptions regarding why and how such activities have arisen in the 1980s and 1990s. Although there are obvious differences between these two cases of what they refer to as "migrant exporting schemes" and "slave importing operations," there are also similarities in the high degree of tacit and active complicity required by a range of people in the sending and destination regions. Similarly, in neither case does "transnational organized crime" of the sort described by many in the news media and among enforcement agencies play a significant role; smugglers and traffickers in both regions are deeply integrated into the social fabric of indigenous settings, though not uniformly so, and are facilitated by a loose network of recruiters, middlemen, actual smugglers, local and foreign financiers, and government officials and police on the take. Though these cases have some unique features that make them unrepresentative of other cases, that is precisely their value: they help keep us attuned to the possibilities disallowed by our assumptions of why and how human smuggling operates, especially as formulated in official rhetoric and media portrayals. They also demonstrate the need to examine the broader historical-sociological forces at play in cases of human smuggling from specific subnational regions, especially those built on a foundation of either failed or abusive/extractive state regimes. These local maladies are augmented by a globalized media and production chain that nevertheless excludes the ability of labor to move freely and by government corruption as both a cause and a consequence of human smuggling.

In Chapter 2, Rey Koslowski examines the challenges posed by human smuggling to states as well as the dilemmas of international cooperation between states to combat human smuggling. He does so by placing the issue of state control in the context of both the process of economic globalization and the politics of linking migration and crime in the policy-making process. States have embarked on multilateral cooperation to combat human smuggling and trafficking by increasing border controls, passing antismuggling and antitrafficking laws, and stepping up enforcement of these laws. If human smuggling is mostly "crime that is organized" by informal transnational social networks rather than just another activity of traditional organized crime groups, as cases studies by Finckenaur, Chin, Kyle and Dale, and Spener indicate, then, Koslowski argues, international efforts to target human smugglers may be much more difficult in practice than anticipated. Moreover, as tighter border controls have the unintended side effects of pushing migrants and refugees into the arms of smugglers, multilateral antismuggling initiatives confront additional challenges, often of their own making. In the end, Koslowski argues that as long as destination states fail to enforce policies that cut demand for smuggled labor, significant reduction of human smuggling is unlikely, and multilateral agreements, which may represent impressive feats of international cooperation, will most likely prove to have much less of an impact than policymakers had hoped.

In Chapter 3, Eric Tagliacozzo examines the sale of human beings for labor purposes during the second half of the nineteenth century and the beginning of the twentieth; namely, he is concerned with the sale and journeys of coolies (laborers) and slaves as they were bought and sold in extralegal ways across the

Malay world. He describes the continuation and expansion of slaving as an institution in the islands of the region, one that went from a sanctioned cultural practice under many indigenous regimes to an illicit form of commerce under moralizing colonial administrations. He argues that these human circuits were a vital and understudied phenomenon of the political economy of the age, linking "centers" and "peripheries," "indigenes" and colonials.

Eileen P. Scully, in Chapter 4, examines the transnational trafficking of women for prostitution from 1850 to the end of the Cold War. Scully reminds us that the issue of trafficking in women and children—which, with regard to people being smuggled across borders, currently gets the most attention in the popular press and politically—is not a new one; it was accompanied then, just as now, by a wide range of efforts by nongovernmental organizations, states, and new multilateral organizations such as the League of Nations and United Nations to control it. The underlying causes of previous forms of trafficking in women (largely a misnomer at the time) flowed directly from large mobile populations of men as indentured laborers and as the new urban workforce, especially the large movement of Asian labor following the abolition of slavery. It is intriguing that two dimensions to trafficking more than a century ago could just as easily describe the topic today: political and economic turmoil in Russia and China fueled significant flows of labor, including prostitutes; and the debates surrounding the definitions and root causes of trafficking and policy recommendations sharply divide into the two camps of those seeking sex-work regulation and those who strongly feel that a prohibition of prostitution will curtail the demand. Ultimately, however, it was the misnamed and racist framework of the "white slave trade" that fell victim to a lack of credibility and hence sustained outrage when it was shown that most of the women in question were neither "white" nor slaves but rather a coethnic community of women attached to overseas laborers. Most appropriate to current actions, projects, and laws being developed, Scully cautions us to consider the unintended consequences of antitrafficking measures such as the Mann Act, most of which served further to assert male control over women.

Peter Andreas presents a fascinating story in Chapter 5 of the development of a state-smuggler symbiosis and the unintended downhill cycles in which state control actions drive would-be migrants into the arms of smugglers, which in turn is used to justify even greater levels of "border buildup." He begins by reminding us that, ironically, it was Mexico's efforts to keep out illegal American immigrants that in part led to the U.S.-Mexican War. The larger point is that ever since that war the United States has either facilitated Mexican labor immigration or turned a blind eye to what has mostly been a low-cost informal affair of crossing the Rio Grande. In the 1990s, the United States sought to deter illegal aliens from crossing through brute force and high technology—as opposed to capturing them once they were across—largely maintaining an ineffective and understaffed program of workforce compliance. The central paradox along this particular border when viewed globally is that it was precisely during the 1990s that tariffs decreased and commercial interpenetration increased between the two neighboring countries. Andreas asserts that instead of migrants and their guides being deterred from making the crossing, their operations have gotten more complex, diverse—and expensive. Thus, the nature of smuggling itself has been transformed from an informal affair to a big business attracting large criminal organizations. By tracing the reciprocal interaction between state policies and clandestine transnational actors, Andreas suggests the multiple ways in which states make smuggling and smuggling (re-)makes states.

In Chapter 6, David Spener proposes an alternative analytical and political framework that views "autonomous migration" as a form of resistance to global apartheid enforced at nation-state borders. Instead of using the terminology of "human smuggling," he defines *coyotaje* as a social process by which migrants hire professional service providers to help them cross international boundaries in the face of states' attempts to exclude them. Drawing on Galtung's concepts of personal violence, structural violence, and cultural violence, he explores complex issues of power and identity in the borderlands of Mexico and Texas.

Ko-Lin Chin, in Chapter 7, describes the social organization of Chinese human smuggling. Using data collected from a survey of three hundred undocumented Chinese in New York and interviews with key informants in the United States and China, he examines the individual and group characteristics of human smugglers, patterns of smuggling operations, and the relationships between alien smuggling, gangs, and organized crime groups. Echoing Finckenauer's findings on human smuggling out of Russia, Chin suggests that most human smugglers are not gang or tong members, although some gang and tong members are involved in the human trade. Moreover, a human smuggling organization can best be described as a small, loosely knit group. Members of the group come from all walks; they are predominantly ethnic Chinese who are not career criminals.

In Chapter 8, Zai Liang and Wenzhen Ye review the historical and demographic trends of international migration from China; there has been a significant increase in immigrants (many of them undocumented) from China's Fujian Province to the New York metropolitan area. Their chapter argues that absolute poverty is not the cause of this new immigration; rather, it is rooted in a unique configuration of historical and contemporary factors. First, since Fujian is on the coast of China, many Fujianese are familiar with life at sea and thus are well prepared for the sometimes dangerous journeys usually to the United States. Second, because of China's transition to a market-oriented economy and remittance from overseas immigrants, the relative income disparities in Fujian have increased over time. This increase has given rise to a sense of relative deprivation among the Fujianese, a primary motivation for seeking fortune abroad. Finally, the existence of a sophisticated human smuggling network throughout the world that uses modern technology facilitates the process of immigrating to New York.

Kamal Sadiq, in Chapter 9, examines flows of illegal migration from and through India and Pakistan to make a much broader argument about the role of documents in human smuggling and trafficking. He demonstrates how state documentation is used to differentiate citizens from foreigners and make individual identity and mobility visible, but he then explains how the same documents are manipulated to conceal visibility from state regulating agencies. He also considers the introduction of biometric features in documents as another regulatory measure but concludes that the gap between state expectations and failed outcomes is due to the lack of understanding of how documents facilitate and inhibit human smuggling.

In Chapter 10, Khalid Koser examines asylum seekers as another major source of contemporary human smuggling often falling between that uncomfortable dichotomy of "freedom fighter" and "evil smuggler"; he suggests that we should not put too fine a point on the distinction between human smuggling as a migration issue and human trafficking as a human rights issue. Asylum seekers straddle this distinction in that they are often escaping human rights violations by seeking out smugglers—much as the Underground Railroad smuggled people out of slavery during the 1800s—but then encounter additional human rights violations along the way. For example, using data from interviews with Iranian asylum seekers in the Netherlands, Koser found that many did not control some of the most basic features of their passage, including how and where they would be smuggled. He explores the historical path to this situation as a series of unintended consequences; reducing legal avenues of migrant workers in Western Europe drove immigrants to seek asylum as the only legal path of entry; this, in turn, led to a set of restrictive control policies for would-be claimants in an attempt to filter out bogus applications; as this cycle deepens, the extreme difficulty of the asylum process has driven both labor migrants and now asylum seekers into the hands of professional smugglers as the only ones able to offer them hope of a life beyond the persecuted and discriminated communities in which they live.

Barak Kalir describes two parallel labor flows to Israel in Chapter 11. The first is a legal flow of migrant workers, who are recruited, transported, and employed by means of a tightly regulated scheme, often based on bilateral agreements between Israel and sending countries. The second is an illegal flow of undocumented migrants, who arrive, find jobs, and settle down by their own initiative and against the official planning of the Israeli government. Based on ethnographic research among legal migrant workers from China and undocumented migrants from Latin America, he argues that seeing illegal and legal migration in opposition to each other is empirically ungrounded and analytically misleading.

In Chapter 12, James O. Finckenauer examines the criminal activities of Russians and others from the former Soviet Union involved in migrant trafficking. He situates "alien smuggling" in the broader context of Russian transnational organized crime in general. This context includes the structures and the scope of criminal activities of the former Soviet criminal organizations engaging in transnational crime. Finckenauer contrasts what we know to be organized crime with what is, for him, better labeled "crime that is organized." Though he emphasizes the lack of hard evidence in this area, he suggests that human smuggling (at least in the case of the Russians) may better represent the latter than the former, a distinction that has implications for transnational law enforcement policies given that large, ongoing criminal organizations are easier to infiltrate and disrupt. Finckenauer suggests that falsely portraying most trafficking from Russia as controlled by the Mafia as organized crime is counterproductive on two counts: first, we lose the possibility of a credible threat among those actually involved; it also diverts attention from the areas of research we need most, especially a better understanding of the consumers of such human commodities and those multiple people who reap the large profits for this trade.

H. Richard Friman describes how smuggled immigrants are socially constructed as threats to the social order in Japan in Chapter 13. Though often referred to as a newcomer to immigration, Japan has, in fact, a long history of public assertions that crime is linked to immigrants or foreigners. In the past, these arguments surfaced during periods of severe dislocation such as the aftermath of the 1923

Tokyo earthquake and the American occupation. A crime-by-foreigner discourse has resurfaced in Japan in the context of increased immigration and high-profile incidents of transnational human smuggling—but in the absence of the severe dislocations of the past. Friman explores the historical and political sources of this resurgent discourse and why it resonates in such a distorted manner. For example, while it is acknowledged that the *yakuza* (Japanese organized crime) have recently turned to human smuggling, the reason most often concerns economic pressure rather than their long history of labor brokering among the still necessary day laborers and other unskilled labor, much of it illegal. In the end, Friman argues that undocumented immigrants—especially Chinese—play an important scapegoat role, one that obscures the continuing need for inexpensive Chinese labor and the unintended effects of antigang legislation resulting in the diversification of *yakuza* operations into human smuggling.

In Chapter 14, Nora V. Demleitner analyzes the current multiple constructions of migrants, coercion, and prostitution in the contemporary period. She argues that the legal construction of victimized migrant women often works at cross-purposes to the goal of curtailing forced prostitution through international trafficking. Noting the aggressive enforcement of migration laws but a lack of policies and laws regarding smuggling and brothel ownership, she argues that the issue of forced prostitution needs to be viewed as a problem caused in part by the current immigration law, reinforced by gender inequalities, and tolerated because of the precarious legal position of the victims. Thus the current treatment of migrant women who prostitute themselves as both illegal and immoral serves to stigmatize them as double outcasts. Demleitner suggests that we also need to learn more about the nature of the global demand for sex services as a global business and, hence, what might be done about the fundamental structure of a world of deep inequalities and restrictive migration policies. The urgent question implicit in Demleitner's chapter is whether states can overcome their focus on migration control and inherently sexist constitutions in order to protect the human rights of those tricked, trafficked, and traded regardless of the degree of their prior knowledge of what lay ahead for them on the other side of the border.

Issues for Future Research

This volume presents a mix of descriptive empirical evidence and conceptual analysis, often providing a much needed historical and comparative context in which to gain a broader perspective. A central theme that emerged naturally from this first set of academic studies on human smuggling was and still remains how state officials and smugglers are locked in an embrace without straightforward solutions, primarily because the causes, social organization, and proposed solutions are much more historically and politically complex than they may at first seem. It is precisely the global nature of human smuggling that requires us to consider the wider social and economic context in which it is flourishing, rather than simply demonizing the smugglers, some of whom provide safe passage out of some very dismal situations and others who prey on the weakest of humanity. Viewing human smuggling as a global phenomenon, we developed a partial list, reinforced by the chapters that follow, of some of the broad issues worthy of further research and analysis. Over the past decade, the emergence of additional issues for further research increasingly became clear, and we describe the issues of moral economy, asylum seeking, and climate change in a bit more detail after the following list:

1. Capital and commodities are increasingly global—labor is not. This is a fundamental tension in the world today, whereby the policies and discourse of free trade abruptly end at the point of labor mobility.

2. Related to the process and ideology of so-called globalization, the demand for cheap or free labor that the smugglers provide resonates with other labor trends of temporary and disposable workers; short-term profitability can be used to justify nearly any action and can even be framed perversely in moral terms as alleviating unemployment among some of the poorer regions of the world.

3. The current state system based on territorial sovereignty but characterized by uneven state capacity is wholly inadequate to the task at hand. This fact is exacerbated by high levels of corruption in some sending, transit, and receiving states.

4. As millions of dollars are beginning to be directed at the root causes of human smuggling and trafficking, a logical approach would be to develop economic and social aid programs in traditional sending regions. However, much of the migration research in general, and the works of the contributors to this volume, indicate that it is not what a person does not have that motivates him or her to leave; it is what that person's neighbor has that compels him or her not to be left behind—that is, *relative* deprivation. Within their national context,

regions with high levels of migrant exporting tend to be some of the most dynamic. In contrast, those being tricked into slavery are more likely to come from more impoverished regions. The challenge in these latter cases is to encourage economic development and political empowerment without reinforcing the power of entrenched local elites.

5. Because we are dealing with a multifaceted social and political phenomenon, the unintended consequences of particular measures in stopping human smuggling are nearly always counterproductive without an integrated approach. For example, a militarized border without effective employer sanctions is ineffective and dangerous to the migrants and sends a message opposite to the one intended. Proposed technological measures of control of "illegal aliens" and labor settings may have consequences for all of us; because people are not intrinsically and obviously illicit in the same way as, say, a kilo of heroin, new methods of categorizing, tagging, and monitoring the world's populations, especially using digital and satellite technologies, will be a tempting, if chilling, solution to overcome the challenge of managing an increasingly highly mobile world.

Moral Economy of Human Smuggling and Trafficking

Human smuggling and trafficking exist because there is demand for smuggled and trafficked labor in receiving countries, whether on farms, in sweatshops, or in brothels. In an analysis of the demand behind human trafficking, Kevin Bales makes the argument that "consumers" of trafficked people operate within a moral economy that allows them to rationalize this activity." In contrast, "human rights are based on the privileging and then codification of the victim's definitions of an action . . . (but) virtually every action that we now think of as a violation of human rights was once defined as acceptable" (Bales, n.d.). Although laws and civilized discourse may increasingly privilege the victims' definitions of the act of paid crossing of an international border and debt repayment through forced labor as a human rights violation, employers and consumers are increasingly operating in a different moral economy that tolerates trafficked labor. Johns may accept the less-than-enthusiastic performance of women trafficked into prostitution for the lower cost of the sex sold relative to that of native prostitutes. Businesspeople who face competitors that lower costs through exploiting trafficked labor may themselves justify hiring illegal migrant workers. This, in turn, increases the demand for illegal migrant labor that inspires desperate people abroad to pay smugglers and be lured by traffickers.

Part of the problem from a consumer's standpoint is that it is difficult for the consumer to distinguish whether products and services are produced by illegal migrants who overstayed their visas, illegal migrants who paid to be smuggled, or a trafficked migrant in debt bondage. For example, the tomatoes in a meal served in an ethic restaurant may have been chopped by a smuggled migrant or by a trafficked migrant working eighty hours per week to repay an enormous debt under threat of violence to his or her family.

Given that the practices of trafficking are so intertwined with smuggling, in practical terms it is often difficult to disaggregate the prevention and prosecution of human trafficking from the prevention and prosecution of human smuggling and illegal migration more generally. Antitrafficking policies that focus on "prevention, protection and prosecution" (e.g., U.S. State Department, 2010: 12–14) may not be enough if they do not deal with the moral economy of the consumer demand for sex with "exotic" foreign women that fuels a growing industry capitalizing on vulnerable illegal migrants. Trafficking prevention through poverty reduction might not be enough if the moral economy remains in place that enables an additional twenty-six million people to be enslaved within their own countries (Bales, 1999). Educating potential victims of traffickers' ploys may not be enough to convince women to stay home when they see the money sent home by those who were smuggled and are working illegally abroad. Given that truly effective measures to stop human smuggling involve major restrictions on employers' access to cheap and compliant illegal migrant labor, one may anticipate significance resistance from powerful interest groups.

Because consumers of cheaper domestic services, restaurant food, fresh vegetables, clothing, and, yes, sex services apparently have little knowledge and/or concerns about the exploitation that goes into the products and services they consume, the moral economy that enables new forms of slavery and trafficking persists and thrives. No matter how much immigration authorities tighten border controls and prosecutors target traffickers and smugglers, as long as there is high demand for illegal migrant labor that inextricably includes the smuggled and the trafficked, it will be very difficult to reduce trafficking.

Asylum and Human Smuggling

The intermeshing of human trafficking and migrant smuggling can raise a quandary for policymakers and human rights advocates with respect to political asylum. Prosecuting the smugglers who transport women bound for forced prostitution may also put out of business those who enable asylum seekers to reach safety. Migrants in search of work are not the only customers for smugglers' services. After the international community turned its back on Europe's Jews at the 1938 Evian Conference, many Jews escaped the Holocaust only by paying smugglers who helped them cross the border into Switzerland. During the Cold War, those who helped Eastern Europeans cross the border into Austria or West Germany were often considered heroes, even if they accepted payment. For doing the same thing today, one may be prosecuted as a criminal. Referring to those Americans who broke the 1850 Fugitive Slave Law and ran the Underground Railroad to Canada as well as Peter Dupre, a British national who smuggled East Germans and Czechs across the Yugoslav border into Austria, a libertarian activist has made the argument that "human smuggling is morally good" (McPherson, 2003). Going back to the smuggler's speedboat, yes, the smuggling of the persecuted Iraqis and Kosovars may be considered "morally good," but the simultaneous smuggling of the Moldovan woman destined into forced prostitution is not. Moreover, smugglers may also be human rights violators. In many cases, smugglers have little regard for the safety of their customers, as boats are often overloaded and, when pursued by the coast guard, smugglers have thrown babies and small children overboard to force their pursuers to stop for a rescue operation that enables escape.

Climate Change and Human Smuggling

An additional complication arises with the moral and legal considerations surrounding current and predicted future growth and forced migration due to the effects of global warming, including more severe climatological events and gradual changes in the ability of some regions to sustain human populations. Popular media reports of up to a billion "climate refugees" (*Climate Refugees,* 2010) by midcentury may or may not come to pass but do signal a turning point in a new framing of an unauthorized, yet immediately understandable, movement and resettlement across international borders. For example, in a growing number of villages in Assam, India, groundwater levels are very low, and farmers are dependent on natural rainfall or *dongs*, traditional water channels that are the main source of irrigation and drinking water. As a result, farmers engaged in water-intensive rice cultivation have been severely affected, sending daughters to cities in search of work, thus placing some in the hands of traffickers ("Young girls face trafficking as lack of rain drives worsening rural poverty," www.alertnet.org/db/an_art/60167/2010/04/5–134544–1.htm). This trend will only further deepen and complicate the moral economy of human mobility and resettlement of forced migrants driven by the myriad effects of global warming.

In sum, continuing to locate the problem exogenously within a transnational crime framework outside the past actions and current conditions of the countries of origin and destination would seem to ensure that, at least in the short run, many more will be tempted into the hands of human smugglers; they will continue to be perceived, correctly or incorrectly, as the only credible hope of attaining the political freedoms and economic opportunities we enjoy in the world's most developed countries. The difficult lesson is that extreme caution is needed before government and nongovernment agencies rush to solve the problem without understanding what "the problem" is beyond the immediate facts of a particular case and without sufficient political will to tackle both its supply and demand dimensions. Unfortunately, as this volume suggests, the phenomenon of human smuggling is exacerbated by multiple sets of interlocking problems such as widening social inequality, state corruption, and ethnic and gender discriminations. Further, all of these are compounded by the contradictions of a contemporary world connected economically and technologically but in no fundamental way integrated politically or culturally. In this sense, human smuggling—in all its guises—is not so much a disease but a symptom of the enormous contemporary disparities in the legitimate mobility of the world's peoples during, ironically, the historical apex of mutual global awareness and interconnectedness.

NOTES

1. See U.S. Department of State, *Trafficking in Persons Report* (various years) at www.state.gov/g/tip/rls/tiprpt/.

2. For a useful discussion of the methodological problems with these estimates, see Laczko and Gramegna (2003) and U.S. Government Accountability Office (2006).

REFERENCES

Altink, S. 1995. *Stolen Lives: Trading Women into Sex and Slavery.* London: Scarlet Press.
Bales, Kevin. 1999. *Disposable People: New Slavery in the Global Economy.* Berkeley: University of California Press.
———. N.d. "Understanding the Demand behind Human Trafficking." Manuscript posted at www.freetheslaves.net/.
Basch, Linda, Nina G. Schiller, and Cristina Szanton Blanc. 1994. *Nations Unbound: Transnational Projects, Post-colonial Predicaments, and Deterritorialized Nation-States.* Langhorne, Pa.: Gordon and Breach.
Beck, Roy. 1996. *The Case against Immigration: The Moral, Economic, Social, and Environmental Reasons for Reducing U.S. Immigration Back to Traditional Levels.* New York: W. W. Norton & Co.
Camarota, Steven A. 1998. "Immigrants in the United States—1998: A Snapshot of America's Foreign-Born Population." Center for Immigration Studies Backgrounder Series, January.
Chin, Ko-lin. 1996. *Chinatown Gangs: Extortion, Enterprise, and Ethnicity.* New York: Oxford University Press.
Climate Refugees. 2010. Documentary film. Climaterefugees.com.
Cole, Deborah. 1998. "Germany Fights Wave of Immigrant Smuggling." Reuters, November 9, 1998.
Cornelius, Wayne A., Philip L. Martin, and James F. Hollifield. 1994. *Controlling Immigration: A Global Perspective.* Stanford: Stanford University Press.
Den Boer, Monica, and Neil Walker. 1993. "European Policing after 1992." *Journal of Common Market Studies* 31 (1): 3–28.
Escobar, Gabriel. 1999. "Immigrants' Ranks Tripled in 29 Years." *Washington Post,* January 9, A01.
"Europe's Smuggled Masses." 1999. *Economist.* February 20.
Free the Slaves and the University of California, Berkeley. 2004. *Hidden Slaves: Forced Labor in the United States,* Free the Slaves and Human Rights Center, University of California, Berkeley, September. www.freetheslaves.net//Document.Doc?id=17 (accessed January 20, 2011).
Ghosh, Bimal. 1998. *Huddled Masses and Uncertain Shores: Insights into Irregular Migration.* Dordrecht: Kluwer Law International.
Global Survival Network (GSN). 1997. *Crime and Servitude: An Exposé of the Traffic in Women for Prostitution from the Newly Independent States.* Washington, D.C.: Global Survival Network.
Hollifield, James F. 1992. *Immigrants, Markets, and States: The Political Economy of Postwar Europe.* Cambridge: Harvard University Press.
Immigration and Naturalization Service (INS). 1998. "INS Arrest Two Fugitives in Largest Alien Smuggling Case." News release, December 4.
———. 1999. "INS Enhances Interior Enforcement Strategy: Plans Deployment of New FY 1999 Resources." News release, March 30.
International Organization for Migration (IOM). 1996. "Organized Crime Moves into Migrant Trafficking." *Trafficking in Migrants, Quarterly Bulletin,* no. 11 (June).
———. 1997. "Trafficking in Migrants: IOM Policy and Activities." www.iom.ch/IOM/Trafficking/IOM_Policy.html (accessed December 2000).

———. 1998a. *Trafficking in Migrants, Quarterly Bulletin,* no. 17 (January).

———. 1998b. *Trafficking in Migrants, Quarterly Bulletin,* no. 18 (June).

ISPAC. 1996. International Scientific and Professional Advisory Council of the United Nations Crime Prevention and Criminal Justice Program (ISPAC) International Conference on Migration and Crime: Global and Regional Problems and Responses. Courmayeur Mont Blanc, Italy, October.

Jenkins, Philip. 1998. *Moral Panic: Changing Concepts of the Child Molester in Modern America.* New Haven: Yale University Press.

Joppke, Christian. 1998. "Why Liberal States Accept Unwanted Migration." *World Politics* 50 (2): 266–93.

Jordan, Ann. 2007. Testimony of Ann Jordan, Director, Initiative against Trafficking in Persons, Global Rights, before the House Subcommittee on Border, Maritime, and Global Counterterrorism, March 20.

Kerry, John. 1997. *The New War: The Web of Crime That Threatens America's Security.* New York: Simon and Schuster.

Kwong, Peter. 1996. *The New Chinatown.* Rev. ed. New York: Hill and Wang.

———. 1997. *Forbidden Workers: Illegal Chinese Immigrants and American Labor.* New York: New Press.

Kyle, David. 2000. *Transnational Peasants: Migrations, Networks, and Ethnicity in Andean Ecuador.* Baltimore: Johns Hopkins University Press.

Kyle, David, and Zai Liang. 2001. "Migration Merchants: Human Smuggling from Ecuador and China to the United States." In *Controlling a New Migration,* edited by Virginie Guiraudon and Christian Joppke. London: Routledge.

Laczko, Frank, and Marco A. Gramegna. 2003. "Developing Better Indicators of Human Trafficking." *Brown Journal of World Affairs* 10 (1): 179–94.

Light, Ivan, and Edna Bonacich. 1988. *Immigrant Entrepreneurs: Koreans in Los Angeles, 1965–1982.* Berkeley: University of California Press.

McDonald, William F. 1995. "The Globalization of Criminology: The New Frontier Is the Frontier." *Transnational Organized Crime* 1 (1): 1–22.

McPherson, Scott. 2003. "Human Smuggling Is Morally Good." Commentary, Future of Freedom Foundation, December 19.

Mickleburgh, Rod. 1999. "Whistle-blower Migrants Offered Landed Status, Aim Is to Catch Snakeheads Who Smuggled Chinese into Canada and to Protect Victims, Caplan Says." *Globe and Mail,* November 27.

MNS. 1998. "More Human Smuggling across the Eastern Border." *Migration News Sheet,* no. 186/98-09 (September), 5.

MTI. 1998. "Conference on Border Control." MTI Hungarian News Agency, April 22.

Nardi, Louis F. 1999. Statement before the Subcommittee on Immigration and Claims, Committee of the Judiciary, U.S. House of Representatives, March 18.

9/11 Commission. 2004. *9/11 and Terrorist Travel: Staff Report of the National Commission on Terrorist Attacks upon the United States.* www.9-11commission.gov/staff_statements/index.htm.

PAP. 1998. "Interior Minister Reports Crime Rise in 1997." Polish Press Agency, February 18.

Passel, Jeffrey S., and D'Vera Cohn. 2010. *U.S. Unauthorized Immigration Flows Are Down Sharply Since Mid-Decade.* Washington, D.C.: Pew Hispanic Center.

Salt, John, and Jeremy Stein. 1997. "Migration as a Business: The Case of Trafficking." *International Migration* 35 (4): 467–94.

Simpson, G. R., D. Crawford, and K. Johnson. 2004. "Crime Pays, Terrorists Find: Group in Europe Smuggles Immigrants and Forges Passports." *Wall Street Journal*, April 14.

Singer, Audrey, and Douglas Massey. 1998. "The Social Process of Undocumented Border Crossing." *International Migration Review* 32 (3): 561–92.

Smith, Paul, ed. 1997. *Human Smuggling: Chinese Migrant Trafficking and the Challenge to America's Immigration Tradition.* Washington, D.C.: Center for Strategic and International Studies.

Stange, Margit. 1998. *Personal Property : Wives, White Slaves, and the Market in Women.* Baltimore: Johns Hopkins University Press.

Stensholt, John. 1999. "Boat People: 'No Bypassing' Rule." *Financial Review,* November 22.

United Nations (UN). 2001. Security Council Resolution 1373. September 28.

———. 2006. "Trends in Total Migrant Stock: The 2005 Revision." United Nations Department of Economic and Social Affairs, Population Division. POP/DB/MIG/Rev .2005/Doc, February.

United Nations Development Programme. 2009. *United Nations Human Development Report 2009, Overcoming Barriers: Human Mobility and Development.* hdr.undp.org/en/media/HDR_2009_EN_Complete.pdf.

United Nations Office on Drugs and Crime. 2010. *The Globalization of Crime: A Transnational Organized Crime Threat Assessment.* www.unodc.org/unodc/en/data-and-analysis/tocta-2010.html.

U.S. Government Accountability Office. 2006. "Human Trafficking: Better Data, Strategy, and Reporting Needed to Enhance U.S. Antitrafficking Efforts Abroad." GAO-06-825. July. www.gao.gov/new.items/d06825.pdf.

U.S. State Department. 2010. *Trafficking in Persons Report 2010.* www.state.gov/g/tip/rls/tiprpt/2010/index.htm.

Wang, Zheng. 1996. "Ocean-Going Smuggling of Illegal Chinese Immigrants: Operation, Causation, and Policy Implications." *Transnational Organized Crime* 2 (1): 49–65.

Winer, Jonathan M. 1997. "Alien Smuggling: Elements of the Problem." *Transnational Organized Crime* 3 (1): 3–13.

Part I / The Global Comparative Perspective

CHAPTER ONE

Smuggling the State Back In

Agents of Human Smuggling Reconsidered

David Kyle and John Dale

Given the immediate policy and enforcement concerns of state agencies, it is unlikely that state representatives and others concerned with developing policies to combat human smuggling will reflect on either states' own role in creating and sustaining human smuggling or the nuances of its historical and sociological foundations. When a causal story is offered by state agencies or media, it usually takes the form of either of two conceptual extremes, one global and the other highly individualistic: first, globalization has created the conditions for greater transnational crime of all sorts, of which trafficking in humans is the most recent illicit global activity; or second, some very ruthless and greedy professional criminals (organized crime) are exploiting the weak and mostly innocent migrants who are either duped or coerced into a clandestine journey. Although there is an important element of truth to these statements regarding some smuggling operations, unfortunately they cover up more than they reveal, simplify more than they illuminate. We take issue with these two general axioms in this chapter through an examination of two very different cases of human smuggling: migrants contracting migration merchants in Ecuador to facilitate a journey to the United States, and young girls and women trafficked from northern Burma to Thailand and held in slavery. These two cases demonstrate the antithesis of the two axioms stated above; first, specific historical actions by politicians and other state actors in both sending and receiving states are largely responsible for the recent increase in global human smuggling, and, second, we need to recognize the extreme diversity of smuggling operations and activities, both among and within sending regions, and how they are integrated into wider regional social structures.

If reporting on human smuggling is rife with the two aforementioned axioms, there is also a well-recognized paradox that academic researchers have been quick to point out: state aggressiveness in combating human smuggling, in the form of tighter border controls and asylum policies, has prompted more people to seek smugglers and others to enter the migrant smuggling business, including ongoing transnational criminal enterprises attracted by the high profits and low risks of this activity. Of course, the rapid increase in U.S. border enforcement activities in the mid-1990s (see Andreas, this volume, Chap. 5) drives up the costs of illegal migration and increases the profits of human smuggling, thereby attracting the attention of criminal enterprises already engaged in other types of transnational smuggling, such as the drug trade. For would-be migrants, what used to be a relatively low-cost, informal affair of crossing the Rio Grande now requires great risks and resources and is less likely to be attempted without some type of professional smuggler. Of course, for those coming from more distant countries this has been the case for some time (Kyle, 2000).

What is telling about the positive correlation between the United States' enforcement actions along the border and the recent increase in the scope and profitability of professional smuggling is that U.S. government representatives, especially from the Immigration and Naturalization Service (INS), not only agree with this assessment but hint that this was the plan all along. However, unlike Andreas's detailed account (this volume, Chap. 5) of the unintended consequences of U.S. domestic politics leading to the militarization of the U.S-Mexican border, which suggests a less than rational policy-making process, the specter of foreign terrorist threats is now consistently mentioned as a significant part of the border deterrence strategies of the 1990s. For example, a recent U.S. General Accounting Office report begins with these two sentences: "Alien smuggling is a significant and growing problem. Although it is likely that most smuggled aliens are brought into the United States to pursue employment opportunities, some are smuggled as part of a criminal or terrorist enterprise that can pose a serious threat to U.S. national security" (May 1, 2000:1). Hence, according to this interpretation, it wasn't the *Golden Venture* smuggling ship that ran aground in 1993 as much as the World trade Center bombing a few months earlier that prompted U.S. government officials to reevaluate border security and strategy. In this scenario, it was desirable for the United States' security interests to diminish the chaos of small-scale mom-and-pop smuggling operations along the border in favor of larger, full-time criminal enterprises. Professional law enforcement techniques rely heavily on infiltration and disruption of stable and quite large criminal organizations rather than small-scale opportunists; in a nutshell, an ongoing professional criminal syndicate presents a much larger and weaker target than two cousins and an uncle moonlighting as migrant smugglers. Thus, by raising the physical and financial costs of a clandestine crossing it was more likely that smaller operations would be driven out of business and migrants would be funneled through (monitored) criminal syndicates.

Interestingly, both of these alternative theories of the United States constructing institutional human smuggling along its border call into question the two axioms of human smuggling reportage, that unfettered globalization is the root cause and that those being smuggled are uniformly the victims of evil smugglers. In the first instance, the concept of technological globalization is much too nebulous and macrosociological to capture the specific actions and political and economic conditions in some regions that have led to increased human smuggling of the type we see today. In the U.S. case, given state complicity in driving would-be migrants into more onerous smuggling operations run by professional criminals who routinely use violent coercion, apportioning all the blame to the smuggler conveniently avoids the moral and political complexity that is a near universal trait of actual smuggling activities. When such complexities do emerge from actual human smuggling situations, such as the prominent case of Cuban boy Elián Gonzalez, depending on one's political agenda the story can be shoe-horned to fit within a preexisting morality story. In the Gonzalez case, it is striking that many who would otherwise be on the side of illegal migration control viewed the mother of Elián, who died in a smuggling operation, not as a victim but as someone who willingly risked her life in order to reach the United States and offer her son a better life. Thus, while the Mexican smuggler helping other Mexicans—many of whom come from indigenous minorities or rural backwaters persecuted by Mexican authorities—find a better economic and political environment in the United States is described as exploitative and cruel when a smuggling operation ends in a death, his Cuban counterparts risking choppy seas in little more than rafts are almost never so described. Once again, the many paradoxes one encounters in the uneven and unbalanced control of people across state borders need to be viewed within the larger political context of conflicting strategic policy goals, of which controlling undocumented labor is only one consideration.

Migrant Exporting Schemes versus Slave Importing Operations

If the case of the U.S.-Mexican border buildup demonstrates how state policies engender professional human smuggling, it is insufficient to explain its more complex sociological and political foundations found in various regions around the world. However, it demonstrates an important point: a narrow focus on the criminal smuggler overlooks a range of people implicated and benefiting from the politics and business of human smuggling. In order to bring some conceptual clarity to the complex social phenomenon of human smuggling, we distinguish between two ideal types: *migrant exporting schemes* and *slave importing operations,* which are exemplified in the cases of Ecuador and Burma, discussed below. One or the other usually predominates in a sending region, though sometimes both together. These conceptual categories draw attention to the entire range of activities at both ends and not simply under what immediate conditions a person is smuggled across a border. The idea is to understand two different kinds of smuggling activities that are profitable, but under different circumstances and with distinct kinds of transnational social organizations.

The primary goal of a migrant exporting scheme is to provide a limited or "package" migration service out of a sending region (see Salt and Stein, 1997). Most of the organizational activity takes place on the sending side, and the contract is terminated once the migrant has arrived at the destination. In some cases, however, financial loans for the smuggling fees become an important source of income after arrival, but the terms of interest and payment and the division of labor vary greatly; the smuggler is not necessarily the loan shark. It is quite common for family members already abroad to lend the smuggling fee for a reduced rate. Such migrant exporting schemes are often characterized by highly irregular, often short-lived criminality, much of it opportunistic. Since many are part-timers, it is not simply a matter of breaking up a stable ring or criminal organization, though there is some evidence that larger criminal syndicates have moved into the migrant exporting business. It may or may not involve high levels of state corruption. Sending states typically find little political will to disrupt such migrant export projects owing to both a lack of criminal law for most related activities and the large sums of migrant remittances. Within such schemes, migrants are often driven to professional smugglers by blocked social mobility, preexisting corruption, and uneven development—not absolute poverty. Racism and sexism are common reasons for perceived ceilings in mobility, though many would be considered middle class within their home communities.

Migrant exporting is more likely money laundering than drug smuggling. The type of flow is not intrinsically illicit—unlike heroin. The principal investors do not have to accompany the commodity physically across the border. The layering process of identity laundering is built into all transactions along the way; once the migrant is integrated by crossing the border, the activity is complete—in contrast, getting heroin across the border is only the beginning because the criminal organization still needs to distribute and sell it in order to reap the bulk of profits. And this is exactly the crucial distinction between a migrant exporting scheme and a slave importing operation.

In a slave importing operation, the goal is to import weak labor, typically minority women, though not always so, for *ongoing* enterprises by relatively stable criminal organizations or even semilegitimate businesses in the destination country. Needless to say, a slave—held in bondage for economic profit—is extremely profitable (Bales, 1999). Unlike a migrant exporting scheme, a slave importing operation nearly always involves corruption of state officials in all countries involved. In most cases, victims of such operations are duped into believing that it is a migrant exporting scheme in which they are about to embark. Slave traders can pretend to be migration exporters precisely because the latter do exist. As with many cons, it is the victim's own complicity in a relatively minor crime (illegal border crossing) that leads to the final snare of the confidence scheme. Tragically, in this case, the migrant (now an illegal alien) is stripped of all legal rights and personal dignity and made to pay off a rolling debt through coerced labor, typically prostitution. Migrants may be held for weeks, months, or years in such conditions, paying off the new debt incurred each time they exchange hands. Given the nature of this enterprise, unlike a migrant exporting scheme, often the victims come from much more dire economic and social situations; it is a combination of their desperateness, political weakness, and lack of strong social networks that leads them to believe the false promises. Such operations are sophisticated enough to have the initial contact person be a seemingly wealthy woman from the same ethnic group as the victim. The recruiter's claims are buttressed by the ubiquitous images of idealized lifestyles of the most developed countries now beamed by satellite around the world through the global media industry.

There is a legal, political, moral, and sociological difference between the two types of smuggling activities we have outlined here. Slaves are slaves; it does not matter what unfortunate decisions were made to place them in the hands of slaveholders. By focusing on the nature of the economic enterprise spanning multiple countries, and not the degree to which a migrant agreed to be smuggled (few are actually kidnapped), we gain a better understanding of what is at stake for those at multiple levels of society who are benefiting from smuggling operations, whether directly or indirectly, and a deeper understanding of their different economic logics may lead to more appropriate policies that go beyond capturing the immediate perpetrators. We next turn to two examples of a migrant exporting scheme and a slave importing operation in order to move from an ideal type to the historical complexities of actual cases.

Ecuador: Migrant Exporting Schemes

Most Ecuadorians abroad are from a single region of Ecuador, the southern province of Azuay, where the most recent development project in a long history of entrepreneurial efforts has come to include migrant exporting. Located approximately 300 kilometers south of Quito over mountainous terrain, the province of Azuay includes Ecuador's third largest city, Cuenca (pop. 330,000), and shares a common social and political history with the neighboring province of Cañar.

Unlike neighboring regions, Azuay is characterized by an early integration with, and dependence on, the capitalist world economy. Azuayans exported cloth during the colonial period. The Azuayan elite relied on ideological control of its nominally independent peasantry, which included unusually large numbers of Spaniards and mestizos compared with the indigenous population. Unlike the rest of Ecuador, Azuay largely avoided the extremes of the colonial *encomienda* system of debt peonage but did not escape it altogether. Throughout the colonial period, policies restricting peasants to *reduciones,* or bounded communities, severely limited their social mobility.

After independence from Spain, the lack of royal authority and Azuay's general isolation meant that local elites could consolidate their political dominance and increase their ideological claims to the region's resources and surplus labor. For example, when the cloth trade in Azuay collapsed in the early 1800s owing to cheap British imports, Azuayan elites actively searched for economic solutions to the crisis that would not fundamentally alter the social status quo. The challenge for elites was straightforward: after several decades of placing little pressure on the Azuayan and Cañari peasantry following the decline of the cloth trade, they needed a peasant cottage industry that furthered the elite's role as intermediaries and could fill a market niche using preindustrial technology and inexpensive raw materials. Thus, local elites deliberately introduced to the region a productive activity—the weaving of straw hats—that would not upset but reinforce the existing Azuayan social structure.

In promoting the new industry, local officials noted the low cost of the straw and other materials needed and also that it was an occupation in which "all hands [could] be put to work, including men and women, elderly and children" (Dominguez, 1991:36). With such a concerted push by the elite and the quick popularity of the hats in sunny Azuay itself, the introduction was a huge success—to the extent that peasants and urban poor were soon weaving hats in nearly every corner of Azuay and Cañar. With the internal demand satisfied, the hats began to be exported for gold miners passing through Panama during the California gold rush of the 1850s (hence the name "Panama hat"); the value of straw hat exports from Ecuador jumped from 117,008 pesos in 1843 to 830,040 in 1855 (Palomeque, 1990).

The weaving of straw hats—planned and instituted by local elites—began a radical transformation that would soon articulate the region into a labor-intensive, industrial bureaucracy, closely linked to the world economy. Though the cottage industry of hat weaving was similar to that of cloth weaving, whereby both raw material and woven product were brokered to the peasantry by middlemen who were, directly or indirectly, employed by urban export "houses," the production and marketing process entailed a greater division of labor on a much larger scale with (as city officials predicted) the participation of both men and women, young and old, each finding his or her production niche. The brokering system itself employs a hierarchy of *comisionistas*, who broker for the export houses, and independent *perros* (dogs), who sell to the *comisionistas* after paying the weaver slightly less for the hat than what the *comisionista* would have paid. Dominguez estimates that at the height of the hat trade in the 1940s as many as 250,000 children and adults from the provinces of Azuay and Cañar were engaged in some activity directly related to making and marketing "Panama hats" (1991).

Although the peasant weavers of Azuay enjoyed an unprecedented freedom in comparison with their counterparts living on haciendas or working in urban sweatshops, their ambiguous class position prevented the achievement of any significant economic or social gains through group mobilization; though thousands were and continue to be exploited at piece rates below subsistence level, this common exploitation as a potential source of group action is outweighed by their conservative position as landowners in direct economic competition with their neighbors—a fact fully exploited by the *comisionistas* and *perros*.

A "long decade" of economic depression in Azuay began with the precipitous drop in Panama hat exports in 1947 and its continuous decline every year until the mind-1960s. Cuenca's principal importer of Panama hats, the United States, began to import cheaper "straw" hats from Asia after World War II.

The impact of the hat industry's decline on Azuay and Cañar was immediate and severe, initiating a quiet revolution of economic disarticulation and social disintegration. For many members of the urban elite not directly connected to the hat trade, any financial losses were compensated by their ability to exploit the new vulnerability of the rural and urban labor force. It was, instead, those diverse groups engaged in some activity related to the hat trade (which at its height included over a quarter of the population) that had to seek external remedies to the immediate economic crisis they were experiencing. While the local and national elite did little to respond effectively to the Azuayan crisis of the 1950s, two groups—the white-mestizo exporters and the rural peasant weavers—began two different types of migration that together would set the stage for a mass exodus in the 1980s and 1990s. It is during the 1950s that the first Cuencanos arrived in New York City, mostly young men of wealthy white and mestizo families directly connected to urban hat export houses. They were looking for ways to capitalize financially on their longstanding connections with U.S. importers—and for adventure (Astudillo and Cordero, 1990). It is also during the late 1950s that regular jet airline service connected Cuenca to New York City via Guayaquil: it was now just as easy for a Cuencano to travel to New York City as to Quito, Ecuador's capital.

These pioneering migration networks notwithstanding, the mass regionwide phenomenon of international migration from Azuay, Cañar, and Morona Santiago (largely populated by Azuayans) that developed during the 1980s cannot be completely accounted for by a geometric increase, that is, a simple "snow-ball" effect of migrants helping family and neighbors to make the multiple border crossings—especially the high number of peasants migrating to New York City directly from the most rural areas. Unlike other historical international flows of documented and undocumented immigrants, there is no evidence of direct recruitment by North American employers to facilitate the considerable financial and legal obstacles of the journey. Yet, in just ten years, the modest international migrations of the 1970s turned into a mass exodus, making it one of the largest groups of undocumented immigrants in the New York City metro area.

This sharp increase in international migration, especially from rural, isolated areas, can be explained only by the reemergence of a centuries-old institution in the region—the usurious middleman, who profits from the economic and political space afforded by a complacent elite and a captive peasantry, in this case, an integrated network of *tramitadores*, or facilitators, who provide the range of legal and illegal services needed to make a clandestine trip to the United States. Instead of mediating the hat procurement for export houses as in the hat trade, *tramitadores* work, directly or indirectly, for unscrupulous travel agencies, which are themselves participants in larger formal and underground networks of migration merchants, or those who profit from some aspect of the migrant exporting business.

Although these facilitating networks are international in scope, they begin with a *tramitador*'s sales pitch to the would-be migrant in his or her home village, not unlike the role played by the *perros* in the straw hat trade. The *tramitador* offers to arrange all the national documents needed to leave Ecuador, visas for intermediary countries, all the physical travel arrangements, and, depending on the type of trip, a falsified U.S. visa or passport. To pay for all these services, which run from $6,000 to $10,000, an amount even the wealthiest of Ecuadorians would balk at, the *tramitador* arranges to have the money lent to the ingenuous peasant by a *chulquero* (smuggler/moneylender), at usurious interest rates of 10–12 percent, compounded monthly, with all land, animals, and possessions of the migrant held as collateral. In addition, numerous local banks and money exchange houses provide the needed financial infrastructure and legal cover for such operations. Local community-based networks of *tramitadores* and *chulqueros* typically are closely related by kinship, relying on social ties with a high degree of trust and loyalty, thus allowing for clandestine capitalism to operate with fewer costs (both monetary and psychological) related to maintaining the financial and legal security of the covert economic activity. For example, in one medium-sized Azuayan town with high levels of international migration, all the moneylenders are members of just five families, and each of these families is further interlocked through marital ties. It should be emphasized that moneylending as an economic institution with a set of rules and customs has been a historical feature of the region even before the rural economy was completely monetized. The vicissitudes of small-scale and subsistence farming among the peasantry, along with the periodic burden of financing an annual religious festival, have traditionally required the services of moneylenders, who are either coethnic villagers or white-mestizo outsiders and whose rates are officially controlled by the state. For example, in times of crop failure, a loan enabled households not only to buy the few necessary household goods but also, most important, to continue to production cycle, which could include temporary coastal migrations and handicraft production. In times of regional scarcity, loans from "outside" the village with one of the urban-based "patrons" often involved usurious practices made possible by the peasant's ignorance and general position of weakness vis-à-vis the patron.

With corrupt local officials and a network of professional forgers, the necessary local and national documents are bought by the *tramitador.* Often the forger's work is so good that U.S. embassy personnel in Quito cannot figure out how the documents can circumvent infrared detectors and laminate safeguards developed by the 3M company (personal communication). Next, working with legitimate travel agents, the *tramitador* makes the travel arrangements, which, broadly speaking, fall into either of two categories: (1) the direct route to New York City, using a "borrowed" passport or forged visa, which also entails a significant amount of cultural coaching on how to look and act like a *residente;* or (2) the tortuous overland route that includes a sophisticated network of Central American and Mexican contacts, "safe houses," and "coyotes" (those who actually lead the migrant across the Rio Grande). Since the Mexican government has made attaining a visa to its country more difficult, sometimes coyotes are also used to get into Mexico through a Guatemalan farm or by boat. At every step of the way, from the financing of the trip in Ecuador to the dependence on a nefarious international network spanning half a dozen countries, the migrant risks being swindled, ailed, deported, robbed, or violently abused, including rape and murder. Not surprisingly, the main task of the *tramitador* is to gain the confidence, whether founded or unfounded, of the potential "client." The price of land is so inflated owing to competition by return migrants in both urban and rural areas that only those who have a U.S. dollar income can hope to purchase a new plot, lending support to the recruiter's sales pitch.

The particular configuration of financial and human resources brought to bear by each migrant on the problem of getting him or her across a border is often as unique as the Azuayan villages and barrios. The financing of the trip usually involves a combination of personal savings, free loans by relatives, interest loans by friends, and usurious loans by *chulqueros*. Similarly, a catalog of the techniques used to get across the U.S. border or obtain a tourist visa could fill a medium-sized book. Kin- and community-based migration networks make use of the information and resources circulating within them, thereby making migration paths fairly consistent within a given social network. In this way, the path taken by a successful migrant pioneer gets repeated and revised within his or her network. Sometimes this evolutionary process may induce a pioneer, who has already made several trips and may be a *residente*, or "green-card" holder, to become an in-network *tramitador*, or coyote, or *chulquero* whose services are provided for a lower fee or even freely (that is, monetarily speaking, though reciprocity of some sort is assumed). Conversely, it is also common for return migrants to lend money to regional intermediaries (of the *perro* mold), who in turn lend at higher rates to professional *chulqueros*, who in turn lend to the new migrant at the highest rate, thus forming a pyramid scheme that requires a constant influx of new migrants to keep capital circulating to the top.

To conclude this section, the impact of mass international migration is nothing short of an economic and social transformation for the province of Azuay. These individual, community, and regional transformations leading to one of the most important mass international migrations from South America are built not on the foundation of either individual decisions or the snowball effect of social networks but rather on a regionwide migrant exporting industry in which a wide range of people play a direct and indirect role, from the re-cruiter to the local banker. The explosive construction of new concrete homes in some rural villages near Cuenca, often filled with a new SUV in the garage and chickens in the upper floors, provides testimony to the general success of the migrant exporting schemes in this region. The sustainability and future changes in the social organization of these schemes are topics for future research.

Burma and Thailand: Slave Importing Operations

A guest staying in one of Myanmar's (Burma) finest hotels may be surprised to learn through an official tourist brochure that Myanmar has a unique natural resource that it would like to offer: its own female virgins (Knowles, 1997; Kyaa Nyo, 1997). A male tourist may therefore be able to experience not only the virgin quality of a mysterious country dotted with hundreds of ancient pagodas, only recently opened to tourism, but also a night with a virgin girl from a rural village who may be as young as twelve years old. If the Myanmar government helps promote its virgins as a local resource for sale, it is not surprising that virgins are also an exportable and highly profitable commodity. The primary destination for young women trafficked out of Myanmar is Thailand, with some eventually continuing on to other destinations.

The transnational trafficking of women and girls between Myanmar and Thailand, while perhaps increasing in overall numbers, is not a new development. As Eileen Scully (this volume, Chap. 4) points out, by the 1890s "networks of varying sophistication and durability" were evident throughout Southeast Asia. Already, as is still the case today, "sexual service to foreigners had been commoditized and stigmatized, the fate of low-born and marginal women." What's novel about the contemporary flow of women from Myanmar to Thailand's sex-work industry is that ethnic minority women from the countryside of Myanmar are in demand by foreign tourists and business travelers (particularly Chinese) in Thailand. This emerging, exoticizing taste for Burmese prostitutes is refined by one further criterion: these women (girls, really) must be virgins. At least, it is Burmese (ethnic Shan) virgins for whom foreign customers traveling in Thailand are willing to pay the most money. Moreover, the states of both Myanmar and Thailand are playing the most proactive role in constituting this demand. H. Richard Friman (this volume, Chap. 13) explains how the state (Japan) plays a constitutive role in the ideological construction of the "snakehead" threat as "foreign" and how the state benefits from this construction both politically and economically. Myanmar and Thailand, however, profit by playing a more direct role in constructing the markets of transnational organized crime that we are describing here. Before turning to Myanmar, to understand the regional and international market for Burmese virgins, we must examine recent economic and demographic changes in Thailand.

In the minds of many Thai citizens, globalization has come to mean currency crisis and unemployment. Joining the prescriptive belt-tightening fiscal austerity discourse provided by the International Monetary Fund has been a more indigenous, nationalist discourse targeting illegal immigration. Curiously absent from the Thai state's remedial discussion of the causes of illegal immigration has been the state's own role in promoting it. In the summer of 1996, when financial analysts worldwide still perceived the Southeast Asian "tiger" economies as roaring, the Thai state issued a cabinet resolution allowing employers in forty-three provinces to register illegal Burmese, Laotians, and Cambodians already living in Thailand to work for two years. The purpose of the resolution was to ease the burden of Thailand's labor shortage. The unanticipated currency crisis, however, engendered a new official policy toward illegal immigration: repatriation of the approximately one million illegal alien workers in an attempt to ease the sharp increase of unemployment among Thai nationals. Most illegal alien workers in Thailand are from Myanmar.

About twenty thousand young girls and boys (age ten to fifteen) are smuggled from Myanmar each year to work in Thailand's sex industry (Mirkinson, 1994: 4). This represents about 10 percent of all prostitutes working in Thailand (Chaipipat, 1997). Most of these youths come from Shan state in the northeastern region of Myanmar, bordering Thailand. According to research presented in Bangkok at a 1997 regional conference on the prevention of human trafficking, the annual illegal income generated by sex workers (of all ages) in Thailand is between 450 billion and 540 billion baht (or roughly US$10 billion).[1] To put these numbers in perspective, this is more money than is generated from drug trafficking. Moreover, Thailand's total state budget was only 1 trillion baht in 1995, prior to the recent currency crisis (Chaipipat, 1997). Complicating Thailand's repatriation policy objective, Myanmar insists that it will not accept illegal workers from its ethnic minority groups now employed in Thailand.

In 1988, a statewide prodemocracy movement emerged in Myanmar to challenge twenty-six years of political repression and economic mismanagement under the military regime that usurped control of the state in a 1962 coup. The military state's crackdown was more dramatic and bloody than that witnessed the following year in Beijing's Tiananmen Square. Western democratic states responded initially to what they identified as human rights abuses by passing economic sanctions against Myanmar. Sorely in need of foreign investment, the military-state regime began to privatize its state-managed natural resources (teak, jade, and oil), abandoning its isolationist economic policy known as the

"Burmese way to Socialism." The state also consented to the demands of the major opposition party, the National League for Democracy, led by Aung San Suu Kyi. Suu Kyi, who has since been awarded the Nobel Peace Prize for her efforts, is the daughter of the national hero Aung San, who was assassinated by the associates of Myanmar's current dictator shortly after he had successfully led the country to democratic independence from the British and Japanese in the wake of World War II. Suu Kyi demanded successfully that the military regime hold fair and democratic elections, and in a 1990 landslide victory she was elected with 82 percent of the vote. The military, however, refusing to honor the results, instead responded by placing Suu Kyi under house arrest and systematically arresting and/or assassinating the newly elected members of her party in each township throughout the state.

As prodemocracy activists from the urban centers of Rangoon and Mandalay fled to the rural Thai-Myanmar border regions to join forces with ethnic minority rebels who had been fighting the state for national autonomy since the initial coup, the Burmese military launched a new campaign to eradicate these rebel strongholds. For the past decade, the military has resorted to a systematic policy of burning local villages along the border, raping and torturing ethnic minority women, forcibly conscripting villagers to serve the military as porters, minesweepers, and human shields in its campaigns to exterminate oppositional groups and coercively enslaving villagers to work on the military state's infrastructural projects. Some of these projects, like the oil pipeline being constructed through Myanmar to Thailand, are financed by transnational corporations like Unocal (based in the United States) and Total (based in France). Such military campaigns and development projects have generated a dramatic increase in Thailand's refugee camps situated along the Thai-Myanmar border.

In contrast to the economic sanctions initiated by Western democratic states (and encouraged by Suu Kyi's National League for Democracy Party), member states of the Association of Southeast Asian Nations (ASEAN), along with China and, of course, transnational corporations with high levels of investment in partnerships with the state-owned Myanmar Holdings Company Ltd., have continued trading with Myanmar under a policy of constructive engagement. Proponents of this policy argue that reviving official development assistance, promoting more investment, and even encouraging nongovernmental associations (NGOs) to provide humanitarian assistance will bring about much needed social and political change in Myanmar. They maintain that isolating the military state regime through economic sanctions is ineffective. In 1997,

ASEAN inducted Myanmar as a new member of its economic regional trading bloc. Myanmar's ruling party celebrated its induction into ASEAN as a solution to its flagging attraction as a site of foreign investment. However, Myanmar was unable to cash in on this opportunity owing to the simultaneous onset of what became dubbed in the international financial press as the "Southeast Asian currency crisis." Myanmar's potential trading allies, such as Indonesia and Thailand, were suddenly subjected suddenly to strict lending criteria imposed by the International Monetary Fund. Overt investment in Myanmar was no longer politically feasible. Yet Myanmar has pursued other sources of unofficial revenue in more clandestine transnational markets of Southeast Asia (and beyond), as illustrated in some of its official tourist brochures promoting another of its putative natural resources: Burmese virgins.

Both men and women from Myanmar concentrated in Thai refugee camps along the border have reported in interviews with humanitarian NGO workers that local Thai officials forced them upon threat of being repatriated to serve as recruiters for organized human smuggling groups engaged in the trafficking of young girls from Myanmar into Thailand's sex industry.[2] The local Thai officials, typically immigration border patrol officers, then receive a bounty from one of the agents of the human smuggling groups. Sometimes the process works the other way around, whereby the agents approach the Thai officials and pay them bribe money to pass without complication through the border checkpoints. These refugee recruiters lead the agents to their home villages in Myanmar. Along the way (and back), the agents pay bribes whenever necessary to Myanmar's military-state personnel. The refugees are needed for their skills in speaking Burmese as well as the local ethnic minority language of the target village in Myanmar. Perhaps most important, the refugees are used to establish the trust necessary for persuading the young girls' families to relinquish custody of their daughters (usually with some form of material compensation) to the Thai officials.

While some girls have a vague idea of the nature of the work they will be doing, they are not aware of the working conditions (particularly the debt peonage) that await them. Upon returning, the local official typically charges 5,000 baht per person brought by agents of the human smuggling operation into Thailand. Brothel owners in Thailand pay the agents, who pay the state authorities, but ultimately the brothel owner charges this same amount to the young girl's debt. As a "virgin," she will earn up to 15,000 baht from one customer. Virgins—particularly Burmese or Shan virgins—command top dollar in many areas of Thailand these days. Most of the demand seems to be coming from Chinese tourists and businessmen. A young girl's "loss of virginity" can be sold several times, until she can no longer pass as a virgin in the eyes of her potential customers. Through a surgical procedure, a girl can also be "revirginized." Thus, the loss of virginity is viewed not so much as an event but rather as a gradual process. Many of these young girls from Myanmar, even prior to entering the sex trade in Thailand, can recount stories of being raped by the Myanmar military. Virgins are highly valued not only for the reduced risk of their having HIV infection but also because in many Asian cultures deflowering a virgin is considered to bestow upon the perpetrator youthful potency and healthful benefits. Burmese and Shan girls are exoticized as special virgins, partly because of the relative isolation of Myanmar for several decades.

The money earned from the commodification of these young girls' virginity is significantly more than that earned by nonvirgins—a status the former are, of course, quickly on their way to assuming. Yet the percentage they actually receive is not even enough to cover their initial smuggling debt. Moreover, the local police regularly raid these brothels (typically consisting of several rooms above a karaoke bar or coffee shop) in order to collect bribe money from the brothel owners, whose business in Thailand is illegal. The cost of these bribes is added to the young girls' debt, along with the cost of their food, clothing, cosmetics, toiletries, occasional health checks, and "rent" (although they typically sleep in the same room, just big enough for a bed and sink, where they service their customers). A "Burmese virgin" can expect to spend an average of eighteen months working simply to pay off her debt to her original brothel owner, or to any subsequent owner who purchases her (and her debt) from that original owner.

It is important to understand that it is not the girl who has paid the bribes to the police all along but rather the brothel owner. This money is not paid simply to prevent the girls from being arrested and deported; it is an informally institutionalized source of income for the police in exchange for their protecting the brothel owner. Sometimes brothel owners or agents will ask the police to arrest certain girls working in their brothel when the owners or agents do not want to give the sex workers the money they owe them. The new Thai policy of repatriating illegal alien workers has not diminished demand for the employment of these girls. It has, however, made it much more difficult for these girls to move into other areas of work and thus to remain in Thailand, once (or if) they have managed to buy back their freedom. Moreover, Thai immigration policy changes have not slowed trafficking but rather have made it easier for the brothel owners and police to threaten these women with repatriation.

Thailand's most recent immigration policy proposal might appear destined for failure (in terms of its putative intent to curb migrant trafficking), but a careful reading between the lines suggests that, in practice, it may serve the state's interests. Thailand's immigration police announced in February 1998 that they had come up with a new strategy to encourage legal and illegal immigrants working in the country to return to their homelands voluntarily: instead of launching crackdowns on illegal workers, immigration police were being instructed to provide travel expenses and free meals to alien workers wishing to return home (Charoenpho, 1998). They argued that this "psychological approach," which focuses only on illegal workers, would be more cost-effective than crackdowns, whereby arrested illegal workers are sent directly to detention centers for months (of free meals). Under the new strategy, authorities would be required to pay only travel expenses and free meals on the day that the workers leave for their countries. In addition, the Thai immigration police, according to the national press, cited their concern for curbing the activities of human smugglers: "To prevent other Burmese immigrants from sneaking through the country [Thailand], Police Lieutenant-General Chidchai said he has liased with non-governmental organizations, the army and concerned agencies to help keep close watch on the movement of human smuggling gangs" (Charoenpho, 1998: 2).

In a move that was meant to be interpreted as "putting their money where their mouth is," the immigration police, in the same report, assured Thai nationals that they had asked Police Region 7 (which is responsible for western provinces bordering Myanmar) to deploy more officials at border passes to prevent the influx of Burmese into the country. This move addresses the common rebuttal bandied in the press that the rate of illegal immigration influx (particularly owing to internal conflict in Myanmar) outpaces that of repatriation. As a solution to preventing illegal Burmese immigration, however, the deployment of more officials at border passes, as we have seen, may serve only to exacerbate the problem. It is precisely such corrupt officials who have been making possible illegal migration from Myanmar through their complicity in human smuggling activities. In fairness to the government of Thailand, its historical and geographical location within one of the world's most volatile regions makes its triple challenges of political stability, economic development, and migration control especially severe. Similarly, few countries in the world are untouched by some degree of official corruption. Nonetheless, the evidence suggests that while Thailand has recently passed laws increasing the penalties for sexual relations with children, the ubiquitous sex industry organized mostly for local consumption and the enormous profits to be gained by investors in the sex trade call into question the notion that women and children trafficked into Thailand and held in bondage are simply the result of some criminal miscreants.

Agents of Human Smuggling Reconsidered

In this section, we examine actors who are common to both of our cases as well as to other cases of migrant smuggling. First, however, in comparing these two differing cases of human smuggling from Ecuador and Myanmar, what is most striking is what is largely missing: "transnational gangsters." Although many point to "transnational organized crime" as the driving social force behind the global increase in human smuggling (see, e.g., Godson and Olson, 1995), it plays only a support role, if at all, in these two cases. Given the nature of the human commodity being smuggled, it is predictable that some human smugglers are members of traditional crime organizations, though by some definitions even corrupt police could be segregated conceptually into the organized crime camp. There is much evidence that most smugglers of migrants around the world simply participate in what Finckenauer (this volume, chap. 12) calls "crime that is organized" but not "organized crime." An additional element to this crime that is organized recalls earlier forms of widespread smuggling; for many around the world participating in migrant exporting and even slave importing is not perceived, as a result of longstanding sociocultural norms, as a "real crime" in the region of origin.

Some migrant smugglers are more akin to the historical "free traders" of an earlier era when important commodities, in this case labor, were highly regulated and usuriously taxed. Migrant smugglers from the region of Azuay are not members of transnational organized crime in any traditional meaning of the term. Most are helping family and neighbors get to New York City. This is a case that illustrates that mass undocumented migration can rapidly increase without organized crime. In contrast, Myanmar presents a case of "state-organized crime" (Chambliss, 1989), entailing the smuggling of an illicit and, to be sure, morally bankrupt commodity. There is all too often a belief that a victim must somehow have deserved her or his fate. Especially on the migrant exporting end of the business, smugglers and moneylenders advertise in newspapers and do little to cover the nature of their business. Moreover, we have seen in the case of Myanmar that even states may subtly advertise to tourists the availability of commodities, the consumption of which are officially designated illicit, such as virgin prostitution. Similarly, it is the parents of young girls who will sometimes sell a daughter for a sum equal to one year's income.

Apart from problematizing the role of organized crime, our two cases implicate other, unusual suspects in the social organization of migrant smuggling: (a) regional elites; (b) states pursuing their official interests and corrupt state officials pursuing self-aggrandizement; and (c) employers at the destination.

Regional Elites

For many developing countries, local economic and political power is concentrated in relatively few regional elite families (Walton, 1977). This is especially striking in the case of Azuay, where such families are still referred to as "the nobles." Since the early 1960s, many elites have adopted the discourse, if not also the strategies, of successive waves of development experts from North America and Europe, especially as foreigners have brought financial and technological aid. Yet the results of the previous modernization period were mixed at best, in large part owing to the unwillingness of regional elites to give up real power and the ideologies of social stratification that legitimize privilege. Hence, we have a common local "development" situation in the 1990s in many parts of the world: great strides in isolated areas that raise expectations for a better life but which do not live up to their promise.

Mass emigration may seem to be the ultimate measure of failure of a regional economy. However, mass transnational migration through an efficient, even rationalized, system of migration commodification and smuggling overcomes the two most important concerns for regional elites in the 1990s: migrant smuggling continues to profit from workers through remittances and curtails political upheaval associated with the broken promises of failed "development" projects.

Not only does the export of people have some of the advantages of other traditional exports, such as backward linkages (e.g., financial services) and forward linkages (e.g., construction), but it also does not have the most significant disadvantage—competition from other regions around the world; migrants represent a global export paradoxically contained within a locally controlled market. Hence, transnational undocumented migration is an unintended consequence of development through modernization—a sort of grassroots development project itself from which many regional elites continue to profit.

States and Corrupt State Officials

The commodification of migration affects sending and receiving states very differently, a fact that points to the real nature of human smuggling and undocumented migration vis-à-vis the saliency of the modern state system. State boundaries add to the value of any commodity needed across borders. Indeed, they are dependent on each other. In the case of human smuggling, sending states have generally viewed migration, whether legal or not, as a positive benefit. Remittances now rival many traditional sources of state revenue. Sending states have even reached out to include migrants abroad in domestic politics and have taken an active role in how undocumented co-nationals are treated in the United States and Europe. The Mexican ambassador Silva Herzog, speaking at the national convention of the League of United Latin American Citizens in Anaheim, California, observed, "It is particularly surprising that at a time of almost unprecedented success in the United States economy . . . the anti-immigration voices have once again taken the high ground. . . . Make no mistake about it, this is racism and xenophobia, and it has a negative impact on every person of Hispanic origin living in this country, regardless of their migratory status" (*Los Angeles Times,* June 26, 1997). Such aggressive campaigning for lessening immigration controls by a Mexican official in the United States is grounded not only in humanitarian concerns but also in the fear that the more than $4.5 billion remittances (ibid.) to families in Mexico every year will recede during a grave economic crisis at home.

Similarly, in Burma, the military government has cried foul because Thailand wants to repatriate Burmese nationals because of backlash against foreigners during a period of economic hardship. Illegal aliens from Myanmar working in Thailand manage to send home substantial amounts of money to their families (substantial, at least, to families living in a country where the annual per capita income is currently about U.S. $150). However, Myanmar's military tends to collect this remitted money through various forms of violence, bribery, and "taxation," which is paid either in cash, labor, or social capital.

Highly publicized in the international media have been the Myanmar military's violent campaigns and practices of coerced labor, extortion, "ethnic cleansing" (rape and murder), and crop burning against its rural ethnic minor-

ity communities living in the border regions of the state (see. e.g., www.soros
.org/burma). We have also noted above how less publicized practices of bribery,
or the payment of "tea money" to state employees, have become informally
institutionalized.

However, the military also collects "taxes" from locals, which are typically
imposed suddenly, as circumstances may dictate. Taxes may be imposed on
particular villages for "beautification projects" (such as patching up ditches in
the villages' dirt roads) purportedly designed to enhance tourism. Those who
cannot pay the tax in cash pay the tax in labor, helping to patch up the roads.
The state also collects taxes from local villages that do not produce the quota
of rice required by the state—even in cases when the state's military campaigns
have destroyed the rice crops, making it impossible for the villagers to meet
such quotas.

When a family within the village has no money to pay these taxes, the state
requires that family to offer a male member of the household to serve either
as a porter (without pay) in the military to fight in campaigns against rebel
ethnic minority armies or in state construction projects. Few of these conscripts
ever return to see their families. It is not uncommon to learn that they have
been literally worked to death. If a poor family has neither the money nor a
male member of the family to serve in the military, it may be able to borrow
the money from either a wealthier family in the village or from the state in
order to hire a neighbor's son to serve in the military for them. In this sense,
the state "taxes" the villagers' social capital.

In short, if the economically poor military state of Myanmar suspects that
there are sources of wealth to be tapped within these villages, it can and does
construct a justification for usurping that wealth. The state understands that a
significant portion of that wealth is sustained through remittances from migrant members of the village working abroad. Thus it is not surprising that the
proposal last year by Thailand's House Committee on Labor and Social Welfare
met with protest from the state of Myanmar. In its effort to alleviate the burden
of continuing to employ illegal workers from Myanmar, Thailand proposed to
tax them all (including ethnic minorities) and remit the money directly to the
state of Myanmar. If Myanmar had accepted these conditions, then it would
have meant that it had also accepted the status of its minority workers in
Thailand—an acknowledgment Myanmar was unwilling to provide. After all,
there was little to gain in doing so: Myanmar already receives at least as much
in remittances by "taxing" local minorities who remain in Myanmar.

In regard to the receiving states, such as the United States, it would seem that the commodification of migration and the increasing use of smugglers would be uniformly negative. After all, some U.S. policymakers have even considered the elimination of birthright citizenship for "illegal aliens." Although employers benefit from falsely documented labor, such benefits cannot be collapsed into the interests of the state. In addition, the economic benefit of both documented and undocumented migration to the U.S. economy on the whole is an area of hot debate.

Unlike private employers, U.S. leaders and policymakers have a variety of pro-immigrant, anti-immigrant, and ethnic communities to contend with and placate (see Freeman, 1994; Joppke, 1998). Although immigration laws must be upheld by the state, and although anti-immigrant voices include some demographic and economic rationales that cannot simply be reduced to racism, there is also a political price for "bashing immigrants." High-profile state agencies can diminish the political fallout of migration controls through a diffusing strategy that relies on a variety of third-party actors such as airlines and privatized detention centers. In a similar manner, a more commodified migration process, also using third parties (i.e., smugglers), allows states to develop a discourse that emphasizes the criminality and evil of alien smuggling rings, which can then be contrasted with hardworking immigrants.

Employers and Slaveholders

North American employers of unskilled urban and farm labor directly benefit from an efficient underground source of labor. Were migrants dependent upon their own social networks to cross borders under conditions of heightened state monitoring, immigrant labor flow might subside. Thus, smugglers might be conceptualized as an extension of, and in some cases a replacement for, labor recruiters. In some undocumented smuggling streams, the migrant, and even the individual smuggler for that matter (see Kyle and Dale, 1999), becomes a sort of indentured servant working for the syndicate or a collaborator. In extreme cases, slavery has returned in the form of garment and sex workers held captive in Los Angeles and New York City. Contemporary slavery, as Bales (1999: 14) pointed out, is not about slave owning but "slave-holding," or complete control over people for economic profit. While this is a useful distinction between older and more contemporary forms of slavery, it is also one that is more disconcerting, since the organization of work around the world under the globalization project has led to greater levels of labor control, practices that are increasingly legitimized as necessary for survival within a competitive global arena. Even when free to find employment on their own terms, illegal immigrants with large usurious debts make an especially docile and hardworking labor force—a point not overlooked by employers or states in receiving countries.

Thus, instead of conceptualizing contemporary slaves as "disposable people," the title of Bales's book, we might instead view them as an extreme, though not uncommon, example of the growing process by which labor is forced underground into invisibility as well as disposability. One could argue that the concept of "disposable people" per se is not particularly novel to the current globalization project but rather has been the lot of much of humanity historically. What is novel is the growing levels of work that is purposively hidden by employers and laborers from the global markets they are seeking to sell in or from the local clientele of "global cities" (Sassen, 1991). Tellingly, all the actors highlighted in this section—local elites, states, and employers—justify their less than honorable actions by invoking some form of the argument "globalization made me do it." Globalization *as an ideology* continues to blur the boundaries of what should be considered exploitative economic behavior first and foremost in the area of labor relations.

Conclusion

Existing studies of transnational human smuggling, its organization, and the actors that sustain this practice are typically shaped by a particularly ahistorical conception of "organized crime"—one that allows no conceptual space for analyzing the organization sources of transnational smuggling provided by, and thus implicating, regional elites, states, and employers (and, hence, consumers). Proceeding deductively from the common assumption that only large-scale transnational criminal organizations are driving increases in the levels of human smuggling fails to elucidate the central, proactive roles played by noncriminal migrants and criminal nonmigrants, including corrupt state representatives, in sustaining and transforming the practice of professional human smuggling. Other studies also suggest that even the premise of the deductive analysis of complex groups of transnational organized crime as necessary to the clandestine activities associated with human smuggling is faulty, especially in cases in which a previous legal activity has been converted to an illegal, heavily penalized one (see Reuter, 1985).

We have used a historical comparative approach in an attempt to under-stand the social organization, political benefits, and economic profitability of contemporary human smuggling as a diverse bundle of activities and partici-pants. Our findings suggest that comparing processes of transnational migrant smuggling across different times and places reveals a wide range of social for-mations implicating a diverse configurations of actors. Yet we have conceptu-alized some significant differences between two fundamental types of smug-gling enterprises: migrant exporting schemes and slave importing operations. Both can be just as deadly for the migrant and place him or her at a great legal and physical risk, but we believe that effective policies need to distinguish among a range of smuggling operations, some which are aiding people to leave situations of political persecution and economic hopelessness and others that deliver them into precisely such circumstances. In broad terms, three themes emerge from this comparison of a migrant exporting scheme and a slave im-porting operation: global diversity, internal organization complexity, and con-tradictory state involvement in human smuggling activities and human rights. Through empirical research, the following chapters help elucidate in diverse ways these three basic operations.

The central argument of this chapter—that the role of criminal syndicates must be balanced with other state and commercial actors with domestic and global interests—was buttressed by the transformation of out-migration from Ecuador just as the first edition was being sent to the printers. Following the dollariza-tion of its economy in 2000, a mass irregular migration to Spain from every region of Ecuador, representing 10 percent of its population, unfolded so quickly that Ecuadorians become the largest immigrant community in Spain by 2004. Strikingly, this irregular mobility arriving by plane did not feature stereotypi-cal smugglers but rather was facilitated by backroom deals by travel agencies and migration merchants lending migrants funds at high interest rates for the cost of the ticket and the approximately $2,000 needed to demonstrate that they were "tourists" (see Kyle and Siracusa, 2005). This was also made possible with complicit Ecuadorian and Spanish state involvement in the conditions and terms of Ecuadorian immigrant labor in Spain, though most were in viola-tion of Spanish labor laws.

In contrast, smuggling routes through Mexico have seen an increase in criminal syndicates involved in drug smuggling with high levels of violence threatening transiting migrants for purposes of kidnapping and extortion

(Kyle and Scarcelli, 2009). The most horrifying example was the 2010 massacre of seventy-two Central American and South American migrants, many Ecuadorian, in Tamaulipas State after allegedly refusing to pay their captors. However, even in these cases, there was no evidence of complicity by the group's smugglers.

NOTES

We wish to thank Daniela Kraiem and John Walton for their editorial scrutiny of an earlier version of this chapter, which was first presented to the annual meetings of the Society for the Study of Social Problems, August 1999, Chicago.

1. These data were presented by the Coalition to Fight Child Exploitation, the Thai Red Cross Society, and Mahidol University's Institute for Population and Social Research.

2. Fieldnotes and audio-taped interviews, February 1998, Thailand. These informants must remain anonymous. The information they provided JD is not the kind of information that their organizations are mandated to collect. These informants—they know who they are—have taken a great personal risk in providing this information, and JD offers them special thanks.

REFERENCES

Albanese, J. 1982. "What Lockheed and la Cosa Nostra Have in Common." *Crime and Delinquency* 28:211–32.
Altink, S. 1995. *Stolen Lives: Trading Women into Sex and Slavery.* London: Scarlet Press.
Andreano, R., and J. J. Siegfried, eds. 1980. *The Economics of Crime.* New York: John Wiley.
Astudillo, Jaime, and Claudio Cordero. 1990. *Huayrapamushcas en USA: Flujos migratorios de la region centro-sur del Ecuador.* Quito: Editorial El Conejo.
Bales, Kevin. 1999. *Disposable People: New Slavery in the Global Economy.* Berkeley: University of California Press.
Basch, Linda, Nina G. Schiller, and Cristina Szanton Blanc. 1994. *Nations Unbound: Transnational Projects, Post-colonial Predicaments, and Deterritorialized Nation-States.* Langhorne, Pa.: Gordon and Breach.
Becker, Howard S. 1998. *Tricks of the Trade: How To Think about Your Research While You're Doing It.* Chicago: University of Chicago Press.
Braudel, Fernand. 1958. "Histoire et Sciences Sociales: La Longue Duree." *Annales E.S.C.* 13 (4): 725–53; reprinted in *Ecrits sur l'histoire,* Paris, 1969.
Chalplpat, Kulachada. 1997. "New Law Targets Human Trafficking." *The [Bangkok] Nation,* November 30.
Chambliss, William J. 1989. "State-Organized Crime." *Criminology* 27: 2.
Charoenpho, Annucha. 1998. "New Way to Repatriate Immigrants: Illegal Workers Lured through Incentives." *Bangkok Post,* February 2, p. 2, col. 1.

Chin, Ko-lin. 1996. *Chinatown Gangs: Extortion, Enterprise and Ethnicity*. New York: Oxford University Press.Dominguez, Miguel E. 1991. *El Sombrero de Paja Toquilla: Historia y Economia*. Cuenca, Ecuador: Banco Central del Ecuador.

Freeman, Gary. 1994. "Can Liberal States Control Unwanted Migration?" *Annals of the American Academy of Political and Social Science* 534: 17–30.

Godson, Roy, and William J. Olson. 1995. "International Organized Crime." *Society* (January/February): 18–29.

ISPAC. 1996. International Scientific and Professional Advisory Council of the United Nations Crime Prevention and Criminal Justice Program (ISPAC) International Conference on Migration and Crime: Global and Regional Problems and Responses, Courmayeur Mont Blanc, Italy, October.

Joppke, Christian. 1998. "Why Liberal States Accept Unwanted Migration." *World Politics* 50 (2): 266–93.

Kerry, John. 1997. *The New War: The Web of Crime That Threatens America's Security*. New York: Simon and Schuster.

Knowles, Joe. 1997. "Come for the Pagodas, Stay for the Virgins." *Might* 15 (March/April): 19.

Kwong, Peter. 1996. *The New Chinatown*. Rev. ed. New York: Hill and Wang.

———. 1997. *Forbidden Workers: Illegal Chinese Immigrants and American Labor*. New York: New Press.

Kyaa Nyo, Maung. 1997. "Myanmar Women." *Today* 4 (December 16–31): 82–84.

Kyle, David. 2003. *Transnational Peasants: Migration, and Markets Networks, and Ethnicity in Andean Ecuador*. Baltimore: Johns Hopkins University Press.

Kyle, David, and John Dale. 1999. "The Social Construction of a 'New' Social Problem: Global Human Smuggling." Presented at the SSSP meetings, "Legislating the Boundaries of Inclusion: Immigration, Citizenship, and the Law," August 6, Chicago.

Kyle, David, and Marc Scarcelli. 2009. "Migrant Smuggling and the Violence Question: Evolving Illicit Migration Industries for Cuban and Haitian Refugees." *Journal of Crime, Law, and Social Change* 52 (3): 297–311.

Kyle, David, and Christina Siracusa. 2005. "Seeing the State Like a Migrant: Why So Many Non-Criminals Break Immigration Laws." In *(Il)licit Flows of People, Objects, and Ideas*, edited by Willem van Schendel and Itty Abraham. Bloomington: Indiana University Press. Light, Ivan, and Edna Bonacich. 1988. *Immigrant Entrepreneurs: Koreans in Los Angeles, 1965–1982*. Berkeley: University of California Press.

McAdam, Doug, Sidney Tarrow, and Charles Tilly. 1996. "To Map Contentious Politics." *Mobilization: An International Journal* 1 (1): 17–34.

McDonald, William F. 1995. "The Globalization of Criminology: The New Frontier Is the Frontier." *Transnational Organized Crime* 1 (1): 1–22.

McMichael, Phillip. 1997. *Development and Social Change: A Global Perspective*. Thousand Oaks, Calif.: Pine Forge Press.

Miller, Tom. 1986. *The Panama Hat Trail*. New York: Vintage Books.

Mirkinson, Judith. 1994. "Red Light, Green Light: The Global Trafficking of Women," accessed December 1, 2000, deepthought.armory.com/~leavitt/women.html.

Morley, Geoffrey. 1994. *The Smuggling War: The Government Fight against Smuggling in the 18th and 19th Centuries*. Gloucestershire: Alan Sutton.

Palomeque, Silvia. 1990. *Cuenca en el siglo XIX: La articulacion de una region*. Quito: Ediciones Abya-Yala.

Reuter, Peter. 1985. *The Organization of Illegal Markets: An Economic Analysis*. Research report, U.S. Department of Justice, National Institute of Justice. February.

Ruggiero, Vincenzo. 1997. "Trafficking in Human Beings: Slaves in Contemporary Europe." *International Journal of the Sociology of Law* 25: 231–44.

Salt, John, and Jeremy Stein. 1997. "Migration as a Business: The Case of Trafficking." *International Migration* 35 (4): 467–94.

Sassen, Saskia. 1991. *The Global City: New York, London, and Tokyo*. Princeton: Princeton University Press.

Schwartz, Herman M. 1994. *States versus Markets: History, Geography, and the Development of the International Political Economy*. New York: St. Martin's Press.

Shapiro, S. 1984. *Wayward Capitalists*. New Haven: Yale University Press.

Smith, D., and R. Alba. 1979. "Organized Crime and American Life." *Society* 16: 32–38.

Smith, Paul, ed. 1997. *Human Smuggling: Chinese Migrant Trafficking and the Challenge to America"s Immigration Tradition*. Washington, D.C.: Center for Strategic and International Studies.

Tilly, Charles. 1985. "War Making and State Making as Organized Crime." In *Bringing the State Back In*, edited by Peter B. Evans, Dietrich Rueschemeyer, and Theda Skocpol, 169–91. Cambridge: Cambridge University Press.

United States Immigration and Naturalization Service. 1998. News Release. September 21. Office of the United States Attorney, Southern District of California, San Diego, Calif., accessed December 1, 2000, www.usdoj.gov/usao/cas/pr/cas80921.2html.

Walton, John. 1977. *Elites and Economic Development: Comparative Studies on the Political Economy of Latin American Cities*. Austin, Tex.: Institute of Latin American Studies.

CHAPTER TWO

Economic Globalization, Human Smuggling, and Global Governance

Rey Koslowski

The rapidly advancing information, communication, and transportation technologies that are driving economic globalization are also propelling international migration and fostering transnational crime. These two aspects of globalization have become intertwined. The international migration of criminals has become a means of expanding local and national criminal organizations into transnational operations, and human smuggling is a form of transnationally organized crime that increases illegal migration.

Although migration scholars might have reservations about analyzing human smuggling because of potentially inflammatory linkages of immigrants to crime, a sober assessment of these linkages is necessary, for despite the relatively meager attention to human smuggling in the migration literature, policymakers have drawn their own conclusions about such linkages and have acted upon them. As a Group of Eight (G8) communiqué noted, "Globalisation has been accompanied by a dramatic increase in transnational crime . . . [that] takes many forms, including . . . smuggling of human beings" (G8, 1998a).

During the 1990s, American and European foreign policymakers placed international migration together with transnational crime in new institutional frameworks set up to deal with the emerging challenges of the post–Cold War world. The Clinton administration restructured the U.S. State Department to more comprehensively address globalization and directed it "to develop a strategy to combat a threat which is a criminal threat, an immigration threat, a human rights threat, and a national security threat, the threat posed by transnational migrant smuggling, alien smuggling, trafficking in persons" (Winer, 1997). These new policy-making organs were focused on the problem of human smuggling as states cooperated within fora such as the European Union (EU) and the G8 as well as within the United Nations and the International Organization for Migration (IOM).

Ironically, as states tighten border controls and asylum policies, they have indirectly prompted more people to get into the smuggling business—increased restriction drives up the costs of illegal migration and increases the profits of human smuggling. Now states are stepping up cooperation to combat transnational criminal organizations and human smuggling in particular. Human smuggling, however, is often "crime that is organized" (Finckenauer and Waring, 1996) rather than a new line of business of easily identifiable traditional criminal organizations. International cooperation to combat human smuggling may provide another demonstration of the challenges posed to states, and international organizations composed of states, when they confront the side effects of globalization.

The argument proceeds in three steps. The first section examines human smuggling in the larger context of the processes of economic globalization that have facilitated both increasing international migration and transnational crime. The second section examines state and multilateral responses to human smuggling as well as the linking of migration and crime in the policy-making process. The third section considers some of the policy dilemmas involved in combating human smuggling, including the difficulties of targeting migrant traffickers and the unintended consequences of tougher border controls.

Economic Globalization, International Migration, and Transnational Crime

Economic globalization has largely been driven by the collapse of Communism and the spread of capitalist economic systems throughout the so-called Second and Third Worlds, combined with the fundamental technological changes that have drastically reduced the cost of communication and transportation (Korbin, 1997). This globalization of economic activities facilitates both increasing international migration and the expansion of transnational crime. Increasing international migration and expanding transnational crime do not simply share a common accelerator in economic globalization and technological change; the very processes of globalization have intensified the very real intersection of these two phenomena.

According to neoclassical economic theory, the liberalization of international capital markets, which has become the hallmark of globalization, should decrease migration (see, e.g., Weintraub and Stolp, 1987; Layard et al., 1992: chap. 1). Recent trends, however, have not always followed neoclassical logic. For example, large-scale direct investment by U.S. companies in South Korea, Taiwan, and China was accompanied by an increase in migration from these East Asian countries to the United States rather than a decrease (Sassen, 1988). Indeed, increased investment in developing countries and increased trade often have the reverse effect than that expected, at least for the immediate term, as has been the case with illegal migration to the United States from Mexico (Massey, 1998). While increased investment may increase the number of available jobs and decrease the wage differentials among developed and developing countries, surplus disposable income often becomes "migration capital" used to pay for international travel and to pay for smugglers who increase the chance of a successful border crossing (Kyle, 1996; Singer and Massey, 1998; Spener, this volume, Chap. 6). Similarly, a large proportion of the Chinese who are smuggled into the United States are from Fujian Province, a coastal province with one of China's fastest-growing regional economies (Liang and Ye, this volume, Chap. 8).

The rapidly advancing information, communication, and transportation technologies that are driving economic globalization and propelling international migration are also fostering transnational crime (see Naim, 2006). There is a long tradition of understanding organized crime in terms of models derived from generalized depictions of the Sicilian Mafia in which criminal hierarchies are dominated by "godfathers" who order foot soldiers to do their bidding. When such criminal activity takes place in two or more countries, it is then considered transnational in nature. In contrast, some criminologists have argued that criminals are more like highly competitive entrepreneurs whose organizations, to the extent that they exist at all, are more like informal trade associations and old boys' networks (Reuter, 1983). Between these two

positions lies the depiction of criminal organizations as underground governments, rather than armies, and as illicit corporations competing in various markets, rather than individual entrepreneurs with informal ties (Naylor, 1995).

In a sense, transnational organized crime groups are not all that different from
transnational corporations (TNCs) in that they both run border-transcending
economic enterprises—the major differences are that TNCs' business is legal
whereas organized crime groups deal in illegal trade (drugs, stolen goods, prostitution) and use illegal means (extortion, theft, money laundering, murder)
to realize their profits (Williams, 1995). Just as technological change has globalized production and markets of legal goods and services, it has a similar
impact on illegal production and markets. As Susan Strange points out, local
and national crime organizations have expanded to global operations; the
expansion is often a response to expanding markets for illegal commodities;
increasing revenue has facilitated favorable treatment by states (i.e., corruption); and the globalization of financial markets and services facilitates the financing of illegal trade and the laundering of ill-gotten gains into "legitimate"
businesses and investment instruments (Strange, 1996: 110–21).

Despite the historical legacy of human smuggling and the recent surge in
cases, migration scholars have been slow to analyze the phenomenon. Part of
the problem is that migrants are all too often implicitly or explicitly identified
with criminality in political rhetoric when in fact migrants are more likely to
be the victims than the perpetrators of crime (see Miller, 1998). For example,
some conservative members of the U.S. Congress are quick to point out that
undocumented aliens are criminals by virtue of their illegal crossing or visa
overstay, and certain European politicians are quick to attribute the spread of
organized criminal activity in Western Europe to increasing migration from
Russia and the successor states of the former Soviet Union. In the face of the
exaggeration of immigrant criminality and the propensity of politicians to
allow immigrants to become scapegoats in the heat of election campaigns, it
is tempting for migration scholars to overcompensate for such knee-jerk reac-
tions by avoiding any discussion of crime among migrants.

Just as it is preposterous to assert that all Sicilian immigrants in the United
States are members of the Mafia, it is also foolish to contend that none are. The
fact of the matter is that local criminal organizations may expand their operations abroad through emigration and recruitment within migrant communities abroad and the transportation and communications revolutions are facilitating this process. For example, the numbers of foreign-born Russians in New

York City and Berlin who are involved in criminal organizations with origins in Moscow may be rather small; however, their activity has expanded the scope of Russian organized crime beyond Russia's borders. Some members of these organizations may be native-born Americans and Germans, but many are indeed migrants from Russia (Finckenauer and Waring, 1996; Finckenauer, this volume, Chap. 12). Mexican drug trafficking organizations have not only supplanted Colombia's Cali and Medellín cartels as the primary suppliers of illicit drugs to the US (CRS 2008), Mexican drug-trafficking organizations control a greater portion of drug production, transportation, and distribution in the United States than any other criminal group and have distribution networks in at least 230 U.S. cities (NDIC, 2008).

It is important to note that the expansion of local gangs to become border-spanning transnational criminal organizations through the migration of members is not always a matter of migration to the advanced industrialized countries of the West from former Communist countries in the East and developing countries of the south. For example, stepped-up enforcement of the U.S. policy of deporting noncitizens who have completed their prison sentences that began in 1996 inadvertently led to the expansion of Los Angeles gangs, Mara Salvatrucha (or MS-13) and the 18th Street gang (or MS-18), to El Salvador. Having fled the Salvadoran civil war as children in the 1980s, these gang members often had few connections to the country of their birth and spoke very little Spanish. The United States deported an estimated twenty thousand young criminal nationals of Central American countries to their "home" countries, often without notifying law enforcement authorities in these countries. Many deportees no longer had close family members and faced bleak job prospects in economies recovering from years of conflict (Arana, 2005). Without jobs but with considerable survival skills learned on the streets of Los Angeles and in U.S. prisons, many deportees turn to crime in an environment characterized by relatively weak civilian law enforcement (Rohter, 1997). Los Angeles gangsters then recruited local Salvadoran youth into the American gang culture and maintained ties with their associates from back in the United States, often returning to the United States illegally. Very quickly MS-13 became pan-Hispanic in membership and established branches in Seattle, San Francisco, Washington, and El Salvador (Sontag, 1997). Information derived from interviews of MS-13 gang members at the time of their arrests indicated that, within a decade, members of MS-13 became involved in smuggling migrants from Central American countries through Mexico to the United States and MS-13 gang members themselves had been smuggled into the United States utilizing the services of established human smuggling networks (Swecker, 2006). Early on, MS-13 established itself on the Mexican-Guatemalan border, where gang members attacked and robbed those migrants heading north to the United States who did not hire MS-13-affiliated smugglers, who charged fees of $5,000 to $8,000 for smuggling migrants to the United States. Then MS-13 expanded its operations into Mexican states all the way to the U.S. border and struck alliances with new Mexican drug cartels in order to help the Mexican cartels to expand their operations in the growing number of U.S. cities in which MS-13 was well established (Arana, 2005).

Finally, it is necessary to point out that members of human smuggling organizations in the receiving countries and the employers who illegally hire the smuggled labor are often themselves migrants. For example, most "enforcers" who collect debts from illegal Chinese workers in New York or the owners of the sweatshops or restaurants who employ them are from the Chinese immigrant community (Chin, this volume, Chap. 7). Similarly, immigrants owned and operated Houston-based "transportation companies" that moved smuggled Mexicans and Central Americans to Washington, D.C. (Moreno, 1998). It is believed that the trafficking of central and Eastern European women to Western Europe is primarily controlled by Russian and Ukrainian organizations; the women are then forced into prostitution by various local gangsters, many of whom are not nationals of the countries in which they operate. For example, Viennese police arrested nationals of Turkey and states of the former Yugoslavia who were holding Hungarian and Slovak women, and, in a major sweep of twenty locations in North Rhine Westphalia, twenty-four women from Eastern Europe were freed from German, Albanian, Turkish, and Italian gangsters (IOM, 1998).

Human smuggling is a form of transnationally organized crime that increases illegal migration, and the international migration of criminals has become a means of expanding local and national criminal organizations into transnational operations. In confronting globalization, policymakers have implicitly, if not explicitly, linked migration and crime, particularly with their focus on human smuggling. Although such linkage has at times been overdrawn for political reasons, the reality of human smuggling by criminal organizations and transnational criminal activity among migrants, not the least being the smuggling and employment of illegal migrants, helps one understand the resonance of such linkages among the publics to which politicians appeal.

Policymaking and Multilateral Cooperation

As declining travel costs reduced the geographical barriers to international travel, visa applications and border controls imposed by states became the primary barrier to entry. When increasing numbers of individuals attempted to enter destination countries without authorization in the 1980s and 1990s, these states tightened their visa and border control policies and also increased the staffing, funding, and legal authority of border guards. As migration destination countries tightened border controls, an increasing percentage of illegal migrants and asylum seekers paid human smugglers for assistance to circumvent border controls or pass through them using fraudulent travel documents. The increase in human smuggling and trafficking was a dark side of the rapid growth of international travel during the 1990s, and it called into question measures taken to facilitate international travel and promote development through international tourism, a small percentage of which became international travel undertaken in order to purchase relatively inexpensive sex with women and children who had been trafficked.

In response, policymakers from major migration destination countries such as the United States, Germany, Canada, Australia, the United Kingdom, France, Italy, and Austria became increasingly concerned with the trafficking in persons, particularly women and children into forced prostitution. Given that measures taken by states to tighten border controls did not necessarily stem the flows of illegal migrants owing to increasingly sophisticated smuggling techniques, migration destination countries increasingly viewed the smuggling of migrants across their borders as a security issue of "uncontrollable" borders.

Although such migration destination states have demonstrated little interest in cooperation to facilitate labor migration, these very same states were very active in efforts to foster international cooperation on human smuggling and trafficking. UN member states, whether primarily countries of origin, destination, or transit, could agree on the evils of trafficking in women and children across international borders. Moreover, most UN member states have come to recognize that they could not collectively combat human trafficking, in which individuals are coerced into forced prostitution and forced labor, if they did not also address human smuggling, in which individuals simply pay smugglers to illegally cross international borders. States to which migrants were increasingly smuggled and trafficked also acknowledged that they cannot combat human smuggling and trafficking on a unilateral or even bilateral basis because human smuggling often involves several transit countries and smugglers and migrants from more than two countries. Many of these states, therefore, have embraced international cooperation on the regional or global level (or both).

Policy making on human smuggling and trafficking evolved in three steps. First, post–Cold War foreign policy making was restructured in a way that elevated international migration and transnational crime to the "high politics" of international security while at the same time associating the two by placing them together in new institutional frameworks. Second, policy initiatives emanating from this restructuring have increasingly focused on the problem of human smuggling in a way that solidifies and justifies the earlier institutional linkages. Third, in combating human smuggling, policymakers have increasingly turned to multilateral cooperation on the regional and global level.

In attempting to deal with post–Cold War policy issues associated with globalization, policymakers in the United States and Europe have often restructured policy-making institutions in ways that associated international migration with transnational crime. For example, Title VI of the 1991 Maastricht Treaty institutionalized intergovernmental cooperation through the Justice and Home Affairs (JHA) Council, the so-called Third Pillar, in which European foreign policymakers put cooperation on migration policy, asylum, and external borders together with cooperation on drugs, fraud, and other issues of law enforcement. Moreover, cooperation in the JHA Council increasingly focused on the growing problem of human smuggling. Similarly, in 1993, the incoming Clinton administration reorganized the State Department to include an Office of the Under Secretary for Global Affairs, which "coordinates U.S. foreign relations on a variety of global issues, including: democracy, human rights and labor; environment, oceans and science; narcotics control and law enforcement; population, refugees and migration; women's issues."[1] Within the portfolio of the Secretary of Global Affairs (now Democracy and Global Affairs), an Office to Monitor and Combat Trafficking in Persons was authorized by Trafficking Victims Protection Act of 2000 and established in October 2001 to support the President's Interagency Task Force to Monitor and Combat Trafficking in Persons.

Human smuggling prompted European Union action as early as 1993, when the JHA Council agreed to a set of recommendations for member states to combat trafficking in women and children (JHA, 1993). The EU and other ministers involved in the Budapest Process dealing with illegal migration as well as representatives from relevant international organizations, such as the IOM, adopted recommendations in areas including "harmonization of legislation to combat trafficking in aliens" and "linkage in trafficking in aliens and other forms of organized crime" ("Conference of Ministers," 1997: 3–6). In January 1998, EU foreign ministers adopted a forty-six-point plan directed at reducing the numbers of Kurds from Turkey and Iraq; the plan describes them as "illegal refugees" as well as "illegal immigrants." The council stated that these migrants "almost always make use of traffickers, of whom the majority appear to be part of organized crime networks, with contacts in the EU" (quoted in "Influx of Kurds," 1998: 4). Twenty of the forty-six points were devoted to "combating illegal immigration," most of which focused on enhanced border control and effective removal (4–6).

In the wake of the September 11, 2001, attacks on the United States, the extraordinary European Council of September 21, 2001, asked member states to strengthen controls at external borders and strengthen surveillance measures provided for in the Schengen Convention (European Council, 2001). Within ten days of the extraordinary European Council, the EU coordinated "Operation High impact," which involved more than 10,000 police officers from 15 member states and 10 candidate countries who apprehended 1,350 illegal migrants and 34 migrant smugglers. Shortly thereafter, the Justice and Home Affairs Council began discussions of developing a common border police force, which would involve the development of a harmonized curriculum for training border control officials and the development of a European border guard school. Police exchange programs and liaison work became increasingly common under the aegis of the Schengen Convention, as, for example, when Germany sent border police to assist in Italy. Although EU member states eventually fell short of establishing a common European border guard or even border guard school, the integration of border management was advanced with agreement in 2002 to establish the European Agency for the Management of Operational Co-Operation at the External Borders of the European Union, or FRONTEX. FRONTEX coordinates the implementation of common policies by member state border police but does not have policy-making or implementing powers of its own. With a staff of two hundred at the end of 2008 and a 2007 budget of 35 million euros, FRONTEX remains relatively small, but it has coordinated an increasing number of joint actions. For example, in the 2008 FRONTEX joint operation HERA off Spain's Canary Islands, 5,969 illegal migrants were diverted back or deterred, and 360 migrant smugglers were arrested (FRONTEX, 2009).

In 1997, the former U.S. Immigration and Naturalization Service (INS) initiated the $8.2 million program Operation Global Reach by opening thirteen offices in sending and transit countries in order to gather information, assist countries in identifying smugglers, provide support for prosecutions, and train law enforcement personnel particularly in order to recognize fraudulent documents. By June 2001, forty overseas offices with 150 U.S. positions had been established and 45,000 host country officials and airline personnel trained. These efforts resulted in the interception of more than 74,000 travelers attempting to use fraudulent documents to transit these countries into the United States (INS, 2001). With the merging of the INS into the Department of Homeland Security (DHS), the offices established under Operation Global Reach have been transformed into "Immigration Overseas" offices and, for the moment, function as platforms for immigration law enforcement by the individual DHS agencies that parts of the "legacy" INS were merged into: U.S. Citizenship and Immigration Services (USCIS), Immigration and Customs Enforcement (ICE), and Customs and Border Protection (CBP). Since the September 11 attacks, these offices have maintained their focus on combating human smuggling and document fraud, but they have also been tasked to facilitate DHS cooperation with the State Department Consular Services in new procedures for security checks on visa applications abroad. In 2004, CBP launched a new initiative in bilateral international cooperation whereby CBP staff work alongside airline personnel as passengers checked in for U.S.-bound flights. As former CBP commissioner Robert Bonner explained, "Essentially, we are developing a proposal to station a small number of CBP inspectors overseas, at some of the major hub airports, to work with and assist the airlines in terms of screening people who may pose a terrorist threat or who may be traveling to the United States with fraudulent or counterfeit passports or other entry documents" (quoted in Aversa, 2004).

The fight against human smuggling became a major focus of the Regional Consultation Group on Migration, composed of Belize, Canada, Costa Rica, El Salvador, Guatemala, Honduras, Mexico, Nicaragua, Panama, and the United States, which met in Puebla, Mexico, in 1996 and in Panama City in 1997. At the third meeting of the group, which took place in Ottawa on March 2, 1998, Colombia, the Dominican Republic, Ecuador, Jamaica, and Peru were invited as observers, as were representatives of the United Nations High Commissioner for Refugees (UNHCR), the Economic Commission for Latin America and the Caribbean (ECLAC), and the IOM. The Regional Consultation Group has encouraged participating states to pass legislation outlawing migrant smuggling and set out to establish a regional network of liaison officers responsible for exchanging information about migrant smuggling. The United States also cooperated with the EU to combat trafficking in women and children from central and East European countries and the Newly Independent States of the former Soviet Union by funding a contract with the IOM to provide education and public information to dissuade Polish and Ukrainian women from getting involved with traffickers (United States and European Union, 1997). In July 1999, the Organization for Security and Cooperation in Europe (OSCE) Parliamentary Assembly adopted a U.S.-initiated "Resolution on the Trafficking of Women and Children" (OSCE, 1999). Moreover, international crime was one of the three major themes of the 1998 G8 Summit in Birmingham, with an explicit focus on the "organized smuggling of people" (U.S. State Department, 1998). Japan joined European countries and the United States in supporting increased efforts to combat human smuggling, having experienced an increase in the smuggling of Chinese into Japan (Kohli and Macklin, 1998).

The League of Nations and then the United Nations have long served as fora for international cooperation against the trafficking of women and children—going back to international cooperation to combat white slavery (see Scully, this volume, Chap. 4). Under the impetus generated by the Bejing UN conference on women and the leadership of certain member states, attention was refocused on human smuggling. Austria took the lead in encouraging fellow UN member states to pass laws that specifically criminalize human smuggling and draft an international convention on the smuggling of illegal aliens (Schuessel, 1997). Such efforts within the UN received support at the May 1998 G8 summit, where leaders called for negotiation of a UN crime convention to be completed within two years (G8, 1998b). In December 1998, the UN General Assembly initiated an ad hoc committee that was charged with drawing up a comprehensive international convention against transnational organized crime and three additional protocols, one of which dealing with human smuggling and another with trafficking in women and children. The committee met six times in 1999 with the objective of meeting the year 2000 deadline for signing the new treaty. Human smuggling and the trafficking in women received high-level attention during the October 1999 opening meetings of the General Assembly. At a meeting hosted by former U.S. secretary of state Madeleine Albright, fourteen women foreign ministers drafted a letter, which they sent to Secretary General Kofi Annan, that called for stepped-up action to combat trafficking and pledged support of the UN Convention against Transnational Crime. The foreign ministers stated, "We recognize the importance of close international cooperation to defeat the traffickers at every stage of their criminal activities" (cited in IOM, 2000).

In November 2000, the UN General Assembly adopted the UN Convention against Transnational Organized Crime, as well as its Protocol to Prevent, Suppress and Punish Trafficking in Persons, Especially Women and Children, and the Protocol against the Smuggling of Migrants by Land, Sea and Air. Once receiving a sufficient number of ratifications, the convention went into effect September 29, 2003, the antitrafficking protocol on December 25, 2003, and the antismuggling protocol on January 28, 2004. As of June 2010, the antitrafficking protocol had 137 state parties, and the antismuggling protocol had 123 state parties.[2]

The objectives of the antitrafficking protocol are to prevent and combat trafficking in persons as well as protect and assist the victims of such trafficking. The objectives of the human smuggling protocol are twofold—establishing the smuggling of migrants as a criminal offense and facilitating cooperation in the prevention, investigation, and prosecution of the crime of smuggling migrants. In order to meet those objectives, the two protocols provide rules for interdicting and boarding ships suspected of carrying illegal migrants, approve of state use of carrier sanctions, and encourage information programs directed at the customers of traffickers and smugglers as well as information exchanges between states that enable more effective law enforcement. The anti-smuggling protocol also calls on states to strengthen border controls and intensify cooperation between border control agencies by establishing and maintaining direct lines of communication, ensuring the integrity of travel documents that they issue, and responding to requests to verify the validity of those documents.

The UN Office on Drugs and Crime (UNODC) functions as the secretariat of the Convention on Transnational Organized Crime, and the UNODC's Global Programme against Trafficking in Human Beings (GPAT) assists countries in their efforts to combat this crime. Additionally, the UNODC launched the Global Initiative to Fight Human Trafficking (UN.GIFT) in March 2007 in order to raise awareness and increase the knowledge base regarding human trafficking; build commitment to partnerships with governments, the international community, nongovernmental organizations (NGOs), the private sector, civil society organizations, and the media; and implement projects to fight human trafficking on a local, regional, and international level.

Created in 1951, the IOM and its predecessors have a long history of work in moving refugees to second countries of asylum, voluntary repatriation of refugees, and the return migration of the highly skilled in order to further development in sending countries. More recently, the IOM emerged as a major actor with respect to international cooperation in the area of human smuggling and trafficking even though it has a smaller membership[3] than the UN and is much more specialized and limited as a forum for migration policy making than regional organizations such as the EU. The IOM played a significant role preparing the way for negotiations that led to the antitrafficking and antismuggling protocols of the UN Convention on Transnational Organized Crime. At a 1994 IOM-sponsored meeting in Geneva, which brought together representatives from source, transit, and destination countries, participants asked the IOM to advance the policy discussions of migrant trafficking, organize regional meetings, collect and disseminate information, analyze the problem of trafficking in women for prostitution, and contribute to policy harmonization (IOM, 1994). Since then, the IOM has been sponsoring regional processes dealing with irregular migration and migrant trafficking in Europe, the Americas, and East and Southeast Asia. While the IOM has emerged as the leading international organization in the area of research and policy dialogues devoted to human smuggling in general,[4] operational programs have primarily focused on trafficking in women and children for forced prostitution, whether in terms of publicity campaigns to discourage women from turning to traffickers or in terms of return programs, with which the IOM is very experienced.

The Dilemmas of Controlling Human Smuggling as a Challenge to Global Governance

Jonathan Winer, the former deputy assistant secretary for law enforcement and crime in the U.S. State Department, presented the problem posed by human smugglers and traffickers to foreign policymakers in terms of increased international cooperation. "We are working with the European Union, the International Organization for Migration, the UN and other organizations to develop international cooperation against traffickers, whose organizations transcend all of our national borders, because in a transnational world, no country can defend its own borders or its people, however big or small, without the co-operation of the entire world" (Winer, 1998: 8). International cooperation to strengthen border controls, criminalize human smuggling where laws against it do not already exist, identify and prosecute human smugglers where they do, and provide information to prospective migrants about the dangers involved in clandestine border crossings are first steps in dealing with the challenges posed by human smuggling. Certain aspects of such cooperation, however, particularly those directed at border control, may potentially exacerbate the problem they were designed to combat. This dilemma arises from a certain misunderstanding of the nature of human smuggling and an underestimation of complex interrelationships between the effects of various migration and refugee policies.

Human smuggling is often depicted in terms of traditional organized crime groups that have added a new line of business to drug smuggling, car theft, and money laundering (IOM, 1996). It may, however, be that human smuggling is more often "crime that is organized" (Finckenauer and Waring, 1996) and committed by people who may have previously not been involved in transnational criminal organizations. Hence, targeting human smugglers for prosecution may be harder to accomplish in practice than it sounds as a policy prescription.

For example, travel agents who sell tickets to migrants without the proper documentation to make the proposed journey legally profit from the illegal transportation of migrants organized by smugglers. Are these travel agents themselves "smugglers" who can be targeted for prosecution? As Ko-lin Chin (this volume, Chap. 7) points out, Chinese migrant smuggling rings are more often than not loose networks of relatives and friends who organize transportation and border crossings for acquaintances as a lucrative business that may even have developed as a supplement to legitimate business. These smuggling networks often use more traditional gangsters involved in other criminal activities such as drug dealing and extortion to enforce debt repayment in the receiving country if necessary; however, enforcers may just be hired hands—thereby outsourcing the dirty work. Law enforcement efforts directed at more easily identified enforcers may not necessarily be very effective in putting out of business the smuggling operations of which they may be a necessary, but replaceable, part.

Another challenge emerges for prosecutors when a group of migrants led by a smuggler is apprehended. It may be very difficult to establish which member of the group is the smuggler. The smuggler may simply say he is a migrant, and the apprehended migrants may be very reluctant to identify the smuggler. As long as they have been well treated, migrants often view smugglers as service providers rather than criminals. Moreover, the smuggler may have given migrants a "satisfaction guaranteed" provision of their arrangement whereby they will be smuggled again if they are not successful in the first or even multiple attempts. Less service-oriented and more violent smugglers may be able to threaten to harm the migrant or his family (or both) if the migrant identifies the smuggler and testifies against him. Finally, prosecuting smugglers in a trial may be a very costly and lengthy process. For example, in the largest smuggling corridor along the U.S.-Mexican border in southern Arizona, Cochise County prosecutors do not try very many human smuggling cases even though Arizona has a specific law against human smuggling. Even if a smuggler can be identified from within a group of smuggled migrants who typically cross the border in groups of ten to fifteen, the entire group must be detained along with the smuggler until the trial is complete. This can take six to nine months and cost the county hundreds of thousands of dollars as well as take up limited jail space. If cases do not involve serious injuries or death, law enforcement officials tend to opt for simply processing those apprehended and returning them to Mexico.[5]

Whether migrant smugglers are gangsters moving into another line of business or businesspeople moving into an illegal activity to help migrants cross borders illegally varies by regions and particular migration flows involved. Winer suggests that in Western Europe and Southeastern Asia "the same criminal organizations may traffic in migrants and narcotics. In other areas, alien smugglers avoid other criminal activities, such as drug trafficking, for which they would risk prosecution and stiff penalties" (1998: 3). For instance, a 1998 study of coyotes who assist crossings of the U.S.-Mexican border found little evidence of collaboration between coyotes and drug traffickers. Border Patrol agents told of some cases of migrants paying their fees by taking along a "small package." This was not a common practice and was not a mode of transporting drugs from producing areas to the border, in large measure because of the high risks associated with drug smuggling (Lopez Castro, 1998: 972).

Over the past decade, smuggling across the U.S.-Mexican border has changed dramatically. The original MS-13 was a Los Angeles street gang that was involved in drug dealing during the 1980s, became transnational in scope in the 1990s, and became involved in smuggling Central Americans through Mexico to the United States in the 2000s. As smuggling fees increased, Mexican drug cartels also became involved in smuggling as well as trafficking in cases when one gang would hijack groups of migrants from other gangs or smugglers held migrants against their will to extort money from them or their families (Boehnke, 2009). Drug smugglers are using smuggled migrants as decoys to divert Border Patrol agents from the path of drug shipments, and migrants are increasingly used as mules to carry backpacks of marijuana across the border. In Arizona, an overwhelmed U.S. Attorney's Office set a de facto threshold of five hundred pounds (or its monetary equivalent in other drugs) for prosecution of a drug smuggling case. This means that Mexican nationals who were apprehended crossing the border carrying a backpack full of marijuana were normally fingerprinted, processed, and returned to Mexico. They may be apprehended doing the same thing again and again until the total amount of drugs seized reaches five hundred pounds.[6]

The communication and transportation revolutions that have facilitated transnational crime provide only a partial reason for the recent increase in cases of human smuggling. Increasing human smuggling may also be an unintended consequence of the stricter visa and border control policies adopted by individual states and, in the case of Europe, more effective EU cooperation on border control and more restrictive policies adopted by countries that aspire to EU membership. Very simply: as more restrictive policies increase the obstacles to crossing borders, migrants turn to smugglers instead of paying the increased costs of unaided attempts that prove unsuccessful.

While stricter visa policies and more effective border controls lead illegal migrant workers to pay for smugglers' services, restrictive border controls and asylum policies have led those who have fled pogroms, secret police, and civil wars to do the same, as explained in the Introduction in this volume. Cases of spontaneous asylum application upon arrival are in a sense a function of loose border controls and the lack of international cooperation on border control. Increasing cooperation to combat human smuggling reduces the opportunity for successful spontaneous asylum seeking by those with a well-founded fear of individual persecution, increases the potential for human rights abuses, and requires stepped-up international cooperation in other areas and increasing demands on international organizations such as the UNHCR and UN Office of the High Commissioner for Human Rights (see Koslowski, 2011, for elaboration).

Moreover, as Salt and Stein (1997) point out, as the human smuggling business expands, the smugglers, rather than the migrants and asylum seekers, make more decisions regarding where their customers actually go. Part of the smugglers' success in getting migrants across borders is the smugglers' ability to change routes and destinations in order to overcome obstacles placed in their way by states. In a sense, the smugglers gather and process information about the weak links in terms of transportation systems, border controls, and liberal visa and asylum policies and then provide it to their customers. Moreover, smugglers often tutor migrants to say certain things to officials that may enable them to claim asylum, for instance, instructing Chinese migrants to claim they participated in the Tiananmen Square protests or that they have been unable to have a family because of China's "one child policy" (Kerry, 1997: 141). This ratchets up the pressure on receiving states to cooperate with one another and to adopt even more restrictivist border control and asylum policies lest their land borders, airports, and harbors be targeted by traffickers as weak links.

Whether stepped-up border controls and stricter visa polices will reduce human smuggling, however, is very unclear owing to the inherent dilemma of control. For example, in response to the implementation of "Operation Hold the Line," "Operation Gatekeeper," and other tougher enforcement of controls on the U.S.-Mexican border in the mid-1990s, fees charged by coyotes soon doubled or tripled, depending on the area of the border, with fees at San Diego reaching $700 in 1998 (De La Vina, 1998). By 2006, with the increased hiring of Border Patrol agents, tightened procedures after the September 11 attacks, the building of fences, and technology deployments, the smuggling fees to cross the U.S.-Mexican border have increased to $3,000 (Lee, 2006). If tougher border controls increase smugglers' fees beyond those which their customers are willing to pay, controls may decrease smuggling. However, if potential migrants are willing to pay the additional costs while at the same time stiffer border controls prompt more migrants to enter into the market, border controls will most likely increase the profits of human smuggling and entice new entrants into the business.

The willingness of migrants to pay more for smugglers' services is perhaps best demonstrated by Chinese migrants who have been smuggled into Western Europe, North America, Japan, and Australia. For example, as Peter Kwong points out, the average fee to be smuggled into the United States rose from a few thousand in the early 1980s to $22,000 in 1988, to some $30,000–35,000 in 1993; yet at the same time the number of those who purchased the smugglers' services grew (Kwong, 1997). Fees have increased to up to $75,000 (Chin, this volume Chap. 7), yet migrants are still willing to pay such exorbitant amounts of money. In this case, such high demand for smugglers' services can largely be explained by the willingness of migrants to incur debts against anticipated future earnings and a border-transcending financial system based on the willingness of family members to ensure repayment and the violent enforcement of debt repayment by criminal organizations in the host country or in China if necessary. "Illegal refugees" who are in fact fleeing for their lives may be even more willing to pay higher prices and incur debts than "illegal migrants." If demand for smugglers' services does not respond to increased prices, stepped-up border controls could lead to increased human smuggling at higher profits, which in turn draw more people into the business. The demand among "illegal migrants" for smugglers' services often depends on anticipated earnings from businesses that are willing to employ smuggled migrants. Hence, increased human smuggling may in large measure be a function of employer demand (Kwong, 1997).

Despite increased employment of smuggled migrants and trafficked forced laborers, enforcement of sanctions against employers for hiring illegal migrant labor in major receiving states has been spotty to say the least (see Miller, 2001), and it has been particularly weak in the United States (Rojas, 1996). The population of illegal migrants in the United States has increased consistently since the early 1990s, despite consistent levels of apprehensions of illegal border crossers and arrests of human smugglers (see Table 2.1). Enforcement of employer sanctions, however, dropped precipitously, thereby reducing the risk and costs to employers of illegal migrants, who, year after year, were increasingly likely to have been smuggled into the United States instead of having crossed the border without any paid assistance.

Indeed, anti–migrant smuggling initiatives of the U.S. government have primarily focused on interdiction on the high seas, targeting smugglers in sending and transit countries, and public information campaigns in sending countries, but little attention has been devoted to reducing demand for smuggled labor. According to a veteran U.S. Border Patrol official, such antismuggling initiatives will not be very effective if they are not paired with demand-reducing actions such as mandatory employer verification of employee eligibility using computerized checks of a Social Security number database, as recommended by the U.S. Commission on Immigration Reform in 1994.[7] An electronic eligibility verification system was included in subsequent legislation, but only in

Table 2.1 U.S. Illegal Migrant Population in Relation to DHS Enforcement Actions

	1997	1998	1999	2000	2001	2002	2003	2004	2005	2006	2007
Est. unauthorized population	5.9M	6.1M	6.5M	8.4M	9.4M	9.2M	9.8M	10.2M	11.1M	11.5M	12.4M
Apprehensions		1.6M	1.6M	1.7M	1.3M	955K	931K	1.2M	1.2M	1.1M	877
Human smuggling investigations											
Arrests	3,381	2,812	4,253	4,139	3,139	3,330	2,663	3,958	2,713	2,154	N/A
Convictions	1,737	1,183	1,199	1,474	1,174	1,252	1,418	491	1,657	1,596	N/A
Worksite enforcement											
Arrests	17,554	13,914	2,849	953	735	485	445	159	251	716	863
Convictions	778	535	297	180	78	13	124	46	188	493	N/A

Source: Estimates of the unauthorized migrant population in the United States for 1997–99 from "Estimates of the Unauthorized Immigrant Population Residing in the United States: 1990 to 2000," Office of Policy and Planning, U.S. Immigration and Naturalization Service, www.dhs.gov/xlibrary/assets/statistics/publications/Ill_Report_1211.pdf; data for 2000–2007 from Passel and Cohn (2008); data on apprehensions, human smuggling, employer sanctions, and enforcement actions from *Yearbook of Immigration Statistics*, years 1997 to 2006, at www.dhs.gov/ximgtn/statistics/publications/yearbook.shtm; 2007 data on apprehensions from 2007 *Yearbook of Immigration Statistics*.

the form of pilot projects in a limited number of states. Eventually, the "Basic Pilot" system became established as a voluntary program available through a Web portal to employers in all fifty states and was renamed "e-verify." Comprehensive immigration reform legislation debated in Congress in 2006 and 2007 included provisions to toughen enforcement of employer sanctions as well as expand electronic employment verification and make it mandatory. After the comprehensive immigration reform legislation collapsed in 2007, the Department of Homeland Security stepped up workplace raids but focused primarily on rounding up illegal migrants instead of arresting and prosecuting employers. Executive orders that made e-verify mandatory for employers who receive federal government contracts were delayed by the incoming Obama administration as it faced a lawsuit against the U.S. government lodged by the U.S. Chamber of Commerce to block mandatory enrollment in e-verify. Labor unions had been a bedrock constituency for strengthening employer sanctions, but at its February 2000 convention the AFL-CIO called for repeal of the employer sanctions law. Labor unions opted to shift their focus to organizing workers regardless of immigration status. Given that both business associations and labor unions support retaining the current weak employer sanctions, if not eliminating them altogether, using employer sanctions and electronic verification systems to combat human smuggling appears increasingly unlikely in the United States.

In the EU, the European Council's January 1998 Action Plan is directed at "tackling the involvement of organized crime," but the council remained mute on the demand for illegal labor by employers. European Commission policy recommendations to combat trafficking in women adopted by the JHA Council focus primarily on judicial and police cooperation directed at smugglers, migrants' labor conditions, and the need for victim support (European Commission, 1996; JHA, 1996), rather than the consumer demand for sex with "exotic" foreign women, which fuels a growing industry that capitalizes on vulnerable illegal migrants. In 1999, Sweden targeted demand by passing a law that prohibits the purchase of sexual services instead of criminalizing prostitution. Subsequently, Finland passed a law that prohibits the purchase of sexual services, but only if the woman is a victim of trafficking. In 2007, the European Commission proposed a directive requiring EU member states to implement systems for effective enforcement of employer sanctions (European Commission, 2007); the European Council and European Parliament arrived at compromise legislation in 2008 that received final approval of the European Parliament in 2009. According to the directive, employers must undertake certain checks before hiring a third-country national. Employers who cannot show that they have done so may be fined, lose subsidies (including EU funding), or be temporarily disqualified from receiving public contracts. EU member states must have criminal penalties available to prosecutors of the most serious cases: repeated offenders, employers of large numbers of illegal migrants, exploitative working conditions, knowingly using the labor of a victim of human trafficking. Although it is much more difficult for illegal migrants to be employed in Europe's much more regulated labor markets and the laws are in place to enforce employer sanctions, it is not clear if there is sufficient political will to follow through with large numbers of arrests of those who employ illegal migrants.

Conclusion

Economic globalization fosters both increasing international migration and transnational organized crime. These two aspects of globalization intersect in the phenomenon of human smuggling, which has in turn drawn the attention of immigration, law enforcement, and foreign ministry officials. North American and European states that have been the primary targets of smugglers and their customers have initiated campaigns to combat human smuggling, and these states have engaged in growing international cooperation aimed against smuggling. Antismuggling initiatives, however, have not come close to matching the recent expansion in the numbers of those smuggled. So far, most states and international organizations have tried to address the problem by increasing migration controls, passing laws against human smuggling, and stepping up enforcement of these laws. Since tighter border controls often yield the unintended consequences of more customers for smugglers and more people entering the smuggling business, the prospects that recent antismuggling initiatives will be very effective remain quite dim. Moreover, since most of these antismuggling initiatives fail to address the demand for smuggled labor, it is unlikely that target states will be able to accomplish much more than the diversion of flows along their borders and among themselves.

Given that sufficient international cooperation in law enforcement and immigration policies to make a significant impact on smuggling may involve major infringements of participating states' sovereignty, one may anticipate a fair amount of resistance to such cooperation from certain political parties of the states involved. Since truly effective measures to stop human smuggling involve major restrictions on employers' access to cheap and compliant illegal migrant labor, one may anticipate significance resistance from powerful interest groups. Because effective worksite enforcement in several countries may involve increased state use of citizens' personal data, which is often perceived as an affront to civil liberties, one may anticipate widespread public outrage.

Nevertheless, the fear of crime, and organized crime in particular, has proven quite effective in moving democratic publics to sacrifice liberties for the sake of their own perceived personal security. Perhaps politicians will prove effective in marshaling popular fears of criminals and the unwanted migrants they bring to galvanize serious international cooperation to curb human smuggling despite the consequences that cooperation may have for state sovereignty, employer profits, and civil liberties. Or, maybe not.

NOTES

1. See www.state.gov/www/global/index.html.
2. For treaty texts, signatures, and ratifications, see "Signatories to the United Nations Convention against Transnational Crime and Its Protocols" at www.unodc.org/unodc/en/treaties/CTOC/signatures.html.
3. As of April 2010, the antismuggling protocol had 127 state parties.
4. In addition to the quarterly bulletin, *Trafficking in Migrants,* see the book by former ILO official and IOM consultant Bimal Ghosh (1998).
5. Author's interviews with law enforcement officials, October 2008.
6. Author's interviews with law enforcement officials, October 2008. Also see Brodesky (2007).
7. Author's interview with Eugene R. Davis, deputy chief Border Patrol agent, U.S. Border Patrol in Blaine, Washington, on November 27, 1999. In a follow-up discussion in February 2009, Davis indicated that his position had not changed; indeed, he was even more adamant that the only way to effectively reduce human smuggling was to reduce demand for illegal migrant labor.

REFERENCES

Arana, Ana. 2005. "How the Street Gangs Took Central America." *Foreign Affairs,* May/June.
Aversa, Jeannine. 2004. "U.S. Wants to Send Customs Agents Abroad." *Manchester Union Leader and New Hampshire Sunday News,* March 2.
Boehnke, Megan. 2009. "16 Immigrants Found inside Small Business." *Arizona Republic,* February 17.

Brodesky, Josh. 2007. "Many Pot Seizures of below 500 Lbs. Go Unprosecuted." *Arizona Daily Star*, October 7.

"Conference of Ministers on the Prevention of Illegal Migration." 1997. *Migration News Sheet*, no. 177/97-12 (December), 3–6.

CRS. 2008. *Mexico's Drug Cartels*. Congressional Research Service Report, February 25.

De La Vina, Gustavo. 1998. "Interview with the New Assistant Commissioner for the Border Patrol, Gustavo 'Gus' De La Vina." U.S. Border Control.

European Commission. 1996. *Communication from the European Commission to the Council and the European Parliament on Trafficking in Women for the Purposes of Sexual Exploitation*. Brussels, COM(96) 567 final.

———. 2007. *Proposal for a Directive Providing for Sanctions against Employers of Illegally Staying Third-Country Nationals*. Brussels, COM(2007) 249 final.

European Council. 2001. "Conclusions and Plan of Action of the Extraordinary European Council Meeting on 21 September, 2001." www.consilium.europa.eu/uedocs/cms_data/docs/pressdata/en/ec/140.en.pdf.

Finckenauer, James O., and Elin Waring. 1996. "Russian Émigré Crime in the United States: Organized Crime or Crime That Is Organized?" *Transnational Organized Crime* 2 (2/3): 139–55.

FRONTEX. 2009. "HERA 2008 and NAUTILUS 2008 Statistics." News Release, FRONTEX Warsaw, February 17.

G8. 1998a. The Birmingham Summit, May 15–17. Communiqué.

———. 1998b. The Birmingham Summit, Drugs and International Crime. Press release, May 16. .

Ghosh, Bimal. 1998. *Huddled Masses and Uncertain Shores: Insights into Irregular Migration*. Doredrecht: Kluwer Law International.

"Influx of Kurds Prompts Adoption of a 46-Point Action Plan." 1998. *Migration News Sheet*, no. 179/98-02 (February), 4–6.

INS. 2001. "INS Global Reach Initiative Counters Rise of International Migrant Smuggling." Immigration and Naturalization Service Fact Sheet, June 27.

IOM. 1994. "International Responses to Trafficking in Migrants and the Safeguarding of Migrant Rights." Seminar, Geneva, October 26–28.

———. 1996."Organized Crime Moves into Migrant Trafficking." *Trafficking in Migrants, Quarterly Bulletin*, no. 11 (June): 1–2.

———. 1998. *Trafficking in Migrants, Quarterly Bulletin*, no. 18 (June).

———. 2000. *Trafficking in Migrants, Quarterly Bulletin*, no. 20 (January).

JHA. 1993. Council of the European Union, "Recommendation on Trafficking in Human Beings." Council press release 10550/93 of November 29 and 30.

———. 1996. Justice and Home Affairs, Joint Action 96/700/JHA. http://europa.eu.int/comm/sg/scadplus/leg/.

Kerry, John. 1997. *The New War: The Web of Crime That Threatens America's Security*. New York: Simon and Schuster.

Kohli, Sheel, and Simon Macklin. 1998. "G8 to Fight 'Slave' Trade into Japan." *South China Morning Post*, May 18.

Korbin, Stephen J. 1997. "The Architecture of Globalization: State Sovereignty in a Networked Global Economy." In *Governments, Globalization, and International Business*, edited by John H. Dunning, 146–71. Oxford: Oxford University Press.

Koslowski, Rey. 2011. "The International Travel Regime." In *Global Mobility Regimes*, edited by Rey Koslowski. London: Palgrave Macmillan.

Kwong, Peter. 1997. *Forbidden Workers: Illegal Chinese Immigrants and American Labor*. New York: New Press.

Kyle, David. 1996. "The Transnational Peasant: The Social Construction of Transnational Migration from the Ecuadorian Andes." Ph.D. diss., Johns Hopkins University.

Layard, Richard, Oliver Blanchard, Rudiger Dornbusch, and Paul Krugman. 1992. *East-West Migration: The Alternatives*. Cambridge: MIT Press.

Lee, Jennifer 2006. "Human Smuggling for a Hefty Fee," *New York Times*, May 28, 2006.

Lopez Castro, Gustavo, 1998. "Coyotes and Alien Smuggling." In *Migration between Mexico and the United States: Binational Study,* vol. 3. Mexico City and Washington, D.C.: Mexican Ministry of Foreign Affairs and the U.S. Commission on Immigration Reform.

Massey, Douglas. 1998. "March of Folly." *American Prospect* (March–April): 22–33.

Miller, Mark. 1998. "The Politics of International Migration and Crime: Reflections on French and U.S. Trends." Presented at the workshop International Migration and Transnational Crime, Rutgers University, Newark, N.J., May.

———. 2001. "The Sanctioning of Unauthorized Migration and Alien Employment." In *Global Human Smuggling: Comparative Perspectives,* edited by David Kyle and Rey Koslowski. Baltimore: Johns Hopkins University Press.

Moreno, Sylvia. 1998. "Legal Attack Targets Vans Carrying Immigrants." *Washington Post,* April 22.

Naim, Moises. 2006. *Illicit: How Smugglers, Traffickers, and Copycats Are Hijacking the Global Economy*. New York: Random House.

Naylor, R. T. 1995. "From Cold War to Crime War: The Search for a New 'National Security' Threat." *Transnational Organized Crime* 1 (4): 37–56.

NDIC. 2008. *National Drug Threat Assessment 2009*. National Drug Intelligence Center, December.

OSCE. 1999. "St Petersburg Declaration of the OSCE Parliamentary Assembly: Resolution on Trafficking of Women and Children." Commission on Security and Cooperation in Europe, Washington, D.C.

Passel, Jeffrey S., and D'Vera Cohn. 2008. *Trends in Unauthorized Immigration: Undocumented Inflow Now Trails Legal Inflow*. Pew Hispanic Center, October 2. http://pew research.org/pubs/978/undocumented-immigration.

Reuter, Peter. 1983. *Disorganized Crime*. Cambridge: MIT Press.

Rohter, Larry. 1997. "Deportees from the U.S. Unwelcome in El Salvador." *New York Times,* August 10.

Rojas, Aurelio. 1996. "Border Guarded, Workplace Ignored." *San Francisco Chronicle,* March 18.

Salt, John, and Jeremy Stein. 1997. "Migration as a Business: The Case of Trafficking." *International Migration* 35 (4): 467–94.

Sassen, Saskia. 1988. *The Mobility of Labor and Capital*. Cambridge: Cambridge University Press.

Schuessel, Wolfgang. 1997. "Statement by Austrian Vice-Chancellor and Federal Minister for Foreign Affairs, Wolfgang Schuessel, to the Fifty-second Session of the United Nations General Assembly, New York, 25 September 1997," Austrian Information Service, Washington, D.C.

Singer, Audrey, and Douglas S. Massey. 1998. "The Social Process of Undocumented Border Crossing among Mexican Migrants." *International Migration Review* 32 (3): 561–92.

Sontag, Deborah. 1997. "Many Deported Felons Return to U.S. Unnoticed." *New York Times,* August 11.

Strange, Susan. 1996. *Retreat of the State: The Diffusion of Power in the World Economy.* Cambridge: Cambridge University Press.

Swecker, Chris. 2006. Statement of Chris Swecker Acting Executive Assistant Director of Law Enforcement Services, U.S. Department of Justice Committee on House Homeland Security Subcommittee on Management, Integration, and Oversight, March 8.

U.S. State Department. 1998. "G-8 Birmingham Summit Overview." Fact sheet released by the Bureau of European and Canadian Affairs, April 30.

Weintraub, Sidney, and Chandler Stolp. 1987. "The Implications of Growing Economic Interdependence." In Organization for Economic Cooperation and Development (OECD), *The Future of Migration.* Paris: OECD.

Williams, Phil. 1995. "Transnational Criminal Organizations: Strategic Alliances." *Washington Quarterly* 18 (Winter): 57–72.

Winer, Jonathan M. 1997. "Operation Global Reach News Conference." Federal News Service, June 19.

———. 1998. "Organized Crime: Smuggling of Illegal Aliens and Trafficking in Women and Children." Speech given at Amerika Haus, Vienna, April 27.

Part II / Historical Perspective

CHAPTER THREE

Trafficking Human Subjects in the Malay World, 1850–1910

Eric Tagliacozzo

In the second half of the nineteenth century, and just beyond this into the beginning of the twentieth century, anyone watching patterns of movement in insular Southeast Asia would have been surprised by the sheer number of people in motion across the region. Many, if not most, of these transiting human beings were migrants, workers, and travelers going about the normal routines of their lives. They were earning a living, visiting kin relations, and sometimes seeing new places, much as local people have done in continuous fashion for many centuries into the past. Yet the erecting of strong state structures for the first time around this period—and with these, vibrant economic enterprises such as plantations, mines, and burgeoning megacities—also meant that a significant number of people were in transit for another reason. Trafficked human beings (those who were transited illegally outside the legal codes of modernizing colonial states) began to move in numbers rivaling the passage of legal human movements. This didn't happen absolutely everywhere in Southeast Asia during this time frame, nor did it happen with equal density in the areas where such movements did indeed occur. But as an evolving pattern of extrajudicial commerce, the trafficking of humans did start to take place on an unprecedented scale.

This chapter looks at the sale of human beings for labor purposes during this roughly sixty-year period spanning the second half of the nineteenth century and the beginning of the twentieth. I am specifically concerned here with the passage and sale of coolies (laborers) and slaves, as they were bought and sold in extralegal ways across the Malay world. I have not focused on the gendered aspect of these trades (prostitution and the trafficking of women) because these specific branches of commerce have been dealt with elsewhere, including by myself (see Warren, 1993; Abalahin, 2003; Tagliacozzo, 2008). Nevertheless, the laborers and slaves dealt with here could be and sometimes were women, as the period sources make clear. First, I lay out the geography and temporality of these trades across the Malay world during this half century, focusing first on the often destitute migrant workers who were trafficked to fulfill the insatiable demand for labor in the region. Second, I examine the continuation and expansion of slaving as an institution in the islands of the region, one that went from a sanctioned cultural practice under many indigenous regimes to an illicit form of commerce under moralizing colonial administrations. I argue that these human circuits were a vital and understudied phenomenon of the political economy of the age, linking "centers" and "peripheries," "indigenes" and colonials in a number of interesting ways.

The Stream of the Laboring Poor

The state-sponsored trade in Chinese labor at the turn of the twentieth century was vast, funneling coolies as far as the Caribbean (for sugar plantations), Australia (for mining), and parts of Oceania and Melanesia (for copra), as well as to many other destinations (Pan, 1992: 47). In Southeast Asia, many planters, mining concerns, and merchants had agents in China and India to secure their necessary labor, which was only sometimes free, and often indentured, under the grimmest of circumstances. Millions of poor laborers passed in these "official" ways down to Southeast Asia, though others, most notably in China, were kidnapped (especially farmers and coastal fishermen), sold (including prisoners taken in interclan battles), or simply duped by traveling recruiters, who then trafficked such men into waiting boats (Thio, 1960; Blusse, 1998: 34–50; Houben, 1998: 51–65). The explosion in prosperity and building in the archipelago, especially in plantations and urban infrastructure projects (such as wharves, rail lines, and tobacco and rubber concerns) made the demand for labor so acute that many were willing to search outside the sanctioned system for the cheap workers they required. This was especially true in places such as Dutch Sumatra and British North Borneo, which had particularly evil reputations as to how coolies were treated (see Pelly et al., 1984: 8–9; Stoler, 1986; and Breman, 1989, 1990, 1992; see also Loh, 1988: 7–54; Heidhues, 1992: chap. 3; and Kaur, 1996: 95–120). Massive disturbances such as the Taiping Rebellion and overpopulation in both China and India often made these concerns irrelevant, however, to hungry multitudes. Several years' worth of laboring, even under the worst of circumstances, was seen as at least an opportunity to eat ("Overzicht van eene Voordracht," 1891: 305–11).

Colonial states in the region tried to combat the illegal passage of people by legislating juridical infrastructures that could combat these flows on the ground. In the Dutch Indies, this meant proclamations such as Staatsbladen, #8 and 9 of 1887, which enacted complete bans on the travel of Indies "natives" to any foreign place for the purpose of laboring. Surveillance on such movements, and Batavia's abilities to ensure that its own subjects were not being trafficked or mistreated, were considered inadequate, even by the state itself. Yet only a few years after these regulations were proclaimed, the demands of overpopulation, especially in Java, overrode such concerns, and the passage of indigenous coolies out of the Indies was again allowed ("Nota over de Uitoeffening," 1907: 3–4). In the British Straits Settlements, the legal edifice built to deal with the smuggling of unwilling or mistreated labor was even larger. Laws regulated the hours and manners of passenger ships' departures and stipulated special instructions and guidelines for the movement of indigenous *perahus,* as well as Chinese junks and sampans.[1] Crimping was specifically (and legally) banned in 1877, in the seminal Crimping Ordinance of that year, while other legislation made special stipulations for the conduct of Chinese and Indian labor through the colony to bordering colonies.[2] It was only around the turn of the twentieth century, however, that strictures were passed looking into the actual mechanisms of the dreaded "lodging houses," and the plight of Netherlands Indies coolies in the Straits in particular.[3] Yet these laws and regulations always managed to be more impressive on paper than they ever were in reality, as Labor Commission Reports from both sides of the Straits make clear.

Official reports from the British in Southeast Asia and similar documents from the Netherlands' colonial government in the Indies show how egregiously standing labor and recruitment practices were breached in the years around the turn of the twentieth century. One of the main reasons for such breaches was that so many coolies (of various ethnicities) were being transited around Southeast Asia during this time. Javanese, Boyanese, Banjarese, "Dayaks," Kelantanese, Tamils, and Chinese were all in motion, sometimes as bonded labor and sometimes as free immigrants (*Labour Commission,* 1891). There was much room in this human maelstrom to take advantage of the system, which many brokers and "barracoons" figured out all too quickly. One of the most important British reports, through the avenue of expert witness testimonies, shows explicitly how secret societies had penetrated the movement of coolies to an enormous degree, transiting Southern Chinese immigrants from place to place (and often under abominable conditions) outside the supervision of the state. It also shows how overseers specifically tried to get labor from more distant locations, so that inducements and opportunities to abscond would be made more difficult.[4] Human beings were graded into hierarchies under these conditions, with Northern Chinese receiving high marks of desirability from labor supervisors and Southern Chinese ("Hailams" and "Macaos," for example) costing much less per head than their northern cousins.[5] Dutch reports also tallied wide abuses of the system, from people being moved under the guise of pilgrimage (but really destined for plantations and mines) to others being spirited out of the Indies ostensibly as "folk-life examples" for exhibitions in Europe. The residents of many places along the north coast of Java, and from southeastern Borneo as well, were told to be particularly watchful for attempts to smuggle laborers to the neighboring English possessions ("Nota over de Uitoeffening," 1907: 9–12).

The plantation and mining district of East Sumatra was one of the main sites for this kind of human labor trafficking outside the surveillance of the state. Huge numbers of Chinese coolies went to Deli and its environs to work on tobacco plantations and in the neighboring tin mines of Siak to the south, as charts kept by the Dutch consul in South China, and by the Sumatra Planters' Committee, make clear.[6] The system to get them there was despised by both the Chinese laborers and the Dutch agricultural enterprises, however, as it relied on coolie-broking middlemen in the Straits and Hong Kong. These agents were quite often less than scrupulous in their procurement methods. Court cases from the Straits, such as *Ramsamy v. Lowe* (1888) and *Apolingam v. E. A. B. Brown* (1893), show how labor traffickers tried to get Straits coolies down to Deli against British laws; other cases show that these illicit movements happened entirely within the English sphere as well, as crimping secreted away immigrants from their true destinations and off to other places, usually locales of grim repute.[7] In January 1890 a riot broke out on the German steamer *Chow Foo* as it carried a huge load of Chinese coolies down to the Straits from South China; the men on board had found out that they were actually being taken to Deli, and not the Straits as had been promised. Thirteen of the men were shot to keep the others in line.[8] Crimping in Penang, also in order to get Chinese coolies to East Sumatra, was just as bad, as Chinese witness statements given to the Straits authorities showed in some detail.[9]

Indian Muslim men were sometimes employed in small sailing craft to pilot these journeys, with the coolies going for thirty-five dollars a head to Chinese subagents waiting in Sumatra.[10] These men were eventually ferried to a large vessel off the coast of Pulau Hantu (Ghost Island), and from there they were transported across the maritime border to the Dutch possessions. Chinese protest petitions were circulated in the Straits when the abuses became particularly bad, and many of the local Chinese accused British police of looking the other way, or of being complicit, and receiving cutbacks to get the men to the Indies.[11] There is good reason to believe that there was a great deal of truth to these assertions: even some Straits administrators admitted that the colony was being used to "entrap coolies for slavery in the neighboring Dutch settlements."[12] With the moral climate changing about issues such as slavery and coolie labor in the last decades of the nineteenth century, these kinds of abuses increasingly were an embarrassment to the Straits government in the larger international arena of Asia.

Reports and Chinese witness statements from Tebingtinggi, also on the coast of Sumatra, show why it often took artifice to induce coolies to come to these areas to work. Chinese woodcutting concerns in this area made a huge business yearly cutting down logs and shipping them back to Singapore for export; one trunk of the timber went for approximately twenty dollars, more than the price of a coolie.[13] Yet the treatment these laborers received, mostly Chinese men funneled in from the Straits, was terrifyingly harsh. A report compiled by the Dutch resident of the east coast of Sumatra took witness statements of various Chinese working in the kongsi; all complained of beatings with fists, sticks, and thick cudgels and prevention of complaints to the police.[14] Yong Siu's testimony of November 13, 1908, told of coolies being denied medicine and forced to undertake labor despite illnesses; four men hanged themselves in his work gang, and he pointed to the photo of another man who was eventually beaten to death. Yong himself finally made his way to a vessel lying at anchor in a neighboring stream and escaped to the Straits, where he told his tale to the authorities.[15] His account was corroborated by other court cases brought before the magistrate in the Straits, which also painted a picture of a porous maritime border being crossed by duped or unwilling coolies in one direction and a few lucky escapees in the other.[16]

Farther down in the Straits, opposite Singapore in the islands of Dutch Riau, the case was much the same. A Chinese sampan that was caught trying to land Chinese coolies there in 1904 illuminated the larger pattern; this particular craft had 161 Hainanese laborers on board, all of whom had been loaded in Guangdong, South China. The officer of Chinese Affairs in Tanjung Pinang, Riau, reported that the ship had false papers and a false destination; it was supposed to have been en route to the Bangka tin mines farther south in the Straits but had tried to land the coolies in Riau instead. Most of these were young men in their teens from the interior of Guangdong; they had been lied to and given false promises and were huddled in the belly of the craft. No passengers had been mentioned on the vessel's manifest either, though the captain eventually told the Dutch that the workers had been brought from Annam (Vietnam). This the officer of Chinese affairs did not believe, as the entire documentation of the craft seemed to have been forged. The papers called the ship the *Khing Tu Li,* but by looking at the small altar to the God of the Sea inside the captain's quarters, where the name of the *wangkang* had to be inscribed, the officer found that it was actually the *Khing Goan Hin.* The shippers had tried to trick the Dutch into thinking that the ship was another craft already on colonial record, but the purpose of the voyage all along was to get the coolies to a secret work site in Riau. The Dutch consul in Hong Kong agreed. He pointed out that the Chinese authorities often saw coolie movements as a way to rid China of "bad elements" and that they didn't care much about illegal passages.[17] Twenty years earlier a similar case was documented in the region when another unregistered junk was shipwrecked in local waters and most of the coolies on board drowned.[18]

The Dutch eventually made much more stringent efforts to get coolies directly from China themselves, a strategy that worked (mainly because of the Deli Planters Lobby's money and influence in Dutch diplomatic circles) after 1890. Yet getting enough labor through legitimate means still remained a problem, even after this date. This can be seen through the maneuverings of the Singkep Tin Company, a Dutch concern on the island of Singkep just south of the Riau archipelago, in the mid-1890s. The Singkep Company's attempts to recruit labor in the Chinese countryside, outside the recently established direct South China–to–Deli funnel, aroused the concern of the formal Dutch authorities. The Hague's consul in Swatow, for example, told his superiors that any transgressions of the present system of labor procurement might make the Chinese nervous and endanger the much larger flows to Sumatra.[19] Yet the company pressed forward with its aggressive program, sending Chinese miners already working for it into the Guangdong periphery in search of able-bodied men to bring down to the Straits. The Malay-language letter of two of these Chinese, Thoe Nam Sin and Tjoa Eng Hay, survives: it shows the conditions under which the company wanted its labor, which included a ban on men from Macao or Chuan-chou (Quanzhou) and a stipulation that the coolies be brought directly down to Singkep and nowhere near Singapore.[20] This last condition was the more earnest of the two: bringing Chinese laborers near Singapore brought them into contact with coolie brokers and the official system, which allowed the workers opportunities to escape and the brokers opportunities to cheat the company. This particular trip to get coolies down to Singkep ultimately failed because of too much resistance from both entrenched Dutch interests and the protective policies of the Chinese.[21] Yet it was only one attempt among many to move men outside the officially sanctioned channels and into lives of labor in Southeast Asia, away from the eyes of the local colonial states.

Conditions in the Dutch tin mines on Bangka and Belitung, two islands farther south in the Straits, eventually became so bad that the Chinese government lodged complaints on behalf of its subjects working there. These islands were two thousand miles away from China, eight to ten days by steamer; they had a resident population of approximately 250 Europeans and 250 Arabs in 1905, alongside 40,000 Chinese.[22] Many of these Chinese worked in mines that were partially self-governing but ultimately responsible to larger Dutch mining companies or the Netherlands Indies state ("Nijverheid en Technische Kunsten," 1911). By 1906, however, the stealthy transport of coolies down to these mines, and their abominable treatment, were arousing the indignation of the provincial Chinese authorities. The viceroy of Guangdong and Guangxi wrote to the Dutch consul in Hong Kong in that year that he knew of such secret enlistments; he warned the consul that this kind of recruitment was forbidden and asked him to work to forbid it.[23] The Chinese press, especially in Hong Kong, was less mild in its approbation. An article published in December

1905 told of brandings on the coolies' thighs and hands and asked why the lives of Chinese were treated as being of no value.[24] The Dutch were quick to respond; under the cover of the name of a Mr. Kien of the Holland/China Trade Company, an article was inserted in the same paper two weeks later denying the validity of the stories.[25] Further protest articles were published in Chinese papers in the Straits, mirroring the earlier complaints.[26] The entire matter shows, however, that both the Chinese government in China and the Dutch authorities in Batavia were well aware of the secret transport of labor across the frontier but were more or less powerless to stop it. Though the viceroy banned the passage of more Chinese coolies down to Bangka in March 1906, there were always other ways to get labor through subterranean channels.[27]

In Borneo, finally, human beings were also trafficked for labor purposes, especially into the domains of the British North Borneo Company in the northern part of the island. Dutch surveillance reports on labor practices in the archipelago singled out North Borneo as a terminus for these sorts of activities, declaring that the company's territory was used repeatedly as work sites for illegally transited labor. Indies coolies who were en route to Sumatra's east coast were sometimes lured to the Borneo plantations by corrupt labor foremen; the Dutch consul in Singapore reported in 1888 that forty coolies were duped in this way by a "Hadji Taip," who landed them on the company's lands instead ("Nota over de Uitoeffening," 1907: 8). The North Borneo Company knew that its territory held an evil reputation as a graveyard for laboring coolies and made sure to sign extradition treaties with neighboring polities to ensure that escapees would be brought back to its shores. Sarawak instituted similar practices throughout the years around the turn of the century.[28] This left nearby ports like Labuan the unenviable task of constantly having to be on the lookout for absconding workers, who often dropped off the side of massive ships like ants in their eagerness to escape their own trafficking.[29] Eventually the company turned to labor sources as far away as South India for the workers it needed, though even other outposts of the extended British Empire in Asia were loath to send their subjects to North Borneo. In 1913, China relented after many long years of complaints and allowed the movement of more settlers to the northern half of the island, though a Chinese supervisor, Dr. T. B. Sia, was required by treaty to accompany the workers to check on their conditions.[30] By the first several decades of the twentieth century, nationalist awakenings in several parts of Asia made such scrutiny highly desirable. Even previously unwilling colonial regimes began to realize the consequences of not improving a system based on mistreatment and near slavery. The traffic in human labor had been going on long enough, and with such a grim reputation, that almost all parties involved now said that coolies needed the protection of emerging international law.

Circuits of Slavery

If coolies smuggled throughout Southeast Asia in the years around the fin de siècle were often treated as little better than livestock, there was another class of human chattel whose plight was arguably even worse. Slaving continued to be practiced in insular Southeast Asia as well, despite the many edicts promulgated against the practice by regional colonial powers. Forms of slavery and debt bondage have existed in Southeast Asia for a very, very long time: one author in particular has outlined the structural reasons that this has been so, pointing to low population densities, cultural tendencies toward vertical bonding, and little extant wage labor as primary reasons for slavery's presence (Reid, 1983: 1–43; Reid, 1993: 64–65). Two other scholars have shown that these were attributes of mainland polities, and by the late eighteenth and early nineteenth centuries, massive slaving expeditions scoured almost all of maritime Southeast Asia as well, moving vast quantities of men and matériel from the Bay of Bengal eastward to New Guinea and as far north as coastal Luzon. By the late nineteenth century, however, these massive movements were halting, partially because slavers were now keeping their human cargoes for themselves (to use for the collection of marine produce and jungle products), while European navies were also cruising more effectively (Warren, 1981: 147, 14; Terweil, 1983: 118–39; Scwalenberg, 1994: 376–84; Means, 2000: 188–89). Even after the highpoint of this phenomenon, however, certain regions continued to export slaves more than others: in the archipelago Bali, Nias, southern Sulawesi and the Batak highlands in Sumatra were some of these places. Though slavery had first been banned in the Dutch dominions in 1818, with the ban renewed with more force in 1860, it was not until 1874 that Batavia started to force indigenous chiefs also to give up their slaves, though these men were then compensated for their losses (van Balen, 1987: 83–96; Reid, 1993: 69, 77).

The 1860 renewal on the ban on slavery in the Dutch Indies abolished the right of Europeans (and Chinese) to own slaves and also abolished slave trading, but these proscriptions were really only enforceable in Java, and not in the Outer Islands. There debt bondage for children was outlawed, and the movement of pawned people across borders was also legislated against, but the realities of Dutch power at this juncture prevented any more serious steps being undertaken in the border residencies (Backer-Dirks, 1985: 57). As the Dutch legal edifice built on these laws evolved, however, Batavia's reach into the Outer Islands grew: competencies given to the Gouvernements Marine, especially, started to give the Dutch a longer arm against slave trafficking in the scattered seas of the archipelago. Staatsblad 1877, #180 and #181, for example, gave the Dutch marine boarding rights on any ship flying the flag of indigenous states (or no flag at all), while other laws tried to push against slavery by various other means.[31] Across the Straits in the English possessions, the British also were moving against slave trafficking, though this was (as with the Dutch) an uneven process. A treaty signed between Singapore and Selangor, for example, specifically mentioned that the latter could not engage in slaving upon Britons or British subjects, but this still gave Selangor plenty of room to deal in other archipelago peoples, notably Bataks from Sumatra.[32] By 1874, the Asian stations of the Royal Navy were receiving specific instructions on how to spot, and deal with, suspected slaving craft. The booklets reveal the legal preoccupations of London in searching out ways to avoid being sued for seizures, as well as its financial acumen in trying to skim tax off these same actions.[33]

Despite these efforts from both colonial camps, slaving was alive and well in insular Southeast Asia in the middle decades of the nineteenth century, especially in many areas along the length of the frontier. Batavia saw the large scale of the slave trade between North Sumatra and the Malay Peninsula as a good reason (or excuse, depending on whose letters one reads) for expansion there in the late 1860s: 8,000–10,000 slaves were said to pass across the Melaka Straits every year, though the British disputed the this number.[34] The British did not dispute, however, that some slaving was indeed happening across the maritime divide, as one correspondence from the resident councilor in Melaka makes clear. In his own jurisdiction, he wrote to the governor of Singapore in mid-1866, slaves were being landed in small boats at night, sometimes onto Melaka rice merchants' own *perahus* far out at sea and other times to the back porches of stilt houses by the beach.[35] In Singapore, farther down the coast, Bugis craft brought human cargoes to Kampung Gelam during the eastern monsoon, a phenomenon reported by men of both Dutch and English nationality. Many of these same Bugis shippers also had interests in slaving farther east, as a huge traffic in humans still managed to take place between Sulawesi and eastern Borneo throughout the 1870s.[36] The perpetrators of most of these sales were Arabs who sailed from Pontianak in western Borneo and had networks and outposts stretching from Sulawesi to Singapore. Farther north, near the terminus of North Borneo and the Sulu Sea, there were also traffickers, some of whom were native to this arena, while others, such as the German captain of the steamer *Tony* named Sachsze, were European.[37]

As early as the 1870s Batavia was trying to turn its rhetoric of emancipation in the Outer Islands into a more coherent reality. One of the ways to do this was to offer money to local chiefs for every slave or pawned person who was freed. This, in conjunction with more coercive representations, did eventually lead to the freeing of large number of bonded people. The first place this was tried was in Sumatra, where twenty thousand people eventually gained their freedom as a result of these inducements by the mid-1870s.[38] On the east coast, slaves could buy their freedom in Deli, Langkat, and Serdang by 1879, though there still were bonded people ten years after that, probably because Batavia did not inject the finances to fully support the program (Kerckhoff, 1891: 757). In Deli, where there were more pawned people than outright slaves, subjects could buy their freedom from the sultan for between thirty-two and sixty four dollars.[39] The practice of keeping such bonded people does seem to have receded over time, though, especially (as the resident of Palembang noted farther down the coast) as inspection tours penetrated farther into the interior.[40] Nevertheless, in some places, such as in southeastern Borneo in the early 1870s, the numbers of pawned people were actually rising, in this case among the residency's Chinese population.[41] Pawning and the "restocking" of these populations also took place through Bugis devices on the western half of the island, as a report in the *Tijdschrift voor Nederlandsch-Indie* makes clear (Kater, 1871: 296–305).

Yet large stretches of the border residencies still remained out of the reach of these programs and colonial "civilizing projects," especially in Borneo. Borneo remained an open field for the trade in slaves, even until a comparatively late date. On the British side of the frontier, the fragmented nature of English authority—split between the Raja of Sarawak, the British North Borneo Company, the sultan of Brunei (who had a British adviser), and Labuan island—encouraged the continuity of trafficking for many years. In Sarawak the Brookes tried to legislate the terms of slavery and bondage to their own advantage by fining any human transfers done outside the jurisdiction of the court. In such a scenario, not only would the "masters" lose money for dealing outside the purview of the state, but the slave would also go free.[42] In the company's dominions on the northern half of the island, however, diaries of company residents in the periphery show how slowly attitudes could be expected to change. William Pretyman's diary at Tempasuk in 1880 described armed combats between parties over stolen slaves, while Resident Everett at Papar made clear that area datus were smuggling Bajaus wherever they wished, in defiance of company proscriptions.[43] In Brunei, London's representative also had his hands full, as area pangerans raided the company's territory for slaves and then attacked British police units that were sent out to arrest the perpetrators.[44] The British consul in Brunei sighed upon hearing news of these depredations, saying that "slave-dealing and kidnapping are a part of Bornean traditions, which must be dealt with by degrees."[45] Even the Straits press expected only slow progress in the matter, pointing out that that it had taken the Dutch one hundred years to deal with the problem in Java and that Brooke still could not abolish it after decades in Sarawak.[46]

On the Dutch side of the enormous land divide, progress was little quicker. In western Borneo, in areas far outside any real Dutch jurisdiction, slavery and slave trafficking went on as they always had, despite local chiefs' signatures on contracts to the contrary.[47] Yet it was primarily in eastern Borneo, along the coast and just a bit inland from these coasts, that slave trafficking managed to survive with greatest tenacity. In 1876, the small polities of Kutei, Pasir, Bulungan, Sambaling, and Pegatan committed themselves on paper against the long-standing area trade in humans. Yet only a few years later, in data collected by the Dutch administration, it became apparent that these sultanates were not living up to their promises (Kerckhoff, 1891: 756). Some Dutch officials felt that this was not for want of trying; the sultans themselves, these authors wrote, could not control their own subjects or hinterlands, which essentially allowed trafficking free reign ("Varia," 1880: 481–83). By 1883, the *Straits Times Overland Journal* was describing whole villages of slaves on the east coast near Berau, despite the Dutch regulations; many of these people worked in area mines and led particularly harsh troglodytic existences underground. Three hundred of these slaves every year were said to be sold at Gunung Tabor, where they were shipped in from the southern Philippines, the result of barter transactions for opium, cloth, and guns.[48] By 1889, the Dutch station commander in eastern Borneo waters was still cruising outside the Berau and Bulungan river mouths, continually on the lookout for more *perahus* carrying slaves.[49]

Yet the remote border forests of Borneo were only one location where forms of slavery and slave trafficking managed to hold on, even until the end of the nineteenth century. Singapore, the central node of all commerce in insular Southeast Asia and the seat of British power in the region, was another. Dutch consuls in Singapore were particularly incensed at the Straits authorities' lack of action on slave dealing through the colony—this despite a wide compendium of laws that had been passed to prevent such abuses. All of this trafficking was on the sly and came in several forms. One manifestation was in the indebtedness some pilgrims managed to find themselves in while trying to undertake the hajj. Many of these pilgrims, particularly Javanese and Boyanese ones, never got farther than Singapore but had bonded themselves to pay their passage to Arabia for several years. The 117 houses of pilgrimage middlemen, known variously as "sheikhs" or "juragans," frequently took advantage of the ten thousand archipelago pilgrims who passed through Singapore every year, and they enlisted them into multiyear "contracts" to pay off their trips, which were little better than slavery. Dutch representatives described these arrangements as remarkably similar to what had befallen "Africans of old," a complaint that the British authorities said was an exaggeration or merely a difference in opinion.[50] There was less of a difference of opinion on other forms of trafficking that passed through the colony, such as Bugis shippers selling slaves from New Guinea in the back streets of Singapore and Javanese females being sold as housekeepers and servants, to both Singapore and Melaka.[51]

It was this latter traffic, the selling of Indies women to rich Chinese merchants and Arabs in Singapore as domestic servants, that caused the Dutch consul to write a letter of protest to the colonial secretary in May 1882. Four women had just sought the protection of the consul on the eighth of that month; three of them, named "Poele, Masmirah, and Karimah," were from Surabaya residency and had been induced by one "Babah Sroening," the supercargo of the steamer *Rosa,* to come with him to Singapore. He had promised to marry all of them (which he could do as a Muslim) and give them jewels; instead, they were brought to the house of Lee Sing Wah on Telok Air Street (who was a partner in the *Rosa*) and sold into domestic slavery. They were never paid a cent for their work and were never allowed to leave their master's house. Finally they were able to run away after another inmate in the house had taken sick and had been beaten for laziness until she died. It was cases like this one that induced Consul Read to bring the matter up again and again with the British, as there were other women, some of them Javanese, others Bugis, who were brought to the Straits against their will and were sold into servitude. A final case mentioned by the consul was of a woman who had been walking as a child in the Netherlands Indies when an Arab man had kidnapped her off a road and brought her to Singapore in a steamer. Some of the women had been in Singapore for years; they had no way to get back home and did not know whom to turn to for help.[52]

Forms of slavery and bondage lived on in Southeast Asia in manifestations such as this for some time and can even (in some circumstances) still be found today (Tagliacozzo, 2002: 193–220). Most slave trafficking in the classic sense, however, of ships with hostages chained to the floor was becoming obsolete by the turn of the twentieth century. Pontianak in western Borneo, for example, which had been mentioned as a center for slaving in the 1870s, was free of such activities by the early 1890s; in Palembang and Jambi, too, such forms of servitude were no longer practiced in 1891, except far inside the interior regions.[53] In Sulawesi there was still pawning of slaves in 1897, while even after the turn of the century scattered Arabs could be found hunting for human cargoes, such as the notorious Said Ali in Toraja.[54] In most parts of the archipelago, however, even in areas that had formerly been slaving centers (such as Bali, Lombok, Kutei, and Aceh), slave trafficking had been pushed back by century's end, although not in a few places such as New Guinea and small parts of the rest of the islands ("Slavernij in Nederlandsch-Indie," 1907: 425–26). Interestingly enough, the Netherlands Indies state, while in the process of abolishing the trade in humans as it expanded into the periphery, was the closest institution left to practicing slavery as the twentieth century dawned. Anthony Reid (1993: 74–77) has drawn attention to the huge size and brutality of Dutch corvée labor in the Outer Islands, not to mention the massive coolie system, which in its own contracts and conditions often treated workers worse than any native "master" ever dared. It was in these circumstances. in which slavery was being abolished under one rubric and more or less continued (unofficially) under another, that the practice of mass movements of human cargoes continued on well into the years of the twentieth century.

Conclusion

By the early twentieth century, most metropolitan Europeans saw the illegal traffic in human beings as morally indefensible; this was a far cry from the 1860s and 1870s, when the passage of human "cargo" was more or less viewed as inevitable in places like Southeast Asia. Yet metropolitan concerns and colonial abilities to enforce change on the ground in the region were often two separate things. The trade in human beings continued on either side of the fin de siècle but was pushed further and further underground by imperial authorities. Coolies were still exploited after this time period but were no longer trafficked outside existing systems as openly as before. Slavery did disappear (for the most part) along the length of regional borders, though this had less to do with interdiction and more to do with a concerted European administrative presence on the frontier. As a broad conceptual category, therefore, the commerce in labor shows the variability of the dance between smugglers and states. Some of these transited peoples found their lives improved immeasurably by the early twentieth century, while others still toiled grimly in different kinds of human bondage.

It would be a mistake, however, to see this period as completely transformative of the ways that human beings were bought and sold in Southeast Asia as a daily part of life. European morals did indeed curb some outstanding cultural norms long practiced in the region, pushing the commodification of human traffic into the margins of economic life. This is undeniably true. Yet even as the twentieth century progressed, it became clear that these changes were uneven across the width and breadth of Southeast Asia and that there are parts of this region where the trafficking of humans still continues unabated. The phasing to postcolonial life after the middle decades of the century did not completely eradicate these trades either—they resurfaced in more sophisticated garb and continue to be practiced today. In this the history of illicit human circuits in the region is one that is still unfolding, even after almost a century of attempts at suppression and eradication has left its uneven mark on the past.

NOTES

Abbreviations
ANRI   Arsip Nasional Republik Indonesia, Jakarta (Indonesia)
ARA   Algemeen Rijksarchief, The Hague (Netherlands)
BNB   British North Borneo Company
CO   Colonial Office Correspondence (Kew, UK)
FO   Foreign Office Correspondence (Kew, UK)
Kyshe   Kyshe's Law Reports, Straits Settlements (Singapore)
MvBZ   Minister, Buitenlandse Zaken (Foreign Affairs, The Hague)
MR   Mailrapport
SSLR   Straits Settlements Legal Reports (Singapore)

I am grateful to Yale University Press for allowing me to reprint some previously published material here that originally appeared in my book *Secret Trades, Porous Borders: Smuggling and States along a Southeast Asian Frontier, 1865–1915* (New Haven: Yale University Press, 2005).

1. See, e.g., *Straits Settlements Ordinances* 1867 #31; 1890 #7; 1868 #14; 1870 #6; and 1883 #5.

2. Crimping was defined as the unlawful sale of laborers for profit. *Straits Settlements Ordinances* 1873 #10; 1877 #2; 1880 #4; 1902 #9; 1910 #30; 1876 #1; 1884 #4; 1877 #3; 1892 #14; 1896 #21; 1891 #8. Chinese coolies had to be photographed by law in Perak as of 1888, as a protection against smuggling. See *Perak Government Gazette*, 1888, 74.

3. *Straits Settlements Ordinances* 1896 #18; 1897 #18; 1908 #21.

4. "Evidence of Tun Kua Hee, a Depot Keeper, 29 Oct. 1890 Sitting," in the *Labour Commission Report,* Singapore 1891; *The Labour Commission Glossary*, Singapore, 1891, under "Javanese and Native Labor," especially the accounts of Mr. Halloway, Mr. Gunn, Count D'Elsloo, Mr. Patterson, Mr. Wittholft, and Mr. Reimer. Indian coolies on estates in Perak in 1870 were absconding (or fleeing) at very high rates—over 20 percent of the total workforce in some instances. See *Perak Governmentt Gazette*, 1890, 572.

5. See "Evidence of D. W. Patterson, Shipping Clerk in Messrs. Guthrie and Co., 27 Oct. 1890 Sitting," in *The Labour Commission Report,* Singapore, 1891.

6. See ARA, Dutch Consul for South China to Chairman of the Planters' Committee, Medan, March 27, 1909, #213, app. 1, in MvBZ/A/245/A.119. The numbers for a range of border residencies are presented and then are blown up for East Sumatra, the main destination for these laborers.

7. For the Deli cases, see "Apolingam v. E. A. B. Brown," 1893, *SSLR*; "Ramsamy v. Lowe," *Kyshe* (1888), IV. For internal transiting of coolies inside British territory and against the law, see "Brown v. Vengadashellum," *Kyshe* (1889) IV, 524, and "Tio Ang Boi v. Hia Ma Lai," *Kyshe* (1887) IV.

8. See the version as printed in the Amsterdam newspaper *De Standaard,* April 11, 1890. See ARA, Dutch Consul Hong Kong to Gov. Gen. NEI, December 22, 1905, #1153, in MvBZ/A/246/A.119.

9. See the official statements provided by "Cheah Sin Ng, Lim Shit, Chew Ah Nyee, Hang Ship Ug, Leong Ship Sam, and Lew Ship Yit," in "Paper Laid before the Legislative Commission, Friday 23 Feb. 1877; Report by Mr. Pickering on Kidnapping Sinkehs," *Straits Settlements Legislative Council Proceedings* 1877, p. 4 of the report.

10. Ibid., pp. 2–3.

11. See the "Proclamation By the People of Canton and Hokkien Province," in the *Straits Observer* (Penang), December 14, 1874, 2.

12. "Report by Mr. Pickering on Kidnapped Sinkehs" *Straits Settlements Legislative Council Proceedings* 1877, 3.

13. ARA, "Chuk Fu's Statement" [February 3, 1909, Contract #17596], in Resident East Coast of Sumatra Report on the Mishandling of Workers at Tebingtinggi Woodcutting Kongsi (n.d.), in MvBZ/A/246/A.119. See also *Surat Surat Perdjandjian Riau* (1970), 215.

14. ARA, Resident East Coast of Sumatra Report on the Mishandling of Workers at Tebingtinggi Woodcutting Kongsi (n.d.), in MvBZ/A/246/A.119.

15. ARA, "Yong Siu's Statement" [November 13, 1908, Contract #17593], in Resident

East Coast of Sumatra Report on the Mishandling of Workers at Tebingtinggi Woodcutting Kongsi (n.d.), in MvBZ/A/246/A.119.

16. See for Tebingtinggi especially "Attorney General v. Wong Yew," *SSLR*, X, 1908, 44, and "Rex v. Koh Chin, Ang Tap, and Ang Chuan," *SSLR*, X, 1908, 48.

17. ARA, Dutch Consul, Peking to MvBZ, May 22, 1905, #593/79; Dutch Consul Hong Kong to Dutch Consul Peking, May 9, 1905, #474/35; GGNEI to Dutch Consul Peking, November 18, 1904, Kab. #48; Officer for Chinese Affairs in Tandjong Pinang to Resident of Riau, March 1904, #4, all in MvBZ/A/246/A.119.

18. ANRI, Maandrapport Residentie Banka 1872 (#98 December).

19. ARA, Dutch Acting Consul, Swatow to Dutch Minister for China, Peking, June 20, 1894, #41, in MvBZ/A/245/A.119.

20. The miners were trying to recruit thirty or forty men according to the letter; they were to be brought directly to the mines in Singkep. Macao and Chuan-chou men were considered physically weak; they were also often considered to be troublemakers. See Thoe Nam Sin and Tjoa Eng Hay's letter, enclosed in ARA, Dutch Consul Hong Kong to New Chief Administrator of the Singkep Tin Co, December 31, 1895, #759, in MvBZ/A/245/A.119.

21. ARA, Dutch Consul, London to MvBZ, October 19, 1896, #43, in MvBZ/A/245/A.119.

22. ARA, Dutch Consul Hong Kong to MvBZ, December 25, 1905, #1156/86, in MvBZ/A/246/A.119.

23. ARA, Viceroy Guangdong and Guangxi to Acting Dutch Consul, Hong Kong, 24th Day, 11th Moon, 32nd Year Guangxu Reign, in MvBZ/A/246/A.119.

24. *Sai Kai Kung Yik Po,* December 11, 1905. The article particularly lays blame upon Chinese who are used as henchmen by the Dutch in the mines. The Dutch themselves also participate in the injustices, leaving the Chinese workers in terrible shape, their bodies and spirits broken by their labors and by the cruelty of their oppressors. The author of the piece then warns that if China were powerful, no one would dare to heap such abuses upon its subjects. In ARA, MvBZ/A/246/A.119.

25. *Sai Kai Kung Yik Po,* December 25, 1905. The rebuttal says that there are untrue statements in the former article; Chinese, rather, have come down to the Dutch Indies for centuries to try to make their fortunes there. Some eventually become wealthy and are able to return home for visits. The article also points out that Chinese foremen supervise the labor and that these men would never allow the inhuman treatments complained of above. In ARA, MvBZ/A/246/A.119.

26. See *Nanyang Chung Wei Pao,* August 21, 1906; August 2, 1906; October 30, 1906; January 11, 1907; January 21, 1907, in ARA, MvBZ/A/246/A.119.

27. ARA, Dutch Consul Hong Kong to MvBZ, December 25, 1905, #1156/86, in ARA, MvBZ/A/246/A.119.

28. See the *Sarawak Gazette,* April 1, 1891, December 1, 1893, April 2, 1894, and September 20, 1895.

29. See CO to BNB Co. HQ, London, January 18, 1889, in CO 144/66, and Act. Gov. Labuan to CO, June 6, 1889, in CO 144/67; also Gov. BNB to BNB Co. HQ, London, June 18, 1912, in CO 531/4.

30. See Gov. Sec. Madras to Gov. Sec. BNB, July 3, 1912, and CO Jacket, October 2, 1912, both in CO 531/4; BNB Co. HQ, London to CO, January 3, 1913, in CO 531/5; BNB Co HQ, London, to CO, June 22, 1915, in CO 531/9.

31. *Staatsblad* 1877, #180, 181; see also *Staatsblad* 1876, #35, 166, 246; *Staatsblad* 1877, #89, 90; *Staatsblad* 1880, #21, 114; *Staatsblad* 1883, #40; *Staatsblad* 1884, #162; *Staatsblad* 1901, #286, 287.

32. Gov, SS to Sec. State India, London, May 21, 1866, #587, in CO 273/9.

33. The Instruction Booklet for 1869 let naval commanders know that "slavery as a legal institution exists in several states with which Great Britain has treaties for the suppression of the slave trade. The mere finding therefore of slaves on board a vessel will not justify an officer in detaining her." See Vice-Admiral Shadwell Circulaire to Ship Commanders, China-Station, April 2, 1874, #86; "Admiralty Instructions for the Guidance of Naval Officers Employed in the Suppression of the Slave Trade," June 11, 1869; and "An Act for Consolidating with Amendments the Acts for Carrying into Effect Treaties for the More Effectual Suppression of the Slave Trade, and for Other Purposes Connected with the Slave Trade," August 5, 1873, all in Public Records Office, London (Kew, UK)/Admiralty/125/#20, China Station General Correspondence (1871–74.)

34. See British Envoy, The Hague, to FO, February 1, 1866, #20, and Gov, SS to Sec. of State for India, London, April 6, #406, both in CO 273/9.

35. Resident Councillor, Malacca, to Sec. of Gov't, Straits, April 10, 1866, in CO 273/9.

36. ARA, Resident West Borneo to GGNEI, April 11, 1871, #32, Secret, in 1871, MR #522; Dutch Consul, Singapore to Col. Secretary, Straits, November 6, 1874, in CO 273/79; ARA, 1870, MR #633; Berigt van de Resident der Zuider en Ooster Afdeeling van Borneo, July 22, 1875, #37, in 1875, MR #655.

37. ARA, Resident West Borneo to GGNEI, April 11, 1871, #32, Secret, in 1871, MR #522; ARA, Extract Uit het Register der Besluiten, GGNEI, August 16, 1879, #1, in 1879, MR #476; also British Consul, Brunei to FO, March 13, 1877, #5 Political, in CO 144/48. Captain Sachsze was well known in local waters as a slaver; he was also sentenced in Singapore at one time for shooting one of his own crew members.

38. *Encyclopaedie van Nederlandsch Indie* (1928), 3:806.

39. ARA, Resident Sumatra Oostkust to GGNEI, August 3, 1875, #1037/10, in 1875, MR #655.

40. ANRI, Algemeen Administratieve Verslag Residentie Palembang 1871 (#64/14).

41. ANRI, Algemeen Verslag Residentie Borneo Z.O. 1871 (#9/2).

42. British Consul, Borneo to FO, February 5, 1883, Consular #7, in CO 144/57.

43. See William Pretyman's Diary at Tempasuk (vol. 72, May 17, 1880), and Everett's Diary at Papar (vol. 73, April 22, 1880), both in Public Records Office, London (Kew, UK)/CO/874/British North Borneo, boxes 67–77, Resident's Diaries (1878–98).

44. See especially Gov. BNB to Consul Trevenen, March 3, 1891, in CO 144/68. As a result of British pressure, the sultan of Brunei was forced to issue a ban on slaving, which particularly mentioned that the company's subjects were now off limits. Sultan of Brunei Proclamation, 26 Rejab, 1308 A.H., in CO 144/68.

45. Consul Trevenen to Marquis of Salisbury (FO), March 31, 1891, #2 Confidential, in CO 144/68.

46. *Singapore Daily Times*, January 4, 1882, 2.

47. ARA, 1877, MR #423.

48. See, e.g., the *Straits Times Overland Journal,* March 26, 1883.

49. ARA, Stations-Commandant Oosterafdeeling van Borneo to Commander, NEI

Navy, November 28, 1889, #898, in 1889, MR #149. See also "Slavenhandel. Slavernij," *Indische Weekblad van het Recht,* #1655, March 18, 1895, 42.

50. Some members of the Colonial Office, in hearing more about the systematic oppression of pilgrims in Singapore, disagreed with the Singapore administration in its dismissal of the Dutch consul's claims. "I feel some doubt whether this question should be allowed to remain uninvestigated," wrote Mr. Meade in the C.O. in early 1875. "The present 'investigation' is next to none at all. Mr. Read (the Dutch consul) may have overstated his case in calling the position of these Hajjis 'slavery.' But it seems to me not very far removed from it." See CO Jacket, Mr. Meade, February 2, 1875; Gov, SS to CO, February 2, 1875, #26; Dutch Consul, Singapore, in "Letter to the Editor," *Singapore Daily Times,* September 21, 1873; and Capt. Dunlop and Allan Skinner to Col. Secretary, SS, September 12, 1874, all in CO 273/79.

51. See *Straits Times Overland Journal,* May 5, 1882, in CO 273/118. The newspaper was glib in its disapproval of the Straits government's efforts to deal with such abuses: "It is very generally believed that the Bugis do a little 'in ebony' from New Guinea on the sly, and that women are frequently brought up from Java and disposed of, at a price, to some of the rich towkays. Of course, our government knows nothing of this. Why should it?" Various other sources confirm both of these transactions.

52. See the details in the fascinating letter by Read, Dutch Consul, Singapore to Col. Sec., Singapore, May 8, 1882, #243, in CO 273/115.

53. ARA, "Verslag Omtrent de Slavernij en den Slavenhandel in de Residentie Westerafdeeling van Borneo over het Jaar 1889," July 17, 1890, in 1890, MR #530; also "Verslag Betreffende Slavernij door de Resident van Palembang" (1891), in 1891, MR #194.

54. ARA, Controleur of the North Coast to Resident, Manado, October 5, 1896, #202, in 1897, MR #438; also ARA, 1902, MR #877.

REFERENCES

Abalahin, Andrew. 2003. "Prostitution Policy and the Project of Modernity: A Comparative Study of Colonial Indonesia and the Philippines, 1850–1940." Ph.D. diss., Cornell University.
Backer-Dirks, F. C. 1985. *De Gouvernements Marine in het Voormalige Nederlands-Indië in Haar Verschillende Tijdsperioden Geschetst 1861–1949.* Weesp: De Boer Maritiem.
Balen, A. van. 1987. "De Afschaffing van Slavenhandel en Slavernij in Nederlands Oost Indië (1986)." *Jambatan* 5 (2): 83–96.
Blusse, Leonard. 1998. "China Overzee: Aard en Omvang van de Chinese Migratie." In *Het Paradijs is Aan de Overzijde,* edited by Piet Emmer and Herman Obdeijn, 34–50. Utrecht: Van Arkel.
Breman, Jan. 1989. *Taming the Coolie Beast: Plantation Society and the Colonial Order in Southeast Asia.* Delhi: Oxford University Press.
———. 1990. *Labour Migration and Rural Transformation in Colonial Asia.* Amsterdam: Free University Press.
———. 1992. *Koelies, Planters, en Koloniale Politiek: Het Arbeidsregime op de Grootlandbouwondernemingen aan Sumatra's Oostkust in het Begin van de Twintigste Eeuw.* Leiden: KITLV.

Heidhues, Mary Somers. 1992. *Bangka Tin and Mentok Pepper: Chinese Settlement on an Indonesian Island*. Singapore: ISEAS.

Houben, Vincent. 1998. "Nyabrang/'Overzee Gaan': Javaanse Emigratie Tussen 1880 en 1940." In *Het Paradijs is Aan de Overzijde*, edited by Piet Emmer and Herman Obdeijn, 51–65. Utrecht: Van Arkel.

Kater, C. 1871. "Iets over het Pandelingschap in de Westerafdeeling van Borneo en de Boegineesche Vestiging aan het Zuider-Zeestrand te Pontianak." *TNI* 2:296–305.

Kaur, Amarjit. 1996. "Tin Miners and Tin Mining in Indonesia, 1850–1950." *Asian Studies Review* 20 (2): 95–120.

Kerckhoff, Ch. E. P. 1891. "Eenige Mededeelingen en Opmerkingen Betreffende de Slavernij in Nederlandsch-Indië en Hare Afschaffing." *IG*, no. 1: 743–69.

Labour Commission: Glossary of Words and Names in the Report of the Commissioners; Index to Evidence and Analysis of Evidence Taken by the Commission. 1891. Singapore: Government Press.

Loh, Francis. 1988. *Beyond the Tin Mines: Coolies, Squatters and New Villagers in the Kinta Valley, Malaysia, 1880–1980*. Singapore: Oxford University Press.

Means, Gordon. 2000. "Human Sacrifice and Slavery in the 'Unadministered' Areas of Upper Burma during the Colonial Era." *SOJOURN* 15 (2).

"Nijverheid en Technische Kunsten." 1911. *Nieuwe Rotterdamsche Courant*, February 12.

Nota over de Uitoeffening van Staatstoezicht op de Werving en Emigratie van Inlanders op Java en Madoera Bestemd voor de Buitenbezittingen of voor Plaatsen Buiten Nederlandsch-Indië. 1907. Batavia: Landsdrukkerij.

"Overzicht van eene Voordracht van J.J. de Groot over dat Gedeelte van China Waar Emigratie naar de Koloniën Plaats Hebben." 1891. *TAG* 8 (1): 305–11.

Pan, Lynn. 1992. *Sons of the Yellow Emperor: A History of the Chinese Diaspora*. New York: Little, Brown and Co.

Pelly, Usman, et al., eds. 1984. *Sejarah Sosial Daerah Sumatra Utara Kotamadya Medan*. Jakarta: Departmen Pendidikan dan Kebudayaan Direktorat Sejarah dan Nilai Tradisional.

Reid, Anthony. 1983. "Introduction: Slavery and Bondage in Southeast Asian History." In *Slavery, Bondage, and Dependency in Southeast Asia*, edited by Anthony Reid, 1–43. St. Lucia: University of Queensland Press.

———. 1993. "The Decline of Slavery in Nineteenth Century Indonesia." In *Breaking the Chains: Slavery, Bondage, and Emancipation in Modern Africa and Asia*, edited by Martin Klein, 64–82. Madison: University of Wisconsin Press.

Scwalenberg, Henry. 1994. "The Economics of Pre-Hispanic Visayan Slave Raiding." *Philippine Studies* 42 (3): 376–84.

"Slavernij in Nederlandsch-Indië." 1907. *IG* 1:425–26.

Stoler, Ann. 1986. *Capitalism and Confrontation in Sumatra's Plantation Belt, 1870–1979*. New Haven: Yale University Press.

Surat-Surat Perdjandjian Antara Kesultanan Riau dengan Pemerintahan (2) V.O.C. dan Hindia-Belanda 1784–1909. 1970. Jakarta: Arsip Nasional Indonesia.

Tagliacozzo, Eric. 2002. "Smuggling in Southeast Asia: History and Its Contemporary Vectors in an Unbounded Region." *Critical Asian Studies* 34 (2): 193–220.

———. 2008. "Morphological Shifts in Southeast Asian Prostitution: The Long Twentieth Century." *Journal of Global History* 3:251–73.

Terweil, B. J. 1983. "Bondage and Slavery in Early Nineteenth Century Siam." In *Slavery, Bondage, and Dependency in Southeast Asia,* edited by Anthony Reid, 118–39. St. Lucia: University of Queensland Press.

Thio, Eunice. 1960. "The Chinese Protectorate: Events and Conditions Leading to Its Establishment, 1823–77." *Journal of the South Seas* 16 (1/2): 40–80.

"Varia." 1880. *TNI* 2:481–83.

Warren, James. 1981. *The Sulu Zone: The Dynamics of External Trade, Slavery, and Ethnicity in the Transformation of a Southeast Asian Maritime State.* Singapore: Singapore University Press.

———. 1993. *Ah Ku and Karayuki-san: Prostitution in Singapore 1880–1940.* Singapore: Oxford University Press.

CHAPTER FOUR

Pre–Cold War Traffic in Sexual Labor and Its Foes

Some Contemporary Lessons

Eileen P. Scully

In early 1995, California papers announced the discovery of a "nationwide prostitution ring" based in San Diego, engaged in smuggling "hundreds of destitute women from Thailand" and selling "them into sexual slavery." Local officials were caught unawares, telling reporters that they had "never heard of a similar case in which foreigners were smuggled into this country for prostitution" (Repard, 1995: B2). A few days earlier, Seattle authorities had also uncovered the local hub "of a national prostitution operation trafficking in Asian women." A police spokesman declared: "We haven't seen this kind of thing in Seattle before" (Whitely, 1995: A1).

For historians, this Orwellian amnesia is both disheartening and provocative: the past is indeed a different country, if not yet a lost civilization. Stepping across the threshold into 2000, we do well to recall the vista that emboldened and confounded contemporaries a full century ago. The new world order of the early 1900s beheld rapid and uneven internationalization, weakening community ties, and unstable great power relationships. These factors collectively abetted a burgeoning traffic in women and children for prostitution, described by contemporaries as the white slave trade. Violence, economic turmoil, and political turbulence pushed local women from Asia and central Europe into brothels as far away as Buenos Aires and Seattle. The collapse of czarism in Russia unleashed successive waves of impoverished refugees, many of them driven into crime and prostitution. As profitability grew, organized gangs and syndicates moved to control supply, demand, and operations, spawning what one American activist described as "a system of gigantic, organized, powerful syndicates, each operating independently, but each depending on the other" (Terrell, c. 1907: 22).

To be sure, there are significant differences between what we bring into the twenty-first century and what awaited those journeying into the 1900s. Recurrence does not mean inevitability or justify indifference; a record of intractability does not make the humanitarian project less compelling. It is hoped, though, that this look at forced migratory sexual labor and its foes in the era before the Cold War will help identify such overlaps and contrasts, while also highlighting how antitraffic groups grappled with many of the same dilemmas bedeviling their counterparts today.

The pre–Cold War history of forced migratory prostitution comprised three distinct periods: (1) the 1840s to about 1895; (2) the late 1890s to World War I; (3) 1919 through World War II.

To the 1890s

The geography and animating forces of modern migratory prostitution were discernible many decades before the white slave trade scare at the turn of the century. The traffic in sexual labor, both coerced and voluntary, took hold in the 1840s and continued to grow and complexify thereafter. Demand was generated by three interlocking developments, all involving the mobilization and migration of large numbers of single males.

The first of these was the deployment of nonwhite, indentured labor to replace African slaves in plantation economies, to fuel extractive industries (such as diamond and gold mining), and to undertake monumental construction projects (such as railroads and canals). Abolition of the slave trade was uneven and sporadic, spanning the whole nineteenth century· for example, the British abolished colonial slavery in 1833 but excluded India, Burma, and Ceylon, then under the control of the East India Company. Revolutionary France abolished slavery in its colonies, reestablished it in 1802, and again abolished it in 1848 (Klein, 1994: 211–13). "Emancipation came at a time when an expanding capitalism was still hungry for labour, and free labour migration was not capable of meeting that demand" (212). This meant the large-scale recruitment of unfree labor in India, China, Japan, Vietnam, Indonesia, and the Pacific islands, "where poverty and landlessness created a pool of willing migrants" (212; Aldrich, 1990: 161).

Together, Asian indentured workers supplied the world with sugar, tea, rubber, minerals, gems, artificial waterways, and railroads. One scholar estimates that a total of 10 million to 13 million Chinese were part of this great labor migration into Southeast Asia, the Americas, the West Indies, and Africa (Tong, 1994: xv–xvii). Western colonial domination in these areas abetted the process; although officials condemned practices such as "black birding," kidnapping, and debt bondage, imperial managers and private concerns effectively combined to transfer labor within and across empires (Aldrich, 1990: 163–64). Indigenous middlemen also played a critical role, bringing labor from the rural hinterlands to transfer points and undertaking "migrant smuggling" to bypass immigration controls against Asians in Western countries, such as the United States.

Second, and concomitantly, was the mobilization and migration of non-Western males within the colonial matrix and Western-dominated world market. At one end of the spectrum, Western imperial enclaves—such as Hong Kong, Singapore, Shanghai, and New Delhi—attracted, and indeed depended upon, the emergence of wealthy, indigenous urban elites. At the opposite end, monetized economies linked to international trade impoverished rural populations, pushing proletarianized peasants into growing cities, into vast colonial armies, or into the migratory labor traffic described above. For example, Spanish rule over the Philippines transformed the city of Manila into a magnet for indigenous "vagrants, vagabonds, and displaced persons" driven from rural areas (Dery, 1991: 475). Concentrations of indigenous males, both rich and poor, most often unattached, provided a ready market for a range of services provided by migratory women, from prostitution to domestic chores.

Third on the demand side was the large-scale, long-distance movement of unattached, wealth-seeking men from Europe and North America, drawn to frontiers, mammoth construction projects, and colonial opportunities. This momentum led to large settlements of single white males, ranging from frontier boomtowns in the American West, Australia, and South Africa to the more socially elevated colonial communities of maritime Asia, such as Hong Kong and the Federated Malay States. The relative ease and affordability of travel, widespread economic depression from the mid-1870s into the 1890s, and great power deployment of personnel throughout the colonial world brought significant numbers of First World men, whose presence irrevocably altered the demographics and sexual economies of non-Western societies.

Together, these three interlocking developments generated an international traffic in sex workers, expanded regional migratory prostitution, and intensified local, indigenous prostitution. At each of these levels—international, regional, and local—women entered the trade under a variety of circumstances, ranging from astute entrepreneurial calculation to entrapment. They operated along a spectrum of autonomy, from full control over their labor conditions to the virtual enslavement of locked brothels.

At the international level, the most important dynamic was the emergence of universal racialized sexual hierarchies: race, ethnicity, and nationality combined to determine women's market value, while also determining men's access to sexual and domestic services. Where racial or colonial domination is exercised, there is a marked "tendency of [the] female body to become symbolic of . . . groups' privilege, something off limits to natives, by way of controlling indigenous groups and intra-foreign gender relations" (Callaway, 1987: 237). Multinational sex markets thus tended to be "highly stratified," with status determined by a "combination of race, ethnicity, education, sociability and sexual skill" (Murphy, 1992: 287). Numerous commentators have discerned in the eighteenth and nineteenth centuries an "exoticist movement" wherein Third World peoples became "the anthropological Other," not only "despised [and] destroyed" but also constituted as a "projection of western fantasies" (Kempadoo, 1998a:10).

The most visible manifestation of this pervasive racialization of sexual hierarchies was the push to supply transported, indentured labor with the sexual services of women of their own race or ethnicity. The cultural preferences of indentured workers dovetailed with the drive among employers and "host" societies to keep white women off limits to non-Western males (Hunt, 1986: 124). The movement of Chinese "coolie" labor to North and South America, the growth of Chinatowns in the United States, and the proliferation of boomtown vice on the American frontier thus brought Chinese prostitutes to the region as early as the 1840s. Chinese women were brought to Latin America, Southeast Asia, South Africa, and Australia—again, to subsidize and reproduce male indentured Asian labor. Japanese women followed in the 1870s, after the Meiji Restoration overthrew Tokugawa feudalism and emigration was decriminalized. Sex workers from Japan could be found in the hundreds in America's Pacific Northwest, Australia, coastal China, and Southeast Asia.[1]

Although initially Chinese and Japanese women tended to venture out on their own initiative, the element of organized coercive procurement increased over time (Ichioka, 1977; Mihalopoulos, 1993; Hirata, 1992). For Chinese women in the American West, there was a brief period (1849–54) of individual agency, entrepreneurship, and consent, and the clientele was primarily non-Chinese (Hirata, 1992). However, by 1854, secret societies or triads had gained full control of the trade, as only they could pay the high cost of the journey, bribe local police, negotiate with Chinatown landlords, and protect the women from pervasive anti-Asian violence (Tong, 1994:10). Procurers, brokers, and secret societies constituted an identifiable network linking the Americas to South China and inland; by 1850, there were well over fifteen hundred Chinese prostitutes in San Francisco's Chinatown alone (Hirata, 1992). Continuing economic distress, political chaos, and social violence in South China ensured rising numbers of recruits not only for prostitution rackets but for the trade in male indentured labor as well. Then, as now, Asian women signed contracts providing for eventual release but were virtually entrapped through trickery and debt bondage; those at the lowest end of the spectrum were worked in sweatshops during the day and brothels at night (Tong, 1994: 73–75).

On the more privileged end of racialized sexual hierarchies, the establishment of white commercial and military garrisons in the colonial world, the opening of various frontier boomtowns, and the commercialization of urban prostitution evident across the globe led also to the migration of sex workers from Western societies. Donna Guy's study of modern Argentina notes that European prostitutes first arrived there in 1797, when a penal ship en route to Australia ended up in the Rio de la Plata after a mutiny; by the 1860s, there was a well-established, easily supplied market for central and Eastern European women, largely under the control of procurers and pimps of their own nationalities (Guy, 1991a: 14–20). Edward Bristow's (1983) authoritative investigation of the trade in Jewish women points to economic distress and the launching of anti-Semitic pogroms in Russia and Eastern Europe after 1860 as the primary "push" factor in the equation. Some went the short distance to western Russia, hoping to earn dowries or help families through difficult economic times (Engel, 1989; Bernstein, 1995). Others traveled greater distances, as suggested by complaints of Singapore newspapers in 1862 about threats to white prestige from "the unwholesome immigration" of immoral women from Eastern Europe (*Straits Times,* May 17, 1862, 1).

Women from Western Europe and North America (the United States and Canada) typically already professional sex workers, traveled to these expanding areas and colonial markets. Chinese sources assert that the earliest European prostitutes arrived with the thousands of British troops sent to fight in the first Opium War (1841–42); however, these women were most likely from Portuguese-controlled Macao in South China (Sun, 1988: 47–48; Porter, 1996). In the 1860s and 1870s, American, British, and French women did undoubtedly join this specialized international migration, following the opening of the Suez Canal (1869), the mid-nineteenth-century establishment of British coaling stations and military garrisons in Asia, and the concurrent inauguration of regular steamship service from Europe and the United States to Asia (Bristow, 1983).

In contrast to both Slavic and indigenous sex workers, American and Western European women generally enjoyed an elite status within the hierarchy of colonial prostitution. In the nineteenth century, these "Occidental" women enjoyed a good living, privileged status (as foreigners exempt from indigenous laws, for example), and substantial control over their working conditions. American women overtly engaged in prostitution in East Asia from the 1860s to about 1900 were typically white, literate, aged between twenty-seven and thirty-five, married at some time, and prostitutes before they arrived. On the run from the law, or pushed out of the U.S. market by younger compatriots and incoming Asian and European women, these older sex workers went out to the colonies to capitalize on the sellers' market within white settler communities. Successfully limiting their clientele to men of their own race, they remained a small but enduring elite in the echelons of migratory prostitution (Scully, 1998). Non-Western courtesan-class women constituted a parallel elite in the nineteenth-century colonial setting, largely off limits to all but wealthy indigenous males (Hershatter, 1989).

White commercial and military colonial establishments and the gathering of unattached males at massive extractive and construction projects not only attracted long-distance migratory prostitution but also expanded and intensified local and regional indigenous prostitution. There is continuing debate around the degree of agency, initiative, and consent involved in the activities of indigenous women in frontier and colonial settings (Butler, 1985; Berger,

1988). This debate over the past is central to ongoing discussions about the post–Cold War traffic in sex workers; Third World activists and scholars reject as cultural imperialism a First World discourse on the phenomenon that depicts non-Western women, past and present, as "ignorant, poor, uneducated, tradition bound, domestic, family-oriented, [and] victimized" (Kempadoo, 1998a:11; Doezema, 1998: 37; Murray, 1998: 59). These commentators promulgate "subaltern understandings and lived realities of sexuality and sexual-economic relations . . . where one can speak of a continuum of sexual relations from monogamy to multiple sexual partners and where sex may be considered as a valuable asset for a woman to trade with" (Kempadoo, 1998a: 12).

It is true that in various historical settings, "sexual bartering, explicit and implicit," has provided "the coin with which women, in so far as they could, converted . . . dependency into a reciprocal relations" (Stansell, 1986: 179). In early modern Southeast Asia, for example, sexual liaison with foreign males was not necessarily a bitter fate. The "temporary wife" of a foreign trader might well have been a woman of high birth, acting as the de facto partner of her husband in local business (Andaya, 1998). Luise White's (1986) well-known work on prostitution in colonial Nairobi makes clear, as well, the complexity, range of activities, and entrepreneurialism termed "prostitution" by contemporaries.

However, over time the ever widening economic inequalities between core and peripheral regions after the 1880s ensured significant wage differentials, making the services of Third World women relatively inexpensive for most First World men across the globe. As noted earlier, an initial phase of agency and initiative among migratory Chinese and Japanese sex workers was quickly overtaken by more coercive, exploitative arrangements (Tong, 1994: 161–63). In the American West, the vast majority of sex workers were impoverished women of color—Asian, African American, Native American, and Latina (Butler, 1985; Hurtado, 1999: 86–88). Western Australia's mining frontier and pearling settlements witnessed similar dynamics, as aboriginal women found themselves driven into the lowest echelons of commercial sex (Hunt, 1986: 137).

In colonial entrepôts, there was a similar long-term degradation of sex work for indigenous women; by the 1890s, sexual service to foreigners had been commoditized and stigmatized, the fate of lowborn and marginal women (Andaya, 1998). Hong Kong provides a good example of the dynamics. Three years after cession to the British, there were an estimated thirty-two brothels in the

"Fragrant Harbor" ("Census of Registration Office," 1845). Procurement was facilitated by the expansion and distortion of customary practices, such as the adoption of female servants (mui-tsai); vested interests—both foreign and indigenous—then tended to defend such customs as essential to social functioning and properly off limits to colonial policing. In 1857, Hong Kong (a crown colony under the Colonial Office) instituted a system for registration and inspection of brothels, compulsory medical examination of inmates, punishment of prostitutes who infected clients, and detention in a Lock Hospital until cured (Miners, 1987: 191). Epidemic levels of venereal disease among British sailors and soldiers led to the implementation in 1867 of amended Contagious Diseases Ordinances. The CDO regime comprised controlled brothels divided racially by clientele, compulsory medical examination for inmates, and expansive police powers.

By 1883, Hong Kong had 1,274 registered female prostitutes; 1,000 of them were Chinese inmates in 78 brothels closed to foreigners ("native brothels"), 220 were Chinese and Japanese women in 39 brothels opened to foreigners and Chinese men ("foreign brothels"), and 54 were foreign women, including American, Australian, and Portuguese (from Macao), described as "voluntary submission women" because they registered voluntarily but lived alone or in small clusters, rather than in brothels, and were unofficially exempted from examination. The number of unregistered prostitutes and "sly" brothels was unknown but thought high (Scully, 1998).

Contemporaries themselves conceded that the ultimate goal of regulated prostitution was to provide "clean native women" for foreign military personnel ("Contagious Diseases Ordinances," 1883). The CDOs, operative from 1857 to 1889, were effectively limited to Asian women servicing foreigners. Hong Kong authorities observed: "It is the foreign houses used by soldiers, sailors and foreign riff-raff where disease and cruelty flourish, and only the most degraded women will enter them except under compulsion" (*Parliamentary Papers*, 26:46).

By the mid-1890s, networks of varying sophistication and durability were evident throughout Asia, the Middle East, the Americas, and Europe. Well-traveled routes included Poland and European Russia to London, Buenos Aires, Rio de Janeiro, North Africa, Saudi Arabia, Turkey, and Syria; France to North and South Africa, South America, the Low Countries, British India; colonial enclaves in East and Southeast Asia; Greece to the Levant; Hungary to Romania; Poland and Austria to Turkey; China and Japan to the United States, Latin

America (especially Argentina and Brazil), Australia, Singapore, Malaya, India, and Hong Kong (Bristow, 1983: 35).

Contemporaries in this initial phase of modern migratory prostitution understood and discussed the problem within several coexisting paradigms: colonial management, immigration politics, social hygiene, and urban angst. Then, as now, public discourse on prostitution became entangled with issues of class, gender, race, and nationality. Across the world, from New York to Moscow, discussions of urban commercial sex served as "the symbol of what was perceived as the social and moral disintegration of society" (Hill, 1992: 17). Regulation and policing tended to pit authorities against one another, as health professionals battled law enforcers and self-appointed vigilantes took on allegedly feeble and corrupt police forces (Guy, 1991a: 35–39; Gilfoyle, 1986: 640). The critique of prostitution emerged as part of a larger assault on urbanization (Lees, 1979: 70). Prostitution became "a metaphor for upper- and middle-class fears about the lower class and the future of the . . . nation" (Guy, 1991a: 44; Gilfoyle, 1986: 645). Typically, regulation of sexual commerce embodied "elite concerns to define the effective boundaries of nationality and citizenship, as well as to discipline working-class women" (Guy, 1991a: 44).

The all-important link between nationality and sexuality in the discourse on migratory prostitution was forged in this early period. In part, this owed to the importance of nationality as a criterion in the state and colonial regulation of prostitution at home and abroad (Guy, 1991a: 14). However, it also arose from the bonding of "respectability" and nationalism in the modern era (Mosse, 1985: 9). "Woman as a national symbol was the guardian of the continuity and immutability of the nation, the embodiment of its respectability" (Mosse, 1985: 18). Although nonindigenous prostitutes had been long entrenched in places such as Shanghai and Buenos Aires by the 1880s, their presence and activities made them lightning rods in debates over nation building and citizenship (Guy, 1991a: 14–16; Scully, 1995, 1998). Prostitutes—homegrown and otherwise—became "the pretexts for defining one nation's sovereignty against another's" and "a focus and symbol in ideological discourse used in the construction, reproduction, and transformation of ethnic/national categories" (Guy, 1991b: 201–2). In colonial and less developed areas, debates about prostitution were infused with ambivalence toward modernity, "Westernization," and Euro-American dominance of the international system (Bernstein, 1995: 8; Hershatter, 1989).

Circa 1895 to World War I

The late 1890s brought the expansion and transformation of migratory, multi-national prostitution. At the same time, the tactics of reform groups and the complex anxieties of contemporaries sensationalized and distorted the phe-nomenon, generating much debate and hyperbole about a worldwide "white slave trade."

The perceptible expansion of migratory prostitution, particularly in colo-nial areas, owed to several factors. There was a sizeable influx of women into China, colonial Asia, and South Africa. Some came from Manchuria, fleeing the chaos of the Russo-Japanese War; others had been driven by urban reformers from the United States and Western Europe. New market demand was stimu-lated by the multinational suppression of the Boxer Rebellion in North China circa 1900, the Boer War, and the Spanish-American-Philippine War. Contem-porary British sources estimated that Shanghai alone had about two thousand non-Chinese prostitutes in the first years of the twentieth century, most of them Russian, Eastern European, and Japanese (Hyam, 1986: 68–69).

This post-1895 phase brought large-scale, organized prostitution, facilitated by improved and more affordable rail and water transportation lines. Itinerant women "attach[ed] themselves to the canteens and hotels," drawing upon those facilities and clienteles, giving politically powerful real estate agents, landlords, and entertainment purveyors a vested interest in the process (van Onselen, 1982: 107–9). The increase of women brought foreign prostitutes out to street-level solicitation and across racial boundaries, making them more visible and more controversial; the increased competition among women led to more elaborate advertising, moving beyond personal introductions and let-ters passed to hotel guests to spectacular promenades and public placards. Policing and regulatory responses exacerbated the situation, as migratory pros-titutes under siege became more reliant on pimps and more vulnerable to cor-rupt officials (Scully, 1998).

The question of migratory prostitution engaged the era's full spectrum of activists, academics, philanthropists, officials, professionals, and social tinker-ers. It was in the late 1890s that public discourse beheld domestic and mi-gratory prostitution as an integrated, international problem to be dealt with multilaterally. In 1898–99, various antiregulationist groups formed the London National Vigilance Association (NVA), which became the nucleus of a broad coalition against the white slave trade (WST); this group asserted the existence of "a highly organized traffic" decoying English women to the Continent.

In fact, this was a rhetorical internationalization of a decades-old regional traffic in English girls to Belgium and France ("Correspondence Respecting Immoral Traffic," 1881). In the 1880s, this intra-European traffic had given limited currency to the term *white slavery* (Bristow, 1983: 35, 36; Nadelmann, 1990: 514).[2] NVA leaders toured the Continent in the 1890s, forming national committees in Germany, Holland, Denmark, Sweden, Russia, Belgium, France, Switzerland, and Austria (League of Nations, 1921: 13). By 1899, the NVA had gathered sufficient momentum for an international conference in London. It was here that the campaign against the WST burst into public discourse, as conferees learned of a European-wide network of procurers and brothels and established an international bureau to coordinate among national committees and disseminate propaganda. By 1904, they had orchestrated an international convention among European states, recognizing white slavery as a juridical concept in international law but limiting signatories to vague pledges to adjust domestic law to punish procurers who had used force or fraud to procure women (Grittner, 1990; Bristow, 1983).

The consensus among historians is that the NVA's internationalist thrust was an adaptation of the tactics and rhetoric of the battle against black slavery from decades back (Bristow, 1983: 37; Walkowitz, 1982: 89). So too was it a reasonable response to the ongoing campaign among public health officials to legalize prostitution worldwide as an anti–venereal disease measure (Nadelmann, 1990: 486, 514–15). This latter dimension was a constant source of tension between abolitionists and regulationists within the antitraffic coalition. Famed abolitionist Josephine Butler criticized the 1899 conference for admitting avowed regulationists. Likewise, Lady Henry Somerset was forced to step down in 1897 as president of the British Women's Temperance Association for remarks to the *Times* endorsing regulated brothels in colonial India.

Any hint of tolerance ran counter to the campaign by temperance and reform groups in London, whose combined force had led to the abolition of the CDOs in Hong Kong and the Straits Settlements and the inauguration of colonial cleanup campaigns in the 1890s. Colonial officials and police resisted the abolitionist push as regards indigenous women, however, arguing that it would generate geometric increases in clandestine prostitution and unmanageable infection rates. The end of the CDOs did not mean the end of tacit regulation, and imperial managers were permitted this de facto policy until the interwar era.

Domestic constituencies back home increasingly required colonial authorities "to make empire respectable," through programs of "native uplift" and a tighter supervision over colonial sojourners themselves, particularly those straddling and blurring racial and cultural boundaries (Stoler, 1989; Levine, 1986; Scully, 1998). An influx of "wage-earning white women in African and Asian colonies" further complicated colonial demarcations, "especially where their work was not within the confines of family—and official attempts to restrict the movements and often the choice of employment of such women were common" (Levine, 1998: 109; Davidson, 1984: 176–79).

In the United States, the judicial expansion of the interstate commerce clause in the 1890s brought trafficking in women under federal jurisdiction (Grittner, 1990: 48–50). American delegates did attend the 1899 London conference but opted not to bring home with them the "white slave trade" phenomenon (40). The United States acceded to the 1904 international convention, but not until 1908. Until 1909–10, migratory prostitution as an issue was manifest in the overlapping domains of nativism, municipal reform, and—to a lesser extent—concern about what the *Stars and Stripes* abetted in the new insular possessions and American communities overseas (Scully, 1995).

In 1906, the American Purity Alliance became the American National Vigilance Committee, later (1913) merging with the American Federation for Sexual Hygiene, to become the American Social Hygiene Association (Grittner, 1990: 51, 61, 14–15). This core group, renamed several times, became the primary U.S. representative at international gatherings and the vehicle of American participation in later League of Nations investigations of trafficking in persons. Notwithstanding sensationalist exposés by such pressure groups, concerns about constitutionality and federal-state divisions kept the United States from signing the 1910 international convention. However, the 1910 Mann Act served the purpose to a certain extent. Aimed at redressing constitutional barriers, the act made it a felony to transport knowingly any woman or girl across state lines or abroad for the purpose of prostitution or debauchery or for other immoral purpose (Grittner, 1990: 86–90). The unintended impact of the legislation was to enhance the power of pimps and procurers over sex workers (Beckman, 1984).

By 1910, the image of the white slave trade conjured up by London purity groups had taken full hold of the American imagination. Lurid stories of sullied white womanhood and organized syndicates linking major cities helped bring on board southerners who otherwise would have argued states' rights in the face of a broad expansion of federal police powers (Grittner, 1990: 90–97). The vision of a vast network of Jewish and French procurers kidnapping and luring white women from Europe and America to service lowly natives and "eastern rich potentates" was captivating, combining as it did racial anxieties, colonial debates, immigration politics, and public morality issues (Feldman, 1967). Similar sensationalism and bourgeois prurience was evident elsewhere, from London to Moscow to Buenos Aires (Grittner, 1990; Bernstein, 1995; Guy, 1991a, 1991b).

Although this image of kidnapped, debauched white women unified disparate groups, in the long run it was counterproductive. Those who might have been able to shut down the traffic as completely as had been the African slave trade were white, metropolitan populations easily outraged by tales of their young pure women brought to the outposts of barely veiled barbarity. However, 99 percent of traffic victims were in fact women of color—broadly defined by contemporaries to include Jews—distributed throughout the world but concentrated in colonial areas.

For Americans—as for Westerners more generally—foreign prostitutes at home were an immigration problem, not an object of sympathy; in the colonial context, they were a class to be despised but tolerated as necessary for sexual stability and military readiness. Metropolitan opinion over the white slave trade did force some changes in imperial management, but only as regards the small cadre among migratory prostitutes known as Occidentals.

Interwar Period and the League

On the eve of war, the agenda agreed upon by the broad coalition of antitraffic groups, enunciated at the 1913 Madrid conference, included (a) efforts by various national committees to push for abolition of licensed brothels universally; (b) initiatives to develop an information bank based on declarations from victims; (c) assisted repatriation and rehabilitation of victims; (d) provision of adequate protection for women emigrants en route; (e) campaign for uniform legislation allowing supervision of employment agencies offering jobs abroad; (f) a push to exclude the question of consent with regard to traffic in minors; (g) full suppression of colonial prostitution; (h) more attention to punishment of procurers and third parties (League of Nations, 1921: 15–16).

When reestablishing ranks in 1919, reformist groups perceived that World War I had "closed, in general, all frontiers, and rendered the traffic in women very difficult. . . . On the other hand, it let loose upon the world violent passions, immorality and even worse disorders" (League of Nations, 1921: 8). In the British colonies—such as Singapore and Hong Kong—European prostitutes had been deported as a wartime measure ("Prostitution in Singapore," 1933). More generally, European emigration decreased noticeably. However, regional and indigenous prostitution had multiplied in response to the continued presence of large military garrisons. Although some earlier lucrative routes were now less traveled, the postwar reopening of commerce and frontiers provided fertile ground for a dramatic increase in the volume and intensity of the traffic in women and children (League of Nations, 1921: 17).

In 1920, the newly established League of Nations took primary responsibility for combating the forced traffic in persons. The racially exclusive and misleading term *white slavery* was abandoned, having come under attack as early as the Brussels and Madrid conferences in 1912 and 1913, respectively (League of Nations, 1921: 55). An officer within the Secretariat was exclusively charged with information gathering and coordination. The assembly assigned to the Secretariat the task of issuing a questionnaire not simply to league members but to signatories of the 1904 and the 1910 conventions, asking what domestic measures had been undertaken to implement these international agreements. In addition, plans were put in motion for the 1921 international conference on the trafficking, to be held in Geneva.

Optimism and expansiveness characterized early league proclamations on the subject. Speakers declared that the "feebleness" of earlier arrangements was "to-day visible to every eye" (League of Nations, 1921: 10). Delegates envisioned a comprehensive, multilateral attack on public and private fronts, to "vanquish this powerful evil" (League of Nations, 1921: 11). However, self-reporting by signatories, annual conferences, and traveling commissions of inquiry constituted, in the main, the league's entire arsenal in this regard. As in diplomatic matters more generally, the league was organically unequipped to force compliance; territorial sovereignty and imperial governance came before collective security.

The dimensions and geography of the interwar traffic can be conveyed by looking at four groups: Occidental, Chinese, Japanese, and Russian. Although the first of these groups was the smallest, it remained the only effective point of access into the conscience and consciousness of Western metropoles. Deported during World War I, Western women returned in the 1920s though in much fewer numbers (League of Nations, 1934). The election of a Labour government in London in 1929 strengthened the hand of domestic reform groups; a planned League of Nations commission visit to Asia and the Middle East turned up the pressure on colonial prostitution (Miners, 1987; "Prostitution in Hong Kong," 1931). Hong Kong officials were warned: "All we can do is to play for time, having at the back of our minds the intention to meet the storm when it breaks," and they took the path of least resistance by targeting Western, rather than indigenous, prostitutes ("Social Hygiene," 1930). In the early 1930s, Hong Kong, Singapore, the Federated Malay States, Ceylon, Malaya, and Palestine closed brothels with European, Australian, and American women; the status quo continued in Syria, Iraq, Persia/Iran, parts of British India, Indo-China, Siam/Thailand, China, Manchuria, Korea, Japan, and Macao (IBSTP, 1934).

The treaty ports of mainland China—Shanghai in particular—were forced to undertake official, if unenergetic, antivice programs in the mid-1920s. However, the byzantine foreign legal system known as extraterritoriality hindered prosecution of either victims or traffickers ("Social Disease, Prostitution," 1935). By the 1930s, even as the number of Occidental women dwindled to double and single digits, a more racially charged version of the white slave trade panic decades earlier took hold back home. Exposés described a huge chain of men passing the women from hand to hand from origin to destinations, warning that *"the prostitution of White women in Asia,* is the cheapening of our White race, in the eyes of the Coloured races, through the medium of the most sacred things it possesses" (Champly, 1930: 278).

The league inquiry commission in the mid-1930s, funded privately by the American Bureau of Social Hygiene, found "an international traffic in women and girls of the Near, Middle and Far East. . . . The bulk of this traffic was in Asiatic women from one country in Asia to another." There were an estimated 17,000 women and girls of many nationalities registered as prostitutes—an equal number of clandestine sex workers—throughout the major cities visited. Only 174 of them were Occidental. Chinese, Japanese (including Korean and Formosan), Eurasians, and Asiatic Russians (east of the Urals) were the most numerous. Smaller groups included Malay, Annamite, Siamese, Filipino, Indian, Iraqi, Persian, and Syrian (League of Nations, 1934).

The Chinese women had been, the league found, recruited from the poorest classes and shipped throughout Asia and the Middle East. There were an estimated 6,000 in British Malaya alone (League of Nations, 1934). Procurers were generally middle-aged or elderly Chinese women, themselves prostitutes, former prostitutes, brothel servants, or brothel managers; traffickers were of the same ilk but posed as maidservants or traveling vendors. Male traffickers were typically "runners" in cahoots with lodging houses, passage brokers, or shipboard employees. The demand was, as it had long been, the large overseas settlements of men. In Shanghai alone, about 100,000 prostitutes operated in the 1930s, in a setting that saw the transformation of what was "essentially a luxury market in courtesans" to one "primarily geared to supplying sexual services for the growing numbers of unattached . . . commercial and working-class men of the city" (Hershatter, 1997: 53, 203).

In the 1920s, Japan's policy was to repatriate its national migratory prostitutes in Singapore, Malaya, India, Hong Kong, and Thailand ("Prostitution in Singapore," 1933). However, in expanding to Manchukuo and thence to China proper, Japan extended its own domestic system of prostitution, staffed by Korean, Formosan, and Japanese women (League of Nations, 1934: 10–13; Lie, 1995: 110–15). Everywhere outside China and Manchuria, Japanese females could not travel without the consent of parents or husbands, and women of the "immoral classes" were barred entirely. The nodal points of regimental prostitution in China were Shanghai, Tientsin, Mukden, Vladivostok, and Harbin.

White Russian women, with few exceptions, were under the control and management of traffickers. Tens of thousands of Russians fled into Manchuria and China after the Bolshevik Revolution; many of the women among them were pawned as prostitutes to local Chinese or went into China and Southeast Asia. Their stateless status and utter destitution pushed them to capitalize on their sexuality, with varying degrees of degradation. White Russian prostitutes comprised the full range of sex labor, from brothel to hostess to mistress (League of Nations, 1934).

As for the United States, by the advent of war in Europe Immigration and Justice Department enforcers of the Mann Act had been made cautionary by constitutional challenges and fiscal constraints (INS, 1914). The U.S. draft act of 1917 included "campfollower" provisions prohibiting prostitution within a prescribed area around military and naval installations (Grittner, 1990: 63). Some Immigration agents saw the wartime hiatus in incoming European prostitutes as an opportunity to "get a better grip on and rid the country of Asiatic aliens" (INS, 1914). However, in general from 1914 until well into the interwar period, Americans came to see the white slave trade as a foreign problem, if not simply the delusion of zealots. With the establishment of the League of

Nations, the United States became a passive presence in the campaign against forced migratory labor beyond American borders.

Casualties of scholarly deconstructionism, interwar foes of trafficking in prostitution are too often dismissed as paternalistic, elitist, racist, misogynist do-gooders more interested in social control than genuine structural transformation. Though representatives of the type are readily found, such a blanket dismissal is unwarranted and counterproductive to current antitrafficking efforts. Then, as now, remedial efforts were undermined by conflicting imperatives, vested interests, the absence of options for victims, and the entrepreneurial opportunism of traffickers.

The modern mind sees in every social problem the medical conundrum: extirpate the roots of a disease or address only the symptoms? In this regard, there are more similarities than differences between then and now. Sociologically minded humanitarians fought for long-term solutions and attention to cognate problems, such as the legal status of women, employment opportunities, punishment of clients and procurers, abolition of licensed prostitution, and so on. Pragmatists and enforcement agencies looked to the symptoms, through heightened scrutiny of travelers, stricter immigration restrictions, and beefed-up policing resources. The disparate worldviews are succinctly summed up in a confrontation between French and Dutch delegates at the 1921 Geneva conference. To the former's suggestion that the league limit its attention to the traffic rather than to prostitution more generally, M. DeGraff impatiently declared: "It is as though you said: we have a cholera Congress but you must not speak of bacilli" (League of Nations, 1921: 69).

Overlapping but distinguishable from this roots-versus-symptoms divide was the clash in the British colonies between universalism and racially infused, paternalistic exceptionalism. Ironically, the cultural relativism now propounded by Third World activists was in this earlier setting a defense of the status quo put forward by colonial offices and indigenous misogynists. When, for example, antitraffic groups pushed for twenty-one as a universal age of consent by way of undercutting those Asian religious and social customs most easily abused by procurers, both British and French delegates obtained a clause by which "in Eastern countries where, owing to climatic conditions and social and religious customs, the above standard of age cannot be applied, the definition of a minor for the purpose of the above provisions . . . shall be fixed by the National Legislatures of those countries" (League of Nations, 1921: 61).

Anticipating the arrival of the league commission of inquiry touring Asia in the early 1930s, the Colonial Office took refuge in the argument that the league's purview was international, not internal.

Finally, remedial efforts ran up against a tension still with us today, that is, between protection and patriarchy. In combating the traffic, delegates suggested a range of measures that clearly crossed the line: special passport requirements for females; bans on women traveling alone; registration with local police when working abroad; forced repatriation and retraining of prostitutes; and the like. Various national governments in Asia and the Middle East enacted legislation, in the name of the international conventions, that banned marriages to foreigners and prohibited female emigration.

Women's groups throughout Europe effectively blocked a league proposal to repatriate women forcibly, saying: "Long experience in the past has shown them that protection sometimes comes to be a hidden form of slavery, a masked tyranny inspired by the best of intention" (League of Nations, 1921: 80). Abolitionists and women's rights groups opposed targeting victims rather than victimizers; jurists noted that as most countries still tolerated prostitution, extradition was not practical or likely; repatriated women tended to return to foreign brothels, thus making the proposition a costly one for governments or private organizations; feminist organizations warned that coercion and restrictions on suspected women would bring abuse and restriction on women in general ("Repatriation of Prostitutes," 1930). The compromise solution was compulsory repatriation of underage prostitutes (IBSTP, 1931).

Pre–World War II efforts to combat the traffic in women and children for prostitution "accomplished, in the final analysis, relatively little toward its objectives" (Nadelmann, 1990: 515). Indigenous women, particularly Eurasians, supplanted migratory sex workers, and a general decrease in trafficking came about as a result of changing "social, economic and demographic conditions" (516). As Ethan Nadelmann has shown persuasively, the WST never inspired a "global prohibition regime" of the sort that spearheaded the eradication of the African slave trade: such a regime turns upon the shift from a common perception of a given activity as legitimate under certain conditions and with respect to certain persons to redefinition of the activity as evil; the delegitimation of government involvement in the activity and the shift to official abolitionist activism; and the erection of effective criminal laws and conventions. This failure owed to a fundamental lack of consensus—still evident today—as to the meaning and morality of prostitution, the ease of concealment, the adaptability of entrepreneurs to changing policing strategies, and the durability of demand (Nadelmann, 1990: 486).

World War II and After

Wartime deployment of troops throughout the colonial world undercut international efforts to control prostitution. Reports in the early 1940s described Singapore as a clearinghouse for traffickers, serving Burma (Myanmar), Ceylon (Sri Lanka), India, Indonesia, Japan, Philippines, and Thailand (IBSTP, 1949). Estimates ranged from 8,000 to 20,000 sex workers in Thailand alone circa 1940, half of whom were concentrated in the metropolitan areas of Bangkok and Dhonburi. Urban and regional markets were supplied from the countryside: "Prostitution is reported to be a big business, operated on a syndicate basis, with supply lines running in and out of Bangkok to most towns and cities in the country" (IBSTP, 1949: 47; League of Nations, 1940/41: 74).

Postwar traffic was nearly all local and regional, with demand generated mostly by standing troops (United Nations, 1948). The new United Nations assumed supervision over international conventions and took on the reporting function earlier performed by league officials. Figures given for the period 1948–50 show this same local and regional concentration: migratory women moved short distances, for example, back and forth from Syria and Lebanon to Palestine/Israel; between Vietnam and Cambodia; Costa Rica and Panama; Somaliland and Aden; France and Poland; between and among Bulgaria, Turkey, Iran, Germany, Greece, Yugoslavia; and the United States, Canada, and Mexico (United Nations, 1952; "International Review of Criminal Policy," 1950).

The primary United Nations response to continued trafficking in sex workers was the 1949 "Convention for the Suppression of the Traffic in Persons and of the Exploitation of the Prostitution of Others." As before, nation-states bore primary responsibility for reporting their own compliance, passing remedial legislation, and dealing with both traffickers and victims (Farrior, 1997: 219–20). Nonbinding provisions and self-reporting allow countries to "gain the moral highground by loudly proclaiming that they have signed a document condemning the buying and selling of women's bodies, when in reality prostitution continues unchecked in their own countries" (Toepfer and Wells, 1994: 92).

Up through the 1970s, the determining factor in multinational prostitution markets in Asia was the large-scale, semipermanent stationing of troops and regularized movement of naval personnel through the region. Since World War II, it has been the U.S. military that has supplied the chief demand for commercial vice in East and Southeast Asia (Tadiar, 1993; Enloe, 1983; Moon, 1997). In the words of one author, "the U.S. presence in the Pacific is . . . a transnational garrison state that spans five sovereign states and the vast expanse of Micronesia" (Bello, 1992: 14). This "transnational garrison state has spawned a subeconomy and subculture that has had distorting effects on the larger economy and culture of the host societies," generating excessive demand for sexual labor and eroticized entertainment (15).

In the 1980s, observers and activists began to detect dramatic qualitative and quantitative changes in sexual trafficking. A decrease in the U.S. military presence in Asia, combined with global economic trends, led countries most dramatically affected to turn to "sex tourism" as a viable, if inhumane, income generator. This sector continued to expand into the 1990s, fueled by the "global restructuring of capitalist production and investment" (Kempadoo, 1998a: 15). Efforts to keep down labor costs and remain competitive had intensified rural displacement and urban unemployment; at the same time, the spread of consumer culture created widespread demand among Third World populations for goods, such as televisions and cars (Kempadoo, 1998a: 16; MacKenzie, 1998). An increased demand for children among customers fearful of AIDS is thus more than met by children themselves seeking disposable income or parents who "deploy the income-generating capacity of their children in order to ensure that the household survives" (Kempadoo, 1998a: 7; Quiambao, 1998).

Free market reforms in Eastern Europe, Russia, Cuba, Vietnam, and the People's Republic of China (PRC) contributed to a resurgence of prostitution in those areas (Litherland, 1995; Pringle, 1998; Langfitt, 1998). "It's like the Klondike during the Gold Rush," one Albanian journalist said recently of war-torn Kosovo (Viviano, 1999: A1). The pre–World War II pattern of women from underdeveloped areas going into wealthier markets continues but is more than matched by movement in the other direction, or from one Third World area to another (Kempadoo, 1998a: 15; Charoenpo, 1998; *Bangkok Post,* July 22, 1998). Long-distance trafficking becomes less necessary with the emergence of areas specializing in sex tourism (Friedman, 1996). Traffickers typically have a diverse portfolio, often involved in narcotics, credit card fraud, money laundering, and so on (MacLeod, 1998).

As in the pre–Cold War era, remedial efforts tend to exacerbate the problem and worsen the conditions under which sex workers operate (Murray, 1998). Stricter immigration controls raise the cost of doing business, allowing organized crime to drive out less organized competitors; increased costs and potentially higher profits push traffickers—and immigrant smugglers more generally—to seek greater control over sex workers, through locked brothels, threats to family members back home, violence, and so on (*Salt Lake Tribune,* June 17, 1994). Continued state reliance on deportation does nothing to diminish the traffic and instead makes women less likely to report their situation and more dependent upon traffickers and pimps.

Most significant, there is even less consensus among antitrafficking groups than before World War II. The prewar divide between regulationists and abolitionists has been complicated by a schism as to whether prostitution may be a legitimate form of labor and prostitutes rational choosers (Doezema, 1998: 37). Various national prostitutes' rights groups have championed this latter interpretation and have found support among Third World academics and activists (Murray, 1998). They reject the nongovernmental organizations' (NGO) and Western media's view of "trafficking . . . as a global conspiracy which can be dismantled through international co-operation and the paternalistic rehabilitation of victims" (Murray, 1998: 62). Although redefining prostitution as work, and migratory prostitutes as workers, may open up new avenues of reform, this ever widening definitional divide portends a repetition of pre–World War II failures.

CHRONOLOGY OF THE CAMPAIGN AGAINST THE WHITE SLAVE TRADE AND THE TRAFFIC IN PERSONS, UP TO 1980

1885   Jewish Association for the Protection of Girls and Women founded in London.
1895   Penitentiary Congress of Paris—search for international agreement and national legislation to deal with conditions known to encourage prostitution.
1899   London Congress—convened by a private group, National Vigilance Association (NVA); reveals to the world the existence of an organization covering all of Europe that had taken the place of isolated procuring, which up to then alone had been dealt with by repressive laws; reveals that underage women had been duped into debauchery abroad. Agreed on need for an international agreement and changes in national laws. Establishment of International Bureau and national committees.
1902   Paris Conference 1902—first diplomatic conference; arranged by French government. Leads to signing of an agreement March 18, 1904.
1904   International Agreement for the Suppression of the White Slave Traffic, March

18, 1904—signatories agree to establish national central authority to collect and share information; bind themselves to general administrative measures regarding vigilance at ports and depots, notification about suspected persons, taking declarations from alien prostitutes to get broad range of information, to protect and maintain victims before repatriation, and to supervise registry offices and employment agencies. Signatories: Brazil, Denmark, India, Italy, Norway, Sweden, Switzerland. In 1908 the United States signs on.

1910   Paris Conference 1910.

1910   International Convention for the Suppression of White Slave Traffic—Austria, Belgium, Bulgaria, Canada, France, Germany, United Kingdom, Hungary, Netherlands, Poland, Portugal, South Africa, Spain, Uruguay. Not ratified by: Belgium, Brazil, Denmark, Italy, Portugal, Sweden. The United States does not accede, arguing constitutional problems. Signatories agree to work for the enactment of national legislation to criminalize and punish procurement of girls and women, either minors or of full age, notwithstanding that the various acts constituting the offense may have been committed in different countries.

1910   Madrid Congress—400 delegates, produces book of relevant laws and ordinances.

1912   Brussels Congress 1912—reveals new facts about children, so "Traffic in Children" added. "White slavery" challenged as racially exclusive.

1913   London Conference 1913—31 official delegates representing 24 countries and between 400 and 500 delegates from national committees. Resolutions concerning need for international legislation prohibiting the employment in theaters, circuses, concerts, and music halls of girls under 16 years of age; with special provision for the protection of girls under age who accept employment abroad to perform in those places of amusement; establishment in each country of an official commission, composed of members of both sexes, to ascertain the extent of the traffic in women and children and its causes.

1919   International Conference at Washington 1919. Respect for women and children the topic.

1919   League of Nations covenant stipulating league oversight of conventions against traffic in women and children.

1920   Conference of 7 Latin American states agreeing to push for cooperation in tracking dangerous individuals.

1921   League of Nations International Conference on Women and Children. Albania, Austria, Belgium, Brazil, Bulgaria, Canada, Chile, China, Czecho-Slovakia, Denmark, Estonia, France, Germany, Great Britain, Greece, Hungary, India, Italy, Japan, Lithuania, Monaco, Netherlands, Norway, Panama, Poland and Danzig, Portugal, Romania, Serb-Croat-Slovene State, Siam, South Africa, Spain, Sweden, Switzerland, Uruguay.

1921   Seventh International Conference for the Protection of Girls (at Neuchatel). This conference made recommendations to the League of Nations, including defining traffic in women as an offense sui generis; criminalizing attempts and preparatory acts; establishing standard age of consent at 21 or higher; punishing internal traffic in same way as international traffic; making punishment as severe as possible.

1921   Convention for the Suppression of Traffic in Women and Children. Seeks to suppress the traffic using three approaches: prosecuting persons who traffic in children, licensing and supervising employment agencies, and protecting immigrating and emigrating women and children.

1926   Slavery Convention. Effort to borrow rights and duties from conventions against arms trafficking. Signatories commit to prevent and suppress the slave trade and bring complete abolition.

1930   Forced Labor Convention. Defined "forced labor" as "all work or service which is exacted from any person under the menace of any penalty and for which the said person has not offered himself voluntarily."

1933   International Convention for the Suppression of the Traffic in Women of Full Age—requires punishment of persons who traffic in women of full age and declares that consent is no defense to the crime of trafficking. Includes colonies and protectorates.

1936   Advisory Committee on Social Questions fuses Traffic Committee with Committee for Protection of Children.

1937   League tries to increase the scope of coverage to full age, either sex, whether or not consent exists, and whether or not person was taken abroad. War interrupts passage of this convention.

1949   UN consolidates the four prior treaties, plus a 1937 League of Nations draft Convention for the Suppression of the Traffic in Persons and of the Exploitation of the Prostitution of Others. Weak enforcement clauses; limited measures. Focuses on punishing procurers, persons exploiting prostitution, and brothel owners.

1957   Abolition of Forced Labor Convention.

1966   International Covenant on Economic, Social and Cultural Rights.

1976   International Covenant on Civil and Political Rights (ICCPR) required signatories to protect citizens against being trafficked for prostitution, by promulgating information about civil rights, imposing penalties, and providing a forum for individual claims. It also established an oversight body, the Human Rights Committee, to monitor compliance.

1979   Convention on the Elimination of All Forms of Discrimination against Women (CEDAW)—includes measures regarding suppression of traffic in women.

Source: Extrapolated from Stephanie Farrior, "The International Law on Trafficking in Women and Children for Prostitution: Making It Live Up to Its Potential," *Harvard Human Rights Journal,* 1997: 10:213; Wanda Grabinska, "Introductory Notes on the Legislative Development of the International Convention for the Suppression of the Traffic in Persons (1899–1949)," International Bureau for the Suppression of Traffic in Persons (IBSTP) Papers, 1955, box 193/6, Fawcett Library, London.

NOTES

1. By the mid-1890s, Japanese officials (under)estimated the numbers of Japanese prostitutes in Southeast Asia as follows: Hong Kong, 100; Singapore, 300; Penang, 200;

Australia, 200; Tonkin, 80; Saigon, 160; British India, 200; Siam, 40. "Japanese Women Abroad," *Japan Weekly Mail,* May 30, 1896, 609.

2. The term *white slavery* was first used in the 1830s by London reformers in reference to East End Jewish pimps, as well as in discussions of the conditions of factory labor for girls. Commentators agree that the phrase was first used by Count de Gasparin at the time of the abolition of the African slave trade and was later repeated by the French writer Victor Hugo in his observation: "In Europe we have another Traffic, not the Black Slave trade, but the White Slave Traffic, which is even worse." By the 1870s, it referred to state-regulated vice and by 1880 had come to include the image of white women kidnapped or lured to foreign brothels (Bristow, 1983: 35, 36; Nadelmann, 1990: 514).

REFERENCES

Aldrich, Robert. 1990. *The French Presence in the South Pacific.* Basingstoke, Hampshire: Macmillan.

Andaya, Barbara Watson. 1998. "From Temporary Wife to Prostitute: Sexuality and Economic Change in Early Modern Southeast Asia." *Journal of Women's History* 9 (4): 11–34.

Assavanonda, Anjira. 1998. "Child Prostitution on the Rise." *Bangkok Post,* September 24.

Beckman, Marlene. 1984. "The White Slave Traffic Act: The Historical Impact of a Federal Crime Policy on Women." *Georgetown Law Journal* 72:1111–42.

Bello, Walden. 1992. "From American Lake to a People's Pacific." In *Let the Good Times Roll: Prostitution and the U.S. Military in Asia,* edited by Saundra Pollock Sturdevant and Brenda Stoltzfus, 14–21. New York: New Press.

Berger, Mark. 1988. "Imperialism and Sexual Exploitation: A Response to Ronald Hyam's 'Empire and Sexual Opportunity.'" *Journal of Imperial and Commonwealth History* 17(1): 83–89, with Hyam's response, 90–98.

Bernstein, Laurie. 1995. *Sonia's Daughters: Prostitutes and Their Regulation in Imperial Russia.* Berkeley: University of California.

Branigin, William. 1999. "A Different Kind of Trade War." *Washington Post,* March 20, A27.

Bristow, Edward. 1983. *Prostitution and Prejudice. The Jewish Fight against White Slavery, 1870–1939.* New York: Schocken Books.

"Brothel Madam Faces Execution." 1998. *South China Morning Post.* November 22, 5.

Burrell, Ian. 1998. "Britain Calls Child Sex Trade Summit." *Independent.* August 4, 7.

Butler, Anne. 1985. *Daughters of Joy, Sisters of Misery: Prostitutes in the American West, 1865–1890.* Urbana: University of Illinois.

Callaway, Helen. 1987. *Gender, Culture, and Empire: European Women in Colonial Nigeria.* Basingstoke, Hampshire: Macmillan.

Capella, Peter. 1998. "Swiss Put Russian 'Mafia Boss' on Trial." *Guardian,* December 1, 14.

"Census of Registration Office." 1845. Colonial Office [CO] 129/12.

Champly, Henry. 1930. *The Road to Shanghai: White Slave Traffic in Asia.* London: J. Long.

Charoenpo, Anucha. 1998. "Thai Girls Lured to Sex Trade in Africa." *Bangkok Post,* August 24.

Chuang, Janie. 1998. "Redirecting the Debate over Trafficking in Women: Definitions, Paradigms, and Contexts." *Harvard Human Rights Journal* 11:65–107.

"Colombia Frees Child Sex Slaves." 1998. *Sun-Sentinel,* September 27, 12A.

"Contagious Diseases Ordinances." 1883. Colonial Office [CO]-129/207, #29 [Microfilm Collection].

"Correspondence, Dispatches, Reports, Returns, Memorials, and Other Papers Respecting the Affairs of Hong Kong, 1862–1881." 1974. *Parliamentary Papers.* China, vol. 25. Shannon: Irish University Press.

"Correspondence Respecting Immoral Traffic in English Girls in Belgium." 1881. British Foreign Office, Belgium No. 1.

"Cuba Cracks down on Vice, Crime." 1998. *Chicago Tribune,* November 2, 6.

Davidson, Raelene. 1984. "'As Good a Bloody Woman as Any Other Bloody Woman . . .': Prostitutes in Western Australia, 1895–1939." In *Exploring Women's Past: Essays in Social History,* edited by Patricia Crawford et al., 171–206. Sydney: G. Allen & Unwin.

DeGroot, Joanna. 1989. "'Sex' and 'Trace': The Construction of Language and Image in the Nineteenth Century." In *Sexuality and Subordination: Interdisciplinary Studies of Gender in the Nineteenth Century,* edited by Susan Mendus and Jane Rendall, 89–128. London: Routledge.

Demleitner, Nora. 1994. "Forced Prostitution: Naming an International Offense." *Fordham International Law Journal* 18:163–97.

Dery, Luis. 1991. "Prostitution in Colonial Manila." *Philippine Studies* 39 (4): 475–89.

Doezema, Jo. 1998. "Forced to Choose: Beyond the Voluntary v. Forced Prostitution Dichotomy." In *Global Sex Workers: Rights, Resistance, and Redefinition,* edited by Kamala Kempadoo and Jo Doezema, 34–50. New York: Routledge.

Engel, Barbara Alpern. 1989. "St. Petersburg Prostitutes in the Late Nineteenth Century: A Personal and Social Profile." *Russian Review* 48 (1): 21–44.

Enloe, Cynthia. 1983. *Does Khaki Become You?: The Militarisation of Women's Lives.* Boston: South End Press.

Farrior, Stephanie. 1997. "The International Law on Trafficking in Women and Children for Prostitution: Making It Live Up to Its Potential." *Harvard Human Rights Journal* 10:213–55.

Feldman, Egal. 1967. "Prostitution, the Alien Woman, and the Progressive Imagination, 1910–1915." *American Quarterly* 19 (2): 192–206.

"France Bids Adieu to 40 Vice Girls." 1999. *Bangkok Post,* April 7.

Friedman, Robert. 1996. "India's Shame: Sexual Slavery and Political Corruption Are Generating an AIDs Catastrophe." *Nation,* April 8, 11–20.

Gilfoyle, Timothy. 1986. "The Moral Origins of Political Surveillance: The Preventative Society in New York City, 1867–1918." *American Quarterly* 38 (4): 637–52.

Grittner, Frederick. 1990. *White Slavery: Myth, Ideology, and American Law.* New York: Garland.

Guy, Donna. 1991a. *Sex and Danger in Buenos Aires: Prostitution, Family, and Nation in Argentina.* Lincoln: University of Nebraska Press.

———. 1991b. "'White Slavery,' Citizenship, and Nationality in Argentina." In *Nationalisms and Sexualities,* edited by Andrew Parker et al., 201–17. New York: Routledge.

Hershatter, Gail. 1989. "The Hierarchy of Shanghai Prostitution, 1870–1949." *Modern China* 15 (4): 463–98.

———. 1997. *Dangerous Pleasures: Prostitution and Modernity in Twentieth-Century Shanghai.* Berkeley: University of California.

Hill, Marilynn Wood. 1992. *Their Sister's Keepers: Prostitution in New York City, 1830–1870.* Berkeley: University of California.

Hirata, Lucie Cheng. 1992. "Free, Indentured, Enslaved: Chinese Prostitutes in Nineteenth-Century America." In *History of Women in the United States,* edited by Nancy F. Cott, 9:123–49. Munich: K.G. Saur.

Honore, Carl. 1998. "Sexual Slavery Growing in Europe." *Milwaukee Journal Sentinel,* December 20, 9.

Hunt, Susan Jane. 1986. *Spinifex and Hessian: Women's Lives in North-Western Australia, 1860–1900.* Nedlands: University of Western Australia.

Hurtado, Albert. 1999. *Intimate Frontiers: Sex, Gender, and Culture in Old California.* Albuquerque: University of New Mexico Press.

Hutchison, Elizabeth Quay. 1998. "'El Fruto Envenenado del Arbol Capitalista': Women Workers and the Prostitution of Labor in Urban Chile, 1896–1925." *Journal of Women's History* 9 (4): 131–52.

Hyam, Ronald. 1986. "Empire and Sexual Opportunity." *Journal of Imperial and Commonwealth History* 14 (2): 34–90.

Ichioka, Yuji. 1977. "*Ameyuki-san:* Japanese Prostitutes in Nineteenth-Century America." *AmerAsia* 4 (1): 1–21.

International Bureau for Suppression of Traffic in Persons (IBSTP). 1931. "International Bureau for Suppression of Traffic in Persons." Box 193/6, IBSTP Papers, Fawcett Library, London.

———. 1934. "Traffic in Women: Official and Non-Official Co-operative Action in Combatting the Traffic in the East." Box 193/7, IBSTP Papers, Fawcett Library, London.

———. 1949. "Post-War Europe as a Field for the Traffic in Women and Children." Box 193/6, IBSTP Papers, Fawcett Library, London.

"International Review of Criminal Policy." 1950. United Nations serial.

Kempadoo, Kamala. 1998a. "Globalizing Sex Workers' Rights." In *Global Sex Workers: Rights, Resistance, and Redefinition,* edited by Kamala Kempadoo and Jo Doezema, 1–28. New York: Routledge.

———. 1998b. "The Migrant Tightrope: Experiences from the Caribbean." In *Global Sex Workers: Rights, Resistance, and Redefinition,* edited by Kamala Kempadoo and Jo Doezema, 124–38. New York: Routledge.

Klein, Martin. 1994. "Slavery, the International Labour Market, and the Emancipation of Slaves in the Nineteenth Century." *Slavery and Abolition* 15 (2): 197–220.

Ko, Michael. 1998. "Mission Possible: Life Skills to Russian Orphans." *Seattle Times,* July 9, B1.

Lakshmanan, Indira. 1998. "Macao Isn't Going Quietly." *Boston Globe,* June 13, A1.

Lamberti, Rob. 1998. "Raids Free 'Sex Slaves' Prostitution Ring Hit in Massive Sweep." *Toronto Sun,* December 3, 4.

Langfitt, Frank. 1998. "China's Freer Market Beckons Old Customer; Prostitution's Return Met by Tax Collector." *Baltimore Sun,* November 17, 1A.

League of Nations. 1921. Records of the International Conference on Traffic in Women and Children, June 30–July 5.

———. 1934. "Commission of Enquiry into Traffic in Women and Children in the East." Summary of the Report to the Council. IV. Social 1934.IV.3.

———. 1935. "Position of Women of Russian Origin in the Far East." A.12.1935.IV 1935. Geneva from Traffic in Women and Children Committee. Social 1935.IV.3.

———. 1940/41. Advisory Committee on Social Questions. Summary of Annual Reports for 1940/41 prepared by the Secretariat, Traffic in Women and Children.

Lees, Andrew. 1979. "Critics of Urban Society in Germany, 1854–1914." *Journal of the History of Ideas* 40 (1): 61–83.

Levine, Philippa. 1986. "Rereading the 1890s: Venereal Disease as 'Constitutional Crisis' in Britain and British India." *Journal of Asian Studies* 55 (3): 585–612.

———. 1998. "Battle Colors: Race, Sex, and Colonial Soldiery in World War I." *Journal of Women's History* 9 (4): 104–30.

Lie, John. 1995. "The Transformation of Sexual Work in Twentieth-Century Korea." *Gender and Society* 9 (3): 310–27.

Litherland, Susan. 1995. "Children—Human Rights." *InterPres Service,* May 16.

MacKenzie, John. 1998. "Sex Industry Booming As Asia Busts." *Scotland on Sunday,* October 18, 21.

Macklin, Simon. 1998. "Hit-List Plan to Combat Child-Sex Tourists." *South China Morning Post,* October 6, 7.

MacLeod, Ian. 1998. "'Chasing Ghosts': The Asian Mafia Explosion." *Ottawa Citizen,* October 25, A3.

McElroy, Damien. 1999. "Portuguese Flee Macao As Their Rule Comes to a Bloody End." *Sunday Telegraph,* January 10, 26.

Mihalopoulos, V. Bill. 1993. "The Making of Prostitutes: The *Karayuki-san.*" *Bulletin of Concerned Asian Scholars* 25 (1): 41–56.

Miners, Norman. 1987. *Hong Kong under Imperial Rule, 1912–1941.* Hong Kong: Oxford University Press.

Moon, Katharine H. S. 1997. *Sex among Allies: Military Prostitution in U.S.-Korea Relations.* New York: Columbia University Press.

Mosse, George. 1985. *Nationalism and Sexuality: Respectability and Abnormal Sexuality in Modern Europe.* New York: H. Fertig, 1985.

Murphy, Brian. 1998. "Inquiry Paints Greece as Prostitution Hub." *Boston Globe,* November 22, A18.

Murphy, Mary. 1992. "The Private Lives of Public Women: Prostitution in Butte, Montana, 1878–1917." In *History of Women in the United States,* edited by Nancy F. Cott, 9:286–98. Munich: K.G. Saur.

Murray, Alison. 1998. "Debt-Bondage and Trafficking: Don't Believe the Hype." In *Global Sex Workers: Rights, Resistance, and Redefinition,* edited by Kamala Kempadoo and Jo Doezema, 51–64. New York: Routledge.

Nadelmann, Ethan. 1990. "Global Prohibition Regimes: The Evolution of Norms in International Society." *International Organization* 44 (4): 479–526.

"NPA to Attend International Meeting on Prostitution." 1998. *Daily Yomiuri,* October 21, 2.

"Paedophile Tourists Face Crackdown." 1995. *Independent,* July 2, 5.

Philps, Alan. 1998. "Welcome to 'Las Vegas of Middle East.'" *Daily Telegraph,* September 17, 26.

Porter, Jonathan. 1996. *Macau: The Imaginary City: Culture and Society, 1557 to the Present.* Boulder, Colo.: Westview.

Pringle, James. 1998. "Owner of Beijing Brothel to Be Shot." *Gazette,* November 19, A24.

"Prostitution in Hong Kong." 1931. C[olonial] O[ffice]-129/533/10.

"Prostitution in Singapore." 1933. C[olonial] O[ffice]-273/659/13.

Quiambao, Cecilia. 1998. "Trading in the Innocent—Child Prostitution." *Bangkok Post,* October 18.

Quilligan, Patrick. 1995. "International Community Acts to Combat Child Sex Exploitation." *Irish Times,* June 1, 10.

Repard, Pauline. 1995. "Ring Importing Prostitutes from Thailand Is Broken Here." *San Diego Union-Tribune,* February 25, B2.

"Repatriation of Prostitutes." 1930. League of Nations archives, United Nations, Geneva, 11b/16984/3293.

Salt Lake Tribune. 1994. June 17, no title, A15.

Sandos, James. 1980. "Prostitution and Drugs: The United States Army on the Mexican-American Border, 1916–1917." *Pacific Historical Review* 49 (4): 621–45.

Scully, Eileen. 1995. "Taking the Low Road to Sino-American Relations: 'Open Door Expansionists' and the Two China Markets." *Journal of American History* 82 (1): 62–83.

———. 1998. "Prostitution as Privilege: The 'American Girl' of Treaty Port China." *International History Review* 20 (4): 855–83.

"Sex Trade Trafficking of Children on the Rise." 1998. *Bangkok Post,* July 22.

Singapore *Straits Times.* 1862. May 17, 1.

"Social Disease, Prostitution Have Been Investigated Many Times in City, Official Says." 1935. *China Press,* July 16, 9.

"Social Hygiene." 1930. Colonial Office-129/522/3. Microfilm Collection.

Stansell, Christine. 1986. *City of Women: Sex and Class in New York, 1789–1860.* New York: Knopf.

Stoler, Ann. 1989. "Making Empire Respectable: The Politics of Race and Sexual Morality in Twentieth-Century Colonial Cultures." *American Ethnologist* 16 (4):634–60.

Sturdevant, Saundra Pollock, and Brenda Stoltzfus. 1992. *Let the Good Times Roll: Prostitution and the U.S. Military in Asia.* New York: New Press.

Sun Kuo-chun. 1988. *Chiu Shang-hai ch'ang-chi mi-shih* (A secret history of prostitution in Old Shanghai). Honan: Ho-nan Sheng Hsin Hua Shu Tien Fu Hsing.

Tabet, Paola. 1998. "I'm the Meat, I'm the Knife: Sexual Service, Migration, and Repression in Some African Societies." In *Global Sex Workers: Rights, Resistance, and Redefinition,* edited by Kamala Kempadoo and Jo Doezema. New York: Routledge.

Tadiar, Neferti Xina M. 1993. "Sexual Economies in the Asia-Pacific Community." In *What Is in a Rim?: Critical Perspectives on the Pacific Region Idea,* edited by Arif Dirlik. Boulder, Colo.: Westview.

Terrell, Rev. F. G. c. 1907. *The Shame of the Human Race: The White Slave Traffic.* Chicago, n.p.

"Thais Account for 90% of Vice Arrests in Hong Kong." 1999. *Bangkok Post,* April 23.

Thompson, Tony, and Nicole Veash. 1999. "Sex Slavery Spreads across UK." *Observer,* March 14, 7.

Toepfer, Susan J., and Bryan S. Wells. 1994. "The Worldwide Market for Sex: A Review of International and Regional Legal Prohibitions Regarding Trafficking in Women." *Michigan Journal of Gender and Law* 2:83–128.

Tomich, Dale. 1988. "The 'Second Slavery': Bonded Labor and the Transformation of the Nineteenth-Century World Economy." In *Rethinking the Nineteenth Century: Contradictions and Movements,* edited by Francisco O. Ramirez, 103–18. New York: Greenwood Press.

Tong, Benson. 1994. *Unsubmissive Women: Chinese Prostitutes in Nineteenth-Century San Francisco.* Norman: University of Oklahoma.

Turnbull, C. M. 1977. *A History of Singapore, 1819–1975.* Kuala Lumpur: Oxford University Press.

United Nations. 1948. Economic and Social Council. "Traffic in Women and Children." Summary of Annual Reports for 1946–47.

———. 1952. Economic and Social Council. "Traffic in Women and Children." Summary of Annual Reports for the Period 1948–1950. Prepared by the Secretariat.

United States. Immigration and Naturalization Service (INS). 1914. A. Warner Parker, Law Officer, to Commissioner General of Immigration, August 7, 1914, 52809–7.

van Onselen, Charles. 1982. *Studies in the Social and Economic History of the Witwatersrand, 1886–1914.* Vol 1. New York: Longman.

Viviano, Frank. 1999. "Albanians Try to Take Over Kosovars' Crime Network." *San Francisco Chronicle,* May 11, A1.

Walkowitz, Judith. 1982. "Male Vice and Feminist Virtue: Feminism and the Politics of Prostitution in Nineteenth Century Britain." *History Workshop* 13:79–93.

Wallen, David. 1995. "Britain Joins the Move against Child Sex Tours." *South China Morning Post,* July 15, 18.

Warren, James. 1993. *Ah Ku and Karayuki-san: Prostitution in Singapore, 1870–1940.* Singapore: Oxford University Press.

Watenabe, Satoko. 1998. "From Thailand to Japan: Migrant Sex Workers as Autonomous Subjects." In *Global Sex Workers: Rights, Resistance, and Redefinition,* edited by Kamala Kempadoo and Jo Doezema, 114–23. New York: Routledge.

Waters, Elizabeth. "Restructuring the 'Woman Question': Perestroika and Prostitution." *Feminist Review* 33:3–19.

"What on Earth?" 1998. *Washington Post.* September 5, A21.

White, Luise. 1986. "Prostitution, Identity, and Class Consciousness in Nairobi during World War II." *Signs* 11 (2): 255–73.

Whitely, Peyton. 1995. "Prostitution Probe: 5 Asian Women Freed." *Seattle Times,* January 31, A1.

Wijers, Marjan. 1998. "Women, Labor, and Migration: The Position of Trafficked Women and Strategies for Support." In *Global Sex Workers: Rights, Resistance, and Redefinition,* edited by Kamala Kempadoo and Jo Doezema, 60–78. New York: Routledge.

Part III / Smuggling from Mexico and China

CHAPTER FIVE

The Transformation
of Migrant Smuggling across
the U.S.-Mexican Border

Peter Andreas

Immigration control across the nearly two-thousand-mile-long U.S.-Mexican border was transformed in the early 1990s from a low-profile and politically marginalized activity into a high-intensity campaign attracting enormous policy and media attention.[1] "The border build up," as one journalist observed, "represents by far the most expensive and prolonged budgetary initiative ever undertaken to reduce illegal immigration" (Suro, 1998: 1). Strikingly, the unprecedented effort to build a police barrier along the border came at the same time that the United States and Mexico were constructing a barrier-free economy. Even though migrant labor was one of Mexico's most important exports and an integral component of the U.S.-Mexico economic integration process, it was noticeably missing from the North American Free Trade Agreement. While most economic barriers were falling during the decade, barriers against the cross-border movement of labor were rising in the form of more intensive policing. These sharply contrasting developments reinforced Jagdish Baghwati's broader observation that immigration controls represented "the most compelling exception to liberalism in the operation of the world economy"

(Bhagwati, 1984: 680). This has been further confirmed by the continued buildup of border enforcement during the past decade.

In this chapter I trace how the interaction between law enforcement and clandestine labor migration across the U.S.-Mexican border perversely generated a more organized and sophisticated migrant smuggling business and how this, in turn, helped to propel a more expansive and intensive border-policing effort. I emphasize that while the relationship between law-evading smugglers and law-enforcing state actors was purposefully conflictive, in practice it was in many ways been unintentionally symbiotic. In short, this is a story about how the state helped to make smuggling and how smuggling helped to (re) make the policing apparatus of the state.[2] I first provide an overview of the emergence and evolution of migrant smuggling across the border and how this intersected with various state practices over time. I then focus on the last years of the twentieth century, characterized by a boom in both immigration control efforts and organized migrant smuggling activity in the U.S.-Mexican borderlands. I conclude with a few observations on border enforcement dynamics in the aftermath of the terrorist bombings on September 11, 2001.

A Brief History of Migrant Smuggling across the U.S.-Mexican Border

If smuggling can be defined as the practice of bringing in or taking out without state authorization, then all population flows involving a clandestine border crossing are by definition a form of smuggling. What has varied across time and place is the degree, nature, methods, and organization of such smuggling. In the case of crossing the U.S.-Mexican border, this has ranged from self-smuggling (i.e., migrants illegally crossing the border without hiring the services of a professional smuggler), to local-level individual smuggling entrepreneurs (the traditional "coyotes"), to highly organized and sophisticated transnational smuggling networks (often specializing in the smuggling of non-Mexicans across the border—such as Chinese and Central Americans).

The first wave of illegal immigration involved self-smuggling from the United States to Mexico. More than a century and a half ago, Mexico unsuccessfully tried to curb illegal American immigration to its northern regions. To a significant extent, the Mexican War was a conflict over immigration and immigration control. After the Treaty of Guadalupe Hidalgo of 1848 and the Gadsden Purchase of 1853, these territories formally became part of the United

States. Large numbers of white settlers (many of them recent European immigrants) moved west to these sparsely populated lands. But while the political boundaries that were redrawn through war remain, the migratory movement has been turned around, with millions of people of Mexican origin populating these areas.

The movement of people across the border remained largely unregulated throughout the nineteenth century. The first real U.S. initiative to restrict migration flows in the Southwest actually targeted Chinese. One side effect of the Chinese Exclusion Act in 1882 was to turn Mexico and the border into a corridor for smuggling Chinese laborers. Boats of Chinese migrants would land south of the California-Mexico border at Ensenada, Guaymas, or Mazatlan. The migrants paid five dollars for the trip to the border and then up to forty dollars to be smuggled into California (Metz, 1989: 365). The migrants also traveled deeper into the Mexican interior and were then smuggled across the border between Juárez and El Paso (Stoddard, 1976: 180). Federal law enforcement officials (called "Chinese inspectors") were deployed to the border area to curb the smuggling of Chinese (McDonald, 1997: 74).

Many Mexicans were informally recruited by U.S. employers to work in southwestern agriculture in the early twentieth century. Whereas legal entry was cumbersome, crossing the border illegally was relatively simple and largely overlooked. The Mexican Revolution, U.S. labor shortages during World War I, and the expansion of southwestern agriculture fueled a further influx of Mexican workers across the border. Restrictions on European immigration in 1921 and 1924 also had the unintended effect of turning the U.S.-Mexican border into a backdoor for illegal European immigrants. Thus, when the U.S. Border Patrol was formed in 1924, with a total force of some 450 officers, the primary immigrants targeted along the border were Europeans and Asians.

An estimated half a million Mexicans entered the United States during the 1920s (Calavita, 1994). When they were no longer needed during the depression era, hundreds of thousands were deported. And when the demand for cheap labor increased again in the 1940s (as a result of labor shortages during World War II), Mexican workers were encouraged to come back. This time the state played a more formal role in the labor recruitment process. The Bracero Program, a guest-worker arrangement in place between 1942 and 1964, was created to provide a cheap source of labor for agribusiness.

The long-term consequence of the Bracero Program was to institutionalize mass labor migration from Mexico to the United States. As one immigration scholar has observed, "by the time the Bracero Program ended, a relationship of symbiosis between Mexican immigrants and U.S. employers had become well-entrenched, facilitated and nurtured by more than 50 years of U.S. policymaking. With the end of the program, employment of Mexican labor went underground as the guest workers of one era became the illegal immigrants of the next" (Calavita, 1996: 289). After the Bracero Program was terminated in the 1960s, Mexican workers continued to be welcomed by employers. Legal sanctions did not worry employers, since the hiring of unauthorized workers was not a felony.[3]

Even as illegal immigration increased rapidly during the 1960s and 1970s, the enforcement capacity of the then Immigration and Naturalization Service (INS) remained limited. Interior enforcement was largely nonexistent, while border controls were minimal. Even as the number of border apprehensions increased from approximately 71,000 in 1960 to more than 1 million in 1978, the budget of the Border Patrol remained less than the budget of many city police departments (Teitelbaum, 1980).

The limited presence and effectiveness of law enforcement meant that migrant smuggling was a fairly simple and inexpensive practice; migrants either smuggled themselves across the border or hired a local border guide. However, the sheer magnitude of the migration flow, competition between smugglers to service this flow, and the dispersion of the flow from agricultural to urban areas meant that smuggling gradually became more organized. As Peter Reuter and David Ronfeldt have noted, "After the termination of the Bracero program in 1965, smuggling of aliens into the United States was conducted by adventurous loners who had little concern for security and by small family-based operations. But the growth and competition for new business, the increased importance of operational skill and security, and the shift from agricultural areas to cities as the destination of many aliens created a need for larger, better organized operations" (1991: 14). Government reports suggest that smuggling organizations had grown substantially in size and complexity by the mid-1970s (Comptroller General of the United States, 1976).

Still, hiring a professional smuggler remained more of a convenience than a necessity. In FY 1970, only 8.4 percent of the illegal migrants caught by the Border Patrol in the southwestern region had attempted entry with the use of a smuggler. This increased to 13.5 percent in FY 1975 (ibid.: 5–6). These statistics probably understate the amount of professional smuggling, since those migrants who hired the services of a smuggler were more likely to evade detection and arrest. Penalties against smugglers remained minimal: fewer than 50 percent of the smugglers caught between 1973 and 1975 were prosecuted, most on a misdemeanor charge (18).

In one study, smugglers report that there was little demand for their services in the 1970s because migrants could easily enter the United States on their own. Smugglers were often hired for special needs, such as the smuggling of women, children, the elderly, and non-Mexican nationals (López Castro, 1998: 970). Using a smuggler to cross the border generally meant a faster and safer trip. This involved some personal risks, but attempting the crossing without a smuggler heightened the possibility of assault by bandits and abuse by the authorities.

Failing as a meaningful barrier, INS control efforts remained largely symbolic (Heyman, 1995). The Border Patrol could cover only a small portion of the borderline. While the INS insisted that "prompt apprehension and return to country of origin is a positive deterrent to illegal reentry and related violations" (INS Annual Report, 1978, cited in Kossoudji, 1992: 161), in practice migrants simply kept trying to cross until they succeeded. Repeated arrests did little more than postpone entry.

As migrants flowed north across the border for work, the Mexican government largely sat on the sidelines. Freedom of exit is guaranteed in the constitution, and the export of excess labor has long been an economic safety valve. Nevertheless, in the late 1970s Mexico, while not blocking the exit of Mexican citizens, began to cooperate with the United States in targeting professional smugglers. This was partly due to the Mexican government's rising concerns over the smuggling of Central Americans to the United States through Mexican territory. During the Carter years, the INS created a special unit called the National Anti-Smuggling Program, which generated increased arrests and prosecutions of smugglers operating on the U.S. side of the border. Mexico, in turn, collaborated by arresting hundreds of smugglers on its side of the line. During the 1980s, cross-border immigration control cooperation continued to focus primarily on the smuggling of third-country nationals through Mexico, especially Central Americans. Nevertheless, smugglers and those being smuggled remained largely undeterred (Nevins, 1998: 326–28).

The most significant U.S. policy response to illegal immigration was the passage of the Immigration Reform and Control Act of 1986 (IRCA). IRCA introduced employer sanctions, authorized an expansion of the Border Patrol, and offered a general legalization program (as well as a special legalization program for agricultural workers). Some two million Mexicans were eventually legalized. IRCA's proponents argued that this supply of newly legalized workers would satisfy the U.S. demand for cheap imported labor, while the employer sanctions would inhibit the hiring of illegal workers. This, at least theoretically, would curb future migration.

IRCA, however, reinforced the very problem the law was promoted to rectify. As one immigration researcher notes, "IRCA stimulated interest in coming to the U.S., and the possibility of obtaining a green card via the legalization programs led to a huge increase in the demand for coyote [smuggler] services" (López Castro, 1998: 970). Those who were legalized under IRCA provided a stronger base for the arrival of new unauthorized immigrants. "By handing out more than 2 million green cards to former undocumented migrants," observes Douglas Massey, "Congress dramatically raised the odds that millions of other family members still in Mexico would themselves enter the United States as undocumented migrants" (1997: 26–27).

The employer sanctions law, meanwhile, provided no effective document verification system. The perverse impact of the law was to generate an enormous business in fake documents. Since IRCA did not require employers to check the authenticity of documents, they could simply continue to hire illegal workers at minimal risk—as long as the documents looked genuine and they made sure to fill out the proper forms. In the short term, IRCA helped to defuse some of the domestic pressure to "do something" about illegal immigration. But the law's failures would help make immigration control an even more daunting task in years to come.

The Intensified Border Enforcement Campaign

As the public mood toward illegal immigration soured in the early 1990s, policymakers from across the political spectrum rushed to outdo one another in proposing tougher control measures. In this heated political context, President Clinton launched an aggressive new campaign to "regain control" of the southwestern border. Noticeably less attention was given to the enormous employer demand for cheap migrant labor or the fact that as much as half of the illegal immigrant population in the country had entered legally (as students or tourists, for example) and then overstayed their visas.

The heightened political status of immigration control was reflected in the dramatic expansion of the INS. The INS budget grew from $1.5 billion in FY

1993 to $4 billion in FY 1999—making it one of the fastest- (and one of the only) growing federal agencies. The single most important growth area was border enforcement. In FY 1998, the INS spent $877 million on border enforcement, up from about $400 million in FY 1993. More than half of the $413 million increase in INS funding from FY 1998 to FY 1999 was allocated for border control.

As a result of its hiring spree, by the late 1990s the INS had more officers authorized to carry a gun and make arrests than any other federal law enforcement agency (*Migration News,* February 1998). Between FY 1993 and the end of FY 1998, the size of the Border Patrol along the southwestern border more than doubled—from 3,389 agents to 7,231 agents. Reflecting the intensified monitoring of the border, total line watch hours for the Border Patrol increased from 2,386,888 in FY 1993 to 4,807,669 in FY 1997 (Bean, Capps, and Haynes, 1999). In addition, as of March 1997, the INS had about 1,300 inspectors at thirty-six ports of entry on the southwestern border. The inspections' appropriations totaled $151 million for FY 1997—a 78 percent increase from FY 1994 levels.

The new border enforcement campaign also involved a massive influx of new equipment, such as infrared night-vision scopes, low-light TV cameras, ground sensors, helicopters, and all-terrain vehicles. The increasingly high-tech nature of border enforcement included a new electronic identification system called IDENT, which stored the fingerprints and photographs of those apprehended at the border. The military also played a supporting role by assisting with the operation of night scopes, motion sensors, and communications equipment, as well as building and maintaining roads and fences. Along the border south of San Diego, for example, army reservists built a ten-foot-high steel wall that extends for fourteen miles. Similarly, in Nogales, army engineers constructed a fifteen-foot tall fence that was nearly five miles long.

Congress assured that the border buildup would continue by passing the Illegal Immigration Reform and Immigration Responsibility Act of 1996. The sweeping immigration law authorized the hiring of 1,000 Border Patrol agents a year, reaching a total force of more than 10,000 by the year 2001. The 1996 law promoted other measures to secure the border, including a sharp increase in the penalties against migrant smugglers. The new sentencing guidelines in some cases called for a doubling of penalties and mandatory minimum sentencing for smuggling aliens for commercial gain.

The border control offensive was based on a strategy designed by the INS in

1993–94 called "prevention through deterrence." By using more physical barriers, surveillance equipment, legal sanctions, and law enforcement agents, the objective was to inhibit illegal entry rather than trying to catch entrants once they have entered the country. The infusion of law enforcement resources at the most popular entry points was designed to disrupt traditional border-crossing methods and routes, forcing migrants to give up or attempt entry in more difficult and remote areas and at official ports of entry.

The deterrence strategy had its origins in Operation Blockade (later renamed Hold-the-Line), which was launched in El Paso on September 19, 1993. Some 450 agents were paid overtime to cover a twenty-mile stretch of the borderline. The sudden show of force led to a sharp drop in attempted illegal entries in the area. Prior to the operation, there were up to 10,000 illegal border crossings per day, and only 1 person out of 8 who made the attempt was apprehended (Ekstrand, 1995). The high-profile operation drew the applause of Washington, the media, and local residents. Importantly, the operation also attracted the attention of political leaders in California, who pushed to reproduce the El Paso "success story" along their portion of the border.

Impressed by the El Paso experience and the domestic support it generated, in 1994 the INS announced a comprehensive plan to apply the "prevention through deterrence" strategy across the entire the southwestern border. The strategy would first target the busiest entry points—the El Paso and San Diego sectors, which in FY 1993 accounted for 68 percent of all southwestern border apprehensions. Thus, El Paso's Operation Hold-the-Line was matched by Operation Gatekeeper south of San Diego in October 1994, which targeted the fourteen westernmost miles of the border (traditionally the location of 25% of all border apprehensions). The strategy would then be expanded to the Tucson sector and south Texas, where migrants were expected to move after the El Paso and San Diego sectors had been secured. As envisioned by the Border Patrol, the strategy would eventually be applied along the entire border (U.S. Border Patrol, 1994).

As predicted, the tightening of border controls in El Paso and San Diego pushed migrants to attempt entry elsewhere along the border.[4] Thus, apprehensions in the El Paso sector remained far below the levels prior to Operation Hold-the-Line but skyrocketed to the west in New Mexico and Arizona. Similarly, apprehensions in the Imperial Beach sector south of San Diego (traditionally the single most important gateway for illegal entry) declined sharply since Gatekeeper began, but arrests jumped in the more remote areas of east San Diego County.

Even though apprehensions reached a twenty-four-year low near San Diego and fell by half in El Paso since 1993, overall apprehensions along the southwestern border were actually up. The Border Patrol made more than 1.5 million apprehensions in FY 1999—an increase of 300,000 over 1993 apprehension levels (*Austin American-Statesman,* November 28, 1999). Although apprehension statistics are notoriously difficult to interpret, it seemed that the border deterrence strategy did more to shift rather than reduce the cross-border flow of migrants.

These shifts in human traffic provided a political and bureaucratic justification to expand the border-policing campaign geographically. Thus, Operation Safeguard was launched in Nogales, Arizona, and Operation Gatekeeper, which first concentrated on the 14 westernmost miles of the border, was extended in October 1996 to cover 66 miles. Similarly, in January 1997 Operation Hold-the-Line was extended 10 miles west into New Mexico. And in late August 1997 the INS announced Operation Rio Grande in southeast Texas, which included setting up portable floodlights, 20-foot watchtowers, low-light video cameras, and high-powered infrared vision scopes along the Rio Grande. As part of Operation Rio Grande, the Border Patrol and the military's Joint Task Force 6 started building 240 miles of roadway, a dozen helicopter pads, and fifty high-intensity lights in the Laredo area (Spener, this volume, Chap. 6).

Meanwhile, the heightened Border Patrol presence between the official ports of entry created more pressure at the ports of entry. Operations such as Gatekeeper prompted attempted illegal entries through the ports of entry, and the INS in turn responded by deploying new port inspectors. Between FY 1994 and FY 1997, the number of INS port inspectors increased from 1,117 to 1,865, representing a 67 percent rise. The added personnel was reinforced by higher penalties for those who attempt entry through fraudulent document use (*Migration News,* February 1997).

The Boom in Migrant Smuggling

Breaking up the traditional routes and methods of clandestine entry turned the once relatively simple illegal practice of entry without inspection into a more complex underground web of illegality. Past entry methods primarily involved either self-smuggling or limited use of a local smuggler. But with the buildup of border policing, the use of a professional smuggler became more of a necessity. The growing reliance on smugglers, a 1997 report of the Binational Study on Migration concluded, "helps to explain why most migrants attempting unauthorized entry succeed despite significantly more U.S. Border Patrol agents and technology on the border" (Binational Study, 1997: 28).

Not surprisingly, as the demand for smuggling services and the risks of crossing the border grew, so too did the price of being smuggled. Prices along some parts of the border doubled and in some cases more than tripled. The smuggling fee could exceed a thousand dollars. The trip from Agua Prieta to Phoenix, for example, cost as little as two hundred dollars in 1994 but reached as high as fifteen hundred dollars in early 1999 (*Arizona Daily Star*, July 11, 1999). The exact price varied depending on location, the quality of service, and the set of services being purchased. As one Border Patrol agent explained, "It's much like a full-service travel agency, all depending on how much you're willing to spend" (*Los Angeles Times*, April 7, 1996). According to the INS, the increase in prices was an indicator that the deterrence effort was effective. Yet higher prices were not necessarily a substantial deterrent, given that smuggling fees tended to be paid for by relatives and friends in the United States rather than by the immigrants themselves (López Castro, 1998: 971). Alternatively, some immigrants may have been given the option of paying off the fee by working in a job arranged or provided by the smuggler (Binational Study, 1997). Although the amount paid to be smuggled across the border was not insignificant, it could be earned back in a relatively short period of time working in the United States.

The most consequential impact of higher prices was to enhance the wealth and power of smuggling groups. As Miguel Vallina, the assistant chief of the Border Patrol in San Diego, noted, "the more difficult the crossing, the better the business for the smugglers" (*Los Angeles Times*, February 5, 1995). INS commissioner Doris Meissner explained in January 1996 that "as we improve our enforcement, we increase the smuggling of aliens that occurs, because it is harder to cross and so therefore people turn more and more to smugglers" (*Federal News Service*, January 12, 1996). But at the same time that Meissner recognized that the Border Patrol had created more business for smugglers, she also emphasized that we are "moving as aggressively as we can . . . so that we can put them [the smugglers] out of business" (Meissner, 1996). The president's

International Crime Control Strategy similarly emphasized the need to target organized smuggling, calling for "aggressive efforts to protect U.S. borders by attacking and decreasing smuggling and smuggling-related crimes" (quoted in Bach, 1999).

Beefed-up policing removed some smugglers but also increased the market position of others. Moreover, many of those arrested were the lowest-level and most expendable members of migrant smuggling organizations—the border guides and drivers who were the "foot soldiers" of the business. Smugglers were first and foremost travel service specialists. And as long as there continued to be a strong demand for their services—which the tightening of border controls and the strong domestic employer demand for migrant labor guaranteed—smuggling would persist. The high profits from smuggling—inflated by law enforcement pressure—assured that there would be smugglers willing to accept the occupational hazards. As one smuggler explained, "Figure it this way. If I work in a factory five days, I make $125 a week. If I take one person across the border, I get $300" (*Los Angeles Times*, May 2, 1992). A good guide could reportedly make $60,000 a year along the border (*San Diego Union-Tribune*, April 28, 1996).

U.S. officials went to great lengths to portray migrants as the victims of smugglers, and they used this both to deflect criticism and to provide a further rationale to crack down on smuggling. Assistant U.S. Attorney Michael Wheat, for example, suggested that "basically, alien smuggling is modern-day slavery. The whole idea behind slavery was moving humans to perform labor. The way the aliens are moved, the way they are treated, this is just a sophisticated form of slavery" (*Los Angeles Times*, February 5, 1995). Migrants, however, generally viewed smugglers as simply a "necessary evil," a clandestine business transaction that they willingly engaged in to evade the expanding border enforcement net. Within Mexico, migrant smuggling was considered a shady business, but one that was seen as relatively harmless (López Castro, 1998: 970). Smugglers, after all, had a clear economic motivation to deliver their "clients" unharmed across the border, since most of the payment was generally made only upon delivery (see Spener, this volume, Chap. 6). Of course, as documented in media reporting, smugglers could be abusive and reckless, and their efforts to bypass law enforcement could place migrants at great risk. Yet smugglers were hired precisely because they generally provided a safer and faster border-crossing experience. Indeed, many smugglers depended on customer satisfaction for future business, since migrants who had a successful experience were likely to recommend their smuggler to other friends and relatives. A smuggler's reputation could matter a great deal.

Smugglers became more skilled as border enforcement became more intensive. As one senior INS official noted, "alien smugglers have developed a sophisticated infrastructure to successfully counteract U.S. Border Patrol operations along the Southwest Border" (Regan, 1997). Those smuggling operations that had the greatest transportation and communication capabilities were the ones most capable of evading arrest, which left small-time smugglers at a competitive disadvantage. Pressured by law enforcement, some smugglers even turned to using commercial trucks to move migrants across the border, blending in with the massive boom in cross-border trucking brought on by the liberalization of trade and transportation. Northbound truck crossings doubled between 1993 and the end of the decade. Overwhelmed by the high volume of cross-border traffic, U.S. port inspectors could realistically search only a small percentage of the trucks crossing the border. Enhanced border policing also prompted smugglers to become more technologically sophisticated. Peter Skerry and Stephen Rockwell noted that "as the Border Patrol pours more resources into night-vision scopes, weight sensors and giant X-ray machines for seeing into trucks, smuggling rings counter with their own state-of-the-art equipment paid for by increased [smuggling] fees" (1998).

Although many of the local freelance entrepreneurs who once dominated migrant smuggling along the border were being squeezed out by the border enforcement campaign, they were being replaced by better organized and more skilled smuggling organizations. One INS intelligence report suggested that many smuggling groups once based in the United States had relocated to the Mexican side, helping to insulate principal leaders from the grasp of American law enforcement (cited in U.S. General Accounting Office, 1997: 42). A federal task force estimated that up to ten to twelve family-based smuggling organizations came to dominate the trafficking of migrants across the border (*Migration News*, June 1998). Of course, it was easy to overstate these claims for political gain. One INS agent even went so far as to say that the border smugglers had become "huge, inter-locked cartels." Such threat inflation made effective media sound bites even if the empirical evidence was thin (*Arizona Daily Star*, July 11, 1999).

Further complicating the challenge of organized migrant smuggling along the border was an unintended result of U.S. efforts to deter the maritime smuggling of Asian migrants. As officials began to target the use of boats to smuggle Asian migrants into the country in 1993, much of the smuggling was diverted to other routes, including land routes through Mexico. The arrival of Chinese smuggling boats (such as the *Golden Venture*) in 1993 attracted a great deal of media attention, sparking a quick law enforcement crackdown. Smugglers reacted by using less visible transportation methods and routes, which in turn has created more work for law enforcement officials. As Meissner noted, "We've stopped that illegal boat traffic, but there are still a lot of people coming from Asia, mainly through Central America and Mexico" (*New York Times,* May 30, 1996). Chinese paid up to thirty thousand dollars for the trip (ibid.). It should be noted that such long-distance smuggling of non-Mexicans was only a small part of migrant smuggling across the southwestern border, but it was by far the most profitable part of the business. For example, a typical boat from China landing in the northern Mexican state of Baja in 1993 carried human cargo worth six million dollars (Rotella, 1998: 75–78).

As migrant smuggling became a more organized and sophisticated enterprise in reaction to tighter controls, this served to justify tougher laws and tougher enforcement. For example, Operation Disruption was initiated in May 1995 to target drop houses used by migrant smugglers in the San Diego area. The operation produced 120 arrests of smugglers and the uncovering of 117 drop houses (*Migration News,* February 2, 1996). The crackdown in San Diego displaced much of the smuggling farther east to the Imperial Valley, as well as to Arizona. The Border Patrol, in turn, responded with a nearly tenfold increase in the number of agents assigned to combat smuggling rings in the area (*Los Angeles Times,* May 10, 1998). Other federal agencies, such as the FBI, also deployed new agents to the border in response to the increase in organized migrant smuggling (*Los Angeles Times,* May 29, 1996).

The number of smugglers prosecuted mushroomed. In San Diego, for example, the busiest federal court in the country for migrant smuggling cases, prosecutions increased from 33 in 1993 to 233 in 1996 (U.S. Department of Justice, 1996). Nationally, the INS presented 1,547 principal smugglers for prosecution of alien smuggling violations in FY 1998—a 19 percent increase from the previous year (Bach, 1999). Tougher sentencing guidelines significantly increased the length of prison terms for smugglers. The INS was also given new enforcement powers to target organized smuggling, such as federal racketeering statutes and the authority to use wiretaps. On the Mexican side of the border, smugglers could be given a ten-year prison sentence. In 1995,

700 smugglers were given prison terms in Mexico, almost a doubling of the 1994 total (*Migration News,* June 1996). Mexico increased prison terms from five years with bond to up to twenty years without bond (*Arizona Daily Star,* July 11, 1999).

The border crackdown, however, failed to cause a shortage of smugglers. One senior official from the Border Patrol's anti-smuggling unit commented that the smugglers "just get paid more for taking more risks" (interview with author, U.S. Border Patrol, San Diego Sector Headquarters, April 8, 1997). And as the risks for smuggling rose, so too did the incentive for smugglers to use more dangerous methods to avoid law enforcement. This partly explained the increase in high-speed chases and accidents that resulted when smugglers try to circumvent INS checkpoints along the highways leading north from the border. It also helped to explain a particularly creative but cruel smuggling trend: because the law did not allow jailing illegal migrants with children, children were sometimes bought, rented, or stolen to facilitate the crossing. The children were then often left to fend for themselves on the U.S. side (*Trafficking in Migrants,* June 1996).

Border corruption also become a more serious problem. Increased enforcement increased the need for smugglers to bribe or buy entry documents from those doing the enforcing. And as smuggling groups became more sophisticated and profitable—as a consequence of the higher demand and cost for their services and the heightened risks involved in providing these services—the capacity and means to corrupt also grew. In one well-known case at the San Ysidro port of entry south of San Diego, U.S. Customs inspector Guy Henry Kmett was arrested for helping a major smuggling ring move migrants through his inspection lane. The three vans busted in Kmett's lane carried Salvadorans, Guatemalans, Dominicans, and an Egyptian. Kmett came under suspicion after the Border Patrol noticed that the vans were parked at Kmett's house the day before. Kmett had spent about $100,000 in cash during the previous year on such items as a swimming pool, computers, and televisions. Law enforcement officials estimated that the Peraltas smuggling organization, which was trying to transport migrants through Kmett's lane, earned $1 million per month for smuggling one thousand migrants per month across the border (*Los Angeles Times,* February 5, 1995).

On the Mexican side of the border, there were numerous cases of official corruption involving migrant smuggling (Rotella, 1998). In one high-profile case, the Mexican migration service's regional head in Tijuana, his deputy, and his chief inspector were all fired and charged with assisting the smuggling of non-Mexican migrants. The Tijuana office reportedly brought in as much as $70,000 weekly from the proceeds of migrant trafficking (*San Francisco Chronicle*, July 11, 1994). It was also reported that Tijuana police took bribes that amounted to as much as $40,000 a month to permit the operation of safe houses where migrants stayed before attempting to cross into the United States (*Los Angeles Times*, February 5, 1995).

The Further Escalation of Border Enforcement after 9/11

As we have seen, the business of migrant smuggling and the business of policing migrant smuggling along the U.S.-Mexico border grew up together and expanded through their interaction. Each law enforcement move provoked a law evasion countermove, which in turn was matched by more enforcement. By the beginning of the twenty-first century, there was little indication that this escalating enforcement-evasion dynamic would end any time soon. Indeed, after the terrorist attacks on September 11, 2001, this dynamic was not only reinforced but further intensified. The security stakes suddenly seemed much higher: U.S. border officials warned that the same groups, methods, and routes employed to smuggle migrants across the border could now potentially be used to smuggle terrorists and weapons of mass destruction. Similarly, the same fraudulent document industry that had long provided identification cards for unauthorized migrants could also potentially provide these services to terrorists.

The heightened importance of border security (Andreas and Bierstcker, 2003) was reflected not only in an infusion of more border control resources but also the reorganization of multiple agencies (including the INS and the Customs Service) under a newly formed Department of Homeland Security—the largest restructuring of the federal government in half a century. This partly consisted of taking the old immigration control infrastructure and adapting it to previously low-priority counterterrorism efforts. It was an awkward fit: the old INS border enforcement system was built to police large numbers of economically motivated, unauthorized migrant workers rather than to detect and deter a small number of determined individuals intending to commit politically motivated violent acts.

The post–September 11 security environment also opened more space for a further militarization of immigration law enforcement on the border. In the past, military units operating along the border were formally limited to assisting antidrug work, but after September 11 the new expanded mission could include targeting illegal immigration. Major military contractors, such as Lockheed Martin, Raytheon, and Northrop Grumman, were also recruited to play a larger role in border control—as one press report put it, "using some of the same high-priced, high-tech tools these companies have already put to work in Iraq and Afghanistan" (*New York Times*, May 18, 2006). For example, in September 2005, border officials in Arizona (which had become the leading entry point for smuggled migrants) unveiled a new unmanned aerial surveillance system based on the satellite-controlled Predator-B spy drone used for military operations in the Middle East and elsewhere. These developments were part of the larger securitization of immigration control issues in the post–September 11 era. Reflecting the shifting priorities, federal prosecutions for immigration law violations more than doubled from 2001 to 2005, replacing drug law violations as the most frequently enforced federal crime.

As part of this new push to secure the border, in 2006 the U.S. Congress also approved the building of a seven-hundred-mile-long border fence and the hiring of thousands additional Border Patrol agents. The size of the Border Patrol had reached some twenty thousand agents by the end of the decade—roughly twice its size since September 11 (and the force had already doubled in size in the 1990s). While these latest enforcement moves have certainly made the border a more challenging and dangerous obstacle (with hundreds of migrants dying each year while attempting the crossing), the most determined migrants and their smuggler guides will most likely be redirected rather than deterred—tunneling under or going around or over the new border barrier. And professional smuggling services can be expected to continue to thrive as migrants become even more dependent on hiring a smuggler to successfully navigate the border crossing.

NOTES

1. For a more detailed analysis, see Andreas (2009).
2. This case is an example of what the sociologist Gary Marx calls the interdependence between rule enforcers and rule breakers. See Marx (1981).
3. In 1952, Congress passed an act that made it illegal to "harbor, transport, or conceal illegal entrants." But employment was not considered harboring. This was the result

of an amendment to the provision (called the Texas proviso), which was a concession to agribusiness interests (Calavita, 1994: 60).

4. For example, apprehensions by the Border Patrol in the San Diego sector fell from 531,000 in FY 1993 to 284,000 in FY 1997, but apprehensions to the east in the El Centro sector jumped from 30,000 to 146,000 in the same period (*Migration News,* July 1998).

REFERENCES

Andreas, Peter. 2009. *Border Games: Policing the U.S.-Mexico Divide.* 2nd ed. Ithaca, N.Y.: Cornell University Press.
Andreas, Peter, and Thomas Biersteker, eds. 2003. *The Rebordering of North America: Integration and Exclusion in a New Security Context.* New York: Routledge Press.
Bach, Robert. 1999. Executive Associate Commissioner for Policy and Planning, Immigration and Naturalization Service. Testimony before the House Judiciary Committee, Immigration and Claims Subcommittee, July 1.
Bean, Frank D., Randy Capps, and Charles W. Haynes. 1999. Testimony for the Hearings of the Subcommittee on Immigration and Claims, Committee on the Judiciary, U.S. House of Representatives, February 25.
Bhagwati, Jagdish N. 1984. "Incentives and Disincentives: International Migration." *Weltwirtschaftliches Archiv* 120 (4): 678–704.
Binational Study on Migration. 1997. *Migration between Mexico and the United States: Binational Study.* Mexico City and Washington D.C.: Mexican Foreign Ministry and U.S. Commission on Immigration Reform.
Calavita, Kitty. 1994. "U.S. Immigration and Policy Responses: The Limits of Legislation." In *Controlling Immigration: A Global Perspective,* edited by Wayne A. Cornelius, Philip L. Martin, and James Hollifield, 55–82. Stanford: Stanford University Press.
———. 1996. "The New Politics of Immigration: 'Balanced Budget Conservatism' and the Symbolism of Proposition 187." *Social Problems* 43 (3): 284–305.
Comptroller General of the United States. 1976. *Smugglers, Illicit Documents, and Schemes Are Undermining U.S. Controls over Immigration: Report to the Congress by the Comptroller General of the United States.* Washington, D.C., August 30.
Ekstrand, Laurie E. 1995. U.S. General Accounting Office. Testimony before the Subcommittee on Immigration and Claims, Committee on the Judiciary, U.S. House of Representatives, March 10.
Federal News Service. 1996. News Conference with Janet Reno and Doris Meissner, Washington D.C., January 12.
Heyman, Josiah McC. 1995. "Putting Power into the Anthropology of Bureaucracy: The Immigration and Naturalization Service at the Mexico–United States Border." *Current Anthropology* 36 (2): 261–87.
Koslowski, Rey. 2001. "The Mobility Money Can Buy: Human Smuggling and Border Control in the European Union." In *The Wall around the West,* edited by Peter Andreas and Timothy Snyder, 203–18. Lanham, Md.: Rowman and Littlefield.
Kossoudji, Sherrie A. 1992. "Playing Cat and Mouse at the U.S.-Mexican Border." *Demography* 29 (2): 159–90.
López Castro, Gustavo. 1998. "Coyotes and Alien Smuggling." In *Migration between*

Mexico and the United States: Binational Study. Research Reports and Background Materials, vol. 3. Mexico City and Washington, D.C.: Mexican Ministry of Foreign Affairs and U.S. Commission on Immigration Reform.

Marx, Gary T. 1981. "Ironies of Social Control: Authorities as Contributors to Deviance through Escalation, Nonenforcement, and Covert Facilitation." *Social Problems* 28 (3): 221–46.

Massey, Douglas S. 1997. "March of Folly: U.S. Immigration Policy under NAFTA." Paper presented at the Meetings of the American Sociological Association, Toronto, Canada, August 8–13.

McDonald, William F. 1997. "Illegal Immigration: Crime, Ramifications, and Control (the American Experience)." In *Crime and Law Enforcement in the Global Village,* edited by William F. McDonald, 65–86. Cincinnati: Anderson Publishing Co.

Meissner, Doris. 1996. U.S. Commissioner of the Immigration and Naturalization Service. Testimony before the Commerce, Justice, State, and Judiciary Subcommittee of the Appropriations Committee, U.S. House of Representatives, May 8.

Metz, Leon C. 1989. *Border: The U.S.-Mexico Line.* El Paso, Tex.: Mangan Books.

Nevins, Joseph. 1998. "California Dreaming: Operation Gatekeeper and the Social Geographical Construction of the 'Illegal Alien' along the U.S.-Mexico Boundary." Ph.D. diss., University of California at Los Angeles.

Regan, George. 1997. Acting Associate Commissioner of Enforcement, Immigration and Naturalization Service. Testimony before the Subcommittee on Immigration Claims, Committee on the Judiciary, U.S. House of Representatives, April 23.

Reuter, Peter, and David Ronfeldt. 1991. *Quest for Integrity: The Mexican-U.S. Drug Issue in the 1980s.* Santa Monica, Calif.: RAND.

Rotella, Sebastian. 1998. *Twilight on the Line.* New York: Norton.

Skerry, Peter, and Stephen Rockwell. 1998. "The Cost of a Tighter Border: People-Smuggling Networks." *Los Angeles Times,* May 3.

Stoddard, Ellwyn. 1976. "Illegal Mexican Labor in the Borderlands: Institutionalized Support for an Unlawful Practice." *Pacific Sociological Review* 19 (2): 175–210.

Suro, Robert. 1998. "Tightening Controls and Changing Flows: Evaluating the INS Border Enforcement Strategy." *Research Perspectives on Migration* 2 (1). Carnegie Endowment for International Peace.

Teitelbaum, Michael. 1980. "Right versus Right: Immigration and Refugee Policy—the United States." *Foreign Affairs* 59 (1): 21–59.

U.S. Border Patrol. 1994. "Border Patrol Strategic Plan 1994 and Beyond: National Strategy." U.S. Border Patrol, Washington, D.C. July.

U.S. Department of Justice. 1996. *Annual Report of the Office of the United States Attorney, Southern District of California.* Washington, D.C.: U.S. Department of Justice.

U.S. General Accounting Office. 1997. *Illegal Immigration: Southwest Border Strategy Results Inconclusive; More Evaluation Needed.* Washington, D.C.: GPO. December.

CHAPTER SIX

Global Apartheid, *Coyotaje*, and the Discourse of Clandestine Migration

Distinctions between Personal, Structural, and Cultural Violence

David Spener

In this chapter I propose a reorientation of the public and scholarly discourse about international migration that takes place autonomously, beyond the pale of state regulation. This discourse, whether engaged in by immigrant advocates or immigration restrictionists, typically uses a terminology and a framing of issues that privilege the perspective of state authorities regarding the phenomenon of cross-border migratory movements. In its stead, I draw upon several concepts in the extant literatures on migration, development, and human rights to offer an alternative framework that views autonomous migration as a form resistance to global apartheid enforced at nation-state borders. Specifically, I focus my analysis on the social process by which migrants hire professional or semiprofessional service providers to help them cross international boundaries in spite of states' attempts to exclude them. In place of the state-centric terms *smuggling* and *trafficking*, I refer to this process as *coyotaje* (from *coyote*, the most commonly used Mexican term for these service providers) and highlight the ways in which it constitutes a survival strategy pursued by migrants. In addition, I direct my attention to how we should understand the question of violence inflicted upon migrants as they traverse the U.S.-Mexican border and how to assess who or what is responsible for that violence. In so doing, I make use of Galtung's (1969, 1990) concepts of personal violence, structural violence, and cultural violence to interpreting the tragedies that too often befall migrants as they pursue *coyotaje* as a border-crossing strategy. Discussion of these issues is based primarily on my field research on the clandestine border-crossing experiences of Mexican nationals in the northeastern Mexico–south Texas migratory corridor in the late 1990s and early 2000s.[1]

Conceptual Framework

In both the scholarly and wider public discourse, clandestine border crossing by migrants is typically discussed in ways that emphasize how it violates laws expressing the right of sovereign nation-states to exclude non-nationals from their territories as they see fit. This framing of the issues fails to recognize how such laws also express international power relations in ways that frequently impose great suffering and deprivation on the part of those whom they exclude. Here I propose an alternative framework that emphasizes how the forcible exclusion of migrants from certain national territories in the world system operates as an instrument of labor control and exploitation, while migrants' clandestine border-crossing practices represent a form of resistance to such control and exploitation.

The division of the world into high-wage, high-wealth, high-well-being regions and low-wage, low-wealth, and low-well-being regions has long preoccupied social scientists. One of the most provocative concepts for interpreting this division to have emerged in recent decades is global apartheid (Kohler 1978, 1995; Richmond, 1994; Alexander, 1996; Booker and Minter, 2001), which emphasizes how the maldistribution of resources and well-being worldwide is strongly correlated with race and nationality. In this perspective, control over the mobility and labor of nonwhite populations at the international level is treated as analogous to the treatment of blacks under the apartheid regime that was in place in South Africa from 1948 to 1994. As the authors employing the apartheid concept have noted, border enforcement, or what Heyman (1999b) refers to as interdiction, plays a crucial role in maintaining global inequalities insofar as it maintains separate social, political, and economic spaces in the world system and also restricts the ability of impoverished residents to move from one region to another in search of higher income and a better standard of living. As I have argued elsewhere (Spener, 2006, 2009), the historical and contemporary operation of the U.S.-Mexican border with regard to Mexican labor can be taken as a specific example of the general operation of a global system of apartheid. Here it is also important to recognize that apartheid operates not only by restricting the physical movement of Mexican workers but also by denying them rights and rendering them vulnerable to exploitation by designating them as illegal if they manage to enter U.S. territory in spite of state efforts to halt them at the border (De Genova, 2002: 429). Thus global apartheid expresses itself in North America as a militarized segmentation of the labor market within a transnational region characterized by a highly integrated market for other goods, services, and capital.

A second concept that guides my research on clandestine border crossing is autonomous international migration, proposed by Néstor Rodríguez (1996: 22) to refer to "the movement of people across nation-state borders outside of state regulations." According to Rodríguez, migrant autonomy means that "working class communities in peripheral countries have developed their own policies of international employment independent of interstate planning." Mexicans pursue this type of migration as a survival strategy in which they actively resist their territorial confinement to a low-wage region of the world economy by crossing the border to work in the United States in spite of the considerable efforts by that country's police forces to prevent their entry. By working in the United States, Mexicans are able to retain a far greater absolute amount of the surplus value their labor creates than they could in Mexico, even as their illegal status and stigmatized racial and cultural characteristics render them vulnerable to superexploitation relative to other U.S. workers. This type of resistance does not have system change as a conscious political goal. Rather, it is a household and community reproduction strategy—that is, it permits workers to support their families above the bare minimum of subsistence that would otherwise be possible in their home countries.

Autonomous international migration can be understood as an example of what James C. Scott (1985) refers to as weapons of the weak, the term he uses to describe the indirect, surreptitious, everyday forms of resistance to domination and exploitation engaged in by subaltern populations around the world.[2] Synthesizing the concepts of autonomous international migration and weapons of the weak and translating them into Spanish, I have given the name *resistencia hormiga* to autonomous Mexican migrants' clandestine border-crossing strategies (Spener 2006, 2009).[3] As has been well documented in the literature on Mexican migration to the United States, the resources that migrants draw upon in order to engage in this type of resistance are principally social and cultural. In this sense, we can think of *resistencia hormiga* as being underwritten by a combination of what Bourdieu (1986) called social capital and Vélez-Ibáñez (1988) has referred to as cultural funds of knowledge that have been accumulated in migratory communities.

Mexican migrants have hired coyotes to assist them with entering and/or obtaining employment in the United States since early in the twentieth century. This assistance—*coyotaje*—has taken two basic forms that have formed integral elements in migrants' practice of *resistencia hormiga* over the years. Bureaucratic-evasion *coyotaje* refers to coyotes helping migrants get around the paperwork requirements and/or applicant queues imposed by the U.S. government to enter and work in the country with its official authorization. We see this type of *coyotaje* in operation when coyotes sell migrants false or impostor documents such as alien registration or Social Security cards to present to employers or when coyotes pay U.S. immigration inspectors to allow migrants to pass through ports of entry or highway checkpoints without presenting documents. Clandestine-crossing *coyotaje* refers to migrants hiring coyotes to guide them across the border and transport them clandestinely some distance into the U.S. interior (Spener 2005, 2009). At the beginning of the twenty-first century a variety of more specific types of both bureaucratic-evasion and clandestine-crossing *coyotaje* were being practiced in the northeastern Mexico–south Texas migratory corridor. In my field research, I found that these types varied considerably in terms of their cost, complexity, availability, safety, and likelihood of success, as well as the extent to which relations between migrants and coyotes were embedded in social relations of trust or involved transactions between anonymous parties with no past or future relationship with one another (Spener 2008a, 2008b, 2009). Regardless of the specific type of strategy pursued, it is important to bear in mind that *coyotaje* as a social process involves autonomous migrants seeking out coyotes in order to carry out migratory agendas they set for themselves. Thus, *coyotaje* is an essential element of migrants' *resistencia hormiga* to global apartheid enforced at the U.S.-Mexican border.

The Dominant Discourse: The State's View of "Alien Smuggling" and the Role of the Media in Disseminating It

The story that U.S. government officials have told about the phenomenon of coyote-assisted border crossings over the past fifteen to twenty years contains a number of recurring elements, which have been widely disseminated in the media. First, coyotes are not referred to as providers of navigation, transportation, and housing services actively contracted by migrants but rather as smugglers or "traffickers[4] of passive victims whom they treat as cargo or commodities. This rhetorical construction links *coyotaje* with other phenomena, such as slavery, indentured servitude, and drug trafficking, that are seen by the public as violent, threatening, and morally reprehensible.

A second element in the official discourse is that smugglers are motivated purely by greed and behave accordingly, showing little to no compassion or concern for the well-being of the migrants they transport, especially if showing such concern would reduce their profits. We find this element at play in accounts of failed border crossings in which migrants are left behind on the trail to die of thirst by smugglers who have lied to them about the rigors they would encounter on the journey, or in which too many migrants are loaded into an old and poorly maintained vehicle leading to a fatal accident when the vehicle is chased by the Border Patrol.

A third element is that as U.S. border enforcement activity has intensified over the past two decades, smuggling has become a much more sophisticated, large-scale, and profitable business that is controlled by a small number of organized-crime syndicates. Smaller-scale and more community-based coyotes are presumed to have been driven out of business by the increased difficulty of the crossing as well by as competition and/or intimidation from organized crime groups. These organized crime groups are said to be involved in prostitution, drug trafficking, and weapons trafficking as well, connoting that the "alien trafficking" business is becoming more like those nefarious businesses in terms of the ruthlessness of its entrepreneurs and their willingness to resort to violence to defend their interests. Some scholars (see, for example, Andreas 2000) have argued that U.S. border enforcement policies and tactics have unwittingly produced this undesirable transformation of the smuggling industry. Elsewhere, I have criticized this portrayal as having prematurely announced the demise of smaller-scale and more community-based *coyotaje* enterprises and failing to acknowledge that U.S. officials made similar claims about smuggling in the 1920s, 1950s, and 1970s, leading one to wonder how many times this "industry" can be transformed into something much more sinister than what it had theretofore been (Spener 2004, 2005, 2009).

A fourth discursive element that has come into play since the terrorist attacks on the World Trade Center and the Pentagon on September 11, 2001, is that the transnational organized crime groups engaged in human trafficking pose a dangerous and imminent threat to U.S. national security. Given these groups' reputed willingness to abandon migrants, execute rivals, sell poisons to children, and force women into sexual slavery, it is suggested that such groups would not hesitate to help terrorist organizations move their members across the border to engage in additional attacks on American soil. This element of the official discourse about smuggling/trafficking found its highest expression in the policy report *A Line in the Sand: Confronting the Threat at the Southwest Border,* whose dubious findings were published in the fall of 2006 by the majority staff of the U.S. House of Representatives Committee on Homeland Security, Subcommittee on Investigations. Here again, it is worth noting that anti-immigrant organizations and politicians made similar claims about the national security threat posed by the smuggling of "subversives" across the United States' "open border" with Mexico in the 1920s and 1950s, when the subversives were said to be Bolsheviks (see Slayden, 1921; American G.I. Forum of Texas and Texas State Federation of Labor, 1953; Samora, 1971). Already by the early 1980s, U.S. officials from President Reagan on down to the sector chief of the Border Patrol in south Texas were warning about infiltration not only by Marxist guerrillas from Central America but also by agents of state sponsors of terrorism in the Middle East (see Loh, 1985; Dunn, 1996).

It is not surprising that government officials, especially law enforcement agents, have a very negative opinion of coyotes, given that coyotes so directly undermine what these officials regard to be one of states' basic prerogatives—the regulation of the movement of people across their frontiers. The success of coyote-assisted migrants in penetrating state borders discredits government claims of effectively protecting national territory against foreign incursions and calls into question the competence and efficacy of officials charged with the enforcement of customs and immigration controls (see Heyman 1999a). Thus coyotes represent not only a challenge to state authority but also a threat to the credibility of state bureaucrats concerned with keeping their jobs and advancing their careers. At the same time, government officials can find the threat posed by coyotes to be a useful tool in protecting or even expanding their personnel and budgets. To the extent that coyotes, along with smugglers of weapons and illegal narcotics, can be successfully portrayed as a substantial and growing threat to national security, with the ability to "outgun" law enforcement authorities on the border, state bureaucrats can justify ever increasing budgets for their agencies to combat the threat. This has been done quite successfully by U.S. law enforcement agencies on the border since the 1980s (see Dunn, 1996; Andreas, 2000).

Beginning with Operation Blockade in El Paso, Texas, in 1993, U.S. authorities have greatly intensified vigilance along the country's border with Mexico by launching a series of military-style operations designed to deter autonomous migrants and their coyotes from staging border crossings in populated urban corridors. In south Texas, this took the form of Operation Rio Grande, launched in Brownsville in the summer of 1997 and subsequently extended upstream toward Laredo (see Spener, 2000, 2001, 2009; Maril, 2004). As a consequence, migrants began to traverse new, longer routes through less populated, more inhospitable country that lay between heavily patrolled urban corridors along the border. Predictably, migrant deaths due to drowning, dehydration, and exposure rose dramatically, as did deaths from accidents occurring when vehicles laden with migrants emerging from the brush after walking around highway immigration checkpoints raced away from the border region, often with Border Patrol vehicles in hot pursuit (Cornelius, 2001; Eschbach, Hagan, and Rodríguez, 2001, 2003; Stop Gatekeeper 2004). When human rights organizations blamed rising deaths on immigration authorities' new enforcement tactics, the authorities attempted to shield themselves from these attacks by pointing to "alien smugglers" as the party responsible for the tragedies befalling growing numbers of migrants. For example, when I interviewed a public affairs agent of the Border Patrol in south Texas in May 2001, shortly after fourteen migrants perished while trekking across the Arizona desert near Yuma, he had this to say: "The Border Patrol did not take those people through Yuma. We don't want them to cross! We don't want them to risk their lives. . . . I mean we're not pushing the people to cross in some other places. It's the smugglers who are the ones deciding where to cross. And they're deciding that they want the group to die rather than get arrested by the Border Patrol. It's up to them! In so many ways."

Moreover, this same agent averred that migrants, far from being the victims, had been the main beneficiaries of the Border Patrol's enforcement operations since the early 1990s. Having more agents guarding the border, he insisted, meant that the Border Patrol could do a more effective job in protecting migrants against victimization by their "smugglers" and other "border bandits" who worked in collusion with them. Identifying "smugglers" as the principal source of violence inflicted on migrants not only diverted attention from the authorities' responsibility for the dangers facing migrants but also enabled these same authorities to cast themselves in the role of the protectors of migrants rather than as their persecutors. Speaking about the question of human "trafficking" elsewhere in the world, Wong (2005) contends that the state-sponsored discourse about the phenomenon emphasizes the need to protect women and other victims of trafficking, whose prevalence is greatly exaggerated to generate moral panic in the public, while state practice in attacking the problem serves first and foremost to reinforce the boundaries that migrants turn to "traffickers" in order to overcome.

My field research on Mexican migrants' clandestine border-crossing experiences in the northeastern Mexico–south Texas migratory corridor at the beginning of the twenty-first century has led me to conclude that these relentlessly negative portrayals of coyotes and *coyotaje* offered by official sources and published in the press are often simplistic and exaggerated and sometimes even quite misleading. In interviews and observations conducted in the northeastern Mexico–south Texas corridor during the 1998–2005 period, I found that (a) coyotes' behavior often could not be neatly categorized as virtuous or villainous; (b) *coyotaje* took a variety of different forms, many, if not most, of which took place outside the direction of organized crime syndicates; (c) relations between migrants and coyotes at times could be relatively friendly and cooperative rather than anonymous and abusive; (d) more than a few migrants were reasonably satisfied with the services provided by their coyotes; and (e) migrants did not necessarily blame their coyotes for hardships and dangers encountered on their cross-border journeys.[5]

Nevertheless, negative characterizations of smugglers and traffickers by government officials dominated media coverage of border issues during this period. There are several reasons why the state's perspective on the phenomenon is disseminated by the media to the exclusion of perspectives that might be offered by other actors knowledgeable about the practices associated with autonomous migration by Mexicans. These are important to understand, since the only knowledge that most U.S. and Mexican citizens have of the social process of clandestine border crossing comes from what they see, hear, and read in the media.[6]

One of the chief reasons that the views of government officials predominate in news coverage of border issues is that their views are taken by the press as newsworthy by virtue of the positions of bureaucratic authority they occupy. In addition, the U.S. Department of Homeland Security is the only institution in south Texas concerned with issues of immigration and border enforcement to have a well-developed public relations infrastructure at its disposal. Needless to say, autonomous migrants and their coyotes have no such public relations apparatus to rely upon to get out their side of the story. Indeed, instead of seeking to influence public opinion about their activities, they do everything possible to protect their anonymity and clandestinity in an effort to evade capture and prosecution by the law enforcement authorities. Thus, while reporters working under deadline on tight budgets find it easy to obtain interviews and information from the Border Patrol, they have to work hard to even locate migrants and coyotes that have information relevant to the news events they are covering, much less interview them in depth. Relatedly, most coyote-assisted border crossings never make the news at all unless they involve a death, an accident, or an arrest of some kind. In other words, successful crossings in which coyotes render services to migrants competently and without abusing them are not called to the public's attention except in those few instances in which journalists are allocated funds and time to undertake special investigative reports. Even in such cases, the legitimating force of the law itself influences reporters' perspectives, especially if some of the most voluble and articulate people they find to interview are law enforcement officials who emphasize the criminality of smuggling as an activity and their own role in upholding the rule of law.[7] In some cases, reporters may defer to law enforcement officials' framing of smuggling issues so as not to jeopardize their access to them as valuable sources of breaking news. In other cases, reporters may not be able to interview migrants and coyotes who have been apprehended by U.S. authorities, since most are returned to Mexico quickly after they have been detained.[8] The legal jeopardy faced by those who remain in custody as suspects or material witnesses gives them little incentive to speak with reporters.

Assigning Responsibility for Violence Suffered by Migrants

As they resist the territorial confinement and material deprivations imposed upon them by the system of global apartheid, migrants confront a variety of forms of violence, both direct and indirect. In order to comprehend and properly contextualize the types of violence suffered by autonomous Mexican migrants who cross the U.S. border clandestinely with the assistance of coyotes, we must employ a definition of violence as an analytical concept that is at once capacious and concise. Following Nevins (2003, 2005), here I employ the definition offered by Johan Galtung, which fulfills these two conditions. Galtung's definition has the advantage of its consistency with many human rights concepts, such as those codified in the Universal Declaration of Human Rights, that contemplate not only acts of physical aggression against persons but also persons being systematically deprived of things vital to their health and development, regardless of whether or not an identifiable individual perpetrator or set of perpetrators is responsible for such deprivation. For Galtung (1969: 168), "violence is present when human beings are being influenced so that their actual somatic and mental realizations are below their potential realizations." To address the question of responsibility, Galtung (1969: 170–71) splits this general concept of violence into two types—personal (or direct) violence, in which there is an identifiable individual actor or set of actors that directly commits acts of violence against a victim or set of victims, and structural violence, in which no individual perpetrator commits a discrete act, but rather the organization of society is such that "violence is built into the structure and shows up as unequal power and consequently unequal life chances." Structural violence, he argues, is roughly synonymous with "social injustice," a concept that is also congruent with policies or acts that violate universally acknowledged human rights. In a subsequent article, Galtung (1990: 291) added the concept of cultural violence to the two types discussed above, which he defined as "those aspects of culture—the symbolic sphere of our existence—exemplified by religion and ideology, language and art, empirical science and formal science (logic, mathematics)—that can be used to justify or legitimize direct or structural violence."[9]

Using Galtung's framework, we can see that most of the attention given to the question of violence against migrants in the public discourse about immigration and border issues in recent years has focused on personal violence inflicted on them by specific actors, especially smugglers. While this public discourse includes a general recognition of lack of adequate economic opportunity in Mexico and ongoing demand for low-wage migrant labor in the United States, it does not typically contemplate these issues as examples of structural violence or social injustice. Nationalist ideology and belief in the rule of law operate as cultural violence to legitimate the prevailing inequalities between Mexico and the United States and provide a rationale for policing the movement of people back and forth across the border between the two countries.[10] Indeed, they combine to "naturalize" the militarized separation of national territories and populations. As I argue below, the discourse about security on the border that focuses on acts of personal violence committed by coyotes against migrants can also be understood as an aspect of cultural violence insofar as it diverts our attention from migrants' resistance to structural violence that takes the form of global apartheid enforced at national borders.

Personal Violence Committed against Migrants: Coyotes and the U.S. Border Patrol

Numerous documented incidents of personal violence committed against migrants by their coyotes in the northeastern Mexico–south Texas border region have been reported in the press since the launching of Operation Rio Grande in the summer of 1997. These have included cases of abandonment on the trail, rape, sodomy, beatings, kidnapping, shootings, and fatal vehicle accidents caused, at least in part, by reckless driving on the part of coyotes (Winingham and Schiller, 1999; Burnett, 2001; Hegstrom, 2001; King 2001; Davis 2004). The most horrific example of this type of violence was the death by hyperthermia and asphyxiation of nineteen migrants who were being transported in the sealed trailer of a tractor-trailer rig near Victoria, Texas, in May 2003 (see Ramos, 2005). It should not come as a surprise that some coyotes would routinely or on occasion commit acts of personal violence against migrants, given that (a) most coyotes are young males in their prime criminogenic years; (b) they guide, transport, and house migrants clandestinely in socially and legally unregulated situations in which migrants are inherently vulnerable to abuse; and (c) they may have real incentives to commit violent acts if they believe they can do so without being subjected to immediate retribution. These incidents, documented in the press, are taken as prima facie evidence of the increasingly violent character of coyotes in the contemporary period of ever intensifying border surveillance, although we should also remember that coyotes in this region have been characterized as ruthless and violent for many decades (see Samora, 1971; Spener, 2005, 2009). Indeed, in spite of the absence of any quantified research data tracking changes in the relative frequency of violent acts committed by coyotes against their customers, coyotes are typically regarded by government officials and the press as intrinsically and uniformly abusive of the migrants they guide and transport, a view that has gone largely uncontested by scholars or human rights advocates. As I have argued elsewhere (Spener, 2008a, 2009), relations between coyotes and migrant communities are often sufficiently socially embedded and characterized by what Portes (1995) has called "bounded solidarity" and "enforceable trust" that migrants are at least somewhat protected from malfeasance by coyotes, though such is not always the case.

During this same period, human rights activists and the press have reported numerous abuses of migrants by U.S. border and immigration enforcement authorities in this region that also fall under the personal violence rubric. These have included beatings and sexual assaults, as well as threats, verbal abuse, shootings, and arbitrary detentions based on ethnicity, including of U.S. citizens (Amnesty International, 1998; Selzer, 1998; Gregor, 2000; Pinkerton, 2000; Maril, 2004; Valley Movement for Human Rights, 2005; "Border Patrol Agent Found Guilty," 2007). Unlike coyotes, U.S. Department of Homeland Security agents are portrayed in the press as nonabusive under normal circumstances, while personal violence committed by agents against migrants is generally portrayed as exceptional. Nevertheless, we should also not be surprised that at least some Homeland Security agents commit acts of personal violence against migrants, given (a) the inherently confrontational nature of their encounters with migrants; (b) the cultural differences between agents and migrants; (c) agents' socialization toward nationalist and even subtly racist attitudes toward migrants; and (d) the fact that agents increasingly apprehend migrants in isolated rural areas in situations in which they may be able to abuse them undetected by other members of their chain of command.

Human rights activists on both sides of the border are well aware of the types of violence that befall migrants at the hands of coyotes, Border Patrol agents, and other law enforcement officials. An activist I interviewed in south Texas in 2001 did not offer an opinion as to who committed more or worse acts of violence against migrants, recognizing only that both coyotes and Border Patrol agents seriously abused migrants on occasion. He did, however, note that it was only the coyotes who were branded as criminals:

> Who are the coyotes? They're people. Just like Border Patrol agents. They're all people. They're both people in a situation where they wield a great deal of power over others. And in such a situation, some will take advantage of that, and some won't. We have some Border Patrol agents who do some really terrible things and some who don't at all. It's just a job, they're going in and putting in their time. I don't see coyotes as a lot different. . . . But as soon as someone is labeled as a criminal, that's used to dehumanize them, no? . . . You apply that to immigrants, hey, they're lawbreakers, they're criminals, they're not human! So, a whole process of dehumanization is opened up. I think it's the same thing with coyotes. If you call them all "evil" then you can do anything you want to them.

No discussion of violence committed against migrants would be complete without a consideration of gender. Mexican women who cross the border clandestinely face serious risk of sexual violence being committed against them by coyotes, law enforcement officials, and other migrants, especially if they are unaccompanied by male family members. Although committing sexual abuse against women is no more intrinsic to the male coyote role than it is to the male Border Patrol agent or male migrant roles, coyotes are typically assumed to be sexual predators, while other migrants and law enforcement agents are not. In this regard, we would do well to recognize that coyotes or Border Patrol agents who commit sexual violence against women do not do so as coyotes or Border Patrol agents per se but rather as men, whose attitudes and behaviors have been forged in a wider culture of violence toward women. In addition, we should bear in mind that there are coyotas as well as coyotes, some of whom specialize in bringing other women across the border. *Coyotaje* may also on occasion serve as a strategy for helping women escape violence in their home communities, as was the case with a young Mexican woman I interviewed who had fled across the border with her toddler son to get away from her battering husband. The woman's mother had arranged for her daughter to cross with the same coyotes who had safely brought her to the United States several years earlier. The woman had found the experience frightening but was delivered unharmed to her destination as promised to her mother by the coyotes. Finally, it is worth noting that in spite of the growth of migration to the United States by Mexican women in recent decades, crossing the border clandestinely without documents appears to remain an overwhelmingly male practice: between 80 and 85 percent of the adult migrants apprehended annually by the Border Patrol in the first five years of the twenty-first century were men (data supplied to author by the U.S. Border Patrol on May 24, 2007).

Structural Violence: The Context within Which Personal Violence against Migrants Occurs

U.S. law enforcement authorities, especially the Border Patrol and the Immigration and Customs Enforcement (ICE) unit of the Department of Homeland Security, play an active and indispensable role in the maintenance of global apartheid with regard to relations between the United States and Mexico. Although global apartheid as a system does not normally involve state agents inflicting direct violence on autonomous migrants, it clearly fulfills Galtung's definition as a form of structural violence against actual and potential migrants insofar as it constitutes an aspect of social structure that denies them access to the means to meet their minimal subsistence needs and/or forces them to engage in high-risk behaviors—such as trekking on foot through deserts—in order to meet them. The immigration and border control apparatus of the U.S. Department of Homeland Security as well as the U.S. attorneys and courts that prosecute the migrant practitioners of *resistencia hormiga* are indispensable elements in the institutionalization of global apartheid—that is, they form part of the structural violence imposed on migrants.

Some analysts have suggested (see, for example, Andreas, 2000: 21–26) that a perversely symbiotic relationship exists between the Border Patrol and smugglers insofar as escalation of border control by the state expands the market and increases revenues for smugglers. This raises the question of how to interpret the role played by coyotes in the structure of global apartheid. Clearly, intensified border enforcement induces more migrants to contract the services of coyotes than might otherwise be the case. In addition, at least some coyotes make mutually beneficial arrangements with agents of the U.S. immigration enforcement bureaucracy to allow them to bring their migrant customers across the border. One could argue, on this basis, that to the extent that migrants are increasingly obliged to contract the ever more expensive services of coyotes and that, as a consequence, coyotes profit from state escalation of border enforcement, the interests of coyotes and the state are somehow allied against migrant interests—that is, that coyotes also form an integral part of the repressive structure of global apartheid.

There are three reasons why I believe such a conclusion is misplaced. First, generally speaking, U.S. law enforcement authorities do not collaborate with or tolerate coyotes but instead dedicate significant personnel and resources to actively pursue, prosecute, incarcerate, and, ultimately, exterminate coyotes and eliminate the practice of *coyotaje*. Second, coyotes do not monopolize clandestine crossing of the border, standing in the way of migrants seeking to enter the United States and extracting a "toll" from them if they wish to pass. Available data suggest that at least through 2003 a large percentage of autonomous Mexican migrants continued to cross the border without contracting coyotes. Third, in spite of the rip-offs and failures that occur, coyotes generally fulfill the terms of their contract with migrants and deliver them to their U.S. destinations after successfully evading apprehension by the authorities in the border region. For this reason, migrants seek the services of coyotes, often based on recommendations from their peers or on personal familiarity with coyotes who operate in their communities, in order to advance their migratory agendas in spite of the obstacles placed in their path by the U.S. government. It is also for this reason, combined with the deprivations and dangers that they face if they stay home, that migrants generally ignore government warnings not to trust coyotes and continue to transact business with them to cross the border.

Instead of concluding that coyotes participate in the enactment of global apartheid and thus in the production of structural violence against migrants, I believe it is more accurate to view the relationship between migrants and their coyotes as a strategic alliance in the social field of border crossing, one of the principal fields in which migrant resistance to global apartheid takes place.[11] This structurally produced alliance is an uneasy and frequently conflictive one that is entered into for practical reasons rather than moral, affective, or political ones. Nevertheless, it is fostered by shared class and cultural characteristics between migrants and coyotes and their confrontation with a common enemy that persecutes them both in nearly equal measure. The fact that some coyotes take advantage of the vulnerability of the migrants who hire them in order to commit serious and unpardonable abuses—and some do—does not contradict the overall argument that migrants and coyotes share common interests and objectives in their everyday battles with apartheid at the border. In this regard, we should remind ourselves that many forms of personal violence are inflicted upon victims by people with whom they are engaged in close relationships—husbands abusing wives, parents abusing children, union shop-floor stewards abusing machine operators, sergeants abusing enlisted men—within societal institutions generally characterized by high levels of in-group solidarity.

We may better understand acts of personal violence committed against migrants by coyotes if we place such acts in the context of the structural violence generated by the escalation of border interdiction by states as part of the system of global apartheid. The escalation of border enforcement affects the relations between migrants and coyotes and the behavior of coyotes toward migrants in several ways. First, as Heyman (1999a) and others have noted, it makes migrants more likely to enter into relations with coyotes get across the border. Second, escalation obliges coyotes to guide migrants through more remote, hazardous terrain for longer distances than was previously the case, with consequent increased danger of accident and death to migrants and coyotes alike. Third, intensified prosecution of coyotes by the authorities with increased penalties upon conviction may give added incentives to coyotes to engage in violent behaviors to protect themselves at the expense of migrants. This may help explain, for example, some of the high-speed chases initiated by Border Patrol and other law enforcement agents in which coyotes at the wheel attempt to escape capture by "bailing out" of the vehicles in which they are transporting migrants and escaping into the brush. Escalation may also lead some coyotes to try to exert more direct physical control over migrants in an effort to avoid detection by authorities, both while in transit and in safe houses, as well as to instill more fear in migrants about the potential consequences of identifying their coyotes to the authorities. Thus government efforts to prosecute coyotes, far from protecting migrants, may actually have the effect of placing them at greater risk. Speaking about the escalation of state border control efforts in Canada and Europe as well as on the U.S.-Mexican border, Sharma (2005: 96–97) notes that the main result of antitrafficking/antismuggling campaigns has been to "make illegalized migrations much more dangerous" and to make "the emergence of modern-day Harriet Tubmans even more unlikely."[12]

One of the forms of personal violence for which coyotes are most commonly blamed is leaving lagging migrants behind on the trail while trekking across the border on foot. Several ambiguities have arisen in my interviews with migrants that complicate assigning blame for such incidents. One issue is whether migrants themselves also share responsibility for leaving a comrade behind, especially given that they typically considerably outnumber their guides in the brush and their guides are not usually armed. Indeed, I have interviewed migrants in San Luis Potosí state who told me of having overruled their coyote when he proposed leaving someone behind on the trail: either he waited for the lagging member of their group, or none of them would continue with him, meaning the coyote and his collaborators would lose all the money they expected to collect from the group, not just the amount corresponding to the individual who would have been left behind.[13] To my surprise, several other Mexican men I interviewed in rural Guanajuato, San Luis Potosí, and in Texas told me they did not necessarily hold coyotes responsible when they left someone behind on the trail. In their opinion, migrants knew that the trek across the border and through south Texas was dangerous and that they needed to be physically strong in order to make it. They knew that coyotes were prone to understating how long a trek might take, and they also knew people from their area who had died making the attempt, even when crossing with "good" coyotes. In their opinion, whether you made it or not depended upon how prepared your own body was for withstanding the rigors of the trek. Coyotes and other migrants in the group had an obligation to try to help their comrades along as they were able, but it wasn't always possible. If you were traveling with a close friend or a relative, that person would stay back with you and help you get out to a road, but you couldn't expect all the others to give themselves up to the Border Patrol. In the extreme conditions of the south Texas brush country, that friend or relative might not even be able to do much to help you. A man from San Luis Potosí whom I interviewed in a Texas city in 2004 had this to say about two men he knew from his hometown:

Arnulfo: Well, there are stories like ours where people didn't suffer too much and there are other stories where people suffered tremendously. For example, about four or five years ago, a friend of mine from home began working as a coyote. Work was scarce, so he began to take people across. And once he brought a family member with him, another one of my friends. It was his uncle. And he died on him on the trail. He had to leave him there in the *monte.* He was an older guy [*era un señor*].
Spener: Was it the coyote's fault or was it simply so difficult that . . .
Arnulfo: No! It's that it was his family member. I don't think it was his fault. He was bringing him along as a family member. He says he left him behind because he just couldn't go on any further. The man himself [i.e., the dying uncle] told him he should just leave him there, he couldn't go on.

Under conditions such as these—imposed by an apartheid state and its agents—we might question whether assigning blame to individuals for these tragedies is actually as straightforward as it is typically made out to be.

In order to better understand why migrants sometimes pardon what outsiders might regard as unpardonable abuses committed against them by their coyotes, we should also consider the way in which global apartheid as a form of structural violence contributes to the worldview and attitudes that migrants hold about life generally and about autonomous migration strategies in particular. In this regard, Bourdieu's (1977) concept of habitus proves useful.[14] Migrants' habitus conditions their border-crossing practices in terms of the risks they are willing to assume and the types of behaviors on the part of their coyotes that they are willing to tolerate. Several generations of migratory experience in Mexico have led to not only the accumulation of considerable stocks of migration-related social and human capital (Singer and Massey, 1998; Phillips and Massey, 2000) but also a set of expectations about border crossing into which aspiring migrants are socialized. This socialization takes place both at the face-to-face level among members of the same social network and through popular culture and the media, in which a variety of forms (e.g., *corridos,* films, telenovelas, public service announcements on television and radio) warn of the dangers of the crossing and of placing one's faith in a coyote.

Other aspects of migration habitus are attributable to migrants' day-to-day experiences of general living conditions as members of the Mexican working class or peasantry. One of the main aspects of these general living conditions is *precariousness,* which manifests itself in inadequate and unreliable income, diet, health care, water supply, sanitation, transportation, and security, all as a consequence of the prevailing international political economy and the state's neglect of its most basic obligations to its citizens. Thus migrants learn to expect and then bear bad conditions as a matter of course in their lives, including as they make heroic efforts to improve their condition by heading north. This, too, we might consider as part of a migratory habitus arising from the historical lack of adequate economic opportunities in Mexico for its working class and peasantry, intensified by the state's pursuit of neoliberal policies that are one of the corollaries of global apartheid. It is in this socialized context that migrants transact business with coyotes. They have been warned that crossing the border is dangerous, that conditions will be harsh, that Border Patrol vigilance is intense, that they may have to make several attempts before reaching their destination, and that some people die on the way. In this sense, the generalized situation of structural violence that constitutes their lived experiences can prepare migrants to "pardon" all but the most egregious abuses committed against them by their coyotes.

Cultural Violence: *Coyotaje* and the Mystification of Structural Violence in Public Discourse

The taking of personal responsibility for one's actions is a fundamental tenet of modern Western morality, especially where harm to another is involved. As the late University of Chicago political philosopher Iris Young (2006:116) noted, the assigning of blame to individuals or discrete groups of individuals for harms caused to others is also a fundamental tenet of Western legal systems. She refers to this approach to assigning responsibility as the liability model: "Under this liability model, one assigns responsibility to a particular agent (or agents) whose actions can be shown to be causally connected to the circumstances for which responsibility is sought. . . . When the actions were voluntary and were undertaken knowingly . . . it is appropriate to blame the agents for the harmful outcomes." When migrants are injured or die as they attempt to enter the United States with the assistance of coyotes, the U.S. legal system typically holds coyotes criminally responsible for these harms. Even in cases in which coyotes are apprehended but no actual harm to the migrants who hired them has occurred, the penalties assigned by U.S. courts are greater if prosecutors can prove that the coyotes knowingly endangered migrants in some way. The rhetoric employed by U.S. law enforcement officials who capture and prosecute coyotes often emphasizes the coyotes' moral culpability for actions that harmed or had the potential to harm migrants. In so doing, these law enforcement officials cast themselves in the role of the protector of migrants and the avenger of wrongs committed against them. They are able to do this because any consideration of the contribution to the harm to migrants by the broader structures of global apartheid of which they form a part is inadmissible in the legal debate over assessing culpability in such cases. In other words, the law enforcement system and the agents who enact it operate with a liability model of justice that prepares them to address problems of personal violence but not the problems of structural violence in which problems of personal violence are so deeply embedded.

The most dramatic example of prosecutorial rhetoric regarding the moral culpability of coyotes not surprisingly comes from the most tragic case involving the deaths of autonomous migrants attempting to enter the United States: the May 2003 death of nineteen people near Victoria, Texas, mentioned earlier in this chapter. U.S. and Mexican authorities identified and successfully prosecuted fourteen defendants who had participated in organizing this fatal journey in one way or another. Prosecutors sought the death penalty for the driver of the rig, a Jamaican immigrant named Tyrone Williams, who they said was the defendant most responsible for the deaths of the migrants. In announcing that his office would seek the death penalty for Williams, U.S. Attorney Michael Shelby said, "Where an act, intentionally undertaken in reckless disregard for human life, directly results in the single largest loss of life in any contemporary smuggling operation, justice and the law demand the accused face the ultimate punishment upon conviction" (quoted in Rice, 2004).

In his opening statement in the first of Williams's two trials,[15] Assistant U.S. Attorney Daniel Rodríguez characterized the "smugglers" as constituting a "criminal enterprise that treated people worse than cattle on the way to the slaughterhouse" and said that Williams was "the most heartless, evil and cruel member of the organization" (quoted in Lozano, 2005a). In his closing statement in Williams's second trial, Rodríguez argued that the "legal status, national origin, and race" of the victims in the case were immaterial to what had happened to them because "the value of a human life in this country is the same." Further, he argued, jurors should "send a message to [Williams]—and not just to him, but to people of his ilk, that justice in this country means justice for all. . . . The only justifiable decision in this case is death. Those people didn't deserve to die" (quoted in George, 2007). Williams's attorney, however, in his closing arguments before the jury in his client's first trial, maintained that "the government has overcharged Tyrone Williams. They looked around and saw a tremendous tragedy, a humongous waste of human life. They saw the sorrow and shame and said somebody needs to pay with his life" (quoted in Lozano, 2005b). At no time in the trial was there any significant discussion of the policies of the U.S. government or the governments of the countries of the dead migrants that prompted nearly one hundred of them to board that truck after stealing across the Río Bravo under cover of night. Neither of the U.S. attorneys quoted above, whose office worked closely with the Border Patrol and ICE to prosecute and jail thousands of migrants for "illegal entry" into the United States through south Texas (see Transaction Records Clearinghouse, 2005), acknowledged any aspect of the government's own apartheid policies in producing the situation leading to the deaths of the migrants. Furthermore, little, if any, of the news coverage of the tragedy itself and the trials that followed it suggested that the policies of the U.S. government were implicated in these deaths in any way. Galtung's concept of cultural violence helps us understand how the omission of a public consideration of the extent of the state's responsibility for the migrants' deaths is possible insofar as the concept calls our attention to the ways in which nationalist ideology and the belief in the rule of law as sacrosanct have come to "naturalize" the militarized separation of territories and peoples. It also helps explain how the state and the media have been largely successful in their attempts to assign unique responsibility for migrant deaths to the coyotes who guide and transport them.

Ultimately, jurors in the second and definitive trial accepted Williams's attorney's argument and rejected the death penalty, although they did find him guilty of "alien smuggling," for which he received a life sentence. One of the jurors in that trial reported that although the jurors had the victims "first and foremost" in their minds, they rejected the death penalty because they believed that Williams expected the people to live, given that he had successfully transported migrants in his trailer before (George, 2007). The jury foreman told reporters that "at no point in time . . . was there intent for anyone to die." Moreover, he said, "As a group, we feel good and at peace with ourselves [and] with our decision" (quoted in Hart, 2007). The decision regarding the death penalty was unanimous and reached without discord among the jurors (Blumenthal, 2007). The journalist Jorge Ramos, in his 2005 book *Morir en el intento,* published almost two years before the jury's decision to spare Williams, believed that the U.S. authorities' attempt to convince a jury of the coyotes' intent to kill the migrants who died in the trailer was destined from the outset to fail: "This was obvious to those who followed the phenomenon of undocumented immigration to the United States. It was very clear that the Victoria case was, simply, an operation that turned out badly, very badly. It is not in the interest of any coyote, no matter how insensitive he is, to have the migrants that he is trying to transport die. As cold as it may sound, coyotes don't get paid for dead migrants. They need them alive" (Ramos, 2005: 134, translated by Spener).[16]

Although the jurors in the Williams trial found the prosecutors to have overreached in seeking the death penalty for the defendant, no public reconsideration took place in the aftermath of the Victoria tragedy of the role played by structural as opposed to personal violence in producing the migrants' deaths. Instead, a few months after the tragedy occurred, the Texas legislature passed HB 2096, a law making certain aspects of human smuggling/trafficking crimes under state law as well as under federal law. The U.S. and Mexican governments, though they could reach no agreement on reforming a broken immigration system between the two countries, launched the Oasis Program to redouble their efforts to dismantle "alien smuggling" and "human trafficking" organizations. The U.S. Border Patrol and the U.S. Attorney's Office in the Del Rio, Texas, area began a policy of "zero tolerance" of "illegal entry," meaning all migrants captured by the Border Patrol would be prosecuted and sentenced to jail time before being formally deported to their country of origin. This included Mexican nationals, who theretofore had been routinely "voluntarily returned" to Mexico immediately following apprehension (Contreras, 2006). Over the next several years, the themes of a border "out of control" and under "assault" by organized bands of criminals, many of whom purportedly were Mexican and Central American "illegals" who entered the country by sneaking across the border, came to dominate the public discourse about migration. Not surprisingly, immigration reform efforts in the U.S. Congress foundered, while calls to build new walls along the border were heeded, the National Guard was called out to assist the Border Patrol in arresting autonomous migrants, and ICE agents were unleashed in raids on immigrant workplaces around the country. The rhetoric that prosecutors employed against the smugglers in the Victoria case is of a piece with this broader discourse of cultural violence that variously serves to justify, mystify, and divert our attention from the underlying structural violence that at once motivates autonomous migration and endangers those who engage in it.

In her theoretical work about global justice, Iris Young (2006: 119) argued that the personal liability model described above was inadequate to address problems of "structural injustice" that transcended international boundaries. To address problems of structural injustice, she proposed developing a social connection model. Such a model would recognize the ways that individuals together bear responsibility for "unjust outcomes" insofar as they contribute to them as a consequence of actions they take within the "diverse institutional processes" that constitute social structures that inflict violence on others. Steps taken toward applying such a model of justice would represent a turn away from a vision of the world in which individuals are uniquely responsible for their own welfare and violence is recognized only insofar as it involves overt acts committed by one individual party against another individual party. It is the type of model we will need if we are ever to begin to dismantle systems of structural violence such as global apartheid. Its adoption and application to the situation facing migrants at the U.S.-Mexican border would also represent a turn away from the cultural violence that criminalizes their nonviolent survival strategies, promotes the demonization and persecution of anyone who assists them in their practice of *resistencia hormiga,* and masks the underlying causes of their suffering.

NOTES

The author thanks Trinity University and the John D. and Catharine T. MacArthur Foundation for generous support of the research and reflection that made the publication of this essay possible. In addition, he acknowledges the helpful comments on this chapter received from participants in the conference titled "Migration and Human Rights in the North American Corridor" held at the University of Chicago in October 2007, as well as the critical comments from two anonymous reviewers from *Migración y Desarrollo.*

1. This qualitative research was limited to the experiences of Mexican migrants from sending regions in Mexico with a long-standing migratory tradition, especially small towns and rural communities in the states of Guanajuato, Nuevo León, and Guanajuato. It was carried out between 1998 and early 2006 in a part of the U.S.-Mexican border region whose characteristics differed substantially from those obtaining in other parts of the region, such as the Alta-Baja and Arizona-Sonora corridors. My informants did not include migrants working in agriculture, where relations between migrants, coyotes, and farm labor contractors may involve considerably higher levels of abuse and exploitation than I encountered in my fieldwork (see Krissman, 2000). For these reasons, the findings and interpretations reported in these pages may not be readily generalized to other populations in other settings.

2. I am not the first scholar to see the utility of Scott's concept to analyzing Mexican migration. Anthropologist Rachel Adler has also described some of the "weapons of the weak" used by the Yucatecan migrants she has studied as they pursue what she refers to as their migratory agendas (2000, 173; 2004, 57–59).

3. My use of this neologism was inspired by two sources. First, in an interview I conducted in San Antonio, a Mexican man described to me how U.S. border enforcement was ineffective because migrants were like ants and would always find "some little hole" in the border to get through. Second, the term *contrabando hormiga* is often used in Mexico and elsewhere in Latin America to describe the small-scale, extralegal movement of merchandise across national borders. *Resistencia hormiga* nicely parallels this usage. In addition, the term *resistencia hormiga* can be seen as a peaceful analogue to the war of the flea tactics (Taber, 1965, 2002) practiced by guerrilla fighters in twentieth century anti-imperialist struggles around the world. See Heyman (1999a) for a more extensive exploration of the analogy between clandestine border crossing and guerrilla struggles.

4. These two terms are often used interchangeably in public discourse, even though they are defined differently under international law. According to the 2000 United Nations Protocol to Prevent, Suppress, and Punish Trafficking, "human smuggling" referred to situations in which migrants paid another party to help them gain illegal entry into a state in which they were neither a citizen nor a permanent resident (Laczko, 2002). It defined "human trafficking" as similar to "smuggling," with the added ingredient of

the "traffickers" taking control over the persons being trafficked in order to exploit them against their will (Laczko, 2002). Although "smugglers" hired by Mexican migrants sometimes in reality turn out to be "traffickers" as defined by the UN protocol, such is not the case for the vast majority of the many thousands of Mexicans who hire a "smuggler" to cross the border annually.

5. Other recent research appears to corroborate several elements of this assessment. A 2006 survey conducted in migrant-sending communities in the Yucatán by a team from the University of California–San Diego found that 92 percent of respondents reported that their coyotes had fulfilled the terms of their agreement with them on their last border crossing, while only 8 percent reported having been abused by their coyotes. Unpublished data from the Mexican Migration Field Research and Training Program, Center for Comparative Immigration Studies, University of California–San Diego, 2006 survey in Yucatán. Received in personal communication from Wayne Cornelius on August 11, 2006.

6. Several of the points I make in this section echo similar arguments Klinenberg (2002) made about press coverage of a heat wave that took place in Chicago in 1995, in which over seven hundred people died. See also Gans (2003) regarding the relationship between reporters and government officials.

7. Nevins (2005) has written cogently about the legitimating power of the law with regard to generating U.S. public support for more stringent border enforcement measures. Here I suggest that reporters are no less likely to have been socialized into the default position that the law represents what is right and just than other U.S. residents and that their reporting reflects and reinforces that worldview.

8. This has always routinely happened with Mexican migrants, who typically are "voluntarily returned" to Mexico within a few hours of their detention by the Border Patrol. Now, with the launching of the binational Oasis Program, Mexican nationals who are purportedly engaging in "alien smuggling" and are captured by U.S. authorities on U.S. soil can be turned over to Mexican authorities for prosecution in Mexico. The reason for doing this is that legal requirements for prosecuting smuggling defendants in Mexico do not include prosecutors having to produce material witnesses to their crimes, as is the case in U.S. federal courts. This aspect of the program may remind readers of the practice of "extraordinary rendition" of terrorist suspects by the United States to third countries where legal protections of defendants are less stringent than in the United States. See Secretaría de Relaciones Exteriores (2005); Cano (2006); Diario de Juárez (2007).

9. Galtung's definition of cultural violence overlaps considerably with Bourdieu's (1977: 191) concept of symbolic violence, which adds the ingredient of euphemization or mystification to Galtung's formulation. In other words, symbolic violence serves not only to legitimate but at times to mask other types of violence by attributing responsibility for them to other than their true sources (see also Imbusch, 2003). In this article, I use the term *cultural violence* to refer to instances of euphemization, mystification, or ignoring of violence, as well as its legitimation.

10. Galtung (1996: 203) himself identified nationalism and legal systems more generally as forms that cultural violence could take.

11. My use of the term *social field* follows Bourdieu and Wacquant (1992).

12. For readers who are not familiar with details of the history of slavery in the United States prior to the Civil War, Harriet Tubman was an African American woman who is

revered for having helped southern slaves escape to freedom in the north as a leader of what was known as the "Underground Railroad."

13. Another example of migrants exerting control over their coyotes on the trail comes from a newspaper report from the Arizona desert. Seventy-seven Mexican and Central American migrants overpowered their guide, who had gotten lost while leading them and attempted to abandon them; they took his cell phone and called 911 to be rescued (Mural, 2005).

14. For Bourdieu (1977: 72), the habitus possessed by individuals consists of a system of "durable and transposable dispositions" that serve as "principles of the generation and structuring of practices and representations" that enable them "to cope with unforeseen and ever-changing situations." People are not typically conscious of the principles that constitute their worldview and guide their actions—their habitus—because they are socialized into them unconsciously. The type of habitus possessed by an individual depends upon the social positions he or she has occupied (class, gender, race, ethnicity, nationality, sexual orientation, and the like) as well as the history that has produced those social positions and their relations to other social positions that exist in the fields of activity in which those positions are located.

15. The first trial ended in a mistrial.

16. None of this, of course, absolves the defendants in the case of any individual responsibility they bore for failing to take sufficient measures to ensure the safety of the migrants they were transporting. Rather, it reminds us to also recognize the role that structural violence imposed by apartheid policies played in the migrants' tragic and needless deaths.

REFERENCES

"Acuerdan México y EU extender el programa Oasis a Coahuila." 2007. *El Diario de Juárez,* June 8.
Adler, Rachel. 2000. "Human Agency in International Migration: The Maintenance of Transnational Social Fields by Yucatecan Migrants in a Southwestern City." *Mexican Studies/Estudios Mexicanos* 16 (1): 165–87.
———. 2004. *Yucatecans in Dallas, Texas: Breaching the Border, Bridging the Distance.* Boston: Allyn and Bacon.
Alexander, Titus. 1996. *Unraveling Global Apartheid: An Overview of World Politics.* Cambridge, England: Polity Press.
American G.I. Forum of Texas and Texas State Federation of Labor (AFL). 1953. *What Price Wetbacks?* Austin, Tex.: American G.I. Forum of Texas and Texas State Federation of Labor (AFL); reprinted in 1976 in *Mexican Migration to the United States,* New York: Arno Press.
Amnesty International. 1998. *United States of America: Human Rights Concerns in the Border Region with Mexico.* New York: Amnesty International.
Andreas, Peter. 2000. *Border Games: Policing the U.S.-Mexico Divide.* Ithaca, N.Y.: Cornell University Press.
Blumenthal, Ralph. 2007. "Jury Spares Driver in Smuggling Deaths Case." *New York Times,* January 19. Electronic edition.

Booker, Salih, and William Minter. 2001. "Global Apartheid." *Nation* 273 (2): 11–17.

"Border Patrol Agent Found Guilty." 2007. *Houston Chronicle,* April 14, B3.

Bourdieu, Pierre. 1977. *Outline of a Theory of Practice.* Cambridge: Cambridge University Press.

———. 1986. "The Forms of Capital." In *Handbook of Theory and Research for the Sociology of Education,* edited by John G. Richardson, 241–58. Westport, Conn.: Greenwood Press.

Bourdieu, Pierre, and Loïc Wacquant. 1992. "The Purpose of Reflexive Sociology (Chicago Workshop)." In *An Invitation to Reflexive Sociology,* edited by Pierre Bourdieu and Loïc Wacquant, 61–215. Chicago: University of Chicago Press.

Burnett, John. 2001. "Immigrant Smugglers." Segment broadcast on National Public Radio's Morning Edition. June 22.

Cano, Luis Carlos. 2006. "Activan plan para combatir tráfico de personas en Juárez." *El Universal,* July 11.

Contreras, Guillermo. 2006. "Immigrants Flooding Del Rio Courts." *San Antonio Express-News,* May 16, 1A.

Cornelius, Wayne. 2001. "Death at the Border: Efficacy and Unintended Consequences of U.S. Immigration Control Policy." *Population and Development Review* 27 (4): 661–85.

Davis, Vincent T. 2004. "Four Accused of Smuggling Migrants." *San Antonio Express-News,* February 24, 1B.

De Genova, Nicholas P. 2002. "Migrant 'Illegality' and Deportability in Everyday Life." *Annual Review of Anthropology* 31:419–47.

Dunn, Timothy J. 1996. *The Militarization of the U.S.-Mexico Border, 1978–1992: Low-Intensity Conflict Doctrine Comes Home.* Austin, Tex.: CMAS Books.

Eschbach, Karl, Jacqueline Hagan, and Néstor Rodríguez. 2001. "Causes and Trends in Migrant Deaths on the U.S.-Mexico Border, 1985–1998." Working Paper Series No. 01-4. Center for Immigration Research, University of Houston.

———. 2003. "Deaths during Undocumented Migration: Trends and Policy Implications in the New Era of Homeland Security." Paper presented at the Twenty-sixth Annual National Legal Conference on Immigration and Refugee Policy in Washington, D.C. www.uh.edu/cir/ Deaths_during_migration.pdf (accessed July 19, 2006).

Galtung, Johan. 1969. "Violence, Peace, and Peace Research." *Journal of Peace Research* 6 (3): 167–91.

———. 1990. "Cultural Violence." *Journal of Peace Research* 27 (3): 291–305.

———. 1996. *Peace by Peaceful Means: Peace and Conflict, Development and Civilization.* Oslo, Norway: International Peace Research Institute.

Gans, Herbert J. 2003. *Democracy and the News.* New York: Oxford University Press.

George, Cindy. 2007. "Truck Driver's Fate in Hands of Jurors." *Houston Chronicle,* January 8. Electronic edition.

Gregor, Alison. 2000. "Immigrant Effort Draws Complaints." *San Antonio Express-News,* February 12, 1A.

Hart, Lianne. 2007. "Driver Gets Life in Prison in Deadly Human Smuggling Case." *Los Angeles Times,* January 19. Electronic edition.

Hegstrom, Edward. 2001. "Local INS Sting Yields 21 Arrests for Smuggling." *Houston Chronicle,* May 15. Electronic edition.

Heyman, Josiah McC. 1999a. "State Escalation of Force: A Vietnam/U.S.-Mexico Border Analogy." In *States and Illegal Practices,* edited by Josiah McC. Heyman, 285–314. New York: Berg.

———. 1999b. "Why Interdiction? Immigration Control at the United States-Mexican Border." *Regional Studies* 33 (7): 619–30.

Imbusch, Peter. 2003. "The Concept of Violence." In *The International Handbook of Violence Research,* edited by Wilhelm Heitmeyer and John Hagan, 13–61. Berlin: Springer.

King, Karisa. 2001. "INS Sting Nets 21 Guilty Pleas." *San Antonio Express-News,* May 15. Electronic edition.

Klinenberg, Eric. 2002. *Heat Wave: A Social Autopsy of Disaster in Chicago.* Chicago: University of Chicago Press.

Kohler, Gernot. 1978. "Global Apartheid." World Order Models Project, Working Paper No. 7. Institute for World Order, New York.

———. 1995. "The Three Meanings of Global Apartheid: Empirical, Normative, and Existential." *Alternatives* 20:403–13.

Krissman, Fred. 2000. "Immigrant Labor Recruitment: U.S. Agribusiness and Undocumented Migration from Mexico." In *Immigration for a New Century: Multidisciplinary Perspectives,* edited by Nancy Foner, Rubén Rumbaut, and Steven J. Gold, 277–300. New York: Russell Sage Foundation.

Laczko, Frank. 2002. "Human Trafficking: The Need for Better Data." Migration Information Source. Electronic newsletter. November 2002. Migration Policy Institute, Washington, D.C. www.migrationinformation.org/Feature/ display.cfm?id=66 (accessed June 15, 2005).

Loh, Jules. 1985. "Aliens Smuggled over Border Come from All Parts of World." *Houston Chronicle.* December 1, sec. 3, p. 10.

Lozano, Juan. 2005a. "Defense Says Language Barrier Kept Driver from Helping Immigrants." Associated Press. March 9. Appeared on the Web site of the *San Antonio Express-News.*

———. 2005b. "Prosecutor in Smuggling Horror Says Driver Blinded by Greed." Associated Press. March 19. Appeared on the Web site of the *San Antonio Express-News.*

Maril, Robert Lee. 2004. *Patrolling Chaos: The U.S. Border Patrol in Deep South Texas.* Lubbock, Tex.: Texas Tech University Press.

Mural. 2005. "Rescate en el desierto." *Mural* (Guadalajara, Jalisco), April 21, 2A.

Nevins, Joseph. 2003. "Thinking Out of Bounds: A Critical Analysis of Academic and Human Rights Writings on Migrant Deaths in the U.S.-Mexico Border Region." *Migraciones Internacionales* 2 (2): 171–90.

———. 2005. "A Beating Worse Than Death: Imagining and Contesting Violence in the U.S.-Mexico Borderlands." ejournals.library.vanderbilt.edu/ameriquests/include/get doc.php?id=349&article=73&mode=pdf&OJSSID=3d4c7cbb5eeb7abcf64ac973cdc91 f2f (accessed September 29, 2007).

Phillips, Julie A., and Douglas S. Massey. 2000. "Engines of Immigration: Stocks of Human and Social Capital in Mexico." *Social Science Quarterly* 81 (1): 33–48.

Pinkerton, James. 2000. "Border Patrol Twice Stops U.S. Judge on Way to Court." *Houston Chronicle,* October 1, 1.

Portes, Alejandro. 1995. "Economic Sociology and the Sociology of Immigration: A conceptual overview." In *The Economic Sociology of Immigration: Essays on Networks, Ethnicity, and Entrepreneurship,* edited by Alejandro Portes, 1–41. New York: Russell Sage Foundation.

Ramos, Jorge. 2005. *Morir en el intento: La peor tragedia de inmigrantes en la historia de los Estados Unidos.* New York: HarperCollins.

Rice, Harvey. 2004. "Feds Seek Death in Immigrant Smuggling." *Houston Chronicle,* March 16. Electronic edition.

Richmond, Anthony H. 1994. *Global Apartheid: Refugees, Racism, and the New World Order.* Toronto: Oxford University Press.

Rodríguez, Néstor. 1996. "The Battle for the Border: Notes on Autonomous Migration, Transnational Communities, and the State." *Social Justice* 23 (3): 21–38.

Samora, Julian, with the assistance of Jorge A. Bustamante F. and Gilberto Cárdenas. 1971. *Los Mojados: The Wetback Story.* South Bend, Ind.: University of Notre Dame Press.

Scott, James C. 1985. *Weapons of the Weak: Everyday Forms of Peasant Resistance.* New Haven: Yale University Press.

Secretaría de Relaciones Exteriores. 2005. "México y Estados Unidos Establecen el Programa Oasis para proteger a los migrantes y procesar penalmente a traficantes y tratantes de personas." Press release. August 17.

Selzer, Nate. 1998. "Immigration Law Enforcement and Human Rights Abuses." *Borderlines* 6 (9). us-mex.irc-online.org/borderlines/1998/bl50/bl50immi.html (accessed October 4, 2007).

Sharma, Nandita. 2005. "Anti-Trafficking Rhetoric and the Making of a Global Apartheid." *NWSA Journal* 17 (3): 88–111.

Singer, Audrey, and Douglas S. Massey. 1998. "The Social Process of Undocumented Border Crossing among Mexican Migrants." *International Migration Review* 32 (3): 561–92.

Slayden, James L. 1921. "Some Observations on Mexican Immigration." *Annals of the American Academy of Political and Social Science* 93 (January): 121–26.

Spener, David. 2000. "The Logic and Contradictions of Intensified Border Enforcement in Texas." In *The Wall around the West: State Borders and Immigration Controls in North America and Europe,* edited by Peter Andreas and Timothy Snyder, 115–38. Lanham, Md.: Rowman and Littlefield.

———. 2001. "Smuggling Migrants through South Texas: Challenges Posed by Operation Rio Grande." In *Global Human Smuggling: Comparative Perspectives,* edited by David J. Kyle and Rey Koslowski, 129–65. Baltimore: Johns Hopkins University Press.

———. 2004. "Mexican Migrant-Smuggling: A Cross-Border Cottage Industry." *Journal of International Migration and Integration* 5 (3): 295–320.

———. 2005. "Mexican Migration to the United States: A Long Twentieth Century of Coyotaje." Working Paper No. 124. Center for Comparative Immigration Studies of the University of California–San Diego. Available at www.ccis-ucsd.org/PUBLICATIONS/wrkg124.pdf.

———. 2006. "Coyotaje as an Everyday Strategy of Resistance to Apartheid at the Mexico-U.S. Border." Paper presented in Cocoyoc, Morelos, Mexico, on October 28 at the Segundo Coloquio Internacional sobre Migración y Desarrollo organized by the Red Internacional de Migración y Desarrollo.

———. 2008a. "Cruces clandestinos: Migrantes, coyotes y capital social en la frontera el noreste de México-sur de Texas." In *La migración a los Estados Unidos y la Frontera Noreste de México,* edited by Socorro Arzaluz, 119–68. Tijuana, Baja California: El Colegio de la Frontera Norte.

———. 2008b. "El eslabón perdido de la migración: El coyotaje en la frontera del sur de Texas y el noreste de México." In *Pobreza y migración internacional: El caso de México,* edited by Agustín Escobar Latapí, 365–417. Mexico City: Casa Chata.

———. 2009. *Clandestine Crossings: Migrants and Coyotes on the Texas-Mexico Border.* Ithaca, N.Y.: Cornell University Press.

Stop Gatekeeper. 2004. "Border Deaths (San Diego to Brownsville)." California Rural Legal Aid, San Diego. www.stopgatekeeper.org/ English/images/graph_death2.gif (accessed June 19, 2006).

Taber, Robert. (1965) 2002. *War of the Flea: The Classic Study of Guerrilla Warfare.* Dulles, Va: Brassey's. Citations refer to 2002 edition.

Transaction Records Access Clearinghouse. 2005. *Prosecution of Immigration Cases Surge in U.S. While Sentences Slump.* Syracuse, N.Y.: Transaction Records Access Clearinghouse. trac.syr.edu/tracins/latest/131/ (accessed March 10, 2007).

U.S. House of Representatives. Committee on Homeland, Subcommittee on Investigations. 2006. *A Line in the Sand: Confronting the Threat at the Southwest Border.* Washington, D.C.: U.S. House of Representatives Committee on Homeland, Subcommittee on Investigations.

Valley Movement for Human Rights. 2005. *In Our Own Backyard: A Community Report on Human Rights Abuses in Texas' Rio Grande Valley.* Harlingen, Tex.: Valley Movement for Human Rights. www.nnirr.org/news/reports/vmhr_report_esp.pdf (accessed July 19, 2006).

Vélez-Ibáñez, Carlos. 1988. "Networks of Exchange among Mexicans in the U.S. and Mexico: Local Level Mediating and International Transformations." *Urban Anthropology* 17 (1): 27–51.

Winingham, Ralph, and Dane Schiller. 1999. "Immigrant Is Found Dead on Train in Frio." *San Antonio Express-News,* April 23. Electronic edition.

Wong, Diana. 2005. "The Rumor of Trafficking: Border Controls, Illegal Migration, and the Sovereignty of the Nation-State." In *Illicit Flows and Criminal Things: States, Borders, and the Other Side of Globalization,* edited by Willem van Schendel and Itty Abraham, 69–100. Bloomington: Indiana University Press.

Young, Iris Marion. 2006. "Responsibility and Global Justice: A Social Connection Model." *Social Philosophy and Policy* 23 (1): 102–30.

CHAPTER SEVEN

The Social Organization
of Chinese Human Smuggling

Ko-Lin Chin

A year after the United States had established diplomatic relations with the People's Republic, China liberalized its immigration regulations in order to qualify for most-favored-nation status with the United States (Dowty, 1987).[1] Since 1979, tens of thousands of Chinese have legally immigrated to the United States and other countries (Seagrave, 1995). U.S. immigration quotas allow only a limited number of Chinese whose family members are U.S. citizens or who are highly educated to immigrate to or visit America (Zhou, 1992). Beginning in the late 1980s, some of those who did not have legitimate channels to enable them to immigrate, especially the Fujianese, began turning to human smugglers for help (U.S. Senate, 1992).

Smuggled Chinese arrive in the United States by land, sea, or air routes (Smith, 1997). Some travel to Mexico or Canada and then cross U.S. borders illegally (Glaberson, 1989). Others fly into major American cities via any number of transit points and make their way to their final destination (Lorch, 1992; Charasdamrong and Kheunkaew, 1992; U.S. Senate, 1992). Entering the United States by sea was an especially popular method between August 1991 and July 1993 (Zhang and Gaylord, 1996). During that time, thirty-two ships carrying as many as fifty-three hundred Chinese were found in waters near Japan, Taiwan, Indonesia, Australia, Singapore, Haiti, Guatemala, El Salvador, Honduras, and the United States (Kamen, 1991; Schemo, 1993; U.S. Immigration and Naturalization Service, 1993), though in the aftermath of the *Golden Venture* incident, the use of the sea route diminished significantly (Dunn, 1994).[2]

U.S. immigration officials estimated that at any given time in the early 1990s as many as four thousand Chinese were waiting in Bolivia to be shuttled to the United States by smugglers (Kinkead, 1992); several thousand more were believed to be waiting in Peru and Panama. American officials maintained that Chinese smuggling rings have connections in fifty-one countries that were either part of the transportation web or were involved in the manufacturing of fraudulent travel documents (Freedman, 1991; Kamen, 1991; Mydans, 1992). According to a senior immigration official who was interviewed in the early 1990s, "at any given time, thirty thousand Chinese are stashed away in safe houses around the world, waiting for entry" (Kinkead, 1992: 160).

Unlike Mexican illegal immigrants who enter the United States at relatively little financial cost (Cornelius, 1989), illegal Chinese immigrants reportedly must pay smugglers about $30,000 for their services (U.S. Senate, 1992). The thousands of Chinese smuggled out of their country each year make human trafficking a very lucrative business (Mooney and Zyla, 1993; Smith, 1997). One case illustrates the point: a forty-one-year-old Chinese woman convicted for human smuggling was alleged to have earned approximately $30 million during the several years of her smuggling career (Chan and Dao, 1990b). In 1992, a senior immigration official estimated that Chinese organized crime groups were making more than $1 billion a year from human smuggling operations (U.S. Senate, 1992). Others suggest that Chinese smugglers earn more— about $3.2 billion annually—from the human trade (Myers, 1994).

Little is known about the organizations involved in smuggling Chinese to the United States. In this chapter, I focus on the group characteristics of human smugglers, the extent of their affiliation with Chinese organized crime and street gangs, and the role of corruption in the human trade.

Research Methods

This study employs multiple research strategies, including a survey of three hundred smuggled Chinese in New York City, interviews with key informants who are familiar with the lifestyle and social problems of illegal Chinese immigrants, a field study in the Chinese immigrant community of New York City, two research trips to sending communities in China, and a systematic collection of media reports.

Group Characteristics

A smuggler I interviewed in 1994 insisted that nobody really knows how many Chinese smuggling groups exist worldwide, but she guessed that there were approximately fifty. Other estimates vary widely, from only seven or eight ("Chinese Social Worker Discusses His Observations," 1990) to as many as twenty or twenty-five (Chan, Dao, and McCoy, 1990; Burdman, 1993a). According to some observers, Chinese people-trafficking groups are well-organized, transnational criminal enterprises that are active in China, Hong Kong, Taiwan, Thailand, and the United States (Myers, 1992; U.S. Senate, 1992; Burdman, 1993b), but there are few empirical data to support this observation.

A smuggler I once asked to characterize a Chinese smuggling network said: "It's like a dragon. Although it's a lengthy creature, various organic parts are tightly linked." According to my subjects, a smuggling organization includes many roles:

- Big snakeheads, or arrangers/investors, often Chinese living outside China, generally invest money in a smuggling operation and oversee the entire operation but usually are not known by those being smuggled.
- Little snakeheads, or recruiters, usually live in China and work as middlemen between big snakeheads and customers; they are mainly responsible for finding and screening customers and collecting down payments.
- Transporters in China help immigrants traveling by land or sea make their way to the border or smuggling ship. Transporters based in the United States are responsible for taking smuggled immigrants from airports or seaports to safe houses.
- Corrupt Chinese government officials accept bribes in return for Chinese passports. Law enforcement authorities in many transit countries are also paid to aid the illegal Chinese immigrants entering and exiting their countries.
- Guides move illegal immigrants from one transit point to another

and aid immigrants entering the United States by land or air. Crew members are employed by snakeheads to charter or work on smuggling ships.

- Enforcers, themselves mostly illegal immigrants, are hired by big snakeheads to work on the smuggling ships. They are responsible for maintaining order and for distributing food and drinking water.
- Support personnel are local people at the transit points who provide food and lodging to illegal immigrants.
- U.S.-based debt collectors are responsible for locking up illegal immigrants in safe houses until their debt is paid and for collecting smuggling fees. There are also China-based debt collectors.

According to data collected in New York City and the Fuzhou area, a close working relationship links the leaders and others in the smuggling network, especially the snakeheads in the United States and China. More often than not, all those in the smuggling ring belong to a family or an extended family or are good friends. If a smuggling group is involved in air smuggling, the group may also need someone to work as a snakehead in such transit points as Hong Kong or Thailand.

When I visited Fuzhou, I interviewed a number of people who belonged to a ring that smuggled Chinese by air. A woman in charge of a government trade unit in Fuzhou City recruited customers and procured travel documents. She interacted only with government officials who helped her obtain travel documents; her assistant dealt with customers directly, recruiting, collecting down payments, signing contracts, and so forth. She recruited a partner, a childhood friend and member of the Public Security Bureau, who was responsible for securing travel documents for the ring's clients. A female relative in Singapore acted as a transit point snakehead. She traveled to countries such as Thailand, Indonesia, and Malaysia to set up transit points in those countries.

The primary leader and investor in the ring, based in New York, was responsible for subcontracting with members of a Queens-based gang to keep immigrants in safe houses and collect their fees after arrival in the United States. If the fee was to be paid in China, the female snakehead's assistant in China would collect it. It was not clear to me how profits were distributed among members of the smuggling ring or how money was actually transferred from one place to another.

Most smuggling groups reportedly specialize in either air or sea smuggling.

According to Zhang and Gaylord (1996), only groups with ties to organized crime groups in Asia engaged in the complicated, large-scale operations of sea smuggling, but snakeheads involved in air smuggling may venture into sea smuggling. A thirty-two-year-old housewife from Fuzhou who left China by boat alleged that her snakehead was involved in both.

Not all smugglers are affiliated with criminal groups, Zhang and Gaylord notwithstanding. A forty-year-old male store owner from Changle described his female snakehead, who specialized in sea smuggling, as "a Taiwanese with good reputation who came to China to be a snakehead. She was involved in sea smuggling for the first time when I was recruited by her. After that, she transported several boatloads of people to the United States. . . . She visited Fuzhou often. After our ship arrived in Los Angeles, [her] husband and a group of people picked us up."

Some U.S. authorities are convinced that Chinese smugglers of immigrants also bring heroin from Southeast Asia into the United States (U.S. Senate, 1992). Senator William Roth Jr., the Delaware Republican who directed a Senate investigation on Asian organized crime, claimed that some human smugglers are former drug dealers (Burdman, 1993a), and there is evidence to support this view. One of the first groups of Chinese to be charged with human smuggling had previously been indicted for heroin trafficking ("INS Undercover Operation," 1985), and a Chinese American who owned a garment factory in New York City's Chinatown was charged with both heroin and human trafficking ("Chinese Merchant Arrested," 1992). Moreover, during an undercover operation, Chinese smugglers offered heroin to federal agents posing as corrupt immigration officers in exchange for travel documents (DeStefano, 1994). U.S. officials also claim that smuggled Chinese are asked by snakeheads to carry heroin into the United States, presumably to finance their illegal passage (Chan and Dao, 1990c). Mark Riordan, INS assistant officer for Hong Kong, suggested that "smugglers make even more when illegals who can't raise the fee carry heroin in exchange for their trip" (Chan and Dao, 1990a: 14).

I asked my respondents whether their snakeheads asked them to carry drugs or to commit crimes to subsidize their illegal passage. Of the three hundred respondents, only one admitted he was asked by his snakehead to transport two bags of opium from the Golden Triangle (northern mountain region of Myanmar, Thailand, and Laos) to Bangkok, Thailand. None of those who left China by sea saw any illicit drugs aboard the sea vessels. It is not clear whether human smugglers are typically involved in heroin trafficking. Based on my interviews, I conclude that only a small number are.

Organized Crime, Gangs, and the Human Trade

Law enforcement and immigration officials in the United States have asserted that Chinese triads, tongs, and street gangs are involved in human smuggling (U.S. Senate, 1992)[3] and claim that Hong Kong–based triads are responsible for the massive movement of undocumented Chinese to the United States via Hong Kong (Torode, 1993a). As Bolz (1995: 148) put it, "Triads have taken over the smuggling of illegal immigrants from smaller 'mom and pop' organizations as an increasingly attractive alternative to drug trafficking because it promises multibillion dollar profits without the same severe penalties if caught."

There is evidence that certain triad members are involved in the human trade. One human smuggler has testified in court that a triad member in Hong Kong was involved in human smuggling (Torode, 1993b), and authorities in California are convinced that the California-based Wo Hop To triad was responsible for the arrival of eighty-five undocumented Chinese on a smuggling boat discovered near Long Beach, California in 1992 ("Many Illegal Chinese Migrants Arrived," 1992). However, no triad member or organization, either in Hong Kong or the United States, has ever been indicted for human smuggling.

U.S. authorities have also claimed that the U.S.-based tongs or community associations, especially the Fukien American Association, are active in the human trade, citing the testimony of New York City police at the 1992 U.S. Senate hearings on Asian organized crime (U.S. Senate, 1992). Leaders of the Fukien American Association, however, have denied that their organization has ever been involved in the illegal alien trade. The president of the association in 1992, labeled by journalists the "Commander-in-Chief of Illegal Smuggling," announced at a press conference that his organization "does not have control over certain individual members and therefore can not be held responsible for their illegal activities. It is unfair to blacken the name of the Fukien American Association as a whole based on the behavior of some non-member bad elements which are not under the control of the Association" (Lau, 1993: 5).

Since 1991 U.S. authorities have also asserted that Chinese and Vietnamese street gangs are involved in smuggling. After a 1991 article in the *San Francisco Examiner* linked Asian gangs and human trafficking (Freedman, 1991), numerous media accounts depicted Chinese gangs in New York City as collectors of smuggling payments. Gang members allegedly picked up illegal immigrants at airports or docks, kept them in safe houses, and forced them to call their relatives to make payments. For their services, gangs reportedly were paid between $1,500 and $2,000 per smuggled immigrant. None of these news articles implied that gangs were involved in transporting immigrants from China to America (Strom, 1991).

After the *Golden Venture* incident, U.S. immigration officials and law enforcement authorities began to view Chinese gang members not as "service providers" to smugglers but as smugglers themselves who were capable of transporting hundreds of illegal immigrants across the Pacific Ocean (Lay, 1993; Wang, 1996) and charged that the Fuk Ching gang was responsible for the *Golden Venture* tragedy itself (Burdman, 1993b; Faison, 1993; Gladwell and Stassen-Berger, 1993; Treaster, 1993). According to the authorities, the gang not only invested money in the purchase of the *Golden Venture* but also was directly involved in recruiting prospective immigrants in China.

In a crackdown on Chinese gangs, members of the White Tigers, the Green Dragons, and the Fuk Ching were indicted for transporting people from borders and coastal areas to New York City and collecting debts for human smugglers. According to court materials in a murder case involving the Fuk Ching gang, Ah Chu, a snakehead, paid a member of the Fuk Ching $500 a head to pick up five illegal immigrants near the Mexican border. Ah Chu also gave the gang member $150,000 to go to California, where he paid a group of Mexicans $500 for each illegal alien they brought in. According to the gang member, Ah Chu was not a member of the Fuk Ching but a partner or friend of the big boss, Ah Kay. The gang member also made two trips to Boston to pick up illegal aliens, transporting seven people by van from Boston to New York City on each trip. For this and for serving time in another case, Ah Kay allegedly paid him $10,000 (Superior Court of New Jersey, 1995).

At the trial, a street-level leader of the Fuk Ching acknowledged that his gang boss paid him $3,000 for transporting 130 illegal immigrants from Boston to New York in a Ryder truck, adding that his gang had smuggled 300 immigrants from China to the United States. Another Fuk Ching defendant testified that he was paid $200 to $300 a week for watching the "customers." However, no Chinese gang members, not even members of the Fuk Ching gang—who were widely believed to be the most active in human trafficking— were charged with transporting illegals from China to the United States. Nevertheless, U.S. authorities completed an undercover operation called Operation

Sea Dragon and concluded that "a highly sophisticated, compartmentalized network of Asian gangs in different parts of the United States" was deeply involved in human smuggling (Branigin, 1996: A12).

When asked what role Chinese gangs play in the human trade, a Chinese American immigration officer told me that in the past Chinese gangs had only collected fees for smugglers but that more recently they have been getting into the smuggling business themselves. They now "plan the trips, invest the needed capital, and collect the debt in America."

Although tongs and gangs are allegedly involved in the human trade, little is known about the nature and extent of their involvement, other than what is suggested by these anecdotal accounts. Nor is it clear whether smuggling operations are sponsored by tongs and gangs jointly or carried out by tong members and gang members on an ad hoc basis. Some observers, including some law enforcement authorities, disagree that smuggling organizations are closely linked with gangs or tongs and regard the connection as, at best, haphazard. One Hong Kong police officer claimed that "some of these people are in triads, but it isn't so organized. It's just a question of a couple of people with the wherewithal to put together a criminal scheme to smuggle illegal immigrants" (DeStefano et al., 1991: 8). Another observer concluded that "contrary to popular belief, people who deal in this business [human smuggling] are normally shop or business owners, not gang or 'Mafia' members" ("Former Smuggler Claims Immigration Graft," 1994: A2).

Asked by a reporter how he was related to members of organized crime, a New York–based smuggler denied any connection between snakeheads and gang members:

> What do you mean by "members of organized crime groups"? These people [debt collectors] are nothing more than a bunch of hooligans who like to bully people in Chinatown. These guys are getting out of control; they are willing to kill people for money. Yet, people like us who are in this business could not conduct our business without them. Most illegal immigrants are decent people; however, there are also some criminals. If I don't hire thugs to collect money, I may not get paid. . . . When the immigrants I smuggle arrive here, my debt collectors will go to the airport to pick them up and lock them up somewhere. They collect the smuggling fees, and I pay them $2,000 per immigrant. (Nyo, 1993: S4)

Willard Myers has also concluded that traditional organized crime groups such as the triads, tongs, and gangs do not dominate the human trade. In criticizing U.S. law enforcement strategies against human smuggling among the Chinese, Myers (1994: 4) suggested that "Chinese transnational criminal activity is carried out as a form of entrepreneurial activity by and among persons who are linked by language (dialect group) and lineage (ancestral birth place), who may or may not be a member or affiliate of an organization recognized by law enforcement."

The testimony of my respondents, although a limited sample, tends to support the conclusion that human smuggling is not closely associated with organized crime, as has commonly been alleged in criminological literature (Maltz, 1994). No doubt members of triads, tongs, and gangs are, to a certain extent, involved in trafficking Chinese, but I believe that their participation is neither sanctioned by nor even known to their respective organizations. *Triads, tongs,* and *gangs* are frightening terms that are often used to generate panic and can result in discrimination against ethnic and racial minorities. The "organized crime and gang" problem is perpetuated by the law enforcement community to justify greater investment in the traditional criminal justice apparatus. The media contribute to this view because organized crime and gang problems are easily sensationalized for public consumption. My data, however, suggest that the Chinese trade in human smuggling is not a form of organized crime but rather a "business" controlled by many otherwise legitimate groups, both small and large, working independently, each with its own organization, connections, methods, and routes. A smuggler once told me, "It's like a Chinese story about eight angels crossing a sea: every angel is extremely capable of achieving the goal due to her heavenly qualities." None of these groups, however, dominates or monopolizes the lucrative trade. When U.S. authorities indicted eighteen Chinese for human trafficking, they found that these defendants belonged to five smuggling groups, with several defendants belonging to more than one group (DeStefano, 1994).

I also found that, contrary to the assertions of Myers (1994), Hood (1993, 1997), and Zhang and Gaylord (1996), that immigrant smuggling is not necessarily dominated by ethnic Chinese from Taiwan but is a global business initiated by Chinese Americans of Fuzhou extraction and supported not only by Taiwanese but also by Chinese and non-Chinese in numerous transit countries. In short, the human trade is in many ways like any other legitimate international trade, except that it is illegal. Like any trade, it needs organization and planning, but it does not appear to be linked with traditional "organized crime" groups.

Government Corruption and Human Trafficking

Reasoning that China is a tightly controlled society, U.S. authorities have suspected Chinese law enforcement authorities, as well, of involvement in the smuggling of immigrants to the United States (Burdman, 1993c; Engelberg, 1994). In such a well-policed state, how could smugglers covertly transport tens of thousands of people and escape the notice of Chinese authorities (U.S. Senate, 1992)? They must either be accepting bribes or be actively involved themselves in transporting people out of China.

An officer of the INS enforcement division told me that "people in the Fujian Public Security Bureau have to be involved in alien smuggling. They take bribes from smugglers and either turn a blind eye on illegal immigration or provide logistical support. The INS has evidence to show that Chinese law enforcement authorities are behind alien smuggling." Some of my subjects made the same point. A female immigrant who was deported back to China by Mexican authorities told me that a group of smugglers transported her and hundreds of others from Fuzhou to a seaport on Chinese military trucks. She believed that the military trucks were used by the snakeheads to avoid inspection by local authorities.

There are many legitimate channels available to Chinese citizens who wish to travel abroad—for instance, advanced study, exported laborers, participating in an official or business delegation, visiting relatives abroad, or joining a Hong Kong or Macao tour. It is reported that Chinese government officials and government-owned travel agencies are actively facilitating the departure of a large number of Chinese immigrants through such means (Burdman, 1993c). To understand how allegedly corrupt officials might be involved in the human trade, one needs to examine the nature and operation of some of the government-sponsored labor and economic affairs organizations in the Fuzhou area.

In China, there is a fine line between illegal immigration and legally exported labor ("Is the Chinese Communist Government Sponsoring 'Labor Export' to Taiwan?" 1989). In the coastal areas, there are numerous government-sponsored labor-export companies that work closely with foreign-based labor-import companies to move tens of thousands of Chinese workers overseas, mainly to Southeast Asian countries where there is a labor shortage (Kwong, 1997). It is not always clear, however, which components of their operations are legal and which are illegal, nor is it always clear whether these companies are involved in the human trade on an organizational level or whether only individual employees are involved unbeknownst to their employers.

Whatever the case, those of my subjects who left China with the aid of a labor-export company professed satisfaction with the company's services. A thirty-five-year-old computer clerk from Fuzhou told this story:

> I sought help from a company, a government agency specializing in exporting labor, to leave China. The company worked along with a company in Singapore to help people leave China as laborers. When I got in touch with the company, it was agreed that I should pay the company $2,000 for a passport and an application fee. After I reached the United States, I would pay an additional $26,000. They told me it would take about seven days to get to the United States and it would be safe. After the meeting with the company, I left China within 24 days. I flew to Singapore from Fuzhou, with a Chinese passport and a Singapore visa. They were all genuine documents. After staying in Singapore for two weeks, the Singapore company provided three of us with photo-sub Singapore passports [passports on which the original holder's picture is replaced with the respondent's picture] to fly to Los Angeles via Germany.

It is possible that employees of these state-run labor-export companies are bribed by snakeheads behind the backs of company officials. A government employee from Fuzhou City said:

> In China, I worked for a government agency [a labor-export company]. The main purpose of the agency was to make money by means of assisting people to go abroad as export labor. I used my position in the company to help a friend obtain tourist passports. My friend told me he was only helping his friends and relatives to immigrate. I wasn't quite sure what was he doing exactly. Later, I learned that those who left China with the passports I provided to him had attempted to go to the United States illegally via a third country. How did that happen? Well, while they were attempting to board a plane in Indonesia with fake travel documents, they were arrested and deported back to China. The Public Security Bureau investigated the case and discovered that I was the one who supplied them with the Chinese passports. They accused me of being a snakehead. My boss ordered me to quit while the investigation was going on. I had nowhere to appeal. In China, the punishment for being a snakehead is severe—equal to the punishment for murderers and drug traffickers. After evaluating all my options, I decided to flee China.

Government employees may play another role in facilitating the illegal movement of Chinese. Since China adopted the open door policy and implemented economic reforms in the late 1970s, the government has sent many official delegations abroad to enhance international ties. Human smugglers seized the opportunity to bribe the people who decide the makeup of these official delegations. A forty-four-year-old male from Changle explained how his big snakehead got him and others included in a business delegation to the United States by writing to officials at the local government department in charge of the visit.

Reports of government employees' involvement in smuggling have also appeared in the Chinese media, as when a newspaper reported that four high-ranking Xian City officials had been convicted of trafficking in people. According to the report, the officials knowingly allowed twenty-three people from Fuzhou to leave China with official passports as members of a business delegation. The report revealed that smugglers paid the chairpersons of the city's Economic Affairs Committee and Foreign Affairs Committee about $90,000 for making the arrangement ("Xian Officials Fired," 1993). Another Chinese media account revealed that the director of the Public Security Bureau angrily denounced "some labor export companies for helping Chinese to go abroad illegally, [who] were in reality 'slave traders' who were only interested in collecting a certain amount of money from the immigrants and allowed the people they helped export to run wild in the world community" (Zi, 1993: S5). In a 1997 media account, 150 officers and soldiers of the Shenzhen Border Patrol Army who were bribed by human smugglers were arrested for allowing more than 8,000 Chinese citizens to leave China illegally ("150 Members of the Shenzhen Border Patrol Army Were Arrested," 1997).

According to a number of my respondents, their snakeheads were either former or active Chinese government employees. One described his snakehead as "a government employee working as a middleman for a big snakehead who was his relative." The snakehead of another respondent "was a government official responsible for recruiting customers locally [who] referred them to his younger brother who lived abroad."

Some government officials in many transit countries are allegedly bribed by human smugglers as well, either to look the other way or to provide help to immigrants (DeStefano, 1997). When asked whether smugglers make kickbacks to immigration police in Thailand, one smuggler replied, "That's the essential part of the business" ("Former Smuggler Claims Immigration Graft," 1994: A2).

One of my respondents said that public officials assisted him in Thailand. "Because we had no documents, we were arrested by the Thai police and detained for seven days. Later, our snakehead bribed the Thai officers to release us." Another respondent recalled how he passed through Thailand: "I got past Thai immigration by means of *maiguan* (buying checkpoint). That is, my snakehead slipped a $100 bill in my passport. A Thai immigration officer took the money, stamped my passport, and I went through."

Immigration officers in other countries were also reported to have accepted bribes from smugglers. In 1993, immigration officers in Hong Kong were involved in a bribery case concerning people trafficking (Gomez and Gilbert, 1993), and in 1995 an immigration officer stationed at the Buenos Aires airport was arrested for aiding Chinese smugglers ("Argentina Government Smashes an Alien Smuggling Ring," 1995).

Some of my respondents reported that Mexican authorities played an important role in facilitating the movement of Chinese to the United States via Mexico. A corroborating newspaper account reported an incident in which Mexican authorities, presumably after being bribed, allowed Chinese immigrants in their custody to "escape." "There were about 300 Chinese confined in a detention center in Mexicali. They were not worried at all because they had been told by their snakeheads that their Mexican guards would all 'fall asleep,' after which they would be transported to the airport for deportation. One night, as predicted by the snakehead, all the guards suddenly 'disappeared,' and the Chinese escaped. They all eventually crossed the border and entered the United States" ("Smuggled Chinese Escaped," 1993: A1). The Washington, D.C.–based Interagency Working Group (1995) also concluded that the trade in illegal immigrants is supported by rampant corruption among officials in various transit countries such as Belize, Panama, Guatemala, and the Dominican Republic.

There is no shortage of evidence that government officials, both within China and at various transit points, help to facilitate the clandestine movement of people abroad.

Since this chapter was first written more than ten years ago, snakeheads—or human smugglers—have continued to clandestinely transport Chinese nationals to the United States. A few things have changed, however. First, the smuggling fee has increased from around $30,000 in the early 1990s to about $75,000 in 2009. Second, snakeheads have virtually abandoned using the sea routes after the *Golden Venture*, a ship carrying almost three hundred illegal aliens, ran aground in New York in 1993. Though snakeheads continue to use the Mexican land route to move large numbers of Chinese into the United States, the majority of illegal Chinese migrants still arrive in the United States by air in small groups. Third, the source of these illegal migrants has extended beyond Fujian Province to include other provinces such as Zhejiang and Liaoning, even though migrants from these provinces are charged significantly less than migrants from Fujian. Fourth, because many Fujianese who were smuggled into the United States in the early 1990s have become permanent residents or citizens, they are sponsoring their children, parents, and brothers and sisters as legal immigrants to the United States. As a result, the demand for smuggling service in the Fujian Province has somewhat decreased. Fifth, there has been a significant increase in the number of Chinese women going overseas to engage in prostitution. These women could be smuggled or trafficked, but they could also be legal immigrants or tourists. There is no evidence to suggest that the minor role of organized crime in the Chinese smuggling or trafficking business has changed over the past decade; Chinese organized crime groups remain relatively inactive in these types of transnational crime. Official complicity in human smuggling and trafficking also has not changed much; government officials in sending, transit, and receiving countries still benefit directly or indirectly from the clandestine movement of people.

NOTES

Support for this research was provided by Grant SBR 93-11114 from the National Science Foundation. The opinions are those of the author and do not necessarily reflect the policies or views of the National Science Foundation.

1. I use *China* to refer to the People's Republic of China, and *Chinese,* unless otherwise indicated, to denote legal or illegal immigrants from, or citizens of, the People's Republic. *Taiwan* refers to the Republic of China on Taiwan, and *Taiwanese* refers to immigrants from, or citizens of, Taiwan.

2. Most Americans became keen observers of the plight of illegal Chinese immigrants in June 1993, when the *Golden Venture,* a human cargo ship with more than 260 passengers aboard, ran aground in shallow waters off a New York City beach. Eager to complete their dream journey to the United States, ten Chinese citizens drowned while attempting to swim ashore.

3. Chinese triads began as secret societies three centuries ago, formed by patriotic Chinese to fight the Qing dynasty, which they considered oppressive and corrupt. When the Qing government collapsed and the Republic of China was established in 1912, triads

degenerated into criminal groups (Morgan, 1960). Most triad societies now have their headquarters in Hong Kong, but their criminal operations have no national boundaries (Booth, 1991; Black, 1992; Chin, 1995). Tongs were established in America as self-help groups by the first wave of Chinese immigrants in the mid-nineteenth century (Dillon, 1962). Historically, tongs have been active in gambling, prostitution, extortion, and violence (Chin, 1990, 1996).

REFERENCES

"Argentina Government Smashes an Alien Smuggling Ring" (in Chinese). 1995. *World Journal,* October 14, A3.

Black, David. 1992. *Triad Takeover: A Terrifying Account of the Spread of Triad Crime in the West.* London: Sidgwick & Jackson.

Bolz, Jennifer. 1995. "Chinese Organized Crime and Illegal Alien Trafficking: Humans as a Commodity." *Asian Affairs* 22:147–58.

Booth, Martin. 1991. *The Triads.* New York: St. Martin's Press.

Branigin, William. 1996. "U.S. Seeks Fugitive Falls Church Man after 3-Year Alien-Smuggling Probe." *Washington Post,* April 21, A12.

Burdman, Pamela. 1993a. "Huge Boom in Human Smuggling—Inside Story of Flight from China." *San Francisco Chronicle,* April 27, A1.

———. 1993b. "How Gangsters Cash In on Human Smuggling." *San Francisco Chronicle,* April 28, A1.

———. 1993c. "Web of Corruption Ensnares Officials around the World." *San Francisco Chronicle,* April 28, A8.

Chan, Ying, and James Dao. 1990a. "Crime Rings Snaking." *New York Daily News,* September 23, 14.

———. 1990b. "Merchants of Misery." *New York Daily News,* September 24, 7.

———. 1990c. "A Tale of 2 Immigrants." *New York Daily News,* September 24, 21.

Chan, Ying, James Dao and Kevin McCoy. 1990. "Journey of Despair: Out of China, into Desperate Debt." *New York Daily News,* September 23, 4.

Charasdamrong, Prasong, and Subin Kheunkaew. 1992. "Smuggling Human Beings: A Lucrative Racket That Poses a Threat to National Security." *Bangkok Post,* July 19, 10.

Chin, Ko-lin. 1990. *Chinese Subculture and Criminality: Non-traditional Crime Groups in America.* Westport, Conn.: Greenwood Press.

———. 1995. "Triad Societies in Hong Kong." *Transnational Organized Crime* 1 (Spring): 47–64.

———. 1996. *Chinatown Gangs: Extortion, Enterprise, and Ethnicity.* New York: Oxford University Press.

"A Chinese Merchant Arrested for Trafficking Heroin and Humans" (in Chinese). 1992. *Sing Tao Daily,* October 10, 32.

"A Chinese Social Worker Discusses His Observations of Alien Smuggling Activity in Fujian" (in Chinese). 1990. *Sing Tao Daily,* July 14, 24.

Cornelius, Wayne. 1989. "Impact of the 1986 US Immigration Law on Emigration from Rural Mexican Sending Communities." *Population and Development Review* 15 (4): 689–705.

DeStefano, Anthony. 1994. "Feds Crack 'Snakehead' Alien Smuggling Ring." *New York Newsday,* November 10, A79.

———. 1997. "Immigrant Smuggling through Central America and the Carribean." In *Human Smuggling: Chinese Migrant Trafficking and the Challenge to America's Immigration Tradition,* edited by Paul J. Smith, 134–55. Washington, D.C.: Center for Strategic and International Studies.

DeStefano, Anthony, David Kocieniewski, Kevin McCoy, and Jim Muvaney. 1991. "Smuggling Rings Victimize Clients." *New York Newsday,* January 6, 8.

Dillon, Richard. 1962. *The Hatchet Men: The Story of the Tong Wars in San Francisco's Chinatown.* New York: Coward-McCann.

Dowty, Alan. 1987. *Closed Borders: The Contemporary Assault on Freedom of Movement.* New Haven: Yale University Press.

Dunn, Ashley. 1994. "After Crackdown, Smugglers of Chinese Find New Routes." *New York Times,* November 1, A1.

Engelberg, Stephen. 1994. "In Immigration Labyrinth, Corruption Comes Easily." *New York Times,* September 12, A1.

Faison, Seth. 1993. "Alien-Smuggling Suspect Eluded Immigration Net." *New York Times,* June 10, A1.

"Former Smuggler Claims Immigration Graft." 1994. *Nation* (Bangkok), November 9, A2.

Freedman, Dan. 1991. "Asian Gangs Turn to Smuggling People." *San Francisco Examiner,* December 30, A7.

Glaberson, William. 1989. "6 Seized in Smuggling Asians into New York." *New York Times,* May 5, B3.

Gladwell, Malcolm, and Rachel Stassen-Berger. 1993. "Human Cargo Is Hugely Profitable to New York's Chinese Underworld." *Washington Post,* June 7, A10.

Gomez, Rita, and Andy Gilbert. 1993. "Immigration Officer Charged over Passport Forgery." *South China Morning Post,* October 20, 1.

Hood, Marlowe. 1993. "The Taiwan Connection." *South China Morning Post,* December 27, 11.

———. 1997. "Sourcing the Problem: Why Fuzhou?" In *Human Smuggling: Chinese Migrant Trafficking and the Challenge to America's Immigration Tradition,* edited by Paul J. Smith, 76–92. Washington, D.C.: Center for Strategic and International Studies.

"INS Undercover Operation Crushes a Taiwanese Alien Smuggling Ring." 1985. *Centre Daily News* (in Chinese), May 9, 3.

Interagency Working Group. 1995. "Presidential Initiative to Deter Alien Smuggling: Report of the Interagency Working Group. Summary." Unpublished.

"Is the Chinese Communist Government Sponsoring 'Labor Export' to Taiwan?" (in Chinese). 1989. *United Daily News,* May 12, 1.

Kamen, Al. 1991. "U.S. Seizes Illegal Aliens from China." *Washington Post,* September 5, A5.

Kinkead, Gwen. 1992. *Chinatown: A Portrait of a Closed Society.* New York: HarperCollins.

Kwong, Peter. 1997. *Forbidden Workers: Illegal Chinese Immigrants and American Labor.* New York: New Press.

Lau, Alan Man S. 1993. Statement by Alan Man S. Lau, chairman of Fukien American Association, at a press conference held at 125 East Broadway, New York, September 28.

Lay, Richard. 1993. "The Gangland Fiefdom of Terror." *South China Morning Post,* June 27, 4.

Lorch, Donatella. 1992. "A Flood of Illegal Aliens Enters U.S. via Kennedy: Requesting Political Asylum Is Usual Ploy." *New York Times,* March 18, B2.

Maltz, Michael. 1994. "Defining Organized Crime." In *Handbook of Organized Crime in the United States,* edited by Robert Kelly, Ko-lin Chin, and Rufus Schatzberg, 21–38. Westport, Conn.: Greenwood Press.

"Many Illegal Chinese Migrants Arrived in the US in Taiwanese Fishing Boats, Triads Are Alleged to Be Behind the Illegal Operations" (In Chinese). 1992. *Sing Tao Daily,* March 6, 23.

Mooney, Paul, and Melana Zyla. 1993. "Bracing the Seas and More: Smuggling Chinese into the US Means Big Money." *Far Eastern Economic Review,* April 8, 17–19.

Morgan, W. P. 1960. *Triad Societies in Hong Kong.* Hong Kong: Government Press.

Mydans, Seth. 1992. "Chinese Smugglers' Lucrative Cargo: Humans." *New York Times,* March 21, A1.

Myers, Willard. 1992. "The United States under Siege: Assault on the Borders: Chinese Smuggling 1983–1992." Manuscript in author's possession.

———. 1994. "Transnational Ethnic Chinese Organized Crime: A Global Challenge to the Security of the United States, Analysis and Recommendations." Testimony of Willard Myers, Senate Committee on Foreign Affairs, Subcommittee on Terrorism, Narcotics and International Operations, April 21.

Nyo, Ming-sen. 1993. "Why So Many Chinese Illegals Coming to the US?" (in Chinese). *World Journal Magazine,* August 29, S4.

"150 Members of the Shenzhen Border Patrol Army Were Arrested for Working for Snakeheads" (in Chinese). 1997. *World Journal,* October 17, A13.

Schemo, Diana Jean. 1993. "Survivors Tell of Voyage of Little Daylight, Little Food, and Only Hope." *New York Times,* June 7, B5.

Seagrave, Sterling. 1995. *Lords of the Rim: The Invisible Empire of the Overseas Chinese.* New York: G. P. Putnam's Sons.

Smith, Paul J. 1997. "Chinese Migrant Trafficking: A Global Challenge." In *Human Smuggling: Chinese Migrant Trafficking and the Challenge to America's Immigration Tradition,* edited by Paul J. Smith, 1–22. Washington, D.C.: Center for Strategic and International Studies.

"Smuggled Chinese Escaped from Mexican Authorities" (in Chinese). 1993. *World Journal,* August 25, A1.

Strom, Stephanie. 1991. "13 Held in Kidnapping of Illegal Alien." *New York Times,* January 2, B3.

Superior Court of New Jersey. 1995. *State of New Jersey vs. Dan Xin Lin et al.* Bergen County, Law Division, Indictment No. S-644–94.

Torode, Greg. 1993a. "Immigration HQ Criticized over Illegals." *South China Morning Post,* February 10, 3.

———. 1993b. "Triads Use HK Agency for Illegals." *South China Morning Post,* March 15, 1.

Treaster, Joseph. 1993. "Behind Immigrants' Voyage, Long Reach of Chinese Gang." *New York Times,* June 9, A1.

U.S. Immigration and Naturalization Service. 1993. "Vessels That Are Known to Have

Attempted to Smuggle PRC Nationals into the United States." Report in author's possession, August 17.

U.S. Senate. 1992. *Asian Organized Crime.* Hearing before the Permanent Subcommittee on Investigations of the Committee on Governmental Affairs, October 3, November 5–6, 1991. Washington, D.C.: U.S. Government Printing Office.

Wang, Zheng. 1996. "Ocean-going Smuggling of Illegal Chinese Immigrants: Operation, Causation, and Policy Implications." *Transnational Organized Crime* 2 (1): 49–65.

"Xian Officials Fired for Receiving Bribes from Human Smugglers" (in Chinese). 1993. *Wen Wei Pao,* November 6, 1.

Zhang, Sheldon, and Mark Gaylord. 1996. "Bound for the Golden Mountain: The Social Organization of Chinese Alien Smuggling." *Crime, Law, and Social Change* 25: 1–16.

Zhou, Min. 1992. *Chinatown: The Socioeconomic Potential of an Urban Enclave.* Philadelphia: Temple University Press.

Zi, Ye. 1993. "The Doom of the Golden Venture" (in Chinese). *World Journal Weekly,* August 15, S-5.

CHAPTER EIGHT

From Fujian to New York

Understanding the New Chinese Immigration

Zai Liang and Wenzhen Ye

One of the most dramatic episodes of illegal immigration to the United States occurred in the early morning of June 6, 1993, when a Honduran ship ran aground off the coast of Queens in New York City. The captain shouted: "The boat is owned by Honduras, jump and swim to the American shore and you will be free." Some of the 286 people on the ship jumped into the chilly Atlantic, but others waited to be picked up by the U.S. Coast Guard (Fritsch, 1993; McFadden, 1993). The ship that carried these undocumented Chinese, called the *Golden Venture* (*Jinse Maoxian Hao*), had traveled some 17,000 miles in 112 days and arrived in New York City via Africa. Most of the 286 Chinese who were aboard came from Fujian (also known as Fukien) Province on the southeastern coast of China and suffered subhuman conditions during the voyage.[1]

Although this was the most publicized incident of undocumented migration from China in the 1990s, it represents only a small chapter in a much larger operation of underground smuggling of Chinese to the United States that started in the 1980s. Chinese immigration to the United States has had a long history and can be dated at least as far back as the middle of the nineteenth century (Nee and Nee, 1972; Tsai, 1983). However, the recent wave of immigration from China has some unique characteristics that deserve analysts' attention. Compared with earlier waves, the current one involves undocumented immigrants who have been smuggled in through a dense network of connections in New York's Chinatown, Southeast Asia, and China. With the help of sophisticated modern technology, the smugglers communicate between locations, make fake documents (such as passports and visas), and find routes that are difficult for the U.S. Coast Guard and immigration officials to detect. They are also able to smuggle people by whatever means possible, such as mingling them with formal delegations using fake passports, entering the United States through Mexico, and landing directly on the U.S. coast (as occurred in Queens in June 1993).

The smuggling business is extremely lucrative given that undocumented migrants pay as much as forty-seven thousand dollars each for the trip. Therefore, any policy measure aimed at stemming the flow of these migrants is likely to encounter difficulty. Despite the tough measures announced by the Clinton administration after the *Golden Venture* fiasco, undocumented immigrants from Fujian continue to enter the country (Butterfield, 1996; Chen, 1998; Holmes, 1998; McFadden, 1998).

Although journalistic accounts are abundant ("China Arrested 256 Snake Heads," 1996; Faison, 1995; Fritsch, 1993; Kinkead, 1992; Lii, 1996a; McFadden, 1993; Noble, 1995; Schemo, 1993a, 1993b; Treaster, 1993) and two novels on human smuggling have been published in China (Cao, 1995; and Li, 1995), the scholarly literature on the illegal migration from China is just emerging (Chin, 1997, 1998; Kwong, 1997; Skelton, 1996; Smith, 1997). Some analysts contend that China's one-child policy has driven people out of Fujian to the United States as political refugees, whereas others argue that poverty in China and relaxed governmental policies are the major factors (Herbert, 1996). On the basis of interviews with illegal immigrants and smugglers, Kwong (1997) presented a compelling account of the smuggling network and the hidden world of undocumented Fujianese in the labor market, especially in New York City. He stated that the heart of the problem is "the ever-healthy demand of American business for vulnerable, unprotected labor" (Kwong, 1997: 6). In contrast, authors of chapters in Paul Smith's (1997) edited volume documented many aspects of the smuggling process: the network connections between migrants and smugglers, the potential of a large volume of illegal migration from China in the future, the relationship between China's large floating population and illegal migration from China, and the experiences of newly arrived undocumented

Chinese. So far the most comprehensive study of illegal migration from China and the social organization of human smuggling is by Chin (1998) who conducted interviews with three hundred illegal migrants in New York's Chinatown.

Despite recent scholarly efforts in this area, several critical questions remain. For example, why have undocumented Chinese migrants come primarily from Fujian instead of other provinces? What are the basic characteristics of Fujian and major immigrant-sending communities that are conducive to international migration? Are immigrants mainly from the bottom of the socioeconomic hierarchy? The complex process of smuggling migrants from Fujian defies simplification and requires the examination of many factors at different levels—individual, community, national, and international.

In this chapter, we examine the causes of the recent surge in migration from Fujian to the New York metropolitan area, drawing on historical documents, secondary statistics from China, a survey conducted in Fujian, and our two field trips to Fujian in 1994 and 1998. First, we briefly review the literature on undocumented immigration to the United States and the significance of immigration from Fujian. Next, we present a profile of several major immigrant-sending communities in Fujian. Then we offer explanations for the flow of undocumented migrants from Fujian. We argue that undocumented migration from Fujian is a continuation of its long-term tradition of international migration. For centuries, Fujian sent a large number of international migrants to Nan Yang (Southeast Asia) and, to a lesser extent, to the United States. Current undocumented migration from Fujian does not stem from absolute poverty. Rather, it is based on a sense of relative deprivation caused by increasing inequality that is driven by China's transition to a market economy and remittance from overseas Fujianese. The involvement of international smuggling organizations has been instrumental in making this undocumented migration possible.

Significance of Recent Fujianese Immigration

Although there has been little research on undocumented immigration from China, there is a large body of literature on undocumented immigration to the United States, particularly from Mexico (Massey et al., 1987; Heer, 1992). The size and patterns of undocumented aliens have been carefully documented along with the impact on the U.S. economy (Massey et al., 1987; Massey and

Singer, 1995; Smith and Edmonston, 1998; Warren and Passel, 1987). The focus on undocumented Mexican immigrants mainly reflects the fact that Mexicans constitute the largest volume of undocumented immigrants to the United States (Espenshade, 1995). Although the most comprehensive volume on international migration (Massey et al., 1998) claims to summarize patterns of international migration in all regions of the world, illegal migration from China in the 1990s is barely discussed.

The recent surge in undocumented migrants from other countries (such as China) provides an opportunity to study this type of migration from a country other than Mexico. We argue that because of the unique geographical position of Mexico and the unique relationship between Mexico and the United States, the findings from studies of Mexican immigrants may not necessarily be generalizable to the patterns of undocumented migration from other countries. Massey et al. (1994: 739) made a similar point: "Far too much research is centered in Mexico, which because of its unique relationship with the United States may be unrepresentative of broader patterns and trends. . . . More attention needs to be devoted to other prominent sending countries, such as the Philippines, the Dominican Republic, Jamaica, Colombia, El Salvador, Korea, and China." Our research is a step in this direction.

Furthermore, in our view, the current immigrants from Fujian differ in many aspects not only from Mexican immigrants but also from earlier Chinese immigrants. Previous waves of immigrants from China came predominantly from Guangdong, a province in southern China, and settled in Chinatowns throughout the United States (Lin, 1998; Zhou, 1992). In contrast, most of the recent undocumented Chinese immigrants have come from rural Fujian and have mainly settled in the New York metropolitan area. The *Golden Venture* fiasco is not an isolated incident, and it indicates a new trend in Chinese immigration to the United States. The exact number of Fujianese in New York is, however, difficult to estimate because many of them are undocumented and therefore are not countable in formal surveys or censuses conducted in the United States. However, Einhorn (1994) estimated that as many as 100,000 Fujianese were living in New York in 1994 and that an additional 10,000 enter each year.

One way to get a sense of the extent of immigration from Fujian is to use the Chinese census and survey data. In a recent paper, Liang (forthcoming) describes the trends of emigration from Fujian over time. According to his findings, in 1990, Fujian had already surpassed Guangdong (29,580 versus 18,688) and ranked third (after Shanghai and Beijing). By 1995, however, Fujian ranked first in the number of emigrants, sending 66,200 people (or 28% of China's emigrant population) abroad, and Guangdong ranked ninth, with only 7,200 emigrants. It should be noted that the number of emigrants identified in Chinese censuses and surveys includes both legal and illegal migrants. It is possible that family members simply do not report that another family member has migrated illegally. Therefore, the number of emigrants for Fujian as reported in Liang's paper is likely to be an underestimate of the actual number of emigrants.

The common destinations for Fujianese immigrants are Japan, Taiwan, the United States, and Australia (Kwong, 1996). Fujianese actually would rather immigrate to Japan because it is much less expensive to go there and the wages are higher than other places. But the only problem is that "the Japanese government routinely deported those arrested back to China after informing the Fujian provincial authorities" (Kwong, 1997: 61). Many Fujianese believe that immigration officials in the United States are much more lenient than those in Japan and Taiwan. Thus some who are unsuccessful in entering Japan or Taiwan try to go to the United States (Ye, 1995). Within the United States, the most frequent final destination of Fujianese immigrants is New York City, partly because smuggling organizations in Chinatown orchestrate the smuggling process and partly because of the availability of jobs in restaurants and the garment industry.

As a result of the large volume of immigrants from Fujian to the New York area, the Fujianese population and community have quickly emerged and challenged the traditional dominance of immigrants from Guangdong. Fujianese have a dense social network, speak their own dialects, and have their own lawyers who help them get green cards and resolve other legal matters. In a stroll along East Broadway in Manhattan's Chinatown, one sees many Fujianese-owned businesses, such as driving schools, dating services, service centers for naturalization, and employment agencies. All these services make the settlement process much easier for the undocumented Fujianese.

What Drives Immigration from Fujian?

Historical Roots and Legacy of Emigration

Fujian is the province closest to Taiwan across the Taiwan Strait and is near such Southeast Asian countries as Singapore, Malaysia, the Philippines, and Indonesia. It had a population of 31 million in 1993. Fujian can be characterized as "a mountain province in Southeast China"; 80 percent of its geo-graphical area is covered by mountains (CMEC, 1993). Because Fujian is also a coastal province, its fishing industry is an important aspect of its economy and employment.

Emigration from Fujian started during the Ming dynasty in the middle of the fifteenth century and gained significant momentum during the Qing dy-nasty in the seventeenth century (Zhu, 1991). Some Chinese emigrated vol-untarily, but millions (particularly those from Fujian and Guangdong) were imported by European colonials to work at their tropical plantations and tin mines (Alexander, 1973; Kwong, 1996).

The large exodus of the Fujianese did not start until after the Opium War, which China lost to Great Britain. As part of the war settlement, China signed the Treaty of Nanking on August 29, 1842 (Spence, 1991). Article 2 of the treaty permitted the opening of five Chinese port cities—Guangzhou, Fuzhou, Xiamen, Ningbo, and Shanghai—for residence by British subjects and their families. Two of the port cities—Fuzhou and Xiamen—are located in Fujian.

The signing of this treaty greatly facilitated the exodus of Chinese laborers (Pan, 1990). This was also a time in which the Industrial Revolution was in high gear. Having abolished the international slave trade, Britain was looking for alternative cheap labor for its colonies. The discovery of gold in California provided a stimulus for the Chinese to emigrate to the United States (Sung, 1967; Zhou, 1992).

With regard to push factors within China, one was the country's unprece-dented population growth during the late Ming and mid-Qing periods. The best estimates suggest that in 1685 China had a population of 100 million. About a hundred years later, in 1790, its population was 301 million—an in-crease of 200 percent (Ho, 1959; Spence, 1991). The rapid growth of China's population created enormous pressure on the forces of production and plunged many people into poverty. This was especially the case in Fujian, about 80 percent of whose geographical area is covered by mountains. Meanwhile, rich merchants and landlords held large tracts of land, which deprived many peas-ants of their means of livelihood (Zhu, 1991). Finally, the Taiping Rebellion (1850–64), which attempted to overthrow the Qing government, also created some uncertainties for Chinese society, especially in the south.

It was under these historical conditions that a large exodus of Chinese emi-grants took place. The majority of Chinese emigrants were either contract la-borers or debtor (indentured) laborers, who had to work a certain number of years to pay off their transportation expenses, after which they would be free. However, whether these Chinese came as contract labor or debtor labor, many of them were actually treated as de facto slaves. This chapter in Chinese history is commonly known as "coolie trade" or "piglet" (Ye, 1995; Zhu, 1991).

From 1845 to 1874, Fujian's level of emigration from the port of Xiamen was modest. Emigration began to increase in 1875 when 16,683 left Fujian, rising to 43,613 in 1885, 105,416 in 1990, 126,008 in 1915, and then dropping to 77,781 in 1920 (Zhu, 1991). Unfortunately, statistics for migration by countries of destination are not available for these years. However, there seems to be a consensus among scholars that the majority of these emigrants left for Southeast Asia and that others went to the United States, Australia, and New Zealand.

The massive Chinese emigration has changed the demography of many Southeast Asian countries and others as well (Poston, Mao, and Yu, 1994). For instance, 80 percent of the Chinese in the Philippines, 55 percent in Indonesia, 50 percent in Burma, and 40 percent in Singapore are of Fujian origin (Zhu, 1991).

Many of the Chinese in Southeast Asian countries have been economically successful (Alexander, 1973). The overseas Chinese also play an important role in the economic development of China by sending remittances back home and by contributing money to educational institutions in China. One of the most prominent Chinese businessmen was Dr. Chen Jiageng, who emigrated from Fujian to Singapore. He founded Xiamen University in Xiamen, Fujian Province, and became a legendary figure of overseas Chinese.

It is because of these earlier emigrants from Fujian that many villages in Fujian are "overseas Chinese villages" (*qiao xiang*) with intensive networks between them and the overseas Chinese of Fujian origin. Thus it is common for Fujianese to have relatives living abroad. As has been shown, emigration is deeply rooted in Fujian's cultural heritage. However, this tradition of emigration came to a halt with the Chinese Revolution of 1949 to 1978 because its citizens were not permitted to leave China.[2]

Escaping Poverty or Relative Deprivation?

Do undocumented Fujianese migrants come to the United States because they are poor in China? Our answer is yes and no. The Fujianese are certainly poor according to the standard of living in the United States, but they are by no means poor compared with people in the rest of China. We first analyze Fujian's economic conditions in relation to the rest of China and then analyze the economic conditions of some of the major immigrant-sending regions within the province of Fujian.

Fujian's level of economic development is closely connected to its geographical position in relation to Taiwan. As the province of mainland China closest to Taiwan, Fujian had long been treated by both China and Taiwan as a military frontier province, and people on both sides of the Taiwan Strait were expecting a war to break out at any time. In fact, the exchange of canon fire between Fujian and Taiwan lasted for about three decades. The tension in the Taiwan Strait began to ease only in the 1970s when Chiang Kai-shek died and his son Chiang Ching-kou assumed power. For this reason, Fujian, which did not have a strong industrial base to begin with, received less investment from the Chinese central government.

However, ever since China initiated the transition to a market-oriented economy in 1978, Fujian has enjoyed a steady economic growth. The quality of life has also improved significantly compared with that in the other provinces. In 1979, China announced the opening of four Special Economic Zones, including Xiamen in Fujian (Crane, 1990), with the intention of attracting foreign investment and stimulating the economy. It is also because of its close proximity to Taiwan that Fujian received a large investment from Taiwan, which further boosted its local economy. In 1992, a year before the ill-fated voyage of the *Golden Venture,* Fujian received $6 billion in foreign investments, whereas other Chinese provinces received on average only half that amount. The investment capital from Taiwan is particularly noticeable: $6.96 billion from 1978 to 1999 ("Experimental Region of Collaboration," 1999). Because of the relatively flexible economic policies and preferential treatment that Fujian has received since 1978, some sociologists classify it as a laissez-faire province, along with Guangdong Province in southern China (Lyons, 1994; Nee, 1996; Parish and Michelson, 1996).

The overall economic prosperity in Fujian since 1978 is further supported by the statistics on per capita income of rural households in various Chinese provinces in 1992. It is more relevant to study per capita income for rural households because most of the undocumented Fujianese migrants are from rural areas. In 1978, when China's transition to a market-oriented economy had just started, the per capita income in rural Fujian households was only about 134 yuan, compared with 133 yuan for China as a whole. What makes Fujian distinctive is that Fujian's rural household per capita income grew at a much faster rate than that of the average province in China. For example, from 1978 to 1988, Fujian's per capita income for rural households increased by 168 percent, compared with 146 percent for rural China as a whole.[3] The difference is even more pronounced for the period 1978–92. During that time, Fujian's rural household per capita income rose by 229 percent versus 179 percent for rural households of China as a whole. As a result, the per capita income of Fujian's rural households rose to eighth place (out of thirty provinces) in 1992 (compared with twelfth in 1978). These data indicate that in contrast to other provinces in China, Fujian has enjoyed a particular advantage in the process of transition to a market-oriented economy. Therefore, at the provincial level, there is no evidence that Fujian is poor compared with the rest of China.

We further examine the economic conditions of major immigrant-sending regions in Fujian—Fuzhou (the capital of Fujian), Fuqing, Changle, Lianjiang, and Pingtan—all of which are concentrated in the eastern part of Fujian and are geographically very close to one another. Fuzhou is a large metropolis with a population of 5 million and is the center of political and economic activities in the province. Fuqing and Changle are extremely close to Fuzhou. Pingtan County is an island off the east coast and is the farthest county from Fuzhou of the immigrant-sending regions. Unlike the northern provinces of China where Mandarin is the standard language, people in Fujian speak many local dialects. Thus a person who speaks the Fuzhou dialect, for example, would not be able to communicate in Xiamen, another well-known city in Fujian that is not in these five regions. However, because of the geographical proximity of these five immigrant-sending regions, they all share a common dialect: the Fuzhou dialect. This common local dialect has implications once Fujian immigrants move to the New York metropolitan area.

Table 8.1 reveals several characteristics of Fujian's five major immigrant-sending regions. Column 3 shows the average salary for urban workers in each region. The average yearly salaries for workers in urban Fuzhou and Fuqing are almost equivalent to the average of Fujian Province as a whole. These data indicate that Fuzhou and Fuqing are not poor by Fujian standards. Workers in the urban areas of the other three regions (Changle, Lianjiang, and Pingtan) are paid slightly lower than the average for Fujian. However, as we discussed earlier, since most undocumented Fujianese are from rural areas, it is more relevant to examine the corresponding figures for such areas.

The per capita incomes for rural households in these immigrant-sending regions are quite different. In fact, with the exception of Pingtan, rural households

Table 8.1   Characteristics of Major Immigrant-Sending Regions
in Fujian Province, 1993

Region	Population (thousands)	Average Salary (yuan)	Per Capita Income (yuan)
Fuzhou city	5,507	4,803	N.A.
Fuqing city	1,101	4,853	1,640
Changle County	654	4,176	1,538
Lianjiang County	613	4,101	1,305
Pingtan County	344	4,101	1,065
Fujian Province	30,992	4,890	1,211

Source: State Statistical Bureau (1994).

in these regions enjoy an advantage in per capita income, especially in Fuqing and Changle. This finding is consistent with the macrolevel portrait of development in Fujian in general. Kristof (1993), a reporter for the *New York Times*, went to Fujian after the *Golden Venture* episode and made similar observations.[4]

If absolute poverty is not the reason for migration, why are Fujianese risking their lives to come to the United States? We argue that a sense of relative deprivation is causing Fujianese peasants to make desperate attempts to migrate. The theory of relative deprivation was first suggested by Stouffer et al. (1949) in their study of army life, especially in relation to promotions during World War II. According to this theory, an individual makes judgments about his or her welfare that are based not only on his or her absolute level of material possessions (such as income) but perhaps more important on the relative level of welfare in reference to others in the community. This sense of relative deprivation has strong implications for an individual's behavior.

In the 1960s and 1970s, the concept of relative deprivation was used to study mobilization and rebellion (see, e.g., Gurr, 1969; Tilly, 1978). More recently, economist Stark and his associates have used this concept to study migration, and the concept is now a major component of the "new economics of migration" (Stark, 1991). In a study of migration from Mexico to the United States, Stark and Taylor hypothesized that "given a household's initial absolute income and its expected net income from migration, more relatively deprived households are more likely to send migrants to foreign labor markets than are less relatively deprived households" (Stark and Taylor, 1989: 4). This hypothesis is supported by data on migration from Mexico (Stark and Taylor, 1989; see also Portes and Rumbaut, 1996).

We argue that the relative deprivation approach has particular relevance for explaining undocumented migration from Fujian Province. China's transition to a market-oriented economy has dramatically increased overall income inequality because many people seized the opportunity to get rich quickly by whatever means possible (Khan and Riskin, 1998; Liu, 1995). The most commonly used measure of income inequality is the Gini index (Xie and Hannum, 1996). A Gini index of .4 or larger is considered to be exceptionally high inequality. The World Bank (1996) reported that China's Gini index was .374 in 1992. More recently, according to a study conducted by the People's University of China in Beijing, China's Gini index was .434 in 1994 (He, 1996). The large and growing value of the Gini index is consistent with the findings from social surveys in China that have suggested that a substantial proportion of respondents have complained about the rising income inequality over time (CND, 1996). The increased inequality in China makes people at the bottom feel a sense of relative deprivation and desperate to find ways to make money and become rich. Going to the United States, through either legal or illegal channels, is an alternative way of getting rich, they think.

With regard to Fujian Province, Lyons (1998) conducted the most systematic study on trends in income disparity in Fujian. Using county-level data from Fujian Province from 1978 to 1995, Lyons analyzed changes in income distribution. He found that the county coefficient of variation (a measure of relative disparity in income) in rural households increased from .209 in 1983 to .273 in 1995. One source of increased relative income disparity is remittance. Although no direct information is available on the amount of remittance sent to Fujian each year, one can gauge the impact of remittance through other channels. As Lyons (1998) argued, part of the remittance was used to start nonagricultural enterprises that have increased rapidly since 1978.

The impact of remittance can also be detected through consumption patterns. One of the ways emigrant households spend the remittance is to build new houses or improve housing conditions. On our recent trip to Changle, one of the major immigrant-sending regions in Fujian, we saw many newly built brick houses. Using data from the 1995 China 1% Population Sample Survey, Liang and Zhang (1999) further analyzed the impact of emigration on housing conditions in Fujian. They found that, controlling for other important sociodemographic characteristics (such education, age, and occupation), families with emigrants are more likely to live in larger houses and have better housing conditions (including the type of cooking fuel used and the availability of a private bathroom and kitchen).

Local Fujianese also like to build fancy tombs for their ancestors to symbolize the good virtue of the ancestors in making the overseas venture possible. We also saw some elementary schools that were supported by money from overseas, many of which bear the names of the overseas Fujianese who donated money for them. The flow of a large amount of remittance also changes the income distribution in the communities, creating a sense of relative deprivation for those Fujian peasants who do not receive it, and provides further impetus for going abroad.

The lavish spending and consumption patterns of Fujianese who return from abroad also contribute to a sense of relative deprivation by the local Fujianese. From the founding of the People's Republic of China to 1977, having a relative abroad was not something of which to be proud. In fact, during the Cultural Revolution of 1966–76, it was a major source of trouble and cause for political persecution. Many families with relatives abroad were accused of spying for foreign countries and therefore severely punished. However, since 1978, China has changed its policy toward the overseas Chinese and has encouraged them to visit China and especially to invest in businesses. As a result, more and more of the overseas Chinese return to visit relatives (*sheng qin*) and to do business in their hometown.[5]

Most of the overseas Chinese of Fujian origin visit relatives during the Chinese New Year. They stay in luxury hotels, bring fancy gifts from abroad, give *hong bao* (red purses, money) to friends and relatives, go to karaoke clubs, and have big feasts in expensive restaurants for relatives. Ye (1995) estimated that almost 80 percent of the customers who stay in hotels in Fuzhou during the Chinese New Year are overseas Chinese of Fujian origin who are visiting relatives. Because of the large volume of overseas Fujianese who visit, some hotels depend on them for business. One manager at a hotel in the city of Fuzhou put it in this way: "To tell you the truth, without the Fujianese returning home for visits, our business could not survive."

Local Fujianese are overwhelmed by how much wealth one can accumulate abroad. What they are rarely told is how hard one has to work to make it and often under subhuman conditions; they only see how glamorous it is to work abroad. The return of the overseas Chinese has particularly motivated peasants in Fujian to migrate internationally because of the extravagant lifestyles that the visiting overseas Fujianese display.

The large volume of emigration and remittance have had a major impact on the local economy. In other provinces of China, it is customary to build the major airport in the capital city of the province. In Fujian, however, the biggest airport was built in Changle, not in the capital city of Fuzhou. In a casual stroll along a street in Changle, one sees many business banners with the word *hua qiao* (overseas Chinese) attached. To accommodate overseas Chinese, several hotels and travel agencies are named *hua qiao* hotels or *hua qiao* travel agencies.

Under such circumstances, migration is perceived as "the thing to do"—the only way that young people can advance economically (Portes, 1997). In some villages in Fujian, almost 90 percent of the young people have gone abroad (Ye, 1995). Young people who are reluctant to go abroad are considered *mei chu xi* (no great future). As more and more people emigrate to other countries, more and more Fujianese communities emerge (especially in New York), which further facilitates the process of migration for other family members from the same communities in Fujian. This is the nature of the cumulative causation of migration, which has been documented clearly in the case of Mexican migration to the United States (Massey et al., 1994).

We have so far discussed changes in income disparity in Fujian from 1983 to 1995 and examined various ways remittances have been spent and their impact on the local economy and in further stimulating more emigration. To substantiate further our argument about relative deprivation, we turn now to the question of who migrated internationally from Fujian. Table 8.2 compares the sociodemographic characteristics of emigrants and nonemigrants from Fujian Province. This comparison is important, because research on Chinese immigration to the United States usually focuses on the Chinese immigrants and rarely examines how immigrants compare with the people who choose to stay. As table 8.2 shows, men are heavily represented in the emigrant population, accounting for 74 percent of the emigrants. The mean ages of the emigrant and nonemigrant populations are similar, but they actually mask a major difference in the age distribution of the two groups. Nearly 70 percent of the emigrants versus 27 percent of the nonemigrants are in the working age of twenty to thirty-four. Another major difference is education. Almost 16 percent of nonemigrants, but fewer than 1 percent of the emigrants, have no formal education. Nearly half of the emigrants have junior high school education, whereas close to 50 percent of the nonemigrants have only an elementary school education. Thus, if education is used as a proxy for socioeconomic status, it is clear that emigrants from Fujian are not at the bottom of socioeconomic hierarchy.[6]

Table 8.2   Sociodemographic Characteristics of Emigrants
and Nonemigrants, Fujian, 1995

Variables	Emigrant (%)	Nonemigrant (%)
Sex		
Male	74.1	50.79
Age (yr.)		
0–14	0.55	29.59
15–19	8.26	8.2
20–34	68.04	27.43
35+	23.14	34.77
Mean Age	29.21	29.03
Marital Status		
Unmarried	37.95	22.41
Married, spouse present	61.22	68.02
Remarried, spouse present	0.55	1.7
Divorced	0	0.65
Widowed	0.28	6.53
Education		
No formal education	0.28	15.88
Literate	0	3.75
Elementary school	27.42	48.23
Junior high school	47.92	22.42
High school	19.39	7.32
Junior college and above	4.99	1.56
Place of Origin		
City	17.36	14.34
Town	17.08	8.33
Rural	65.56	77.33

Source: Liang and Zhang (1999).

Culture of Seafaring

Unlike earlier Fujian emigration to either Nan Yang (Southeast Asia) or the United States, the current illegal immigration is highly risky. For example, the *Golden Venture* traveled 112 days, passing Thailand, going through Africa (Kenya and the Ivory Coast), and finally reaching Queens in New York City (Schemo, 1993b). The Fujianese aboard suffered from the lack of food and poor nutrition, isolation, and extremely poor sanitary conditions (Schemo, 1993b; 1993a). It is hard to imagine that the average Chinese could endure such an ordeal. Do Fujianese have any particular characteristics that make them exceptionally risk taking? We argue that their familiarity with sea life facilitates the voyage to the United States.

The sea is a way of life for many Fujianese. Because Fujian is located on the southeastern coast of China, many Fujianese depend on fishing for a living. They are more familiar with life at sea and are not afraid of its difficult conditions. Mr. Chen, a fisherman in Fujian, said: "There is a risk of not being able to return for every fishing trip. But how can you catch fish without going to the sea? For me, going to America is just like another fishing trip." Another informant expressed it this way: "I am from Changle, we are sons of the sea. Our life depends on the sea for generations. . . . My wife does not worry about me when I go on a fishing trip for days because she knows I am going to be ok" (cited in Xin 1993). This unique way of life and culture helps the Fujianese overcome the fear of a voyage of several months and of enduring the conditions that would perhaps be unbearable for most non-Fujianese.

The deep connection with sea life can be traced throughout in Fujianese history and in Fujian's folklore. A well-known Chinese scholar of the Ming dynasty wrote: "Hai zhe min ren zhi tian ye" [sea is the field for Fujianese] (Wang, 1994: 4). Because of the lack of arable land, the Fujianese have for many years earned their living by fishing. There is also a saying that Fujian has a silk road on the sea. During the Ming dynasty, Fujianese took advantage of several port cities and the ready availability of good-quality lumber for ship-building to transport silk and cotton from Jiangsu and Zhejiang Provinces for export to other countries (Wang, 1994).

The most famous folktale is of Mazu, the sea goddess. Legend has it that Mazu always helps people through hardships and, in particular, rescues fishermen when they face crises at sea. Even today, before fishermen in Fujian go fishing, they pray to Mazu to protect them. This tradition has been carried over to the Fujianese immigrant community in New York. In February 1999, during the annual parade of the Lunar Chinese New Year in Flushing and Manhattan's Chinatown, we observed floats carrying statues of Mazu.

History and folklore are suggestive of the Fujianese's close attachment to the sea, but they are not a substitute for a rigorous and systematic analysis. Therefore we measured the importance of the fishing industry in the current Fujianese economy. Compared with other provinces in China, the fishing industry accounts for 17 percent of the total agricultural output in 1992—the highest proportion among all the provinces of mainland China (SSB, 1993). The fishing industry is clearly more important in Fujian than in other provinces. Moreover, the total value of the fishing industry output places Fujian in fourth place behind Guangdong, Shandong, and Zhejiang (all coastal provinces) (SSB, 1993).

The importance of fishing is even more evident if one looks at the five immigrant-sending regions—Fuzhou, Fuqing, Changle, Lianjiang, and Pingtan. On average, more than half (54%) the agricultural output value is related to fishing industries of these regions (SSB, 1994). This is particularly the case for Lianjiang and Pingtan Counties, whose fishing outputs account for 69 percent and 75 percent of the total agricultural outputs, respectively (SSB, 1994).

Despite the unique economic structure in the immigrant-sending communities, which is dominated largely by fishing-related industries, the rich historical evidence, and folklore linking Fujianese culture with sea life, we are by no means suggesting that most emigrants are fishermen before their departure.[7] Instead, we argue that life at sea is familiar to many Fujianese who live in these regions and that this familiarity prepares them well for the sometimes dangerous journey to the United States or other destination countries.

Snake People and Snakeheads

Given the significant income and wage differentials in Fujian, the Fujianese are clearly motivated to migrate to the United States. However, many Fujianese cannot make the journey on their own. Many players assist in this process: snakeheads, or *she tou* (smugglers), who organize the entire smuggling process; corrupt Chinese officials, who make sure that the Chinese Coast Guard conveniently disappears when ships carrying illegal immigrants leave for international waters (Kwong, 1997); contacts in many transit countries who arrange for charter flights to the United States or are subcontracted to help the immigrants across the U.S. border; enforcers in New York whose task is to threaten and torture illegal immigrants until they pay their debts; and, finally the snake people, or *ren she*[8] (the illegal migrants), who usually endure long journeys to and harsh working conditions in the United States. The smuggling of undocumented Fujianese is a complex and difficult operation that does not succeed without an extremely careful plan and collaboration around the globe.

The snakeheads are much more sophisticated than the "coyotes" who help Mexicans cross the U.S.-Mexican border. Their organizations are transnational and have access to the most advanced technology for communication. Their passport and visa factories have the capacity to make fake passports of any country, fake visas to the United States, and any other documents that are needed. They are also able to obtain the most up-to-date information and plan the best possible routes for smuggling people.

The smuggling process typically begins in the communities in Fujian, where smugglers go to recruit potential migrants. Most experts in the study of human smuggling believe that the mastermind of today's smuggling organization is located in Taiwan (Kwong, 1997; Myers, 1997). Such earlier smuggling was pretty much a mom-and-pop operation with limited contacts around the globe and involved smuggling only a few individuals at a time. These operations were run mostly by Cantonese, people from Guangdong Province, another coastal province not far from Fujian (Myers, 1997). However, it was not until the "Taiwan connection" was established that smugglers had access to sophisticated technology and were able to transport large numbers of people with high rate of success.

The ability to establish a global smuggling network seems to be an unintended consequence of the Cold War. After the defeat of the Kuomintang (KMT) by Mao Zedong's People's Liberation Army in 1949, KMT head Chiang Kaishek was preparing to regain mainland China when the opportunity arose. As an integral part of this strategy, the Intelligence Bureau of the Military National Defense (IBMND) was cultivating all its connections among those who fled China (many of whom had connections with criminal organizations [Kwong, 1997]). According to Myers (1997) and Kwong (1997), with funding and training from the CIA, the IBMND turned the KMT Third Army in Myanmar and Thailand into "Chinese Irregular Forces," who were alleged to be involved in heroin production and export. In the late 1950s, again with further support from the CIA, Taiwan expanded its technical and economic assistance to countries in Africa, Central and South America, and the Caribbean islands. "Thousands of Taiwanese were transferred to work in aid programs . . . and many thousand more Taiwanese emigrated to these obscure countries" (Myers, 1997: 106). Although there is no direct evidence of the Taiwan government's involvement in human smuggling, there is no doubt that Taiwanese crime organizations have taken advantage of the foundations laid by the Taiwan government, and the U.S. law enforcement officials strongly suspect that Taiwan's military and intelligence communities are involved in and profit from the human smuggling trade (Kwong, 1997: 87). In any event, it is clear that smugglers have a dense network that reaches every part of the world: Fujian, Taiwan, Hong Kong, the Golden Triangle (northern mountain region of Myanmar, Thailand, and Laos), Latin America, Africa, and New York's Chinatown.

The Taiwanese have another advantage in smuggling Fujianese to the United States other than geographical proximity: the cultural linkage between Fujian and Taiwan. Many people in Taiwan (80% by some estimates; see "Experimental Region of Collaboration," 1999) are the descendants of Fujianese who migrated to Taiwan many years ago. Though the local dialects are not entirely identical, the Taiwanese and Fujianese have many similar cultural traditions, such as praying to the sea goddess Mazu for safety. This cultural homogeneity facilitates communication and builds a sense of trust, which is essential for smuggling people thousands of miles away from their homes.

There are several strategies for smuggling snake people into the United States. One strategy is to use fake documents that allow them to land directly at airports in the United States. In this case, the snake people first buy fake Taiwanese, Singaporean, Malaysian, or South Korean passports to apply for U.S. visas as citizens of these countries. Often through travel agencies in the United States and China, snake people also mingle with different delegations from China. The only difference is that snake people will simply disappear upon arrival at the destination. Often they are picked up by the smugglers and assigned to work in restaurants or garment factories in the New York metropolitan area. This strategy continues to be used. On December 27, 1997, eight Fujianese were about to board Air China Flight 981 from Shanghai to New York's JFK airport. Chinese immigration inspector Chen Haiyin noted that all eight Fujianese held Chinese passports and U.S. immigration visas but looked suspicious, so she detained them for further inspection of the documents. It turned out that all eight visas were forged ("$120,000 Bought 8 Pages," 1997).

The second strategy requires snake people to pass through transit countries in other parts of the world before they reach the United States. Some snake people travel on foot and by bus from China's Yunnan Province (southwestern China) to Thailand and other Southeast Asian countries and then take flights to the United States (Liu, 1996; Myers, 1997). "Between eastern and western processing and holding centers, more than 43 countries played a transit role in airborne and seaborne smuggling" (Myers, 1997: 117). Mexico is a major transit country for snake people. Once they arrive in Mexico, local subcontractors take them across the U.S.-Mexican border.

Another variation of this channel is for snake people to arrive in Canada using Hong Kong passports, since holders of Hong Kong passports do not need visas to enter Canada. Once in Canada, the snake people will be transported to the United States. On December 10, 1998, Doris Meissner, the commissioner of the Immigration and Naturalization Service, announced the crackdown of a smuggling ring that had brought more than thirty-six hundred illegal Chinese immigrants into the United States over the previous two years (Chen, 1998; Holmes, 1998). The ring, consisting mainly of Chinese and members of a Native American tribe, transported immigrants through an upstate New York Indian reservation that was guarded minimally by the U.S. Border Patrol.

Another strategy is to smuggle snake people by sea. Snakeheads often use crumbling freighters or fishing vessels owned by Taiwanese. Between 1991 and 1993, thirty-two ships with a total of fifty-three hundred Chinese were found in the waters of Japan, Taiwan, Indonesia, Australia, Singapore, Hawaii, Guatemala, El Salvador, Honduras, and the United States (Chin, 1996: 157). In sum, whatever strategies snake people use to enter the United States, it is clear that they cannot make it to the United States without the involvement of snakeheads.

New York's Chinatown plays a pivotal role in this process as well. For a good part of this century, crime and gang activity have been part of life in New York's Chinatown (Chin, 1996; Kwong, 1996), but it was not until recent years that members of Chinatown's organized crime organizations became involved in smuggling immigrants from China, among other things (Cooper, 1996).[9] In New York, the smugglers (often in the name of "welcoming and receiving organizations") are responsible for picking up the snake people and escorting them to Chinatown for employment and sometimes sending them to work outside New York if opportunities are available. They also make sure that all snake people are taken care of by enforcers to collect the smuggling fees. In some cases, enforcers use severe physical torture and sometimes sexual abuse to collect the smuggling debt (Chin, 1997; Kwong, 1997).

Summary and Discussion

This chapter has striven comprehensively and systematically to examine undocumented immigration from China's Fujian Province. It first provided a historical overview of emigration from Fujian Province, showing that emigration from Fujian is not a new phenomenon. This historical legacy has stimulated contemporary out-migration because of the lifestyle overseas Fujianese display when they visit Fujian. What is new, however, is the extremely dangerous form this new migration has taken. One important fact that has often been overlooked is that since they live on the east coast of China, many Fujianese are used to life at sea and risk taking as a way of life. This trait makes them particularly good candidates for being snake people.

We suggest that the sense of relative deprivation driven by China's transition to a market economy and the large amount of remittance sent to Fujian are other critical factors in the decisions of Fujianese to immigrate to other countries. Even though the standard of living in Fujian has risen, people at the bottom of the income hierarchy feel poorer than they actually are when they see others getting rich so quickly. In addition, our data clearly show that people who live in these immigrant-sending communities are not poor compared with those in the rest of China or in the rest of Fujian. We suggest, as Massey (1995) pointed out, that in one way or another China's transition to a market-oriented economy has planted some seeds for migration.

What distinguishes Fujianese immigration from other cases (such as the Mexican) is the heavy involvement of the transnational smuggling network. Although the involvement of this network increases the success rate of smuggling, it also increases the cost, which makes this type of migration not accessible to everyone. However, this pattern began to change recently. During our fieldwork in the summer of 1994, we found that snake-heads have started using some new tactics in recruiting potential snake people. For example, they send women with children to chat with potential snake people, which makes the recruitment less threatening, and recruiters often tell potential snake people stories of success of former townspeople to show how easy it is to go to the United States and become rich.

There have also been some changes in the way smugglers collect money. Although the smuggling fee in most cases is still $30,000–$35,000 or even higher, the way snakeheads collect money is different. Some snakeheads do not collect any money until the snake people arrive in the United States (most likely New York City). Other snakeheads lend snake people some money before the departure, which makes the emigration option very attractive. Over time, snakeheads seem to make offers that are difficult to refuse, and because of the high success rate, more and more Fujianese are drawn into the process of illegal migration to the United States.

The entry of large numbers of Fujianese into New York and especially their concentration in Manhattan's Chinatown have implications for the ethnic economy and politics of the city. Increasingly, the Fujianese, as new blood in Chinatown, are playing a greater role in the Chinese community and in many ways are rivaling the old-timers from Guangdong and Taiwan. Lii (1996a, 1996b,

1997) noted that Fujianese have taken control of almost all the takeout places in the New York area that used to be owned by ethnic Chinese from Guang-dong and Southeast Asia. The entry of a large number of Fujianese immigrants is also providing a new source of labor for the garment industry, which often pays less than the minimum wage (Kwong, 1996). Furthermore, there has been a heavy concentration of Fujianese immigrants in some sections of Man-hattan's Chinatown; for example, some have called East Broadway "Fuzhou Street" (Cooper, 1996; Kinkead, 1992). At the same time, there is also evidence that Fujianese are expanding their businesses to Texas and Indiana (Einhorn, 1994).[10]

The emergence of the Fujianese community introduces new dynamics of "transnational politics" in Chinatown. Most Fujianese are pro–mainland China. In contrast, the Chinatown old-timers are more likely to be pro-Taiwan. So, for the first time in 1995, a Fujianese-led organization (the United Chinese Asso-ciations of New York) celebrated China's National Day on October 1 (Kwong, 1996), but the Chinatown old-timers (led by the Chinese Consolidated Benevo-lent Association) continued to celebrate October 10 ("double 10" as some call it), the day of the birth of the Republic of China. So far both celebrations have been peaceful. However, Tommy Chan (the deputy inspector of the Fifth Pre-cinct, where Chinatown is located) is caught in the middle of these "transna-tional politics" and tries to keep a balance between the pro-Taiwan Cantonese old-timers and pro–mainland Fujianese newcomers (Lii, 1996b). As more and more immigrants from Fujian arrive each day, the extent of "transnational politics" is likely to be further intensified.

In this short update, we would like to discuss two trends that are worth noting for understanding long-term consequences of international migration from Fujian Province to the United States now and in the years ahead.

First, since our original article was published nearly ten years ago, many Fujianese immigrants have gotten married and had children in the United States. Among many of these Fujianese parents there is a pattern of sending their American-born children to their hometowns in Fuijan. When we talked to local officials in these migrant-sending towns, they often jokingly said that the issue is so important that it will affect Sino-U.S. relations (all American-born children are U.S. citizens). These children often stay in China until they are school age and are then sent back to the United States to attend elementary school. It will be interesting to examine the short-term and long-term consequences of this experience for these second-generation immigrants.

In the United States, a major new pattern of employment for Fujianese has developed. Instead of working in New York City's Chinatown, increasingly large numbers of Fujianese immigrants have found work in nongateway destinations. In one way, this reflects the Fujianese saturation of the restaurant market in New York City. At the same time, the establishment of many new Chinese restaurants in nongateway destinations is meeting the job demand generated by a large supply of Fujianese immigrant workers. Although the first destination of Fujianese immigrants may still be New York City, more often than not their first employment location is in another state. This shift in patterns of employment offers opportunities for immigrant workers but also presents challenges because nongateway locations often do not have services that are associated with gateway destinations, such as a hometown association, bilingual services and education, and bilingual church services. It is important to examine how immigrants fare under this new regime of employment and settlement.

NOTES

An earlier version of this chapter was presented at the 1996 annual meetings of the American Sociological Association, New York City, August 21, 1996, and a conference at the New School for Social Research in 1997. We thank Hector Cordero-Gozman, Josh DeWind, Greta Gilbertson, Sean-Shong Hwang, Peter Kwong, Pyong Gap Min, and Philip Yang for their helpful comments and constructive suggestions on earlier versions of this chapter. This project is supported, in part, by grants from the National Institute of Child Health and Human Development (1R55HD/OD3487801A1 and 1R29 HD34878–01A2) and Queens College Presidential Research Award, whose support is gratefully acknowledged.

1. Among the 286 people aboard the *Golden Venture,* 10 died trying to swim to shore (Faison, 1995): 246 were from Fujian and 40 were from Wenzhou in Zhejiang Province (also on the east coast) (Kwong, 1994).

2. During the late 1950s and 1960s, however, many Fujianese escaped to Hong Kong in search of political and economic freedom.

3. Statistics used in this paragraph have been adjusted for inflation.

4. Some even go further in arguing that it is precisely because of Fujian's recent economic growth that some peasants are able to pay snakeheads (smugglers) large sums of money to emigrate (Xin, 1993; Ye, 1995).

5. Obviously only Fujianese immigrants who have already obtained green cards are able to return.

6. We also compared the socioeconomic and demographic characteristics of emigrants in the 1995 sample survey conducted in Fujian with Chin's (1997) sample selected from illegal migrants in Manhattan's Chinatown and found that the results are amazingly similar.

7. Our field trips in Fujian suggest that many people switched from fishing to other types of businesses because the fishing industry has been declining in recent years owing to overfishing.

8. According to Xin (1993: 131), these terms were first used by people from Guangdong, who initiated the process of undocumented migration to the United States. Legend has it that if one transports a single snake, it is easy for the snake to die on the road. But if one transports many snakes together, they will rely on one another and are likely to survive to their destination. Historical records also suggest that the indigenous Fujianese used snakes as totems for worship (Wang, 1994: 15).

9. Chin's (1998) recent research implies that human smuggling is not so much organized crime as crime that is organized. Chin argued that although certain members of organized crime groups are involved in human smuggling, it is not clear that their participation is sanctioned by their organizations.

10. During the course of our research, we also came across Fujianese who are working in Connecticut and Rhode Island.

REFERENCES

Alexander, Garth. 1973. *The Invisible China: The Overseas Chinese and the Politics of Southeast Asia.* New York, Macmillan.

Butterfield, Fox. 1996. "Three Are Indicted in Plot to Smuggle Chinese Aliens into New York." *New York Times,* October 10.

Cao, Guilin. 1995. *To Du Ke* (Human smuggling). Beijing: Modern Publishing House.

Chan, Sucheng. 1990. "European and Asian Immigration into the United States in Comparative Perspective, 1820s to 1920s." In *Immigration Reconsidered: History, Sociology, and Politics,* edited by Virginia Yans-McLaughlin, 37–75. New York: Oxford University Press.

Chen, David. 1998. "China to Chinatown, Via Canada." *New York Times,* December 20, Metro Section.

Chin, Ko-lin. 1996. *Chinatown Gangs: Extortion, Enterprise, and Ethnicity.* New York: Oxford University Press.

———. 1997. "Safe House or Hell House?: Experiences of Newly Arrived Undocumented Chinese." In *Human Smuggling: Chinese Migrant Trafficking and the Challenge to America's Immigration Tradition,* edited by Paul J. Smith, 169–95. Washington, D.C.: Center for Strategic and International Studies.

———. 1998. "The Social Organization of Chinese Human Smuggling." Paper presented at conference titled "International Migration and Transnational Crime," Rutgers University at Newark, May 15.

"China Arrested 256 Snake Heads in 1995." 1996. *People's Daily,* overseas ed., January 29.

China Map Editorial Committee (CMEC). 1993. *Handbook of Updated Chinese Maps.* Beijing: China Map Press.

China News Digest (CND). 1996. "Survey of 40 Cities in China." August 23.

China Population Census Office (CPCO). 1993. *Tabulations from 1990 China Population Census*. Beijing: China Statistics Publishing House.

China Population Sample Survey Office (CPSSO). 1997. *Tabulations from 1995 China 1% Population Sample Survey*. Beijing: China Statistics Publishing House.

Cooper, Michael. 1996. "New Mission for Lin Ze Xu, Hero of Old." *New York Times,* June 2.

Crane, George T. 1990. *The Political Economy of China's Special Economic Zones*. New York: M. E. Sharpe.

Einhorn, Bruce. 1994. "Send Your Huddled Masses, and a Hot and Sour Soup." *Business Week,* November 14.

Espenshade, Thomas. 1995. "Unauthorized Immigration to the United States." *Annual Review of Sociology* 21:195–216.

"An Experimental Region of Collaboration between Fujian and Taiwan Was Established." 1999. *People's Daily,* overseas ed., March 15.

Faison, Seth. 1995. "Asian Gang Members Arrested in Kidnapping." *New York Times,* March 22.

Fritsch, Jane. 1993. "One Failed Voyage Illustrates Flow of Chinese Immigration." *New York Times,* June 7.

Gurr, Ted Robert. 1969. *Why Men Rebel?* Princeton: Princeton University Press.

He, Qinglian. 1996. "Analysis of Social Stratification in China." *China News Digest,* July 26.

Heer, David. 1992. *Undocumented Mexicans in the United States*. ASA Rose Monograph Series. New York: Cambridge University Press.

Herbert, Bob. 1996. "Freedom Birds." *New York Times,* April 5.

Ho, Pingti. 1959. *Studies on Population in China: 1368–1953*. Cambridge: Harvard University Press.

Holmes, Steven A. 1998. "Ring Is Cracked in Smuggling of Illegal Chinese Immigrants: Route Ran through Indian Land in New York." *New York Times,* December 11. Metro Section.

Hood, Marlowe. 1997. "Sourcing the Problem: Why Fuzhou?" In *Human Smuggling: Chinese Migrant Trafficking and the Challenge to America's Immigration Tradition,* edited by Paul J. Smith, 76–92. Washington, D.C.: Center for Strategic and International Studies.

Institute of Modern Chinese History of Chinese Academy of Social Sciences (IMCH-CASS). 1983. *Modern Chinese History* (in Chinese). Beijing: China Youth Press.

Khan, Azizur Rahman, and Carl Riskin. 1998. "Income and Inequality in China: Composition, Growth, and Distribution of Household Income, 1988–1995." *China Quarterly* 154:222–32.

Kinkead, Gwen. 1992. *Chinatown*. New York: HarperCollins.

Kristof, Nicholas. 1993. "We Think of the U.S. as a Kind of Heaven." *New York Times,* July 21.

Kwong, Peter. 1994. "China's Human Traffickers." *Nation,* October 17, 422–25.

———. 1996. *The New Chinatown*. Rev. ed. New York: Hill and Wang.

———. 1997. *Forbidden Workers: Illegal Chinese Immigrants and American Labor*. New York: New Press.

Li, Fangfang. 1995. *Two Beijing Playboys in New York* (in Chinese). Beijing: Qunzhong Press.

Liang, Zai. Forthcoming. "Demography of Illicit Emigration from China: A Sending Country's Perspective." *Sociological Forum.*

Liang, Zai, and Toni Zhang. 1999. "Emigration and Housing Conditions in Fujian, China." Paper presented at the annual meeting of the Population Association of America, New York City, March 26.

Lii, Jane H. 1996a. "The Chinese Menu Guys." *New York Times,* sec. 13, pp. 1–2 and 11–12, "The City." July 28.

———. 1996b. "The Tightrope of Tommy Chan." *New York Times,* sec. 13, pp. 1–2 and 8–9, "The City." October 20.

———. 1997. "The New Blood in Chinatown: on the Eve of Hong Kong Takeover, a Revolution Takes Hold in Lower Manhattan." *New York Times,* "The City." June 22.

Lin, Jan. 1998. *Reconstructing Chinatown: Ethnic Enclave, Global Change.* Minneapolis: University of Minnesota Press.

Liu, Ningrun. 1996. "The Gangsters on the Black Trail." *China Times,* no. 7.

Liu, Xiaozhu. 1995. "Income Distribution in Chinese Society." Working paper series no. 2. Beijing: China Strategic Institute.

Lyons, Thomas. 1994. "Economic Reform in Fujian: Another View from the Villages." In *The Economic Transformation of South China,* edited by T. P. Lyons and Victor Nee, 141–68. Cornell East Asia Series no. 70. Ithaca, N.Y.: Cornell University East Asia Program.

———. 1998. "Intraprovincial Disparities in China: Fujian Province, 1978–1995." *Economic Geography* 74:405–32.

Massey, Douglas S. 1995. "The New Immigration and Ethnicity in the United States." *Population and Development Review* 21:631–52.

Massey, Douglas S., Rafael Alarcon, Jorge Durand, and Humberto Gonzalez. 1987. *Return to Aztlán: The Social Process of International Migration from Western Mexico.* Berkeley: University of California Press.

Massey, Douglas S., Jaquin Arango, Graeme Hugo, Ali Kouaouci, Adela Pellegrino, and E. Edward Taylor. 1994. "An Evaluation of International Migration Theory: The North American Case." *Population and Development Review* 20:699–751.

———. 1998. *Worlds in Motion: Understanding International Migration at the End of the Millennium.* New York: Oxford University Press.

Massey, Douglas S., and Audrey Singer. 1995. "New Estimates of Undocumented Mexican Migration and the Probability of Apprehension." *Demography* 32:203–13.

McFadden, Robert D. 1993. "Chinese Abroad Are Seized for Illegal Entry." *New York Times,* June 7.

———. 1998. "Illegal Immigrants Seized after Jersey Shore Landing." *New York Times,* June 1.

Meyers, Willard H., III. 1997. "Of *Qinqing, Qinshu, Guanxi, and Shetou:* The Dynamic Elements of Chinese Irregular Population Movement." In *Human Smuggling: Chinese Migrant Trafficking and the Challenge to America's Immigration Tradition,* edited by Paul J. Smith, 93–133. Washington, D.C.: Center for Strategic and International Studies.

Nee, Victor. 1996. "The Emergence of a Market Society: Changing Mechanisms of Stratification in China." *American Journal of Sociology* 101:908–49.

Nee, Victor, and Brett De Bary Nee. 1972. *Longtime Californ': A Documentary Study of an American Chinatown.* Stanford: Stanford University Press.

Noble, Kenneth B. 1995. "In California, Smuggled Refugees of Golden Venture Protest Long Detention." *New York Times,* December 2.

"$120,000 Bought 8 Pages of Copy Paper." 1997. *Xinmin Evening News.* http://www.hsm .com.cn/html/fztd.htm

Pan, Lynn. 1990. *The Sons of the Yellow Emperor: A History of Chinese Diaspora.* Boston: Little, Brown.

Parish, William, and Ethan Michelson. 1996. "Politics and Markets: The Dual Transformations." *American Journal of Sociology* 101:1042–59.

Portes, Alejandro. 1997. "Immigration Theory for a New Century: Some Problems and Opportunities." *International Migration Review* 31:799–825.

Portes, Alejandro, and Ruben G. Rumbaut. 1996. *Immigrant America: A Portrait.* Berkeley: University of California Press.

Poston, Dudley L., Jr., Michael Xinxiang Mao, and Mei-Yu Yu. 1994. "The Global Distribution of the Overseas Chinese around 1990." *Population and Development Review* 20:631–45.

Schemo, Diana Jean. 1993a. "Chinese Immigrants Tell of Darwinian Voyage." *New York Times,* June 12.

———. 1993b. "Survivors Tell of Voyage of Little Daylight, Little Food, and Only Hope." New York Times, June 7.

Skelton, Ronald. 1996. "Migration from China." *Journal of International Affairs* 49 (2): 434–55.

Smith, James P., and Barry Edmonston. 1998. *The Immigration Debate: Studies on the Economic, Demographic, and Fiscal Effects of Immigration.* Washington D.C.: National Academy Press.

Smith, Paul J., ed. 1997. *Human Smuggling: Chinese Migrant Trafficking and the Challenge to America's Immigration Tradition.* Washington, D.C.: Center for Strategic and International Studies.

Spence, Jonathan D. 1991. *The Search for Modern China.* New York: W. W. Norton.

Stark, Oded. 1991. *The Migration of Labor.* Cambridge, Mass.: Basil Blackwell.

Stark, Oded, and J. Edward Taylor. 1989. "Relative Deprivation and International Migration." *Demography* 26:1–14.

State Statistical Bureau (SSB). 1993. *China Statistical Yearbook.* Beijing: China Statistics Press.

———. 1994. *Fujian Statistical Yearbook.* Beijing: China Statistics Press.

Stouffer, Samuel A., E. A. Suchman, L. C. DeVinney, S. A. Star, and R. M. Williams Jr. 1949. *The American Soldier: Adjustment during Army Life.* Princeton: Princeton University Press.

Sung, Betty Lee. 1967. *Mountain of Gold: The Story of the Chinese in America.* New York: Macmillan.

Tilly, Charles. 1978. *From Mobilization to Revolution.* New York: Random House.

Treaster, Joseph B. 1993. "Behind Immigrants' Voyage, Long Reach of Chinese Gang." *New York Times,* June 9.

Tsai, Shih-shan Henry. 1983. *China and the Overseas Chinese in the United States, 1868–1911.* Fayetteville: University of Arkansas Press.

Wang, Yaohua. 1994. *Overview of Fujianese Culture* (in Chinese). Fuzhou, China: Fujian Education Publishing House.

Warren, Robert, and Jeffery S. Passel. 1987. "A Count of the Uncountable: Estimates of Undocumented Aliens in the 1980 Census." *Demography* 24:375–93.

The World Bank. 1996. *World Development Report 1996: From Plan to Market.* New York: Oxford University Press.

Xie, Yu, and Emily Hannum. 1996. "Regional Variation in Earnings Inequality in Reform-Era Urban China." *American Journal of Sociology* 101:950–92.

Xin, Yan. 1993. *Hell in Paradise* (in Chinese). Beijing: Tuanjie Press.

Ye, Wenzhen. 1995. "An Analysis of Illegal Immigration from Coastal Region of Fujian Province." *Historical Study of Overseas Chinese* (in Chinese) 1:28–36.

Zhou, Min. 1992. *Chinatown: The Socioeconomic Potential of an Urban Enclave.* Philadelphia: Temple University Press.

Zhu, Guohong. 1991. "A Historical Demography of Chinese Migration." *Social Sciences in China* 12:57–91.

Part IV / The Many Dimensions of Human Smuggling and Trafficking

CHAPTER NINE

Have Documents, Will Travel

Kamal Sadiq

There are no "undocumented" immigrants in this world. As beneficiaries of human smuggling or as victims of human trafficking, immigrants are rarely undocumented—most possess some form of documentation. In fact, characterizing them as "undocumented" is symptomatic of the many ways in which we have misunderstood the process of human smuggling and trafficking. Possession of documentation, fake or real, is critical to human trafficking, human smuggling, and illegal immigration. Yet states rely on the same state-authorized documentation to regulate, control, and monitor such unwanted flows. Are documents a tool for the regulation of labor mobility, or are they a means to circumvent state control of labor flows?

Documents are vital for any labor mobility—illegal immigration, human smuggling, or trafficking—yet their role is largely ignored.[1] In both coerced and voluntary flows an individual requires a passport, an identification card, or a birth certificate to cross state boundaries and become a part of its sex or labor industry. State-authorized documents such as passports and national identity cards are central to state regulation of illegal labor flows. Documents mark mobile populations. However, dependence on state-mandated documents opens the path to a counterstrategy—the acquisition of fraudulent documents to facilitate human smuggling and trafficking. How can documents, fake or real, both regulate and facilitate illegal human flows?

In this chapter, I examine the illegal labor flows from India and Pakistan to illustrate the tension between the two roles of documents in human smuggling and trafficking—as a regulator and as a facilitator—and I argue that the gap between state expectations and failed outcomes is due to the lack of understanding of these dual roles. Together, India and Pakistan are the sources of some of the largest illegal human flows in the world. They also represent varying institutional capacities and cultural challenges to labor regulation common to developing countries. With the second-largest population in the world, the largest concentration of the poor, and flexible institutional practices to identify and organize an expansive citizenry, India is a major source of smuggling and trafficking in the world. Across the border, Pakistan is a theater in the "war on terror," allowing radical Islamists and Afghans to both infiltrate its territory and travel abroad. India and Pakistani states appear dual faced in their expectation of what documents can achieve in terms of controlling human mobility. I begin by investigating the role of state documentation in safeguarding the popular and territorial sovereignty of the state, an effort that calls for separating eligible citizens from ineligible "foreigners." Next, I examine how state documents make individual identity and mobility visible ("Now You See Them"), and I then show how the same documents are manipulated to conceal visibility from state regulating agencies ("Now You Don't"). In the penultimate section, I analyze the introduction of biometric features in documents as another regulatory measure that may not succeed in its goals.

Seeking Control

Why do states seek national identity documents? State-mandated documents are expected to manage the flow of humans, including their social and economic activity. National identity documents aim to protect the territory, especially its benefits, from foreigners. The twentieth and the twenty-first century are distinct in the number of projects launched by states as part of their state-making efforts to create a national document that could exclude outsiders definitively. Nazi Germany, the Communist states of Eastern Europe and the former Soviet Union, the oil-rich monarchies of the Middle East, and the liberal economies of Asia, such as Singapore, all created national identity cards and passports to mark and monitor the location of their citizens—where they lived, where they worked, and where they traveled. De facto, such documents circumscribe foreigners by excluding them from full local benefits, rights, and protection. For some states, creating national identity documents was a sign of efficient policy making and a smooth economy. Knowing who is eligible for state benefits is the beginning of good policy making, domestically. Hence, documenting eligible members and distinguishing them from ineligible outsiders—both internal and external—created better policies for poverty alleviation, health services, education, and suffrage. In addition, this led to more efficient databases, which made for smoother banking and financial transactions. Yet other states justified the need for domestic political order to counter restive minorities, insurgents, and international criminals. So, for example, Middle Eastern states wanted to secure their citizenry from the influence of democratic practices, norms of gender equality, respect for non-Arab minorities, and labor activism.

The Communist states were no different. Former Romania and East Germany were paranoid about liberal norms and capitalist "conspiracies" influencing their citizenry—hence the need for surveillance of every movement of their own people.[2] Whether to mark and catalog populations for economic gains or to track their movements, passports and national identity cards have become a central feature of modern state building. I call this web of institutions processing identity information—name, address, age, gender, educational level, ethnicity, physical features, a photograph—the infrastructure of citizenship. The state creates an infrastructure of citizenship. A variety of documents identify the individual at various life stages, and they all make up this infrastructure of citizenship. There is a hierarchy of documentation within this infrastructure. At the very top of this edifice lies the passport—but the acquisition of the passport relies on the authentication of other identity documents such as birth certificates, high school diplomas, and marriage certificates. India and Pakistan, like many developing countries, have a decentralized culture of documents below the passport—each document a node in the larger infrastructure of citizenship. These nodes, or "feeder" documents, authenticate individual identity at various governmental levels and hierarchies and are commonly used for a variety of socioeconomic purposes. A feeder document is any document, paper or plastic, real or fake, seemingly state authorized and posing as a proof of identity and location such that it gives access to other identity documents authorized by the state. Consequently, the state-mandated documents, part of the infrastructure of citizenship, are meant to distinguish citizens from outsiders, those eligible for benefits and travel and those excluded. Only a citizen possesses *national* identity papers; outsiders are ineligible.

Many developing states have difficulty marking their own citizenry, finding it equally difficult to identify foreigners—how then do you distinguish between the two? If the state is unable to identify individuals, how can it regulate their movement or protect their rights when they are illegally absorbed into the local sex industry or domestic servitude? With documents, state institutions can identify the age of victims particularly in charging brothel owners, smugglers, and traffickers with rape and child servitude. According to a national survey in India by the National Human Rights Commission (2004: 1: 81–82), children constituted 20.7 percent, or one-fifth, of the brothel population, though only 4.7 percent of those trafficked reported their age to be under eighteen years. Most survivors record their age as above eighteen years because of bullying and coaching by exploiters. A case study on age notes how child victims are made to say they are above eighteen years of age. This permits human smugglers and brothel owners to avoid rape charges resulting from sexual exploitation of underage victims. Most victims do not possess documents to verify their biographical details. If they do, documents such as birth certificates or work permits have false personal information and are held by the trafficker, smuggler, or brothel owner. The exploiters are able to threaten helpless victims with prison time on grounds of fake documents and false information. Additionally, victims feel vulnerable without documents—unable to travel or prove their identity far away from home. Human smuggling/trafficking groups manipulate identity documents of victims to bypass state regulation of their illegal travel and criminal activities.

Traffickers and smugglers, like illegal immigrants, often follow traditional migratory routes. They move with their victims from Bangladesh and Nepal to India and onward to the rich Persian Gulf states of the Middle East. At each stage, a document—a visa, passport, work permit—verifies their identity and travel itinerary. Both trafficking and smuggling require intimate knowledge of legal entry/exit procedures and utilize legal entry and exit systems to facilitate illegal immigration (National Human Rights Commission [India], 2004: 1:180–81). These systems include family reunification programs and student and tourist visas. In each case, an individual produces false documentary proof that he or she is genuine family or a student or tourist. Once smugglers and victims enter the state legally using false pretenses and identities, they can move internally to other destinations, work without permission, or overstay visa restrictions. Another path is to exit the state legally with a genuine passport but enter another state illegally on a fake visa. The receiving state is fooled by the genuine passport, even though the visa is fake (but a good copy). Lastly, fake documents can be used for both illegal exit and entry, as they shield the true identity of the victim and the trafficker.

Smugglers and traffickers recognize that if one has the right documents, one can travel anywhere. It does not matter whether the documents are real but fraudulently acquired or they are outright fakes. If state agencies are unable to tell the difference, they have created a state-validated individual. In countries with a weak infrastructure of citizenship, any document that looks authentic will pass as real at points of entry. For example, the Pakistani Federal Investigation Agency arrested two human traffickers, Mohammad Qadoos and Hameed Ullah, and discovered a passport unit at their "travel agency" with fake and genuine British, Pakistani, and Afghani passports ("FIA Arrests Two for Human Trafficking," 2004). The genuineness of some of the passports could not be confirmed. If the top Pakistani investigative agency was unable to determine the authenticity of Pakistani passports, did it matter whether they were real or fake copies? Similarly, a recent government of India report on birth certificates has this to say: "There is wide variation in their format and design across the states and even within a state. In many cases, it is not clear from the appearance of the certificate as to whether it has been issued by a Government body or not" (Office of the Registrar General of India, Government of India, 2003: 9).

Until 9/11, Pakistani municipal and district offices issued a variety of documents vouching for individual identity, each with a different logo, letterhead, and marker—some of these outdated, others new. This lack of uniformity in identity documents distributed by different levels of the state made it even more difficult for border police or army personnel to distinguish between a counterfeit document and an authentic one. In India, until 9/11, regional passport offices were not networked; therefore an individual could obtain two legitimate passports by applying to two different passport centers. Each regional office was unaware of passport distribution by the others. Multiple state-authorized travel documents were being obtained without detection. Even when state authorities could detect manipulation, for reasons of ethnic affinity or political and monetary benefit they overlooked the violation of state laws. Documents along with sympathetic or corrupt officials enabled illegal and criminal individuals to enter a state and participate in its criminal industry.

I call the illegal possession of seemingly state-authorized identity documents to travel and settle abroad "documentary citizenship" (Sadiq, 2009). With documentary citizenship, victims of human smuggling/trafficking appear as legitimate travelers or citizens of host states—eligible for entry and rights that come with such status. Both the victim and the smuggler/trafficker pose as legitimate individuals, authorized by the state. Since the infrastructure of citizenship is dependent on the biographical information supplied by individuals, manipulation or falsification of such details on a passport or birth certificate— that is, documentary citizenship—violates the national sovereignty of host states. Territorial sovereignty of states is undermined by the breaching of state boundaries. Smugglers and traffickers, or any unwanted individuals, utilize false documents to enter another state, undermining its ability to police and control its territorial border. Documentary citizenship also violates national sovereignty by compromising the sanctity of citizenship—those ineligible for employment, criminal or otherwise, are able to live as common citizens. For example, women and children illegally trafficked from Bangladesh and Nepal utilize fake documents to settle in India. Afghan women and children are commonly trafficked to Pakistan, where they adopt local paperwork and identities. Finally, documentary citizenship muddles the rights regime for the state: victims appear as criminals, offenders appear as bystanders, and law enforcement agencies are expected to prosecute and deport those most vulnerable. Such violations undermine a state's moral and legal sovereignty.

But how is sovereignty compromised? What is the connection between documents and security? In what ways do state documents filter unwanted immigrants? Alternatively, in what ways do human smuggling organizations employ documentary citizenship to undermine national security? The ability to use such documents and bypass state regulation is ubiquitous in developing countries. The issue is at the heart of all discussions on state security in international relations, and yet very few have analyzed the connection between documents and security, even as some of the most dangerous immigrants and travelers—terrorists, criminals, smugglers, and traffickers—are appearing at the borders of states bearing identity documents that appear legal but are fraudulently acquired.[3] If the world is to deal with this problem, it must understand how fraudulently acquired documents are challenging the sovereignty and security of states and how they shape and transform the process of international smuggling and trafficking in developing countries.

Now You See Them

In the literature on international relations, immigration, human smuggling, and trafficking, the individual is assumed to be visible—we know or have the capacity to identify each individual in the international system. International relations scholars may make analogies between the individual and the state or between the characteristic of an individual and his or her group—in each case the characteristics, identity, and location of the individual are assumed. The international system functions on the visibility of persons. And yet, the only way we know an individual's identity and location is through the paperwork he or she holds. Documents make individuals visible and knowable to states within the international system. International mobility of individuals hinges on this verification.

The sending state validates biographical information through standardized paperwork; this validation legitimizes an individual's nationality and locality, verifying that he or she resides in a particular territory or address and is of a certain anthropomorphic type. Documents thus embody individual identity, making the individual visible to the state. Each document confirms a distinct activity or category. Different categories/activities produce different documents, but an individual does not possess more than one, the primary assumption being that there can only be one document per person.

Documents work in the following ways: individual "X" is screened and validated by institutions of the state when born, entering school, graduating, getting married, exercising franchise, or receiving welfare benefits. Each activity produces a document identifying the individual as "X," which is distinct from any identity documents produced for other individuals (e.g., identity document "Y" belonging to individual "Y"). With identity document "X," individual "X" makes entries into multiple state records as "X" when traveling within the state or crossing international borders. "X" was here today, "X" applied for a visa, "X" crossed the border, and so on and so forth. Depending on the level of institutionalization, individual "X" may be screened exhaustively or minimally. However, every verification exercise assumes that the document representing "X" actually identifies the individual named "X." Every time travel document "X" is verified, state authorities know the ethnic identity, citizenship, and location of "X" through the documentary record he or she produces. A trail of individualized documents follows each person.

In this way, state documents are threat "neutralizers"—they create safe, identifiable individuals whose travel record poses no threat to the state. Verification from different authorities validates the safe and secure presence of an individual. Standard documents operate as international treaties/institutions— mutually agreed-on international norms that foster trust and reciprocity among states. Documents reflect trust between states as well as trust in an individual validated by the state. Each document is issued on behalf of the state. Officially, passports are issued on behalf of a country's president by the Ministry of Foreign Affairs or other government department, such as the U.S. State Department. Only a legitimate school authority can supply a high school certificate. The birth certificate can be obtained only from government officials in charge of birth and death registration. This is precisely why traffickers, smugglers, and other criminals lose their eligibility for passports, visas, ration cards, and other such state-authenticated documents.[4] These individuals are no longer deemed "safe" and may lose their travel rights. International norms and regulations require all states to ensure that their safe travelers possess standardized documentation. So, in order for state documentation to be effective, a functioning and comprehensive civil registration system identifying members must exist because it allows the host state to trace a traveler's origin. The host can determine eligibility for entry into its territory only if the sending state can verify an individual's identity. Documents embody the individual's living record and therefore convey trust in the registration system of states.

However, with increasing global human smuggling, trafficking, and migration, an individual's racial/ethnic profile embedded in state documentation is a record of his or her territory, location, and lack of criminality.[5] One could be a female-child Nepali being trafficked to India and yet hold an adult Indian passport under a fake name, or be a smuggled Bangladeshi and hold an Indian, British, or Malaysian identity card. A legal regime verifying state paperwork allows for subtle ethnic and racial profiling of suspected traffickers, smugglers and victims of such flows. Hence, the spread of state documents means that police and border officials at points of entry are constantly performing a balancing act when monitoring individuals—they have to be impartial to an individual's race, religion, ethnicity, and language while also conducting racial and ethnic profiling of the immigrating individual.

Why is this significant? Because states, even liberal states, use racial and ethnic profiling to weed out unwanted and criminal immigrants. Ethnic profiling is one way of identifying an individual who may pose a security threat. Whether it was the "criminal tribes" in the British India of the twentieth century or whether it is the current international criminal networks trafficking and smuggling humans from China, India, Bangladesh, Afghanistan, Thailand, or Eastern Europe—in all cases the state monitors gangs and individuals by their ethnic, racial, and linguistic markers. There is a correlation between particular ethnic groups and an apparent security threat. Albanian, Chinese, Thai, and Afghan traffickers are detected at points of entry because of their ethnic affiliations. Distinguishing particular ethnic groups as adverse to state stability is part of a larger security apparatus, which attempts to screen and regulate specific ethnic communities. But in today's international system, how does one racially or ethnically profile, given an increasingly multiethnic environment? Naturally, this can be only done through standard documentation: "In the absence of telltale markers such as language or skin color—which are themselves inconclusive as indicators of one's national identity, of course, but which nonetheless frequently have been taken as such—a person's nationality simply cannot be determined without recourse to documents. As an ascribed status, it cannot be read off a person's appearance" (Torpey, 2001: 269). Documents, paper or plastic, are imprinted with an individual's identity characteristics. In order to confirm an identity, you no longer need to look at the individual but merely examine his or her identity documents. For example, many Islamic and African states include ethnic identity and religious information in documents such as the passport. Yet it is also true that passports of Western states do not overtly contain ethnic information. However, the trail of documents leading to the passport (or the national identity card) does give detailed information on an individual's ethnic origins: parents, grandparents, place of birth, age, type of marriage ceremony (religious or civil). The documents, directly or indirectly, give gatekeepers all the ethnic/racial information they need to screen the individual. A passport may not contain ethnic or racial information, but the background documents that accompany such national documents often provide the necessary ethnic/racial/biographic information.

This documentation process is the modern transformation that now facilitates human mobility between states. Through documentation one can verify whether an individual is actually an Indian, Pakistani, Afghan, or Thai.

Embedded in documentation are mechanisms for ethnic/racial profiling, which allow states to confirm ethnic identity and nationality. Documentation makes the individual traveler "visible."

In developing countries, the systematic structure of recording and authenticating individuals moving between states is inoperative or is insufficient. This is the case primarily when documents are no longer a reliable marker of an individual's ethnicity, identity, and travel record. Security is compromised in such cases. If the international system is based on one identity and ethnic profile per person, the entire system is compromised if individual "X" possesses documents containing information on individual "Y" while individual "Y" may or may not possess such paperwork or even exist. Here individual "X" will travel as "safe" individual "Y," and authorities depending on such documentation will assume the individual is "Y" not "X." Adopting the safe identity of "Y," "X" too becomes a safe traveler.

Now You Don't

In contrast to safe and visible immigrants are "unwanted" migrants. These immigrants consist of dangerous criminals, smugglers, traffickers, terrorists, insurgents, or political-cultural threats. When dangerous smugglers and traffickers enter a territory posing as safe immigrants, they have been validated by documentary citizenship. The system of safe and secure ethnic/racial profiling breaks down, and the acquisition of fake or real documents makes the true identities of victims and traffickers alike "invisible." Biographical information such as age, ethnicity, location, and nationality as well as travel records are now manipulated for smooth entry into another state.

The threatening feature of illegal entry was recognized by Jeremy Bentham very early. According to Bentham, the "danger" comes from those who can "conceal their movements" from the institutions of the state (Bowring, 1962: 557). Illegal human flows are a challenge to national security because of their dual characteristics—providing invisibility while facilitating movement. How is this invisibility achieved? Seemingly real documents, fake or real, bypass state control and allow illegal entrants to conceal their actual identity and travel history, thus enabling them to settle down in a host country.[6] If the individual is a member of a criminal organization, out to traffic human beings, the individual can keep doing "business" traveling under the assumed identity without state detection. The individual's real identity remains invisible to the state. Importantly, the same is true for the victim of human trafficking. So while the purpose of state documents was to make individuals visible to the state, the reverse is actually occurring. Documentary citizenship enables legitimate international travel for victims of trafficking and traffickers as gangs are able to obtain real and seemingly legal documents through fraudulent means.

Legal travel between two states occurs even as the real identity of the individual is invisible to the state. For example, on June 19, 2007, in Karachi, Pakistan, Rasheed Ahmed attempted to board a Muscat-bound flight with official documents in another name ("'Human Trafficker' Arrested." 2007). In 2004 Ahmed had obtained a national identity card and passport in the name of Mohammad Naeem, who had died in 1998. Earlier, the United Arab Emirates had blacklisted Ahmed for his involvement in the trafficking of young boys for camel racing, to no effect. Since documents permit travel, they enable exploitation in all its forms. Underage boys are trafficked from Bangladesh to India by land and then flown to the Middle East to become camel jockeys (National Human Rights Commission [India], 2004: 1:165). Documents are falsified in these cases as in others—to bypass state agencies.

The threat "neutralizer" function of fake, or real but fraudulently acquired, state documents allows anyone in the possession of such documents to appear safe, secure, and legitimate. The situation is further complicated by individuals who are harmless travelers, those who, for example, use fake documents because they cannot afford the time and money needed to obtain authentic verification. How does a border patrol agent, or immigration official, at the airport distinguish between a traveler with criminal intent (i.e., those who smuggle or traffic) and individuals who are nonthreatening? Despite the best efforts of both sending and receiving states to document populations accurately, criminal flows occur.

According to a 2004 report on trafficking by the National Human Rights Commission of India (1:86, 110,154), brothel owners in India make sure that women change their name, ethnic community, and sometimes caste when jailed for soliciting. The report notes a deliberate attempt by the brothel owner to change the name of the victims in state documents while bailing them out of prison. This ensures a new identity, so that multiple cases do not apply to the same individual. In the report, over 40 percent of the respondents had changed their name at least once at the behest of the brothel owner. The report notes how trafficked women are "registered" by the police. Once a trafficked victim is brought to a new brothel, the local police "makes note" of her presence by accepting a bribe from the brothel owner. If the victim is a minor, the bribe is higher. Documents process an underage child as an adult, a foreigner as a national—all for a price commonly agreed on by the brothel owner and state officials. It is the nexus between traffickers, fraudulent documents, and corrupt state officials in developing countries that enables the anonymous exploitation of women and children.

Major smuggling, trafficking, and terrorist groups in India and Pakistan are aware that for international travel there is a strong fraudulent passport network running from Dubai to Peshawar to Karachi, to Delhi to Mumbai, to Kuala Lumpur, and to Bangkok that facilitates regional travel, ultimately giving the network the ability to reach the West. Traffickers maintain international links through the use of fraudulent travel documents. For example, in a recent survey (National Human Rights Commission [India], 2004: 1:154), close to 20 percent of traffickers admitted to visiting at least one other country for purposes related to trafficking (80% of the respondents refused to answer). The majority of the respondents among traffickers (84.4%) acknowledged that their overseas trip was for buying or selling girls. Underage male children were also trafficked for begging in Saudi Arabia and nearby Persian Gulf states. Places listed by respondents as sites of trafficking included Nepal, Bangkok, Kenya, South Africa, England, and several Persian Gulf countries.

Immigrant and criminal networks utilize false documentation to weaken the capacity of states to segment the political realm—that is, to erect and maintain boundaries around national and territorial sovereignty (Brubaker, 1992). Traveling on false documents generates invisibility to state agencies and is therefore as vital to smugglers, traffickers, terrorists, insurgents, and oppositional groups as it is to illegal immigrants. They all share a need to bypass state regulation and keep their real identities concealed as well. For human smuggling operations the ability to bypass state monitoring while remaining anonymous is vital—their ability to acquire arms, counterfeit technology, and modes of transportation must remain clandestine in nature. Central to these international networks are operatives who specialize in preparing travel documentation.

Common to most smuggling/trafficking operations are photo-substituted travel documents. These can be genuine documents obtained through fraudulent means that have biographical information altered after the point of acquisition. For example, passports with valid travel visas can be lent to other individuals for a fee. In Gujarat, India, Sakina Ahmad (from the state of Bihar) lent her passport with a valid American visa to Babuben Patel for 100,000 rupees (Mukherjee, 2004, 9). The same passport could be used by multiple individuals. Such was the case with the passport of Yunus Ramaiya, which had already been used once to send an individual to the United States and was being reworked to send yet another migrant abroad. Mind you, these were all genuine passports that had undergone photo substitution. These operations were conducted by "travel agents" who act as middlemen between individuals seeking to travel abroad and those seeking to earn money by lending their documents. Others conceal travel history by purchasing genuine passports under aliases or false identities with the help of corrupt officials. Bribing passport staffers to alter biographical information before the acquisition of a genuine passport assures further authenticity. Often human smuggling and trafficking organizations have operatives within national identification offices, expediting the entire process. However, the most common way human smuggling and trafficking organizations manipulate state identity documentation is through forgery. Tremendous improvements in the quality of forging techniques have taken place over the past decade, primarily owing to the professionalization and expansion of the underground market and improvements in counterfeit technology. For smugglers, traffickers, and their victims, traveling abroad under a new false identity overcomes most verification systems and cursory background checks and, importantly, gives access to any visa-free entry arrangement that the adopted country may have with other states. In short, by covering one's identity through false identity and travel documents, the individual ensures smooth international travel. Both the trafficker and the victim become invisible to, and hence hidden from, the surveillance institutions of the host state.

How widespread is the manipulation of travel documents for human smuggling and trafficking in India and Pakistan? In 2001, India had only 20 million registered passport holders worldwide, with a total population of over 1 billion (Jha, 2001). Two years later, the figure had increased to 25 million (Baruah, 2003). In short, only about 2 percent of individual "Indians" can be identified by their passport.[7] As the Indian economy liberalizes with a large middle class moving abroad, Indians working overseas or individuals planning on traveling abroad generally constitute a large percentage of these passports. It is important to note that the majority of these passport holders do not live in India. According to a recent annual report of the Ministry of External Affairs (2007: 175), in just a matter of twelve months, over 4 million passports were issued

Table 9.1   Individuals Caught Traveling on Fake Documents at Major Airports in India, 1997–1999

Year	Delhi	Mumbai	Calcutta	Chennai	Amritsar	Trivendrum	Total
1997	420	1,483	198	223	70	59	2,453
1998	553	1,328	217	269	42	57	2,466
1999	534	1,086	082	175	59	43	1,979

Source: Response by Mr. I. D. Swami, minister of state, Ministry of Home Affairs, Government of India, to Starred Question No. 425 regarding "fake passports, visa rackets," Parliamentary Proceedings, Lok Sabha, December 19, 2000. http://164.100.24.208/lsq/quest.asp?qref=14861.

in India. In 2005, 3.57 million passports were issued (Ministry of External Affairs, 2006: 167). Clearly, there is a rising trend in both the acquisition and manipulation of documents as Indians travel abroad. Replace a photograph, a name, an age, personal details, travel history, and you will have an entirely new person traveling abroad. Figures from the late 1990s on the number of individuals detected with forged documents based on data from six major international airports in India are shown in Table 9.1.

In 2005, a senior government minister revealed in the Parliament that 2,331 individuals were caught traveling on fake travel documents at major Indian airports between January 2004 and June 2005.[8] Despite common use of fraudulent passports and travel documents in India, very few individuals are caught with fraudulent documents. Most cases of detection occur at major airports. However, many are not caught, thus explaining the successful emigration of illegal immigrants from India to a variety of destinations abroad. For example, the state of Kerala in southern India sends large numbers of immigrants to the gulf states in the Middle East—many are smuggled. Tellingly, in just six months in 2005, airport authorities arrested seventy-seven returning Indians from the gulf states for using fraudulent passports. State police acknowledge that substituting digitally imposed photographs in passports is common among Indians working in the Persian Gulf (Anand, 2005). Such Indian passports cost them a little less than a thousand dollars.

Widespread documentary citizenship enables both the entry of "foreigners" into India and "Indians" into other states. It is not beyond imagination for an unwanted immigrant or a foreign smuggler or trafficker to travel abroad posing as an "Indian." After all, the minister of state for external affairs acknowledged in Parliament the following cases of fake Indian passports being acquired by noncitizens: one Indian passport acquired by an Afghan in 2001;

two passports acquired by Sri Lankans in 2002; eleven Indian passports by Afghans in 2000 and 2002; one passport by a Bangladeshi in 2002; one Indian passport by a Pakistani in 2002; two passports by Pakistanis in 2006.[9] This acquisition opens the possibility of both native Indians and foreign Afghans, Bangladeshis, and Pakistanis traveling abroad as "Indians."

Yet cases of successful prosecution are rare in an environment of widespread documentary citizenship. The 2005 annual report from India's domestic intelligence agency, the Central Bureau of Intelligence, observes the prosecution of fourteen officials from the passport office in Delhi and its collaborators for "fraudulently issuing passports and additional passport booklets with different photographs of various persons on forged documents" (Central Bureau of Investigation, 2005: 22). Another official from the passport office in Jaipur was prosecuted for corruption (ibid., 9). The 2006 annual report highlights legal action against another senior passport official for distributing passports and passport booklets with different photographs under the common Indian name of Rohit Kumar (Central Bureau of Investigation, 2006: 26). In this manner, different individuals in the photographs could travel abroad under the name Rohit Kumar. Such rare prosecution of state officials, complicit in the production and distribution of fake passports and documents, is like a tap on the hand.

Compared with the situation in India, that in Pakistan is absolutely critical. Almost 12,000 passports were being issued per day in 2007, according to the director general of the Immigration and Passports Department (Bhagwandas, 2007). Yet one 1 of every 100 applications for the new computerized national identity card was based on *fake* documents. Over 160,000 such fake applicants were detected by the National Database and Registration Authority (NADRA). Just a few years earlier, Interpol was supplied the details of over 32,000 stolen or missing passports ("Revelation of Stealing of 32,000 Passports." 2003). The Pakistani government, under close scrutiny after 9/11, is aggressively chasing criminal networks that traffic guns, drugs, and women and operate under fake or real Pakistani national identity cards and passports. With the correct amount of money, incentives, and network connections, almost anyone can get a Pakistani passport. Human smugglers operating from "travel agencies" swap photographs, personal descriptions, travel history, and identity documents making individuals appear to be legitimate Pakistani document holders. Reportedly, 582 individuals in 2003 and 523 individuals in 2004 were caught traveling abroad with fake Pakistani documents ("291 Pakistanis Arrested for Traveling Illegally," 2005). According to a report, 160 individuals, many of whom were

Afghan refugees, were smuggled to Europe on fake Pakistani and British passports (Ahmad, 2004). Members of a "travel agency" provided the travel documents. According to a February 2007 report, 300 Afghans on Pakistani documents were discovered performing the hajj, the Muslim holy pilgrimage to Mecca ("300 Afghan Hajis Being Deported Today," 2007). Some were detected before they left Pakistan and were still allowed to travel to Saudi Arabia. Two months later, a report notes the return of 638 Afghans who had performed the hajj in Saudi Arabia on fake Pakistani documents ("638 Afghans Deported for Fake Haj Papers," 2007). Sher Mohammad, an Afghan, felt it was easier to get Pakistani documents and travel abroad as a Pakistani than to travel legally from Afghanistan. Pakistani authorities were "deporting" such Afghans to Afghanistan—but what does deportation mean in a region with porous borders and document substitutable identities?

Stolen passports from immigration centers have become a regular feature of the Pakistani government, with over 41,000 blank copies stolen in the past fifteen years, almost half of which, 21,000 blank passports, were stolen in the past five years (Ijaz, 2005). The sheer frequency with which such passports have been stolen (Table 9.2) prove the lucrative nature of fake travel documents—any address, name, and travel history can be entered, thus tailoring to individual illegal or criminal needs.

Cross-examination of Afghans by the Pakistani Federal Investigation Agency revealed the involvement of Pakistani embassies abroad in cases of stolen and missing passports. Investigations exposed the complicity of Pakistani embassy staff in Middle Eastern states in issuing Pakistani passports to Afghans with

Table 9.2   Stolen Blank Pakistani Passports, 1999–2001

Year	Number of Stolen Blank Passports and Location
1999	185 blank passports from the Muzaffarabad passport office and 1,960 passports from the Dera Ismail Khan office Total: 2,145 stolen
2000	1,112 blank passports from the Sialkot office; 2,200 from the Quetta office; and 2,160 copies from the Abbottabad office Total: 5,472 stolen
2001	2,120 blank passports from the Multan office; 1,000 blank passports from the Gujranwala office and 2,200 passport books from the railway authorities in Peshawar Total: 5,320 stolen

Source: Wajahat Ijaz, "Interpol Seeks Data about Lost, Stolen Passports," *Dawn,* August 5, 2005.

fake Pakistani national identity cards ("Afghans with Fake NICs Get Passports," 2003). Human smugglers and traffickers are using documentary citizenship to smuggle Bangladeshis and Afghans into Pakistan, even as Afghans are traveling on Pakistani passports to Europe and the Middle East—all challenging the territorial and national integrity of Pakistan.

Ironically, many members of the Pakistani Hazara and Pashtun tribes have successfully settled in Australia by posing as Afghan asylum seekers— documentary citizenship is common to both Afghans and Pakistanis (Ansari and Bucha, 2002). A common Afghan tactic is to carry two passports on the journey, destroy the Pakistani passport at sea, and then claim political asylum on the Afghan passport. To the neutral eyes of international immigration officials, it is impossible to tell the difference between a Pakistani and an Afghan Pashtun, or a Pakistani and an Afghan Hazara. During 2000–2001, the Pakistani government learned that the country was receiving Bangladeshi, Indian, and Iranian nationals deported from other states—all Pakistani passport holders (Ali, 2004).

"Pakistanis" with fake documents are a global phenomenon. No one, not even the Pakistani state, knows whether these individuals are native Pakistanis or foreigners posing as Pakistanis. In the past three years, 1,264 Pakistanis were arrested in thirty-one countries for using fake documents and visas (Table 9.3). A national identity card was introduced by different branches of the Pakistani government in the 1970s. However, illegally obtaining a fake or real but fraudulent passport, identity card, driver's license, or birth certificate is oftentimes much easier that acquiring one legally. It is unlikely that either the earlier or the current computerized effort at a national identity card and passport is sacrosanct. For example, it is common practice among the elites and criminals in Pakistan to have multiple passports—one set for traveling to the Middle East or other Muslim countries, another for United States and other Western countries.[10] Whenever travel information has to be hidden, a separate passport is a must. For example, after 9/11, people traveling to the United States can avoid showing their travel history to Middle Eastern states by simply using a clean passport. All this entails a slight modification of the name—for instance, from Abdul Ali to Syed Abdul Ali or Abdel Ali with an "e." Mind you, these are all genuine, authorized passports issued by complicit national authorities bearing legitimate visas. If states rely on documents for identification and travel regulation, such practices will become even more common among human traffickers and smugglers. The prevalence of documentary citizenship demonstrates the

Table 9.3   Pakistanis Caught Using Fake Documents and Visas, 2004–2007

Country	Number of Individuals Caught	Country	Number of Individuals Caught
Britain	428	Sri Lanka	10
Saudi Arabia	311	Egypt	7
Germany	88	Portugal	6
Singapore	87	Mauritius	6
France	52	India	5
Japan	38	Azerbaijan	4
Poland	28	Slovakia	4
Italy	28	Bahrain	3
Canada	25	Kuwait	2
Austria	24	Qatar	2
Norway	19	Syria	2
Malaysia	18	Serbia	1
Croatia	18	Romania	1
Denmark	17	Tunisia	1
United States	16	Kenya	1
Hong Kong	12		

Source: Statement by Pakistani foreign minister Khurshid Mehmood Kasuri in the Pakistani Senate. See "1,264 Pakistanis Detained in 31 Countries," *Dawn,* January 20, 2007.

adaptability of illegal human flows; will the introduction of biometric schemes restrict such criminal behavior?

A Biometric Future?

The desire for illegal entry generates the complicity of state agencies. Even with the introduction of biometric schemes, gatekeeping sectors of the state will continue to be operated by human personnel. For an individual to erase a past criminal record, corruption must be utilized. Since only a border patrol agent, immigration official, or bureaucratic staffer has the authority to access state verification databases, it is corrupt individuals in these positions who are complicit in acts of illegal entry. Stricter regulations of standardized documents at points of entry will not only raise the cost of travel but also increase the payoffs to complicit state officials. However, if an individual has no prior record of criminality, militancy, or terrorism and has a fresh record of biometric signifiers, he or she will be able to enter the state smoothly with out any red flags going off. In addition, if this individual has criminal intent but a clean record, it will be impossible to stop his or her entry based on the clean record. The system of regulation makes it impossible to distinguish between those with criminal motivation and those without among the millions seeking entry. However, these are all ways of entering the state using smugglers through state-authorized entry points. An individual could also enter illegally, through unguarded parts of the border—land, sea, or air—and then once across the border could use fake or real documents to establish a trail of legitimate entry and settlement.

Biometric systems do not take into account political affiliations or motivations—they are based purely on phenotypic characterizations. An individual's past history and experiences are not taken into account either; those are part of the traditional paper record. Moreover, these aspects of one's life can be altered by forged documentation. False birth certificates, school degrees, voting stubs, employment references, marriage license(s), and address confirmation(s) are all part of a fake paper trail creating a "safe individual." Monitoring those aspects of an individual's life that are critical for the purpose of regulating entry into other states is impossible for the sending state. The criminal and undesirable criteria that make an immigrant unwanted are precisely the business of human smuggling operations in creating a safe paper trail that bypasses state regulation. Phenotype characteristics from the biometric system will only work with the history of the individual provided through traditional records. Biometric systems will ensure that once an individual's phenotype is identified with criminal or other unwanted records, he or she will be unable to enter the state through state-guarded entry points. He or she will have to create an alternate identity with a new set of fingerprints, iris scan, and other biometric identifiers—which through complicity of state officials can be entered into the appropriate database. It was no surprise when Pakistan's National Database and Registration Authority recently discovered many entry operators producing national identity cards with duplicate fingerprints ("Nadra Employees Caught in Fake ID Cards Racket," 2007).

Alternatively, individuals can enter through unregulated parts of the land, sea, or air border. And some, without any identification history or record of biometric measures, can act on behalf of a criminal, militant, or terrorist organization, as can individuals with a safe record of travel. Human smuggling and trafficking will continue to undermine state security through documentary citizenship.

Conclusion

The rise of documentary citizenship reveals the emerging features and trajectory of illegal human travel. First, documents have come to embody individual identity because states increasingly utilize them for the regulation of human mobility. Second, owing to varying institutional capacities amid expanding citizenries, state documentation is open to manipulation and fraud. Third, if eligible citizens and ineligible "foreigners" obtain similar documents, unambiguous identification of victims, criminals, and nonthreatening travelers is unfeasible. Finally, the acquisition of fake or real documents facilitates illegal travel—documents are the backbone of unwanted human mobility.

Documentary citizenship assaults state authority over territory and citizenship, since unverified individuals can enter and settle without detection. Dependence on state documents for the regulation of human mobility has the unintended consequence of breeding invisibility, achieved through the very documentation meant to regulate illegal flows. The introduction of biometric measures adds another layer of safeguards but produces other challenges. Computerized databases with biographical profiles and anthropomorphic identifiers generate incentives and pressures for complicity at every level. Illegal access to networked circuits risks the privacy and anonymity of individuals like never before. States face an uphill struggle as illegal human flows employ fraudulent documentation to facilitate illegal travel.

NOTES

Many thanks to Richard Friman, Ryan Harvey, Rey Koslowski, Simon Reich, and Tamara Zaman for their feedback and encouragement. I am grateful to the Smith Richardson Foundation for awarding me their generous Junior Faculty Grant. Thanks to several units at the University of California, Irvine, for funding my research: the Center for Global Peace and Conflict Studies, Center for the Scientific Study of Ethics and Morality (CEM), and the Center for Asian Studies.
    1. An exception is the recent work of Koslowski (2000).
    2. Extreme surveillance is remarkably captured in a recent German film—*The Lives of Others* (2006).
    3. See, for example, Eldridge et al. (2004), Ginsburg (2006), and Koslowski (2005).
    4. A ration card is a paper document issued by the state agency responsible for distributing subsidized grains (rice, lentils), sugar, kerosene, and other basic commodities to the eligible poor. Ration cards are an integral part of the antipoverty program in India.
    5. Critics will point out that for many states a racial or ethnic profile is not part of a

person's official identity documentation, that some states may include ethnic identity information in travel documents but others do not. Not true. If one looks carefully into the trail of documents that finally lead to a passport, one will find almost all the racial or ethnic information one needs. Information such as the names of a person's parents or birth place is often intended to reveal such information. Law enforcement personnel, immigration authorities, and border police are all trained to look into the trail of documents for such information.

6. Estimates of illegal immigrants in the United States, much as in India, range from 10 million to 20 million. In Pakistan a range of figures in the millions is often cited. The recently released report by the Pew Hispanic Center notes how illegal immigration forms a large component of migration to the United States in spite of the tighter border security measures and resources employed by the most powerful state in the world. See Passel and Cohn (2008).

7. See Ministry of External Affairs (2007: 175). In appendix 4 of that report, there are many more passports issued than applications received. This discrepancy can be attributed to a particular city issuing a larger number of passports than would otherwise be the case because it issued passports to individuals whose applications were submitted in another city. Such discrepancy can also hide real documents under assumed identities being issued fraudulently to individuals. In states where such data is never collected or never centrally organized and made public, the scope for passport-type documentary citizenship is enormous.

8. Response by Sriprakash Jaiswal, minister of state, Ministry of Home Affairs, Government of India, to Unstarred Question No. 3260 regarding "Fake Passports/Visas," Parliamentary Proceedings, Lok Sabha, August 16, 2005. http://164.100.24.208/lsq14/quest.asp?qref=15007.

9. Response by Mr. E. Ahamed, minister of state, Ministry of External Affairs, Government of India, to Unstarred Question No. 2321 regarding "fake passports to foreign nationals," Parliamentary Proceedings, Lok Sabha, August 29, 2007. http://meaindia.nic.in/mystart.php?id=220213101.

10. Confirmed in conversations with various Pakistani elites.

REFERENCES

"Afghans with Fake NICs Get Passports." 2003. *Dawn*, June 6. http://archives.dawn.com/2003/06/06/nat28.htm.

Ali, Azam. 2004. "Alien Nations." *Jang*, December 5.

Ahmad, Shafiq. 2004. "Two Confess to Human Smuggling," *Dawn*, January 12. http://archives.dawn.com/2004/01/12/nat23.htm.

Anand, G. 2005. "Forging of Indian Passports Rampant in the Gulf." *The Hindu*, June 10. www.thehindu.com/2005/06/10/stories/2005061002390700.htm.

Ansari, Massoud, and Sanna Bucha. 2002. "Perilous Journey." *Newsline* (Karachi), special report, March 2002.

Baruah, Amit. 2003. "Database Lists 25 m Passport-Holders." *The Hindu*, January 28.

Bhagwandas. 2007. "Passport Dept, Nadra Cross Swords over Dues." *Dawn*, November 29. http://archives.dawn.com/2007/11/29/local2.htm.

Bowring, John. 1962. *The Works of Jeremy Bentham*. Vol. 1, *Chapter XII Problem IX Principles of Penal Law*. Reproduced from the Bowring edition of 1838–43. New York: Russell and Russell.

Brubaker, Rogers. 1992. *Citizenship and Nationhood in France and Germany*. Cambridge: Harvard University Press.

Central Bureau of Investigation. 2005. *Annual Report 2005*. New Delhi: Government of India.

———. 2006. *Annual Report 2006*. New Delhi: Government of India.

Eldridge, Thomas R., et al. 2004. *9/11 and Terrorist Travel*. Staff Report of the National Commission on Terrorist Attacks upon the United States. August. www.9–11commission.gov/staff_statements/index.htm.

"FIA Arrests Two for Human Trafficking." 2004. *Dawn*, January 6. http://archives.dawn.com/2004/01/06/nat21.htm.

Ginsburg, Susan. 2006. *Countering Terrorist Mobility*. Migration Policy Institute. www.migrationpolicy.org/pubs/MPI_TaskForce_Ginsburg.pdf.

"'Human Trafficker' Arrested." 2007. *Dawn*, June 20. http://archives.dawn.com/2007/06/20/top16.htm.

Ijaz, Wajahat. 2005. "Interpol Seeks Data about Lost, Stolen Passports." *Dawn*, August 5. http://archives.dawn.com/2005/08/05/nat5.htm.

Jha, Nilanjana Bhaduri. 2001. "Government in No Position to Check Passport Fraud." *Times of India* (New Delhi), September 22.

Koslowski, Rey. 2000. "The Mobility Money Can Buy: Human Smuggling and Border Control in the European Union." In *The Wall around the West: State Borders and Immigration Controls in North America and Europe*, edited by Peter Andreas and Timothy Snyder, 203–18. Boulder, Colo.: Rowman and Littlefield.

———. 2005. *Real Challenges for Virtual Borders: The Implementation of US-VISIT*. Migration Policy Institute. *www.migrationpolicy.org/pubs/Koslowski_Report.pdf*.

Ministry of External Affairs. 2006. *Annual Report 2005–06*. New Delhi: Government of India.

———. 2007. *Annual Report 2006–07*. New Delhi: Government of India.

Mukherjee, Sauruv. 2004. "For Rs 1 Lakh, Get Passport with US Visa in Guajarat." *Times of India* (New Delhi), December 21.

"Nadra Employees Caught in Fake ID Cards Racket." 2007. *Dawn*, November 17. http://archives.dawn.com/2007/11/17/local3.htm.

National Human Rights Commission (India). 2004. *A Report on Trafficking in Women and Children in India, 2002–2003*. New Delhi: National Human Rights Commission (India), UNIFEM, Institute of Social Sciences.

Office of the Registrar General of India, Government of India. 2003. "National Conference of Chief Registrars of Births and Deaths: Proceedings of the Conference." New Delhi: Government of India Press.

Passel, Jeffrey S., and D'Vera Cohn. 2008. *Trends in Unauthorized Immigration: Undocumented Inflow Now Trails Legal Inflow*. Washington, D.C.: Pew Hispanic Center, October. http://pewhispanic.org/reports/report.php?ReportID=94."Revelation of Stealing of 32,000 Passports." 2003. *Jang* (Rawalpindi, Pakistan), September 9. Source: BBC Monitoring © British Broadcasting Corporation 2003, Record Number: 0FECE3F9C7EDF5A6. In Urdu. http://docs.newsbank.com (accessed June 15, 2006).

Sadiq, Kamal. 2009. *Paper Citizens: How Illegal Immigrants Acquire Citizenship in Developing Countries.* New York: Oxford University Press.

"Six Hundred Thirty Eight Afghans Deported for Fake Haj Papers." 2007. *Dawn*, April 5. http://archives.dawn.com/2007/04/05/nat9.htm.

"Three Hundred Afghan Hajis Being Deported Today." 2007. *Dawn*, February 13. http://archives.dawn.com/2007/02/13/local3.htm.

Torpey, John. 2001. "The Great War and the Birth of the Modern Passport System." In *Documenting Individual Identity: The Development of State Practices in the Modern World*, edited by Jane Caplan and John Torpey, 256–70. Princeton: Princeton University Press.

"Two Hundred Ninety One Pakistanis Arrested for Traveling Illegally." 2005. *Dawn*, December 11. http://archives.dawn.com/2005/12/11/nat22.htm.

CHAPTER TEN

The Smuggling of Refugees

Khalid Koser

There are several reasons that a separate chapter on refugees can contribute to an overall understanding of global human smuggling. First, in certain parts of the world—particularly Europe—a significant proportion of all those smuggled subsequently claim asylum. There is also scattered evidence for quite large-scale smuggling of people to neighboring countries from conflict zones, including from Afghanistan, Iraq, and Somalia, who may not apply for any legal status but are certainly fleeing in refugee-like circumstances. Second, while smuggling exposes all migrants to dangers and risks, smuggled refugees face particular vulnerabilities. Third, the smuggling of refugees poses special policy challenges for destination states: on the one hand, controlling their borders and combating irregular migration constitute an important component of state sovereignty; on the other hand, most states have made international commitments to respecting the right to asylum and protecting refugees.

The version of this chapter written for the first edition of this book used a small empirical case study to illustrate in particular the policy dilemmas relating to the smuggling of refugees (Koser, 2001). This chapter updates the earlier version by drawing mainly on academic articles and policy reports published in the intervening period. An immediate observation is that while there has been a significant increase in research on migrant smuggling in the past five years (for example, see the 2006 Special Issue of the journal *International Migration*) there has been very little research that looks specifically at the case of refugees. In further contrast to the earlier version, this chapter also considers in greater depth some of the more conceptual issues that arise in analyzing the smuggling of refugees.

Concepts and Data

The smuggling of refugees—a distinct migrant category—is a subset of the wider phenomenon of migrant smuggling, which is in turn a subset of the broad category of irregular (or "illegal") migration. Significant conceptual challenges and data problems are confronted by research, policy, and analysis on irregular migration in general (Koser, 2006), and these are magnified as the focus is narrowed first to migrant smuggling and then still further to the smuggling of refugees.

Concepts

Smuggling of people and trafficking in human beings are now distinct criminal offenses that have been defined by the international community in the so-called Palermo Protocols to the United Nations Convention on Transnational Organized Crime. Trafficking of human beings is defined as "the recruitment, transportation, transfer, harbouring or receipt of persons, by means of the threat, or use of force or other forms of coercion, of abduction, of fraud, of deception, of the abuse of power or of a position of vulnerability or of the giving or receiving of payments or benefits to achieve the consent of a person having control over another person, for the purpose of exploitation" (United Nations Office on Drugs and Crime, 2004: 42). The smuggling of people is defined as "the procurement, in order to obtain, directly or indirectly a financial or other material benefit, of the illegal entry of a person into a state Party of which the person is not a national or a permanent resident" (54–55). In reality, however, the distinction can be more difficult to ascertain, particularly in the case of refugees. One of the underlying contrasts between the Palermo Protocol definitions, for example, revolves around the concept of choice—victims of trafficking are assumed not to have given their consent, whereas people who are smuggled are considered to have willingly engaged in the enterprise.

But in the circumstances in which refugees flee their countries—to avoid persecution or threat to life—it can be difficult to draw quite such a clear line between choice and coercion. Refugees may not be forced to engage smugglers, but if smuggling represents their only route out of harm's way, it is hardly a voluntary decision. Helping people escape violence can be considered an invaluable service for which it is justifiable to charge a fee. From another perspective, charging that fee might be viewed as exploiting the situation of a desperate person.

Another reason that it can be hard to distinguish smuggling from trafficking in reality is that one can transform into another. When a migrant pays for only part of the journey in advance, for example, the possibility for exploitation after arrival in the destination country is opened up (Bhabha, 2005). It might be reasonable to assume that this scenario is particularly likely to occur for refugees, who have to move quickly and are so desperate to escape that they may be willing to take the risk of being indebted to a smuggler.

The conceptual challenges of distinguishing what smuggling comprises are compounded in this case by the challenges of defining who is a refugee. Once again there is a very clear legal definition: a refugee is someone who, "owing to well-founded fear of being persecuted for reasons of race, religion, nationality, membership of a particular social group, or political opinion, is outside the country of his nationality, and is unable or, owing to such fear, is unwilling to avail himself of the protection of that country." As is explained in the next section, there can be circumstances in which people who have been recognized as refugees are subsequently smuggled to another country. In most cases, however, people are smuggled first and then apply for asylum as a refugee after arriving. In certain parts of the world, especially Western Europe, an increasing proportion of people who apply for asylum do not satisfy the criteria for definition as a refugee and do not receive that status. Some may receive alternative, temporary forms of protection, but most are turned down outright and expected to return home. An immediate conceptual challenge is therefore to distinguish asylum seekers from refugees.

In addition, because they have been smuggled, these people also fall into the separate migrant category "irregular migrant." As is discussed later in this chapter, arriving in a country without authorization should not by law have an impact upon a refugee claim, although in reality there is evidence to suggest that it may. An additional conceptual challenge, nevertheless, is to distinguish refugees from other irregular migrants.

Data

Analysis of the smuggling of refugees is further hampered by a serious lack of data, making it difficult to identify trends or to compare the scale of the phenomenon in different parts of the world. One reason is conceptual—as explained above, it can be difficult to distinguish smuggling from trafficking and refugees from other migrant categories.

Another reason is methodological. Most research on migrant smuggling to date has been on the basis of interviews with migrants in destination countries. Many smuggled migrants remain in destination countries with no legal status and are likely to avoid speaking to the authorities for fear of detection. In contrast, applying for asylum necessitates engagement with the authorities. Most asylum seekers, nevertheless, are very reluctant to admit to either authorities or researchers that they were smuggled and thus arrived without authorization, for fear of jeopardizing their claim (even though in law this should not be the case). In theory those recognized as refugees might be willing to admit how they arrived, as they now have secure legal status, but sensitivities remain.

There has also been some significant research on smuggling in transit countries—especially in central and Eastern Europe—in recent years (Salt and Hogarth, 2000; Neske, 2006; Jandl, 2007). Even if migrants are willing to be interviewed in transit, they have not arrived in their intended destination country and so have not yet applied for asylum. They may be fleeing life-threatening circumstances—and they may or may not be willing to admit that—but they are not legally refugees.

Besides migrants themselves, the other main source of information and data on migrant smuggling is the authorities—accessed, for example, through reviews of official statistics or interviews with border guards. But these sources depend on migrants self-reporting their means of movement (smuggling or trafficking), their current status, and their intentions regarding whether to apply for asylum. There are good reasons for migrants, including refugees, not to provide accurate information on any of these aspects.

Numbers and Geography

Taken together, a lack of conceptual clarity and shortage of reliable data mean that it is virtually impossible to provide accurate estimates of the scale of refugee smuggling (or indeed, any other form of migrant smuggling) or patterns and trends in movement. By necessity this section can provide only rough indications.

Numbers

There is a broad consensus that as the number of international migrants has increased so too has the global scale of irregular migration (Global Commission on International Migration [GCIM], 2005). Most estimates of irregular migration are at the national level. It is thought, for example, that there are more than 10 million irregular migrants in the United States, accounting for nearly one-third of the foreign-born population there. More than half of these irregular migrants are Mexican, and a significant proportion have been smuggled across the border. It is also estimated that there are between 3.5 million and 5 million irregular migrants in the Russian Federation, originating mainly in countries of the Commonwealth of Independent States (CIS) and Southeast Asia. Up to 20 million irregular migrants are thought to live in India today (Koser, 2006).

Other estimates are provided on a regional or global scale. Half of all migrants in both Africa and Latin America are thought to be irregular. It has been estimated that overall some 2.5 million to 4 million migrants cross all international borders without authorization each year (International Centre on Migration Policy and Development, 2004). It is reckoned by the Organization for Economic Co-operation and Development (2004) that between 10 and 15 percent of Europe's 56 million migrants have irregular status and that each year around half a million undocumented migrants arrive in the European Union (EU). There are, however, considerable variations in the figures provided.

Just as with irregular migration in general, it is impossible to enumerate accurately either human trafficking or migrant smuggling. Figures usually provided relate to people who have been found and who admit to having been smuggled or trafficked. The problem is that no one knows what proportion of trafficked and smuggled people is actually found. It seems reasonable to assume that many are never known to the authorities. The U.S. State Department does publish annual estimates of human trafficking. It estimated that between 600,000 and 800,000 women, children, and men were trafficked in 2004 alone. Of this total, about two-thirds of victims were trafficked within Asia (260,000–280,000) and within Europe (170,000–210,000) (U.S. Department of State, 2005).

The most widely quoted figure for the scale of migrant smuggling in Europe was produced as long ago as 1994 by Widgren (1994). It is worth briefly rehearsing how he arrived at his numbers (Salt and Hogarth, 2000). He estimated in 1993 that there were 240,000–360,000 illegal migrant entries in Western Europe. The figure was calculated on the basis of extrapolations of how many illegal migrants were apprehended in a destination as a reflection of the known number of migrants apprehended in transit countries on their way to that destination. Analysis of border control data showed about 60,000 apprehensions. Based on discussions with border control authorities, Widgren then estimated that at least four to six times that number entered their destination undetected. Of this total, Widgren further estimated that between 15 and 30 percent had used the services of smugglers during part of their journey, amounting to a total of between 36,000 and 108,000 smuggled migrants in 1993.

If Widgren's multipliers are applied to more recent data on border apprehensions in Europe, the estimate needs to be updated significantly. Approximately the same ranges—of between 250,000 and 350,000 illegal migrants, of whom between about 35,000 and 100,00 have been smuggled—are reached using data only for Germany, Austria, and the United Kingdom (Koser, 2003).

At the same time, Widgren made a separate calculation for the proportion of asylum seekers who had been smuggled. In 1993 there were about 690,000 asylum seekers in Western Europe, of whom Widgren estimated about half were not in need of protection. Of those without a well-founded claim for asylum, Widgren estimated that between 20 and 40 percent had been smuggled, amounting to between 70,000 and 140,000 smuggled asylum seekers in Western Europe in 1993.

Two observations are worth making on Widgren's estimates on asylum seekers. First, it is interesting that he made an estimate only of the smuggled proportion of those asylum seekers whose applications he guessed to be unfounded. The limited available research suggests that there are no grounds to assume a distinction in terms of their interaction with smugglers between those who do and do not have a well-founded claim for asylum. In an admittedly small-scale study, for example, Morrison (2001) found a high incidence of smuggling among a group of respondents who had been granted refugee status in the United Kingdom.

Additionally, it is significant that Widgren estimated first that there were more asylum seekers in Europe than illegal migrants and second that a greater proportion of asylum seekers (without a well-founded claim) than of illegal migrants had been smuggled (20–40% compared with 15–30%). According to his lowest estimation, a total of 106,000 smuggled migrants were composed of 70,000 asylum seekers—amounting to 66 percent. At his highest estimations, a total of 248,000 smuggled migrants were composed of 140,000 asylum seekers—amounting to 56 percent. In other words, asylum seekers accounted for the majority of those who were smuggled into Europe.

What is more, there is evidence that in fact a significantly larger proportion of asylum seekers than estimated by Widgren have used smugglers since he made his estimate. The German Federal Refugee Office estimated in December 1997 that about 50 percent of asylum seekers in Germany were smuggled into the country. Meanwhile the Dutch Immigration Service upgraded its estimate of 30 percent in 1996 to between 60 and 70 percent in 1998 (Mavris, 2002).

Geography

From around the world there are scattered reports of the smuggling of refugees and asylum seekers: the International Organization for Migration (IOM) estimated in 2006 that three thousand Afghani refugees had been smuggled into Tajikistan in the preceding years (IOM 2006). The Afghans and Iraqis who were smuggled aboard the *Tampa* and other ships to Australia subsequently applied for asylum, although none were eventually granted refugee status in Australia (Maley, 2001; Brolan, 2002).

It is reported that an increasing proportion of Iraqis fleeing the current crisis and seeking asylum in Sweden have been smuggled there (Ekman, 2007). There has also been an increase in the smuggling of unaccompanied children from northern Iraq to Sweden (Väyrynen, 2003). It has been suggested that the majority of Kurds applying for asylum in Greece have been smuggled there overland (Papadopoulou, 2004). As insecurity increases on the main roads between Iraq and Syria, it has also been asserted that even Iraqis fleeing to neighboring countries may soon have to pay smugglers (Al-Khalidi, Hoffman, and Tanner, 2007).

There have also been press reports of smuggling of people fleeing the recent conflict in Somalia. And it was estimated in 2003 that up to 250 unaccompanied children were smuggled out of Mogadishu every month heading for the United Kingdom or North America to try to claim asylum.

Such reports lend themselves to very limited analysis—refugee smuggling appears to be a global phenomenon that can take place over a range of distances from crossing local borders to movements between continents. While

Table 10.1   A Typology of Refugee Smuggling

Refugee "Type"	Main Geographical Focus	Smuggling Associations
Asylum seekers	Europe	Limited research indicates that the majority may be smuggled
Resettled refugees	Australia, Canada, United States, Scandinavia	May have been smuggled to the initial host country, but no evidence of smuggling to resettlement countries
Prima facie determination on a group basis	Africa, Middle East, Asia	Payments/bribery to cross local borders reported to be common, but does not usually take the form of organized smuggling; some may subsequently be smuggled onward
Onward movements	Europe	May have been smuggled to initial asylum country and likely to have been smuggled onward

there is insufficient evidence to provide an empirical overview of global patterns and trends in refugee smuggling, it is possible to develop a basic typology of refugee smuggling that has certain geographical characteristics (Table 10.1).

With the notable exception of Scandinavia, most European countries do not have resettlement quotas for refugees, effectively meaning that in order to claim asylum there a refugee needs to make his or her own away. Various studies have demonstrated how a range of immigration controls—from border enforcement to restrictive visa regimes—have had an impact on asylum seekers as much as other migrants, with the result that increasing proportions of asylum seekers arriving in Europe arrive without authorization and often through smuggling (Overland, 2007). Only a proportion of these are eventually recognized as refugees.

In contrast, most refugees in North America as well as Australia are resettled there. They are deemed to satisfy the criteria for refugee definition in host countries in their region of origin and then selected for resettlement as refugees and transported to the final destination. While some of them may have been smuggled to their initial host country, there is no reason they would subsequently need to be smuggled to their final destination, as they are relocated there formally and with international assistance. There have been some reports of corruption with regard to the resettlement selection process, but this does not constitute smuggling, as the actual movement across borders takes place legally.

In situations of mass exodus—typically in Africa, although also in Afghanistan and more recently in Iraq—refugees are generally not screened individually to check whether they satisfy the refugee definition criteria. Instead, a prima facie determination of their status is made on a group basis. There are reports in these situations of people having to pay or bribe officials to cross borders, but there is little evidence of organized smuggling across borders from conflict zones.

Some people who have either applied for asylum or been recognized as refugees in one country subsequently attempt to move to another, usually richer country, not through formal resettlement programs but individually and almost always without authorization. This phenomenon of "onward movement: is often also referred to as "irregular secondary movement." Analysis of statistics on the origins of asylum applicants in industrialized states indicates that a large proportion have already been recognized as refugees in host states in their region of origin (United Nations High Commissioner for Refugees, 2006). A Swiss Migration Forum (2005) study of onward movement of Somali refugees demonstrated that many of them did not want to move beyond their region but that protection issues, a lack of social amenities, and confinement to camps effectively forced them to.

Causes of Refugee Smuggling

From the recent research and publications on migrant smuggling, three principal frameworks for explaining the phenomenon have emerged. With certain limitations, each also applies to refugee smuggling.

One focuses on underlying causes (Castles and Miller, 2003; Koser, 2006). Growing developmental, demographic, and democratic disparities, compounded by the global jobs crisis, provide powerful reasons to move. The segmentation of labor markets in advanced economies is creating an increasing demand for migrant workers there. The communications revolution has made people more aware of opportunities elsewhere, and a revolution in transportation has made moving long distances cheaper and easier. Migration networks and the growth of a migration industry add further momentum. For these sorts of reasons, it is argued, more people than ever before want to move, but because of restrictive immigration policies, there are proportionately fewer legal opportunities for them to do so. The demand for irregular migration has increased as a result, and migrant smugglers have cornered the emerging market.

To what extent does this framework also apply to refugee smuggling? For refugees the principal underlying cause of flight is conflict, although it is also worth observing that very often there are inextricable links between conflict, poverty, and underdevelopment, making it at times difficult to discern any single motivation for refugee flight. While the majority of refugees still settle in neighboring countries, an increasing proportion seek asylum farther away, mainly in industrialized countries. The prospect of a better life—including the possibility of working—appears to be one reason; another is to join family and friends. Limited research also suggests that some refugees have the time to assess information about prospective destinations and make a positive choice, although many leave so quickly and in such desperate circumstances that they cannot (Gilbert and Koser, 2006). And restrictive immigration policies have also had an impact on asylum seekers. The outcome, as for migrants in general, is that refugees trying to move long distances and enter an industrialized country often have little alternative but to employ a smuggler.

A separate but related explanation for migrant smuggling focuses specifically on the role of policies and views the growth of migrant smuggling as an unintended consequence of restrictive immigration policies (Castles, 2004). Research in this vein has not been able to establish a causal link between restrictive policies and the growth of migrant smuggling. But it has shown how one of the principal functions served by smugglers is to overcome obstacles that have resulted directly from these policies, especially in the form of visa restrictions and border controls. The argument is that were these obstacles to be removed—for example by increasing opportunities for legal migration—the services of smugglers would no longer be required, or at least demand for them would be reduced. Very similar conclusions have been reached in research on the impact of asylum policies (Koser, 2000; Väyrynen, 2003).

A third explanation expands the migration industry concept contained within the first. It draws on the "business model" of migration that conceives of migration as a business comprising "a system of institutionalized networks with complex profit and loss accounts, including a set of institutions, agents and individuals each of which stands to make a commercial gain" (Salt and Stein, 1997: 467). Migrant smuggling (and human trafficking) constitutes the illegitimate side of this business. According to this model, the profit motive creates an almost irrepressible momentum within the migration business, and migrant smugglers actively recruit clients to turn a profit (Bilger, Hofmann, and Jandl, 2006). The extent to which this last explanation also applies to refugees is least clear, as there has been no research whatsoever on how refugees enter the smuggling process.

The first of these three explanations might be characterized as macrolevel (it concerns underlying structural features) and the second and third mesolevel (respectively, the role of policy and intermediaries). What is striking is that explanations for migrant smuggling have rarely analyzed the microlevel of individual or family decision making. Each of the above explanations implies why individuals decide to employ the services of smugglers: because they are desperate to escape poverty and repression, because policy changes leave them with little option, or because they are actively recruited by the migration industry. But none really explains the decision.

On the face of it, for most migrants, the decision to voluntarily employ a smuggler voluntarily makes no sense given the potential risks involved. Possible explanations are that they are unaware of the risk involved or that the potential benefit outweighs the perceived risk. The decision is, however, probably easier to explain for refugees, for whom just about any risk is worth taking, as the alternatives—death, persecution, imprisonment, and so on—are so bad.

Consequences of Refugee Smuggling

While the risks associated with human trafficking are almost always greater, migrant smuggling is certainly not risk free. Refugees confront many of the risks faced by other migrants too, but their particular status brings additional vulnerabilities.

The Risks of Migrant Smuggling

A large number of people die trying to cross land and sea borders without being detected by the authorities—as many as 2,000 migrants each year trying to cross the Mediterranean from Africa to Europe and 400 trying to cross the U.S.-Mexican border (GCIM, 2005). Smuggled migrants—especially women—can be confronted with discrimination, are obliged to accept the most menial informal-sector jobs, can face specific health-related risks (Gushulak and Mac-Pherson, 2000), and are often at risk of exploitation by employers and landlords (Gencianos, 2004). Smuggled migrants with irregular status are barred from using the full range of services available to citizens and migrants with regular status and do not always make use of public services to which they are entitled—for example, emergency health care (Le Voy, Verbruggen, and Wets, 2004).

Smuggled migrants can also confront forms of economic insecurity (Koser, 2001). The costs of migrant smuggling vary enormously according to factors such as origin and destination country, mode of transportation and the number of people being moved (Petros, 2005) but are reported to be at least US$20,000 to move from Asia to Europe and much more to move to North America. Unsurprisingly, most would-be migrants do not have access to such significant sums and are obliged to turn to friends or relatives for financial assistance. Many subsequently leave their country with virtually no money yet sometimes need to subsist for long periods in transit. After arriving in their destination country, they may be under pressure to find work immediately in order to pay debts to friends or relatives from whom money had been borrowed initially. Many work illegally in transit and destination countries, which in turn can heighten their vulnerability to deportation.

The role of smugglers in influencing the destinations of some migrants can also give rise to a source of what might be described as social insecurity. Most migrants want to head for countries where they have family, friends, or at least ethnic communities to support them (Herman, 2006). But some end up in other destination countries—chosen by smugglers—and in this way they effectively become isolated from potentially supportive social networks (Koser, 2001).

Refugee-Specific Smuggling Risks

Smuggled refugees confront all of the risks mentioned above, but their status as refugees (or asylum seekers) brings added insecurities, in particular those of a political nature.

One of the main sources of political insecurity for any asylum seeker arises from the threat of deportation. On the one hand, the 1951 United Nation Convention on Refugees stipulates that refugees should not be penalized on the basis of their means of arrival in a country of asylum. The implication is that once asylum seekers have entered the asylum procedure their involvement or otherwise with smugglers should have no bearing on their applications. On the other hand, it is quite clear that on certain political and media agendas asylum seekers are increasingly becoming synonymous with irregular migrants. There is a concern among human rights activists that asylum seekers who can be shown to have been smuggled may not be allowed to begin the asylum procedure and face the threat of deportation as irregular migrants (Morrison, 2001). For example, in the United Kingdom recent grounds for rejecting asylum applications have been reported to include the failure to present supporting documentation and the presentation of fraudulent documentation. Yet empirical research has identified both of these as specific outcomes of smuggling.

Another source of political insecurity that arises particularly in the context of the EU is the possibility under so-called readmission agreements of returning asylum seekers to countries outside the EU that they can be demonstrated to have transited and require them to apply for asylum there. Iranian asylum seekers, for example, have often been returned from Europe to Turkey; yet regular deportations of Iranian asylum seekers from Turkey still take place. Similarly, a readmission agreement has been negotiated by the Dutch government with Romania so that asylum seekers can be returned there. Romania, however, is one of several central and Eastern European countries still considered by many authorities to be ill equipped to receive and protect asylum seekers properly.

The international community recognizes that refugees require specific legal protection, especially against being returned home against their will. Despite the evidence that refugees can be smuggled, the form of protection afforded to trafficked individuals in the Palermo Protocols is nevertheless far greater than that for the smuggled. The Trafficking Protocol addresses the need for protection of trafficked persons in considerable detail and provides for a broad range of protective measures, while the Smuggling Protocol contains minimal reference to protection needs for smuggled persons.

During the negotiations for the Palermo Protocols the United Nations High Commissioner for Refugees (UNHCR) and the Office of the High Commissioner for Human Rights (OHCHR) inserted a "savings clause" to ensure that the instruments did not undermine the rights, obligations, and responsibilities of states under international human rights and humanitarian law, including in particular the principle protecting refugees from being returned to a place where their lives or freedom could be threatened (non-refoulment). It remains to be seen, however, "whether the savings clause is enough to prevent the two protocols from being used to undermine the already precarious refugee protection regime" (Gallagher, 2002).

Policy Implications

Four approaches to combating migrant smuggling can be discerned, and often they are employed in combination. One is to strengthen borders through measures such as more physical border controls, biometric tests, and extended visa regimes. A second is to disseminate information about the risks entailed in employing a smuggler in countries and subregions from which significant migration occurs. A third is a set of longer-term policies concerned with reducing incentives to move in an irregular fashion in the first place. These include achieving development targets to increase security and livelihoods in origin countries, as well as increasing the opportunities to move legally. A final approach is to target smugglers directly—for example, using intelligence services, working in collaboration with authorities in origin and transit countries, and offering incentives for migrants to provide testimonies.

Each of these can be problematic in the case of refugee smuggling. Restrictive policies run the risk of excluding refugees as well as other irregular migrants. Disseminating information in a conflict zone is usually impractical and in any case fairly pointless, as most refugees have few options but to flee, if necessary paying a smuggler to do so. Addressing root causes is a laudable long-term goal but does not reduce the immediate need for refugees to flee violence. And when smugglers really do represent the only way out for refugees, restricting their activities may restrict the possibility for refugees to escape and survive. Overall the policy dilemma is how to stop migrant smuggling without also closing the door on asylum.

This dilemma might be at least in part resolved through three policies (Koser, 2001). One is in-country processing—whereby refugee status determination takes place in the country of origin—or alternatively in-country protection of refugees in safe havens. The only reason refugees need to employ smugglers is that they need to move. If movement can be eliminated from asylum, so can smugglers. Proceeding from the same logic, a second option is processing and protection in a country in the refugee's region of origin, one to which legal access can be guaranteed. A third is to reintroduce in Western Europe and extend elsewhere resettlement quotas for refugees. Another reason refugees employ smugglers is that they have no legal alternatives. Quotas would mean that at least a proportion could enter asylum countries legally.

Conclusion

Focusing on refugees in this chapter has contributed to an overall understanding of global human smuggling in four main ways. First, it has illustrated challenges—such as those regarding concepts and data—that beset research on human smuggling in general. Second, it has pointed to thematic gaps in research—for example, on explaining why and how migrants make the decision to voluntarily employ a smuggler. Third, it has made the case for the need to extend current explanatory frameworks to cover the specific causes and consequences of refugee smuggling. Finally, it has identified specific policy dilemmas that indicate the need for more refined policy making on migrant smuggling as a whole.

REFERENCES

Al-Khalidi, A., S. Hoffman, and V. Tanner. 2007. *Iraqi Refugees in the Syrian Arab Republic: A Field-Based Snapshot.* Washington, D.C.: Brookings–Bern Project on Internal Displacement.

Bhabha, J. 2005. *Trafficking, Smuggling, and Human Rights.* Migration Information Source. Washington, D.C.: Migration Policy Institute.

Bilger, V., M. Hofmann, and M. Jandl. 2006. "Human Smuggling as a Transnational Service Industry: Evidence from Austria." *International Migration* 44 (4): 60–93.

Brolan, C. 2002. "An Analysis of Human Smuggling Trade and the Protocol against the Smuggling of Migrants by Land, Air and Sea (2000) from a Refugee Protection Perspective." *International Journal of Refugee Law* 14:561–73.

Castles, S. 2004 "Why Migration Policies Fail." *Ethnic and Racial Studies* 27 (2): 205–27.

Castles, S., and M. Miller. 2003. *The Age of Migration.* New York: Guildford Press.

Ekman, I. 2007. "From Iraq to Sweden—Human Smugglers Have a Package to Suit All Refugees." *International Herald Tribune,* February 13.

Gallagher, A. 2002. "Trafficking, Smuggling and Human Rights: Tricks and Treaties." *Forced Migration Review* 12:25–28.

Gencianos, G. 2004. "International Civil Society Cooperation on Migrants' Rights: Perspectives from an NGO Network." *European Journal of Migration and Law* 6:147–55.

Gilbert, A., and K. Koser. 2006. "Coming to the UK: What So Asylum-Seekers Know about the UK before Arrival?" *Journal of Ethnic and Migration Studies* 32 (7): 456–71.

Global Commission on International Migration (GCIM). 2005. *Migration in an Interconnected World: New Directions for Action.* Geneva: GCIM.

Gushulak, B. D., and D. MacPherson. 2000. "Health Issues Associated with the Smuggling and Trafficking of Migrants." *Journal of Immigrant Health* 2 (2): 67–78.

Herman, E. 2006. "Migration as a Family Business: The Role of Personal Networks in the Mobility Phase of Migration." *International Migration* 44 (4): 191–230.

International Centre on Migration Policy and Development. 2004. "Irregular Transit Migration in the Mediterranean: Some Facts, Figures and Insights." Presented to the Dialogue on Mediterranean Transit Migration, Vienna, February 5–6.

International Migration. 2006. 44 (4): 39–230.

Jandl, M. 2007. "Irregular Migration, Human Smuggling and the Eastern Enlargement of the European Union." *International Migration Review* 41 (2): 291–316.

Koser, K. 2000. "Asylum Policies, Trafficking and Vulnerability." *International Migration* 38 (3): 91–112.

———. 2001. "The Smuggling of Asylum Seekers into Western Europe: Contradictions, Conundrums and Dilemmas." In *Global Human Smuggling: Comparative Perspectives,* edited by D. Kyle and R. Koslowski, 58–74. Baltimore: John Hopkins University Press.

———. 2003. "Reconciling Control and Compassion: Human Smuggling and the Right to Asylum." In *Refugees and Forced Displacement,* edited by E. Newman and J. Van Selm, 181–94. Tokyo, UNU Press.

———. 2006. "Irregular Migration." In *The Politics of Migration,* edited by B. Marshall, 44–57. London: Routledge.

Le Voy, M., N. Verbruggen, and J. Wets, eds. 2004. *Undocumented Migrant Workers in Europe.* Brussels: PICUM.

Maley, W. 2001. "Security, People-Smuggling and Australia's New Afghan Refugees." *Australian Journal of International Affairs* 55 (3): 351–70.

Mavris, L. 2002. "Human Smugglers and Social Networks: Transit Migration through the States of Former Yugoslavia." New Issues in Refugee Research, Working Paper 72. UNHCR, Geneva. December.

Morrison, J. 2001. "The Trafficking and Smuggling of Refugees: The End Game in European Asylum Policy?" New Issues in Refugee Research, Working Paper 39. UNHCR, Geneva. April.

Nadig, A. 2002. "Human Smuggling, National Security and Refugee Protection." *Journal of Refugee Studies* 15 (1): 34–52.

Neske, M. 2006. "Human Smuggling to and through Germany." *International Migration* 44 (4): 121–64.

Organization for Economic Co-operation and Development. 2004. *Trends in International Migration—SOPEMI 2004 Edition.* Paris: OECD.

Overland, G. 2007. "The Illegal Way In and the Moral Way Out." *European Journal of Philosophy* 15 (2): 186–203.

Papadopoulou, A. 2004. "Smuggling into Europe: Transit Migrants in Greece." *Journal of Refugee Studies* 17 (2): 120–34.

Petros, M. 2005. *The Costs of Human Smuggling and Trafficking.* Global Migration Perspectives 31. GCIM. www.gcim.org/attachements/GMP%20No%2031.pdf.

Salt, J., and J. Hogarth. 2000. *Migrant Trafficking and Human Smuggling in Europe: A Review of the Evidence with Case Studies from Hungary, Poland and Ukraine.* Geneva: IOM.

Salt, J., and J. Stein. 1997. "Migration as a Business: The Case of Trafficking." *International Migration* 35 (4): 467–94.

Swiss Migration Forum. 2005. "Movements of Somali Refugees and Asylum Seekers and States' Responses." Paper presented to at Convention Plus Forum, Geneva.

United Nations High Commissioner for Refugees. 1951. *Convention Relating to the Status of Refugees.* Geneva: UNHCR.

————. 2006. *The State of the World's Refugees.* Oxford: Oxford University Press.

United Nations Office on Drugs and Crime. 2004. *United Nations Convention against Transnational Organized Crime and the Protocols Thereto.* Vienna: UNODC.

U.S. Department of State. 2005. *Trafficking in Persons Report.* Washington, D.C.: U.S. Department of State.

Väyrynen, R. 2003. "Illegal Immigration, Human Trafficking and Organized Crime." UNU WIDER Discussion Paper 2003/72. UNU, Helsinki.

Widgren, J. 1994. "Multilateral Co-operation to Combat Trafficking in Migrants and the Role of International Organizations." Discussion paper presented to the IOM Seminar "International Responses to Trafficking in Migrants and the Safeguarding of Migrant Rights," Geneva.

CHAPTER ELEVEN

Uncovering the Legal Cachet of Labor Migration to Israel

Barak Kalir

It appears straightforward and commonsensical to oppose illegal migration to legal migration. While illegal migration has been put high on the "public enemy" list of most Western countries, legal migration is considered to be the orderly way to enter, work, and potentially settle down in another country. Illegal migration is often seen and analyzed as the "dark side" of global human flows. It is closely associated with the operations of human traffickers and smugglers and with the ensuing brutal exploitation of indentured labor. Legal migration, in contrast, is associated with regulations, paperwork, and bureaucratic supervision. In fact, many policymakers and experts advocate the drafting of legal schemes for the importation and employment of temporary migrant workers as an important means for countervailing illegal migration. Common wisdom commands, they argue, that when states facilitate employers' access to temporary migrant workers, the demand for undocumented migrants diminishes, and with it the incentive for people to undertake illegal migration in search for work in those countries.

In this chapter I challenge this premise by examining two parallel labor flows to Israel. The first is a legal flow of migrant workers, who are recruited, transported, and employed according to a tightly regulated scheme, often based on bilateral agreements between Israel and sending countries. The second is an illegal flow of undocumented migrants, who arrive, find jobs, and settle down by their own initiative and against the official planning of the Israeli government.

Based on ethnographic research among two representative groups in Israel—legal migrant workers from China and undocumented migrants from Latin America—I argue that seeing illegal and legal migration in opposition to each other, or as two antidotes on a continuum, is empirically ungrounded and analytically misleading. Empirically, and against all conventional thinking, it is migrant workers from China who must pay an informal fee of around US$25,000 to recruitment companies, while undocumented migrants from Latin America operate independently of any migration industry and pay little more than the airfare that takes them to Israel. Once in Israel, indebted migrant workers are subjected to a highly restrictive employment scheme, which conduces to their systematic exploitation by local employers to a degree that led some critiques to define the situation of migrant workers in Israel as a "contemporary form of slavery" (Ellman and Laacher, 2003). In contrast, undocumented migrants are free to sell their labor for competitive salaries in the local market. They thus earn higher salaries than migrant workers and suffer much less from exploitation by Israeli employers. Finally, owing to the restrictive Israeli employment scheme, thousands of migrant workers lost their legal status and ended up being deported from Israel. At the same time, thousands of undocumented migrants settled down, and some even managed to legalize their status in Israel.

I thus argue that much of what we consider to constitute global human smuggling is taking place under the guise of legal flows of labor migrants. It is therefore analytically misleading and even unscrupulous to uncritically reproduce in our research the formalistic distinction that states draw between legal and illegal migration. Instead, we must examine what really happens on the ground under the formal authority of the state. We must put to the test the assumption that regulated flows of migrant workers are *per definition* an improvement on the process that characterizes illegal migration. Otherwise, we might contribute to the "legal fiction"—that is, a formalistic facade—that characterizes states' migration regimes and does little in practice to regulate the labor market, protect the rights of migrant workers, and curtail illegal migration.

It is a truism that gaps inevitably exist between the ideal reality that laws ordain and the actual reality that is created on the ground through social interactions. Yet revealing and analyzing the emergence and particular shape that these gaps take on in each migration regime are key to understanding paradoxical situations such as the one I describe in Israel. As Miller (2001) has convincingly shown, it is often the case that the major problem in the management of labor importation schemes is not a lack of laws but the failure of officials and law enforcers to implement existing laws and to bring to justice those who violate them. In the words of Giorgio Agamben: "Today we see how a maximum anomy and disorder can perfectly coexist with a maximum of legislation" (Raulff, 2004: 612). The "disorder" that is created by the chronic failure of states to enforce laws and protect rights is symptomatic, in the case of labor flows, of the deeper failure of states to treat migrant workers as political subjects. Migrants who cross the territorial borders of states are often unable equally to cross and penetrate the mental borders that are more firmly held by state officials and most legal members of nations.

A Complementary Dimension: From Il/legality to Il/licitness

To analyze the gap between existing laws and their implementation in practice, we need to complement our distinction between legality and illegality with a distinction between licitness and illicitness. While it is the letter of the law that determines il/legality in the management of migration regimes, it is the social perceptions of those who are involved in the actualization of migratory processes that define il/licitness. I take my cue here from the work of van Schendel and Abraham (2005), who offer a matrix of "spaces of competing authorities" (Table 11.1). The matrix juxtaposes the formal political authority of states (legal-illegal) and the nonformal social authority of members in societies (licit-illicit). While states hold the capacity to define that which is il/legal

Table 11.1   Spaces of Competing Authorities

	Legal	Illegal
Licit	(A) Ideal State	(B) Underworld/Borderland
Illicit	(C) Crony Capitalism / Failed State	(D) Anarchy

Source: Reprinted from van Schendel and Abraham (2005: 20, table I.1).

under their jurisdiction, members in society can nonetheless perceive things/actions/flows to be licit, given their subjective viewpoint and position as actors.

Whereas a complete overlap between state's legal definitions and people's perceptions produces an "Ideal State," a negative overlap produces a state of "Anarchy." Yet the interesting insights and use value of this matrix can be found in the mismatches it highlights. Cell (C) captures "legal but illicit" situations, in which the laws of the state permit illicit corporative conduct, like money laundering in the Cayman Islands or an "Enron Stage of Capitalism" in the United States, that nurtures close—and often corruptive and corrupting—ties between politicians and private businesses. In its extreme, cell (C) represents a situation in which the state is no longer able to define and defend the "legal" against the "illicit" and therefore ceases to exist as an effective political unit of organization. Cell (B) calls attention to "illegal but licit" situations, in which people routinely and knowingly act not in accordance with the official law but in a way that they consider to be—within their social and spatial context—justifiable and rightful. The two prime examples here are the underworld (as in markets for counterfeited goods) and the borderland (as in the illegal cross-border practices that constitute an integral part of the daily life and livelihood of people who reside in the vicinity of international borders).

When applied to immigration flows, this analytical framework enables us to probe and talk about what really happens on the ground. Mismatches of the "illegal but licit" kind explain, for example, why human smugglers in many countries are defined as dangerous criminals by law but are seen as folk heroes and skilled professionals by millions of people who seek their services (see Kyle and Dale, this volume, Chap. 1) or why undocumented migrants' presence and employment are defined by states to be illegal even though they are often being routinely employed by millions of ordinary citizens in their homes, as well as by private companies in many sectors. The lack of enforcement of migrant workers' rights constitutes an "illegal but licit" situation from the perspective of law enforcers, who are assigned to protect migrants' rights but often deliberately refrain from doing so because they consider it to be an unimportant or unworthy task.

Mismatches of the "legal but illicit" kind characterize many government schemes for the employment of migrant workers. These schemes often unreasonably give greater priority to the interests of private businesses over the rights of migrant workers. The design of such schemes by policymakers is often influenced by the lobbies of powerful employers. When these schemes are implemented, as was the case in Israel, employers are endowed with absolute power vis-à-vis migrant workers. The latter are often obliged to work exclusively for specific employers, who can then take advantage and threaten workers with dismissal if they resist overwork. While employers break no law, their conduct is perceived by all workers, and arguably by most objective observers, as immoral and socially unacceptable. In fact, independent organizations such as state comptrollers, nongovernmental organizations (NGOs), central banks, and the media often criticize governments heavily for adopting unfair schemes.

The Israeli Labor Importation and Employment Scheme: What's in a Law?

The state of Israel has been internationally recognized (United Nations Resolution of 1947) and legally established (Declaration of Independence, 1948) as a Jewish state. Israel's declared purpose has been to serve as a "home" for Jews worldwide. Accordingly, Israel actively encourages the immigration of Jews, while it ideologically rejects the immigration of non-Jews. However, in the early 1990s, as the first intifada led to a dramatic reduction in the number of Palestinian workers in the Israeli economy, the political lobbies of organized Israeli employers in the agricultural and construction sectors succeeded in pressuring the government to engage for the first time in its history in the importation of non-Jewish migrant workers.[1] This move was condemned by several political parties in Israel as a betrayal of Zionist ideals, and it prompted the government to rectify its commitment to the Jewish character of Israel by vowing to prevent non-Jewish workers from settling down in the country.

Starting in 1993, Israel began importing migrant workers from different countries, mainly in Asia (e.g., Thailand, the Philippines, Nepal, India, and China) and East Europe (e.g., Romania, Bulgaria, Moldova). Migrant workers were designated chiefly for jobs in three sectors: construction, agriculture, and caregiving for elderly and/or disabled people. At first, work permits to migrant workers were issued on a very limited basis. Yet, under pressure from employers, the government increased the number of permits more than tenfold within three years: from 9,600 in 1993 to 103,000 by 1996. By the year 2000, there were 113,000 temporary migrant workers in Israel, constituting 11.5 percent of the total Israeli workforce in the private sector (Bank of Israel, 2000). Throughout the 2000s, the number of migrant workers in Israel remained around 100,000.

The Recruitment Scheme

The process of recruiting qualified migrant workers abroad and importing them to Israel was relegated by the state to authorized, privately owned manpower agencies. The Israeli Law of Employment (1959) strictly forbids employers or manpower agencies, in Israel or abroad, to charge migrant workers for the right to work in Israel.[2] The profit of these agencies is supposed to come from the fees that they charge to the Israeli employers who contract their services. Yet in practice Israeli manpower agencies, often working together with local recruitment agencies abroad, charged expensive informal fees from recruited migrant workers. Charging informal fees to migrant workers, although illegal, became a huge profit-making business in Israel (Hotline for Migrant Workers and Kav La'oved, 2007). In the early 2000s Israeli manpower agencies were making an estimated average profit of US$3,000 for each migrant worker they provided to Israeli employers (State Comptroller, 2003: 649). Consequently, the incentive for Israeli manpower agencies to import as many migrant workers as possible was high.

Competition among manpower agencies over the "right" to provide Israeli employers with migrant workers soon emerged and intensified. Agencies not only waived the fee that employers should have paid them but also offered employers kickbacks for the "right" to provide them with workers from abroad. Employers often received a few hundred dollars for each migrant worker who was brought for them to Israel. Big companies, which gave manpower agencies the "right" to provide them with hundreds of migrant workers, could receive more than a million dollars for it.

Severely criticizing the government for its ineptness in confronting the actions of manpower agencies, the state comptroller asserted, "The state and its citizens suffer from these practices . . . the financial benefits from charging migrant workers with fees for coming to work in Israel creates a temptation to pressure for more work permits than is necessary, and for the unlawful dealing of work permits" (State Comptroller, 2003: 649). Yet, as repeated journalistic and police investigations found out, manpower agencies powerfully lobbied the government to set higher quotas of migrant workers, using bribes to officials in key ministries as one prominent means to achieve this (Kav La'oved, 2000. *Yediot Aharonot,* October, 7, 2001; *Haaretz,* February 26, 2002). A former adviser for the Israeli government on the issue of migrant workers, Hertzel

Hagai, expressed his frustration with the process, remarking in a sarcastic way that "the major profit in Israel from migrant workers is coming from their very importation rather than their employment" (*Haaretz*, October 2, 2002).

Employers, too, were encouraged by the kickbacks to demand from the government more migrant workers than they actually needed. Employers then often ended up with superfluous migrant workers, whom they either arbitrarily dismissed after a short while or "sold" to employers in sectors that were not entitled to an allocation of migrant workers. The "selling" of workers is strictly illegal under Israeli law and amounts to human trafficking. Yet in the few cases in which the police captured migrant workers who were "sold" to other employers, those workers were arrested and deported for violating their contract, while the employers involved were hardly ever indicted.

The Employment Scheme

Allegedly in order to ensure that migrant workers would never settle down, Israel issued work visas for migrant workers for a period of one or two years, often with the possibility to extend them up to a maximum of five years. Migrant workers were allowed to work only in a designated job and for an exclusive employer, whose name appeared in their work visa. Any violation of these strict terms, including the dismissal of migrant workers for whatever reason by their employer, instantly invalidated the work visa of migrant workers, who then had to leave the country.

Migrant workers were habitually kept close to their working site and separate from larger Israeli society; construction workers were often lodged at the sites on which they were working, agricultural workers were accommodated in caravans placed at the perimeters of the fields they cultivated, and caregivers resided in the home of the person receiving care. Migrant workers' social isolation and physical proximity to their working environment not only had an alienating effect but also rendered workers "ready-on-demand" for their employers. Workers were under constant supervision and could enjoy recreational activities only when employers permitted it. In addition, migrant workers could not be joined by their families. Fearing that it would promote their settlement, Israel prohibited the partners, and particularly the children, of migrant workers from joining them. This prohibition was explicitly mentioned in migrant workers' contracts and firmly monitored by state officials. It was, moreover, made clear to migrant workers that if they were to form matrimonial or even romantic relationships while in Israel, they would be dismissed and sent back home.[3]

The bureaucratic caging, which effectively bound migrant workers to exclusive Israeli employers, became publicly known in Israel as the "binding arrangement." Some Israeli scholars (Rosenhek, 1999; Kemp, 2004) defined migrant workers as "captive labor," borrowing the term from Calavita (1992), who studied the situation of Mexican workers in the United States. Indeed, in Israel, migrant workers found themselves in an extremely vulnerable position when many employers began to take full advantage of the "binding arrangement." Employers routinely violated the contracts of migrant workers and threatened that any complaint to law enforcement institutions would lead to their dismissal. The fear of being dismissed has led many migrant workers to endure severe working conditions and harsh exploitation.

Employers commonly paid workers much less than had been agreed upon in contracts. Some especially ruthless employers held up the salaries of migrant workers for a few months, only to then dismiss them arbitrarily and force them to leave the country without paying their salaries. When migrant workers refused to leave and insisted on payment, employers often called on the police to arrest their migrant workers, who by then had lost their legal status. The police regularly arrested and deported workers before the dispute over their salaries would be resolved in court (for more on these forms of exploitation, as well as others, see Drori and Kunda, 1999; Schnell, 2001; Hotline for Migrant Workers and Kav La'oved, 2003, 2004; Kemp, 2004). Indeed, Israeli law enforcers did very little to protect migrant workers' rights. Inspectors in the Ministry of Labor, who had responsibility for supervising the conditions of migrant workers, seriously neglected the enforcement of their rights (Yanay and Borowosky, 1998). The state comptroller claimed that "in practice, employers that accommodated foreign workers in improper conditions are not being penalized" (State Comptroller, 1996: 494). The Bank of Israel (2000) reported that between 1996 and 2000 an average of 56 percent of migrant workers were unlawfully paid below minimum wage. Other labor laws were also widely violated by employers with no serious precautions taken by the state (Schnell, 2001).

This entrenched exploitation also impinged on migrant workers' civil rights. Israeli employers often confiscated the passports of their workers in order to exercise even greater control over them. Confiscating passports constitutes a criminal offence in Israel that carries a penalty of up to one year in prison (Penal Law, Art. 376-a). Some Israeli NGOs assisted hundreds of migrant workers in complaining about the confiscation of their passports; nevertheless, the police took little, if any, action to follow up on these complaints and bring the violating employers to court. Israeli authorities actually collaborated with employers on this unlawful practice. Officials from the Interior Ministry, who were responsible for checking migrant workers' passports upon arrival, commonly returned the passports not to workers but to their employers, who then kept them (Association for Civil Rights in Israel, 1997).

The Case of Chinese Migrant Workers: Legality as Liability

In 1992, Israel and China officially established diplomatic relations. Soon afterward, Chinese workers started to reach Israel: at first only a few hundred, but since 1996 thousands have arrived each year. According to the Israeli records, more than 30,000 Chinese workers reached Israel on a work visa in the period between 1995 and 2004 (Ministry of Industry, Trade, and Labor, 2005). The recruitment of workers from China should be seen in a broader context of exponentially growing economic ties between the two countries. According to the Chinese embassy in Tel Aviv, the Sino-Israeli bilateral trade increased from US$50 million in 1992 to US$3 billion in 2005, and more than eight hundred Israeli companies are currently doing business in China.[4]

Most Chinese workers in Israel are men aged thirty to forty-four who have been initially mainly recruited from villages across the southern province of Fujian. In later years recruitment has spread to other provinces like Jiangsu, Anhui, and Hubei. Chinese workers come from a poor economic and educational background, commonly quitting school at the age of fifteen and beginning to work to contribute to their household's income. Their pre-migration salary was around US$100 per month from work in construction or agriculture (Kalir, 2009; Li, 2009). In Israel, Chinese workers are predominantly employed (around 90%) in the construction sector, where they can earn between US$800 and $900 per month.[5]

According to the agreement between the two countries, around forty Israeli manpower agencies are authorized to recruit workers in China, but they must always collaborate with Chinese authorized labor export companies (Berman, 2007). From a purely formalistic perspective, the recruitment of Chinese workers is processed in an orderly manner by Israeli and Chinese authorized companies, in full compliance with official procedures and state institutions. Nevertheless, in practice, this is far from being the case.

According to Israeli regulations, migrant workers must sign a detailed contract before they reach Israel and must receive a copy of it in their own language. However, Chinese recruitment companies take advantage of the fact that many Chinese workers are illiterate and/or desperate to emigrate; recruitment companies, then, offer no written contract to migrants who are too afraid to insist on it or are ignorant about their right to a contract. From a survey conducted by Israeli NGOs among forty-three Chinese migrant workers it appears that 12 percent of them never signed a written contract, and among those who did sign a contract, 45 percent never received a copy of it (Hotline for Migrant Workers and Kav La'oved, 2007: 22). The Israeli regulation regarding the signing of contracts could have been easily enforced, for example, by the Israeli embassy in Beijing before it issued work visas. However, as the Israeli consul in Beijing told me: "I never know what kind of contracts they sign and what is written in them. For me, such contracts do not exist" (interview, December 2007).

From my own interviews with Chinese workers in Israel it appears that the only meaningful contract they sign in China is with the recruitment company. This contract is a sort of "insurance policy" specifying that the migrants must work only for the Israeli employer that is indicated in their contract and that, in return, the recruitment company guarantees to pay back a part of the informal fee in the event that migrant workers are deported from Israel during the first year of work.

Out of all labor migrants in Israel, Chinese workers pay the highest informal fee to recruitment companies (Berman, 2007). From my interviews with Chinese workers it appears that this informal fee stood at around US$5,000 in the mid-1990s, US$10,000 in the year 2000, and as much as US$25,000 in the year 2008.[6] To pay the informal fee almost all Chinese workers depend significantly on loans from usurious moneylenders who charge an interest rate of 1–3 percent per month. Recruited workers pay the informal fee under the table to Chinese companies. Almost half of the fee then makes its way to the hands of Israeli manpower agencies. The money, I learned from interviews, is often transferred by means of hidden financial schemes in order to conceal it from the Israeli police and tax authorities. The other half of the fee is retained by the Chinese labor companies as profit.

In Chinese law, while there is no mention that charging fees from recruited workers is legal, there is equally no prohibition of such practice. As several scholars have documented, labor export in China is by no means contained by regulations that are drafted by the central government in Beijing (see Biao, 2003; Li, 2004). Since the 1980s the central government has gradually lost its monopoly in regulating emigration of workers to the local level. Some local governments, being more concerned with demonstrating economic growth, positively view and actively facilitate emigration, including irregular emigration, as means for creating a flow of remittances and raising the local standard of living (Thunø and Pieke, 2005). As Biao (2003: 24) reports, irregular emigration services are "sometimes regarded as local development strategies, and are, therefore accorded a certain degree of legitimacy."[7] Only a thin line is drawn in China between the legal work of officially authorized companies and the illegal work of the informal migration industry. In fact, from the perspective of many Chinese migrant workers to Israel such a line does not exist at all. They perceive the payment of informal fees to be licit. Yet, instead of there being an institutional attempt to offset such unlawful practices, there is a systematic collaboration on both the Chinese and Israeli sides to maintain the situation as it is.

Undocumented Migration in Israel: A Blind-Eye Policy

In the early 1990s, when the Israeli government debated its decision to import migrant workers, there were signs that the market was beginning to embrace its own informal solution to the demand for cheap labor. In 1990 the Israeli state comptroller had already reported the emergence of undocumented migration of non-Jewish workers to Israel. In response, the Israeli Parliament moved to pass the Foreign Workers Law: Unlawful Employment, which defined the criminal aspects and the corresponding penalties for those who engaged in the unlawful employment of undocumented migrants. Nevertheless, an increasing number of undocumented migrants reached Israel from 1993 onward. Although the exact number has been widely contested and politicized, since the late 1990s most sources estimated the number of undocumented migrants at around 150,000 (see Schnell, 1999; State Comptroller, 1999; Kav La'oved, 2000).

Undocumented migrants entered Israel from four continents and more than ninety countries (Ministry of Labor, 2002: 5). Most of them entered on a legal tourist visa and then overstayed it. Israel faced particular difficulties when try-ing to tighten its visa and entrance regime for tourists. Apart from the fact that tourism was a vital source of national income for Israel, the religious signifi-cance of the Land of Israel, especially for Christians, made it problematic to prevent the entry of those who wished to visit it for allegedly religious pur-poses. A much less popular way for undocumented migrants to enter Israel was by trespassing its national borders or by using falsified documents. These op-tions were initially only rarely used, not least because of Israel's international image as a beleaguered country that exercises tight border controls owing to its sensitive security situation.[8]

Undocumented migrants could easily find employment in Israel because of a structural unanswered demand for cheap labor. Israel originally decided to allocate permits for migrant workers only to employers who were, according to official records, dependent on Palestinian labor before the outbreak of the first intifada. However, it is estimated that in the early 1990s around fifty thou-sand Palestinians regularly worked in Israel without official permits (Schnell, 2001). Since employers of undocumented Palestinians could not put forward to the government their demand for migrant workers, they instead sought undocumented migrants. In addition, tens of thousands of middle-class fami-lies employed undocumented migrants as domestic workers. One survey among the Israeli middle and upper classes showed that 55 percent of these house-holds employed domestic workers (*Yediot Aharonot,* December 30, 2002).

Undocumented migrants in Israel were not bonded to one employer and could thus offer their labor in the black market for competitive salaries. Em-ployers of undocumented migrants knew that exploitation would lead workers to search for a better workplace. Thus employers often exercised "utilitarian opportunism" in their working relations with undocumented workers—that is, employers treated workers with fairness and even kindness, which ensured workers' continuous employment under conditions that were still very profit-able for employers.

Undocumented migrants were freed from all kinds of restrictions that ap-plied to migrant workers. They often rented an apartment in Tel Aviv or other big cities and commuted to their job daily. They thus lived away from the monitoring eye of their employer and had daily access to recreational activities after working hours. While migrant workers could not be joined by their fami-lies, undocumented migrants often brought their spouse and children to live with them in Israel. Undocumented migrants also interacted with other Israelis

apart from their employers. These interactions induced the expansion of social networks that improved the social as well as economic position of undocumented migrants. It sometimes led to friendship and even marriage with
Israelis.

The relative ease with which tens of thousands of undocumented migrants
entered Israel, found jobs, and began to settle down clearly indicates an Israeli
blind-eye policy. Officially deciding to limit the number of migrant workers,
the Israeli government found it a convenient intermediate solution to connive
in the steady flow of undocumented migrants into the country. While undocumented migrants satisfied the demand for cheap, flexible, and disenfran-
chised labor, the government could expediently present itself not as the cause
of this development but rather as its victim.[9] Although the government always
vowed to expel tens of thousands of undocumented migrants, in practice,
until the year 2002 only a tiny fraction of the total undocumented migrants in
Israel were deported each year (see fig. 11.1).

Deportation campaigns were undermined by failures to properly budget for
a necessary extra police force, juridical personnel, and detention facilities. One

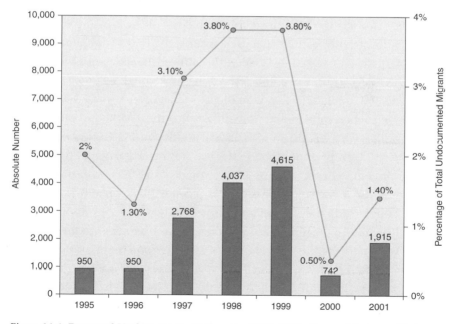

Figure 11.1. Deported Undocumented Migrants, 1995–2001. *Source:* Ministry of Labor,
2002.

high-ranking police officer described the government's recurring underfunded deportation plans as "amusing" (*Yediot Aharonot,* January 3, 2002).[10]

The Case of Undocumented Latino Migrants: The Advantages of Illegality

When Israel began to import migrant workers, it never recruited laborers from countries in Latin America. Nevertheless, in the early 1990s the first undocumented Latino migrants reached Israel. Latinos customarily needed no more than US$4,000 in order to get to Israel. The Israeli authorities regularly required tourists from Third World countries to be in possession of a return ticket to their country of origin, hotel reservations for their visiting period, and financial proof of their ability to sustain their stay in Israel. Either joining an organized tour or independently booking a roundtrip flight and a hotel in Israel cost approximately US$2,000 for people in Latin America. To demonstrate financial solvency tourists needed to show a valid credit card, traveler checks, or sufficient cash (around US$2,000).

Latinos rented apartments initially in the poor neighborhoods of southern Tel Aviv, Israel's economic capital. They worked mostly as domestic servants and office cleaners in the affluent northern parts of the city and its middle-class suburbs. Latinos earned salaries of around US$1,000–$1,500 per month. In many of the conversation I had with Latinos, the ease with which they could enter Israel, find work, and settle down was noted. Latinos clearly had the impression that Israel was not enforcing a strict entry regime. With respect to the Israeli deportation policy, notwithstanding the devastation experienced by individuals who fell victim to it, most Latinos considered it to be a "symbolic policy"; Latinos understood that Israel was mainly paying lip service to its commitment to deport all non-Jewish workers from the Jewish state.[11] Here is how Juanito, a twenty-nine-year-old undocumented migrant from Chile, put it: "I don't think they [Israeli authorities] really want to get us out of here. I'm in this country for nine years and I never had a problem to find a job or rent a place. In these nine years I only saw that more and more Latinos arrived, and they all find jobs. They [Israeli authorities] know we are here, they even know where we live. But they know we do the jobs that they [Israelis] don't want to do, so they don't mind that we are here." Before long, Latinos in Israel began to call on their relatives and friends to join them there. Since would-be migrants were not dependent on *tramitadores* and *coyotes* to arrange the migration trip for them, making the decision was easy. The inexpensive cost of this migration trajectory was also very appealing, and loans could easily be arranged from relatives in Israel (see Kalir, 2005) Subsequently, many Latino families were reunited after the initial immigration of one of the spouses, while numerous new households were formed when single Latino migrants met and got married in Israel. The children of Latinos often attended public Israeli schools. Several head teachers in Tel Aviv neither shared, nor conformed to, the official antagonistic approach of the government toward undocumented migrants. Instead they followed professional ethics, based on universalistic and humanist values, and admitted the children to their schools.

In the late 1990s, the number of Latinos in Israel was estimated to be around twelve thousand. Despite their undocumented status as migrants, Latinos were able to enjoy a much improved livelihood, rich family and social life, and even a religious scene that included numerous makeshift evangelical churches. It was not uncommon for me in the years I spent doing fieldwork among Latinos to hear them voicing positive judgments on their lives in Israel and their interactions with Israelis.[12] The case of Latinos in Israel thus buttresses the need to call into question our axioms regarding the (negative) realities of "self-smuggled" migrants (see Kyle and Dale, 2001).

Massive Deportation: The Israeli Response to Its Failing Migration Regime

The Israeli migration regime of non-Jewish workers was bound to collapse, as it increasingly led to an unsustainable economic and political constellation. In 2001, the Israeli Research Center for Social Policy unequivocally stated in a special report, "The blunt exploitation of legal foreign workers is so severe that it is better for them to give up their legal status and remain to work illegally" (Schnell, 2001; see also Amir, 2002). Indeed, a survey that the Ministry of Labor conducted among undocumented migrants showed that 73 percent of former migrant workers improved their salaries once they left their exclusive employers; 45 percent also reported an improvement in the treatment they received from their new employer (Ministry of Labor, 2001· 50) The survey also revealed that 53 percent of all undocumented migrants used to be legal migrant workers. This practically meant that the Israeli labor importation scheme was not fighting illegal migration but was rather a major contributor to this phenomenon, as it forced tens of thousands of migrant workers into illegality.

This absurdity reached its peak in 2001, when close to 12,000 Chinese migrant workers arrived in Israel (in former years this number stood at around 2,000 migrant workers per year). Exploitation and early dismissal by employers led most of them to become undocumented day workers. Chinese newcomers were often encouraged to opt for undocumented work by their relatives and friends in Israel who had already been working successfully in this fashion and could help them to find "black" jobs. Chinese workers often stood at certain crossroads that became known among Israeli employers and ordinary citizens, who sought undocumented workers. Some Chinese gradually acquired a workable command of the Hebrew language and a circle of trusted Israeli employers, who regularly contacted them on their mobile phones, thus relieving them from the risk involved in standing at crossroads.

At the same time, the visual evidence for the advanced settlement of undocumented migrant families, mostly from Latin America, Africa, and the Philippines, rendered it indefensible for the government to continue practicing a blind-eye policy. An aggravated public opinion with respect to the government's management of the flow of migrant workers, and a rising level of unemployment among Israeli workers, have led Israeli politicians to move toward the massive deportation of undocumented migrants. In September 2002, a special Immigration Police was established, with a clear task of deporting 50,000 undocumented migrants in its first year of operation. The interior minister at that time, Eli Yishai, bluntly expressed what he believed to be the ultimate goal: "I want everybody who is not Jewish out of this country" (*Maariv*, November 25, 2002). This time a substantial budget was allocated for executing the task, and more than seventy officers and four hundred field agents were recruited.[13] In addition, special courts now operated within detention centers and ruled on cases of arrested undocumented workers. The Immigration Police managed to deport around 25,000 migrants, creating a ripple effect of intimidation that induced an estimated 55,000 more undocumented migrants to exit the country (*Haaretz*, January 1, 2004).

Determined to deport undocumented migrants, the Immigration Police regularly ignored the law and resorted to the use of illegal methods, which included knocking down doors with heavy hammers and breaking into suspects' apartments in the middle of the night, often without warning. Suspects were handcuffed and loaded onto vans or buses as if they were dangerous criminals. Reports by NGOs and the media detailed the recurrent mismanagement of authority by the Immigration Police and the general trampling of migrants' rights throughout the deportation process (e.g., Hotline for Migrant Workers and Kav La'oved 2003, 2004; Willen, 2007; see also *Jerusalem Report,* May 21, 2003 *Yediot Aharonot,* November 6, 2003).

Once suspected undocumented migrants were arrested, the legal procedures for dealing with them were not always followed. From one report, which surveyed the legal treatment of 111 detainees (mostly Chinese), it appears that in 46 percent of the hearings that were held in detention centers there was no presence of a translator and detainees could not understand what was said; nor could they present their version. Consequently, a number of detainees were sentenced for deportation because they allegedly refused to cooperate with the court. Some of these cases were reversed once a translator was found and it became clear that the detainees were very happy to collaborate and give their side of the story (Hotline for Migrant Workers, 2003).

The Israeli law stipulates that detainees must be brought to court within two weeks from the day of their arrest or else they should be unconditionally released. The above-mentioned report documents many cases in which detainees were held in custody for longer than fourteen days without seeing a judge. Appeals by the NGO to authorities in the detention centers, as well as to officials from the Interior Ministry, were never answered. Finally, the report also mentions numerous cases in which suspected undocumented migrants were deported without ever being brought before a court.

By the end of 2005, after three year of operations, a spokesperson for the Immigration Police proudly reported that the number of undocumented migrants who left Israel stood at 150,752 (*Haaretz,* January 13, 2006). Tens of thousands of Chinese and other migrant workers were thus first forced by the unjust Israeli labor importation regime to become undocumented migrants and then aggressively deported from the country.·

The Accountability of the State for Its Failing Migration Regime

Different state and nonstate actors repeatedly alerted successive Israeli governments to the structural and legal failings of the labor importation scheme. These actors included, among others, Israeli academics, activists in NGOs, the state comptroller, and the Bank of Israel, which as early as 2000 concluded that the "binding arrangement" was counterproductive to the national economic goals of Israel (Bank of Israel, 2000).

Israel's insistence on keeping the importation scheme intact provides a strong indication for the sway of "crony capitalism" over its economy. Israeli employers in the construction and agricultural sectors are historically well organized and exercise significant political power on any ruling government through powerful lobbies. It was indeed because of pressure from these lobbies that the binding arrangement was applied by Israel in the first place and in later years kept integral (see Bartram, 1998, 2005).

Although equating the management of the labor importation scheme in Israel with "crony capitalism" is accurate, it falls short of explaining the way in which numerous officials, police agents, and even some judges operated separately from one another but all in a concerted fashion, which led to the systematic violation and trampling of migrant workers' rights. Moreover, the illegal manner in which Israel has conducted much of its massive deportation campaign must raise the following question: How can the state of Israel get away with its illegal conduct vis-à-vis migrant workers? To arrive at an answer to this question, we must first delineate the accountability field in which Israel operates. There are five potential fronts in which Israel might stand accountable for its conduct vis-à-vis migrant workers. In the following subsections I address the influence of each front on the conduct of Israel.

Migrants' Sending State

China could undoubtedly exercise some political and economic leverage on Israel in trying to influence its exploitative policies and illegal actions vis-à-vis Chinese migrant workers. It is nevertheless clear that China chooses not to interfere with the Israeli handlings of its labor migration regime. In my interview with the Chinese consul in Israel, he offered the official Chinese view of the scheme: "In China we call it a win-win-win situation. All sides win out, China is able to export workers, Israel is happy to receive cheap workers who are willing to do the jobs Israelis don't want to do, and the migrants can earn and save a lot of money for their families" (February 2007).

When I asked the consul whether he was aware of the widespread exploitation of Chinese workers by Israeli employers, he opined that "everything goes well if they [Chinese workers] don't do illegal things." When I asserted that according to most independent sources, like academics and journalists but also some Israeli state institutions, the blame for the systematic exploitation of migrant workers lies with Israeli employers, unfair Israeli regulations, and a lack of enforcement of workers' rights by Israeli authorities, the consul laconically reacted: "If the problem is with the Israeli employer we try to call him and solve it."

Toward the end of the interview I carefully asked about the informal fees that workers pay recruitment companies in China. The consul first dismissed my claim as sheer rumors, but when I insisted that my knowledge in this matter comes from interviews I personally conducted with Chinese in Israel, the consul had this to say:

> Listen, in China we have now a free market economy. You probably know that lately we even joined the WTO. It is the market which decides if people will go abroad, not the government. So they pay these fees to agencies, but they still earn a lot of money, otherwise they wouldn't have come here, right? People know how much they have to pay and they can decide if it is good for them to emigrate. Usually, what they pay to agencies is equivalent to two years of work in Israel. But they stay here longer, often even five years, the rest of the time they work and earn money for their families. If they had to work four years to pay agencies they would probably not come here. Did they also tell you how much they save? You know what? It is not a win-win-win situation; it is a win-win-win-win situation. [Laughing out loud at his gag.] The agencies also win, but it is still a good deal for all sides.

This statement demonstrates not only that the consul is fully aware of the informal fees that migrants must illegally pay but that he sees it as an unproblematic issue.

International Law, Conventions, Treaties

Israel is a signatory to UN conventions that define and safeguard the working and living conditions of migrant workers, including the Migrant Worker Convention (1975) of the International Labour Organisation and the United Nations International Convention of the Rights of All Migrant Workers and Members of their Families (1990). Yet, as Scully (this volume, Chap. 4) illustrates lucidly by following historically failing international attempts to combat the trafficking in sex workers, a UN convention can hardly be enforced on individual nation-states that sign it in order to gain the moral high ground while in practice they do little to fight related practices within their jurisdiction.

Indeed, Israel has regularly ignored UN resolutions and violated international conventions whenever they seemed to interfere with what Israel perceived to be its national responsibility. Israel's immigration regime is closely tied to its aspiration to maintain a Jewish state, and it is therefore definitively considered an internal affair by the state. For example, despite much pressure from the international community, Israel has refused for decades to allow the return of the Palestinian inhabitants of Israel who fled the country in 1948. Notwithstanding the general unreceptive approach of Israel toward international law, some of the changes that were facilitated by Israeli NGOs' appeals to Israeli courts (see next subsection) might have succeeded owing to an increased accountability to an emerging global discourse of human rights (Soysal, 1994; Sassen, 1999, 2002; Cornelius et al., 2004). The fact that Israel refrained from deporting the children of undocumented migrants, and accordingly also allowed "undocumented mothers" to remain in Israel, is perhaps the clearest evidence for the influence of human rights on the Israeli policy.

Israeli Courts

The most effective way to influence changes in the Israeli policy vis-à-vis migrant workers has proven to be legal appeals to Israeli courts. Such appeals against the state, the Interior Ministry, the police, and employers of migrant workers were mainly filed by lawyers working for Israeli NGOs. These appeals concerned particular cases of individuals whose rights were violated, as well as more general appeals against the legal validity of the binding arrangement or certain deportation procedures. Israeli courts often upheld the rule of law in particular cases against Israeli employers, and in some cases the High Court accepted the many objections of NGOs against the Israeli labor importation-deportation schemes. In this respect, some of the important decisions by Israeli courts include ordering temporary halts on deportation campaigns, reducing the period of time in which detainees must be brought before a judge, setting clear regulations for healthcare insurance for migrant workers, and allowing the possibility for migrant workers who were dismissed to find new authorized Israeli employers and avoid deportation.

While it appears that Israeli courts played an important role in protecting the rights of migrants, a study of hundreds of Israeli court resolutions concludes that "courts above all enforced the 'binding arrangement.' In fact, leaving one's employer was seen [by judges] as a violation that deserves its punishment [deportation]. Migrant workers were often described as 'unaways' who took the law into their own hands" (Gill and Dahan, 2006: 375).

In 2002 six different NGOs jointly appealed the Israeli High Court in demand of a complete abolition of the binding arrangement. In 2006, after four years of court procedures, the judge ruled in favor of the NGOs' appeal, revoked the binding arrangement, and ordered the government to draft new regulations for the employment of migrant workers.[14] Yet here again, Gill and Dahan (2006) contend that the legal procedure was allowed to be stretched for over four years, not least because the High Court often extended more time for the state attorneys to prepare their arguments. In these four years most undocumented migrants were deported from the country.

Civil Society

The precarious situation of migrant workers and the perilous lives of undocumented migrants were never left completely unchallenged. Most counter-hegemonic calls for revoking the binding arrangement, and for introducing the legalization of status for non-Jewish migrants according to secular criteria, came from a small group of Israeli civil society actors, which included several NGOs, human rights activists, journalists, artists, and left-wing politicians. These civil actors used Israel's democratic characteristics, which included freedom of association, freedom of speech, and the government's (limited) accountability to Israeli laws and international conventions. In addition to their appeals to Israeli courts, activists offered migrants practical and legal assistance and attempted to drum up public opinion for their cause through the media, cultural events, and public demonstrations.

Public Opinion

The general public opinion toward migrant workers should be considered as a larger context for legitimization in which the state operates. Surprisingly perhaps, pubic opinion in Israel was initially considerably supportive and tolerant toward non-Jewish migrant workers (Bar-Tzuri, 1996).

However, Israeli public opinion was proven to be highly responsive to the state's nationalistic rhetoric. Since the government launched its first deportation campaign in 1996, it regularly alleged that non-Jewish migrants were corrupting the Jewish character of the state, as well as increasing criminality and causing unemployment among Israeli workers. Consequently, support for migrant workers all but collapsed among the general Israeli public (Nathanson and Bar-Tzuri, 1999; Schnell, 1999). Just before launching a massive deportation campaign in 2002, the head of the Foreign Workers' Desk in the Interior Ministry warned, "The state won't be able to deal with the Chinese community because most of its members are violent, and they have nothing to loose. We will finally reach a situation in which the state won't be able to defend its sovereignty against them" (*Yediot Aharonot*, February 26, 2002).

It is fair to assume that some Israelis were influenced purely by the state's rhetoric, while others, especially unskilled workers, might have actually suffered from competition with an increasing number of migrant workers. Indeed, an in-depth study found that disadvantaged populations in Israel (low income, low education, high unemployment) were most likely to endorse economic discrimination against migrant workers (Semyonov, Raijman, and Yom-Tov, 2002). However, the study further discovered that Jewish Israelis expressed significantly more hostility toward migrant workers than did Arab Israelis, although the latter were more prone to suffer from competition with migrant workers. It was thus concluded that the attitudes of Jews are also motivated by "the ideological commitment (among Jews) to preserve the Jewish character of the State . . . non-national workers are evaluated not only as economic competitors, but also as a threat to the very essence of the social and political order of the state and to its national (Jewish) identity" (Semyonov, Raijman, and Yom-Tov, 2002: 428). Thus, while the state acted in a discriminating and illegal manner against non-Jewish workers, there was hardly ever a public outcry about the legitimacy of such actions, which were considered to be licit by most Jewish Israelis.[15]

Migrant Workers as Nonsubjects

To further analyze the accountability of states, I would like to return to the matrix of "competing authorities" by van Schendel and Abraham (2005) and carefully examine its contours. The matrix mostly treats the state in its capacity as the legislator to define il/legality. States' definitions of il/legality then qualify the actions of people and correspond, or not, to the social perceptions of different groups. The matrix thus limits our conceptualization of the state to its role as the producer of il/legality, while it reserves for people in society the role of actors.

Yet the juridical capacity to define il/legality is distinguishable, both theoretically and in practice, from the executive authority of states. Executive authority is manifested and practiced through the actions of the personnel in various state institutions—e.g., police agents, ministers, judges, civil servants. We should thus examine the state as an actor in the realm of what it has defined

Table 11.2 Modalities of Legitimation for State Dominion

	Legal	Illegal
Licit	(A) Legitimate Rule	(B) Undisputed Legitimacy
Illicit	(C) Crisis of Legitimacy / Authoritarian Regime	(D) Occupation

to be il/legal. This exercise amounts to a reverse in the directionality of the relationship between the two protagonists in the matrix. Consider a matrix whereby the state (designated by the column heads "Legal" and "Illegal") is treated in its executive capacity while the public/society (designated by the stub entries "Licit" and "Illicit") is the qualifier of state actions (Table 11.2).

Cell (A) represents a complete overlap between the actions of the state and the view of the public regarding these actions, thereby producing an ideal legitimate rule. Cell (D) represents an illegal takeover of the state that is met with a total disapproval by society. Such illegitimate occupation of the state can be external (when it is performed by another hostile state [or states]) or internal (when a coup d'état is led by a minority group that lacks greater support in society). Owing to its inherent illegitimacy, occupation must rest on constant intimidation and the use of force.

Cell (C) stands for a situation in which the state acts in a legal fashion but the populace perceives it to be illicit. We are then faced with a crisis of legitimacy that can be resolved in different ways. In a democratic regime such a crisis can lead to new elections that will renew legitimacy in the elected government. When the crisis is deeper, encompassing the very existing type of regime, we face a potential regime change of the kind we recently saw in Nepal (from a monarchy to a parliamentary democracy), in Georgia (from one-party Soviet system to a multiparty democracy), or in Venezuela (from Western type of democracy to a socialist type). If a crisis in the legitimacy of a governing elite is not resolved, we can usually expect that the regime will gradually become authoritarian, relying on coercion rather than consent.

Yet most relevant to my discussion in this chapter is the case captured in cell (B). It highlights the possibility for illegal state actions to be perceived as licit by the majority in society. In this peculiar situation of "undisputed legitimacy," as I call it, the state can expand its actions beyond the restrictions of its own laws without suffering any loss to its legitimacy. The most prominent example of this eventuality is when a state launches a military offense on another state, against international law and/or against its own constitution, but nevertheless receives popular support from the public for its actions. The U.S. preemptive wars in Afghanistan and Iraq are a case in point. The passing of the Patriotic Act is another, more sophisticated example whereby the state seeks to expand the law to encompass illegal actions that it already takes and for which it receives wide public support.

Notably, situations that fit into cell (B) usually occur in times of national emergencies. In fact, the legal option for governments to declare martial law is an institutionalized recognition of the need of the state political elite to enjoy an undisputed legitimacy in times of severe danger, either internal or external, to the very existence of the state and/or to the safety of its citizens. Given that cases captured in cell (B) usually represent states of emergency, it is interesting to note that many of the actions that states take to combat undesired immigration belong in the same category—for example, the building of physical barriers, the passing of Draconian exclusionary regulations, the deployment of the army or special police force to strategic areas, and so on. Discursively, states often portray flows of immigrants as constituting a national threat. It is allegedly a threat to the sustainability of states' infrastructure (hospitals, schools) and resources (welfare), as well as the integrity of the nation and its "culture."

Pierre Bourdieu (1996) argued that Weber's classic definition of the state as holding the monopoly over the legitimate use of violence should be supplemented by its dominance over symbolic power. With this Bourdieu wishes to draw our attention to the power of the state to shape the social categories through which members in the polity perceive their experiences and the actions of the state. In other words, the state, according to Bourdieu, "is not only 'out there' in the form of bureaucracies, authorities, and ceremonies. It is also 'in here,' ineffaceably engraved within us, lodged in the intimacy of our being in the shared manners in which we feel, think, and judge. Not the army, the asylum, the hospital, and the jail, but the school is the state's most potent conduit and servant" (quoted in Wacquant, 1996: xviii).

Israel has historically insisted on a marked representation of its Jewish character on a symbolic level (e.g., a flag with the Star of David, a national hymn that praises the return of Jews to Israel). Moreover, national belonging in Israel is overwhelming determined by one's Jewishness. The validity of the state's Jewish character is being naturalized by the state and internalized by most Israeli citizens through the Israeli education system, the army, and the celebration of national festivities and remembrance days such as the Holocaust Day.

The symbolic power, which is invested in shaping Jewish Israelis' perceptions, leads the majority of them to recognize non-Jewish migrants as invalid subjects of the Jewish state. Even when Israelis show sympathy toward migrants, they usually conceive the bigger picture in a way that is neatly captured in the following quotation from one of my Israeli informants: "I have nothing against them [non-Jewish migrants], many of them are very honest people who come here because they want to take care of their poor families in their countries. But when they come here they know they come to a Jewish state. They know and take the risk involved. So when Israel decides that they have to leave and deport them, what do they expect? They have to go back to their countries. I'm sorry but it's Israel's right." According to the prevalent perception in Israel, non-Jewish migrant workers do not belong in Israel, and they are consequently never fully registered as real political subjects in the mindscape of Jewish Israelis. This dynamic is amplified in the case of undocumented migrants who are often seen as transgressors who disregard the law and disrespect the national sovereignty of the state. Undocumented migrants' illegal actions and status justify, in the eyes of many citizens, the hard-line approach of the state, including the "right" to use illegal methods against them.

We can therefore conclude that the illegal but licit actions of the state against migrant workers are by and large the result of hermetic mental borders that are produced by the state and are imprinted onto citizens' mind-sets. The greater an overlap in the attitude toward migrants exist between the state's formal approach and people's social perceptions, the greater the chance is that the state will enjoy undisputed legitimacy as it acts against migrants, even in an illegal manner.

Of course a total overlap hardly ever exists. As I have shown, Israeli civil society actors clearly managed to escape the symbolic power of the state and persistently fought to change Israel's treatment of migrant workers. Astutely, civil society actors compared the Jewish history of ethnic persecution to the situation of many non-Jewish migrants in Israel. This dreadful contrast effectively touched upon the very sensitivity that had historically led most Israeli politicians to establish and closely protect the Jewish state. It consequently led many liberal politicians, as well as right-wing conservative ones, to amend existing regulations and eventually to support the legal incorporation of some non-Jewish migrants as citizens. Among the "lucky few" who in the end became Israeli citizens were many Latino families, but not a single Chinese migrant.

Concluding Remarks

In lieu of a conclusion I would like to point out two counterintuitive, albeit evident, developments that underline the case study I described here. First, many of the practices and outcomes that we traditionally associate with illegal migration and human smuggling are now largely characterizing regulated flows of legal migrant workers. I do not wish to overdramatize my claim by arguing that the situation of undocumented migrants becomes less horrendous in comparison with that of legal migrant workers (although this was the case in Israel). I simply want to highlight that legal migration is increasingly being degraded, in practice, to the standard of illegal migration, instead of replacing it with a qualitatively different type of migration. In other words, the difference between legal and illegal migration is oftentimes a formalistic one, and maintaining this distinction might actually serve to clean our conscious from the need to change the lived realities of migrant workers in substantive ways.

In the case of *illegal* Chinese migrant workers in the United States, Kwong (2001: 250–51) has argued that more punitive legislation regarding their employment only renders these workers more attractive for American businesses because "illegal aliens continue to be cheaper, more pliable, and more dependent on their employers than legitimate labor." In Israel, as I have shown, the same statement can be said about the situation of *legal* Chinese migrant workers. This happens, in both cases, because of a chronic lack of enforcement of migrant workers' rights and a tolerance of employers' unlawful conduct. Trying to understand this chronic lack of enforcement leads me to my second point.

Many scholars have suggested a number of factors that weaken enforcement of existing regulations in the migration field, not least the influence of "crony capitalism" on the conduct of many politicians and law enforcers who cater to the special interests of employers in labor-intensive sectors. Yet if we do not want to believe that every official, police agent, judge, employer, or ordinary citizen who is doing little to help protect the rights of migrant workers is directly involved in a national scam against these non-national laborers, we should recognize a more fundamental civil and humane failure in our societies—that is, the failure to recognize migrant workers as political subjects, even if it is for a limited period in which they work and live in our country.

In recent years there has been a growing trend, led by the Italian philosopher Giorgio Agamben (1998), to equate the position of extremely marginalized groups, such as refugees or prisoners in Guantanamo Bay, with the Roman figure of the *homo sacer*. *Homo sacer* is a depoliticized human, someone who is not a member of the political community and over whom the sovereignty of the state does not apply. *Homo sacer* can therefore be killed with no punishment but not sacrificed. It is the nonbelongingness and exteriority of *homo sacer* that allows us to construct a link between membership in a political community and sovereignty over a territory.

Several scholars who study migration have picked up in recent years on Agamben's ideas; however, they mostly apply them to the precarious position of undocumented migrants (e.g., Rajaram and Grundy-Warr, 2004; Ellerman, 2009). While I value such efforts to elucidate the marginal position of millions of undocumented migrants in the world (see Kalir, 2010), I would argue that we should include in such conceptualization the position of many legal migrant workers whose rights and life conditions often mean little to the majority of members in states. This indifference toward those who are categorized as not belonging to the political community is by and large a consequence of the commodification of labor, which effaces the human factor in what is perceived to be "labor transactions." The problem we face is thus of a great magnitude. We are not in need of new or better laws but of a population that treats workers who are defined as nonmembers—whether legal or illegal—as political subjects. This task of raising political and legal consciousness is better entrusted to educators and social leaders rather than to police agents and opportunistic politicians.

NOTES

1. For more on the process that led the Israeli government to make this decision, see Bartram (1998), Schnell (1999), and Rozenhek (2000).

2. In 2006, the law was amended to allow recruitment agencies to charge migrant workers a fee of up to US$700.

3. This last sanction was never mentioned in contracts, as it contradicted basic civil and human rights and could never withstand a legal appeal; nevertheless, it was infor-

mally mentioned to migrant workers and enforced by employers and the government (see Pilovsky, 1999).

4. See www.chinaembassy.org.il/eng/ (accessed April 26, 2007).

5. Around 10 percent of Chinese migrant workers are employed in factories, agriculture, and caregiving for disable people. Around a hundred Chinese "chefs" are recruited for work in kitchens of Israeli-owned Asian restaurants.

6. The eagerness of Chinese to go to Israel has to be seen in the wider context in which much higher prices (sometimes around US$100,000) are paid in China for getting to other, more attractive migration destinations like the United States and the United Kingdom.

7. There are many more countries around the world that consider the export of commodified labor as a development strategy; see Kyle and Siracusa (2005) on the involvement of states in "migrant-exporting schemes."

8. By 1995 it became known that human smugglers and traffickers operated from Egypt, getting migrants, mainly from Africa but also from former Soviet countries, stealthily across the border into Israel. Many of the smuggled migrants were women from Eastern Europe who were misled by criminal organizations, which promised them a legal permit to work in Israel as secretaries or cleaners but instead forced them to work as prostitutes in Israeli sex clubs. Much has been written about this phenomenon in the Israeli media, and official reports were also prepared by NGOs and government departments (see *Maariv,* September 21, 1995; *Yediot Aharonot,* November 13, 2002, and May 23, 2003; Hotline for Migrant Workers, 2003).

9. An unofficial policy of permissible undocumented migration to ensure a ready supply of labor to sectors in the national economy is found among many Western countries (cf. Zolberg, 1990; Jones-Correa, 1998; Kyle and Siracusa, 2005).

10. In the United States, Calavita (1992) describes how Congress, influenced by the special interests of farmers, underfunded for years the Immigration and Naturalization Service and thus disenabled its agents to enforce the unlawful employment of undocumented migrants in the agricultural sector.

11. The adoption of "symbolic policy" by states in the case of undocumented migrants is of course not unique to Israel and can be found in the United States (cf. Heyman, 1995; Cornelius et al., 2004) and different countries in Europe (cf. Bade, 2004).

12. For more on the lived realities and advanced settlement of undocumented Latino migrants in Israel, see Kalir (2010).

13. See Andreas (2000) for the ways in which the business of illegal migration and the business of law enforcement are interlinked and expand because of each other.

14. In May 2005, probably in anticipation of the court's ruling, the government introduced a new set of regulations to replace the binding arrangement. However, as a detailed report concludes, the new system fails to remedy most related problems, and the exploitation of migrant workers, as well as the customary payment of informal fees, is still the norm. The failure of the new system echoed a similar failed attempt to amend the situation in 2002, under the "closed skies" policy, which promised to stop the importation of new migrant workers and instead relegalize those in Israel who lost their status (for a detailed account of these failures, see Berman, 2007).

15. It might even be that the public does not overtly legitimize the state actions vis-à-vis migrant workers, but by not voicing contempt, expressing rejection, or mobilizing resistance, it nonetheless connives with the unjust actions of the state.

REFERENCES

Agamben, G. 1998. *Homo Sacer: Sovereign Power and Bare Life*. Stanford: Stanford University Press.

Amir, S. 2002. "Overseas Foreign Workers in Israel: Policy Aims and Labor Market." *International Migration* 36 (1): 41–57.

Andreas, P. 2000. *Border Games: Policing the U.S.-Mexico Divide*. Ithaca, N.Y.: Cornell University Press.

Association for Civil Rights in Israel. 1997. *Annual Report*. Jerusalem. (Hebrew)

Bade, J. K. 2004. "Legal and Illegal Immigration into Europe: Experiences and Challenges." *European Review* 12:339–75.

Bank of Israel. 2000. *Press Release*. December. (Hebrew)

Bartram, D. 1998. "Foreign Workers in Israel: History and Theory." *International Migration Review* 32 (2): 303–25.

———. 2005. *International Labor Migration: Foreign Workers and Public Policy*. New York: Palgrave Macmillan.

Bar-Tzuri, R. 1996. "Foreign Workers in Israel: Conditions, Attitudes and Policy Implications.: In *The New World of Work in an Era of Economic Change*, edited by R. Nathanson. Tel-Aviv: Friedrich Ebert Foundation. (Hebrew)

Biao, X. 2003. "Emigration from China: A Sending Country's Perspective." *International Migration* 41 (3): 21–48.

Berman, Y. 2007. "Binding Migrant Workers to Corporations." Tel Aviv: Hotline for Migrant Workers and Kav La'oved.

Bourdieu, P. 1996. *The State Nobility: Elite Schools in the Field of Power*, Cambridge, England: Polity Press.

Calavita, K. 1992. *Inside the State: The Bracero Program, Immigration and the INS*. New York: Routledge.

Central Bureau of Statistics. 2000. *Statistical Abstract of Israel*, Jerusalem: CBS.

———. 2002. *Statistical Abstract of Israel*, Jerusalem: CBS.

———. 2007. Press release. July 30, 2007.

Cornelius, W. A., T. Tsuda, P. L. Martin, and J. F. Hollifield. 2004. *Controlling Immigration: A Global Perspective*. Stanford: Stanford University Press.

Drori, I., and G. Kunda. 1999. "The Work Experience of Foreign Workers in Israel: The Case of Filipino Caregivers, Thais in Agriculture and Rumanians in Construction." Discussion Paper No. 100, Golda Meir Institute.

Ellermann, A. 2009. *Undocumented Migrants and Resistance in the State of Exception*. Paper presented at the European Union Studies Association meeting in Los Angeles, April.

Ellman, M., and S. Laacher. 2003. *Migrant Workers in Israel: A Contemporary Form of Slavery*. Copenhagen and Paris: International Federation for Human Rights and the Euro-Mediterranean Human Rights Network.

Gill, A., and Y. Dahan. 2006. "Between Neo-Liberalism and Ethno-Nationalism: Theory, Policy, and Law in the Deportation of Migrant Workers in Israel." *Misphat Umimshal* 10 (1): 347–85. (Hebrew)

Heyman, J. M. 1995. "Putting Power into the Anthropology of Bureaucracy: The Immigration and Naturalization Service at the Mexico-United States Border." *Current Anthropology* 36 (2): 261–87.

Hotline for Migrant Workers. 2003. *For You Were Strangers: Modern Slavery and Trafficking in Human Beings in Israel.* www.hotline.org.il/english/pdf/For_you_were_strangers _2nd_edition_Eng.pdf.

Hotline for Migrant Workers and Kav La'oved. 2003. *Immigration Administration or Expulsion Unit? www.hotline.org.il/english/pdf/Hotline_and_Kav_Laoved_paper_on_Immigration _Police_May_2003_Eng.pdf.*

———. 2004. *Immigration Police as Means for Employers to Exploit Their Workers.* www .hotline.org.il/hebrew/pdf/Kav_Laoved_%2526_Hotline_report_A_tool_in_the _hands_of_employers_053104.pdf. (Hebrew; accessed January 3, 2009).

———. 2007. *Freedom Inc.: Binding Migrant Workers to Manpower Corporations in Israel.* www.hotline.org.il/english/pdf/Corporations_Report_072507_Eng.pdf.

Jones-Correa, M. 1998. *Between Two Nations: The Political Predicaments of Latinos in New York City,* Ithaca, N.Y.: Cornell University Press.

Kalir, B. 2005. "The Development of a Migratory Disposition: Explaining a 'New Emigration.'" *International Migration* 43 (4): 167–96.

———. 2009. "Finding Jesus in the Holy Land and Taking Him to China: Chinese Temporary Migrant Workers in Israel Converting to Evangelical Christianity." *Sociology of Religion* 70 (2):130–56.

———. 2010. *Latino Migrants in the Jewish State: Undocumented Lives in Israel.* Bloomington: Indiana University Press.

Kav La'oved. 1998. *Newsletter.* May. (Hebrew)

———. 2000. *Newsletter.* July. (Hebrew)

Kemp, A. 2004. "Labour Migration and Racialisation: Labour Market Mechanisms and Labour Migration Control Policies in Israel." *Social Identities* 10 (2): 267–92.

Kemp, A., R. Raijman, J. Resnik, and S. Schammah-Gesser. 2000. "Contesting the Limits of Political Participation: Latinos and Black African Migrant Workers in Israel." *Ethnic and Racial Studies* 23 (1): 94–119.

Kwong, Peter. 2001. "Impact of Chinese Human Smuggling on the American Labor Market." In *Global Human Smuggling,* edited by David Kyle and Rey Koslowski, 235–53. Baltimore: Johns Hopkins University Press.

Kyle, D., and J. Dale. 2001. "Smuggling the State Back In: Agents of Human Smuggling Reconsidered." In *Global Human Smuggling,* edited by David Kyle and Rey Koslowski, 30–57. Baltimore: Johns Hopkins University Press.

Kyle, D., and C. A. Siracusa. 2005. "Seeing the State Like a Migrant: Why So Many Noncriminals Break Immigration Laws." In *Illicit Flows and Criminal Things: States, Borders, and the Other Side of Globalization,* edited by W. van Schendel and I. Abraham, 153–76. Bloomington: Indiana University Press.

Li, M. 2004. "Re-emergence of Labour Brokers in China Today: The Xiamen Example." *Indian Society of Labour Economics* 47 (3): 565–81.

———. 2009. "Making a Living at the Interface of Legality and Illegality: Chinese Migrant Workers in Israel." *International Migration.* doi: 10.1111/j.1468-2435.

Miller, Mark J. 2001. "The Sanctioning of Unauthorized Migration and Alien Employment." In *Global Human Smuggling,* edited by David Kyle and Rey Koslowski, 318–36. Baltimore: Johns Hopkins University Press.

Ministry of Industry, Trade, and Labor. 2005. *Newsletter 46.* (Hebrew)

Ministry of Labor. 2001. "Foreign Workers without Work Permits in Israel: 1999." Discussion paper no. 5.01. Manpower Planning Authority, Jerusalem. (Hebrew)

———. 2002. "Foreign Workers without Work Permits Deported from Israel in 2001." Manpower Planning Authority, Jerusalem. (Hebrew).

Nathanson, R., and R. Bar-Tzuri. 1999. "A Survey of Public Opinion towards Workers from Foreign Countries." In *The New Workers: Wage Earners from Foreign Countries in Israel*, edited by R. Nathanson and L. Achdut, 90–118. Tel-Aviv: Hakibbutz Hameuchad. (Hebrew)

Pilovsky, L. 1999. "The Role of Manpower Agencies in the Treatment of Foreign Workers in Israel, and Their Connections with Government Institutions." In *The New Workers: Wage Earners from Foreign Countries in Israel*, edited by R. Nathanson and L. Achdut, 41–89. Tel-Aviv: Hakibbutz Hameuchad. (Hebrew)

Rajaram, P. K., and C. Grundy-Warr. 2004. "The Irregular Migrant as Homo Sacer: Migration and Detention in Australia, Malaysia, and Thailand." *International Migration* 42 (1): 33–64.

Raulff, U. 2004. "An Interview with Giorgio Agamben." *German Law Journal* 5 (5): 609–14.

Rosenhek, Z. 1999. "The Politics of Claims-Making by Labour Migrants in Israel." *Journal of Ethnic and Migration Studies* 25 (4): 575–95.

———. 2000. "Migration Regimes, Intra-state Conflicts, and the Politics of Exclusion and Inclusion: Migrant Workers in the Israeli Welfare State." *Social Problems* 47 (1): 49–67.

Sassen, S. 1999. *Guests and Aliens*. New York: New York Press.

———. 2002. "The Responsibility of Citizenship: Emergent Subjects and Spaces for Politics." *Berkeley Journal of Sociology* 46:4–25.

Schnell, I. 1999. *Guidelines for Policy Making towards Foreign Workers in Israel*. Jerusalem: Israeli Centre for Political and Social Research. (Hebrew)

———. 2001. *Foreign Workers in Southern Tel Aviv–Yafo*. Jerusalem: Floersheimer Institute for Policy Studies. (Hebrew)

Semyonov, M., R. Raijman, and A. Yom-Tov. 2002. "Labour Market Competition, Perceived Threat, and Endorsement of Economic Discrimination against Foreign Workers in Israel." *Social Problems* 49 (3): 416–31.

Soysal, Y. N. 1994. *Limits of Citizenship: Migrants and Postnational Membership in Europe*. Chicago: Chicago University Press.

State Comptroller. 1996. *Annual Report* no. 46. Jerusalem. (Hebrew)

———. 1999. *Annual Report* no. 49. Jerusalem. (Hebrew)

———. 2003. *Annual Report* no. 53. Jerusalem. (Hebrew)

van Schendel, W., and I. Abraham. 2005. *Illicit Flows and Criminal Things: States, Borders, and the Other Side of Globalization*. Bloomington: Indiana University Press.

Thunø, M., and F. N. Pieke. 2005. "Institutionalizing Recent Rural Emigration from China to Europe: New Transnational Villages in Fujian." *International Migration Review* 39: 485–514.

Wacquant, L. J. D. 1996. Forward to *The State Nobility: Elite Schools in the Field of Power*, by P. Bourdieu, ix–xxii. Cambridge, England: Polity.

Willen, S. 2007. "Towards a Critical Phenomenology of "Illegality": State Power, Criminalization, and Abjectivity among Undocumented Migrant Workers in Tel Aviv, Israel." *International Migration* 45 (3): 8–36.

Yanay, U., and A. Borowosky. 1998. "Foreign Workers in Israel: Rights and Access to Welfare Services." *Social Security* 53: 59–78. (Hebrew)

Zolberg, A. R. 1990. "Reforming the Back Door: The Immigration Reform and Control Act of 1986 in Historical Perspective." In *Immigration Reconsidered: History, Sociology and Politics,* edited by V. Yuns-McLaughlin, 315–37. Oxford: Oxford University Press.

CHAPTER TWELVE

Russian Transnational Organized Crime and Human Trafficking

James O. Finckenauer

The criminal activities of Russians and others from the former Soviet Union are today of serious concern to many nations. Not the least of these nations are the newly independent states formed after the collapse of the USSR in 1991. In the relatively short time since that cataclysmic event, crime emanating from the former Soviet empire has swept across national borders into Eastern and Western Europe and moved east to Afghanistan, China, and Japan, south to Israel, and across the Atlantic to Canada and the United States. A looming threat of Russian organized crime and what is called a global "Russian Mafia" has become fixed in the minds of many—especially those in the media and law enforcement.

As attention to and concern about a Russian Mafia have risen, a certain mythological quality has enveloped how it is perceived (See, e.g., Rosner, 1995; Finckenauer and Waring, 1998; and Rutland and Kogan, 1998). In their article "The Russian Mafia: Between Hype and Reality," Rutland and Kogan concluded that there is a "myth of the Russian mafia" that fits with a long-standing demonic image of Russia itself (1998: 1). Hollywood and the news portray Russian criminals as more clever, devious, and ruthless than the criminals of any other nation. Why this hype? Because, they say, there are many in Russia today who have vested interests in maintaining an especially ominous image of organized crime as being mafia or mafialike. These are interests that have something to gain from the existence of a Russian Mafia—be it bigger budgets, selling newspapers, or a scapegoat to blame for policy failures. Those interests include the Russian police, the Russian president, the reformers, opposition politicians, journalists, international advisers, and even organized criminals themselves (2).

Many of these same pressures and interests—and for some of the same reasons—exist in the United States as well. Now that the original Italian Mafia threat on our shores has receded, what better replacement to galvanize political support for law enforcement and to sell newspapers, books, and movies than exotic criminals from the former "evil empire"?

Here I want to look at this Russian organized crime, or mafia, threat. And I want to do so with respect to a particular type of crime that has itself become very visible on the global scene—a type of crime that is viewed with a special kind of horror because of its insidious nature and the special vulnerability of its victims. The crime is that of human trafficking and its associated exploitation and victimization of women and children. The most flagrant type of victimization occurs when women and children are smuggled for commercial sexual purposes. The sex industry that exploits these victims encompasses everything from old-fashioned prostitution to escort services, topless dancers, massage parlors, video porn, and child pornography. It is estimated to be a multibillion dollar business (see, e.g., Robinson, 1998).

In order to look at the role of Russian organized crime in trafficking women and children for commercial sexual exploitation, we need to consider a number of broader questions, beginning with just what is organized crime and what is the current picture with respect to organized crime in Russia? Then, what is the transnational nature of this crime? Are there any indications that Russian organized crime per se is engaged in people smuggling? Finally, are there such indications with specific respect to the trafficking of women and children for the sex industry? In each instance we should ask what do we actually know and how do we know it?

Let me also clarify the use of the term *Russian* in the context of this discussion. Undoubtedly it would be more precise to refer to all peoples from what was formerly the USSR as former Soviet—more precise, but a bit cumbersome.

The same is true of attempting to break down the hundreds of specific ethnic identities of all such peoples. I thus adopt the conventional use of the term *Russian* to refer to all former Soviet peoples and activities (including crimes and criminals), while recognizing that the use of this term is strictly for convenience's sake.

Although Russia, most especially Moscow, is in fact the epicenter of organized and transnational crime from that part of the world, many of those involved in that crime are not ethnic Russians. Indeed, Armenians, Belarussians, Chechens, Jews, Georgians, and Ukrainians, among others, account for a considerable share. Russian officials, journalists, and scholars with whom I have spoken have pointed out this misnomer, and some have suggested Eurasian organized crime as a more accurate descriptor. I grant their concern but will leave that discussion for another day.

Definition and Overview of Russian Organized Crime

True organized crime is much more than just crime committed by organized groups. It is also more than what might be called professional organized criminality (Amir, 1996). Beyond being simply crime that is organized, *organized crime* has a number of additional defining attributes. These attributes include the structure and continuity of criminal networks engaging in crime—structure that facilitates committing certain kinds of crimes. Then there is the sophistication of the crimes and the skill levels required to carry them out; the violence (and a reputation for violence) that is systematically used to attain and retain monopoly control of criminal ventures; the capability to mount multiple and simultaneous criminal enterprises; and a capacity to corrupt political and legal authorities.

Criminal groups or organizations can likewise be defined by their capacity to do harm—economic, physical, psychological, and societal harm (Maltz, 1990). Those criminal organizations that qualify as true organized crime groups have significant capacity for these types of harm. On the other hand, small ad hoc groups do not have the harm capacity that would make them sophisticated criminal organizations of the type to constitute organized crime. Although their individual victims are certainly harmed, such groups do not have the capacity to carry out the serious, long-term economic, physical, psychological, and societal harm that marks real organized crime. Instead, they are most typically somewhat amorphous collections of individuals, usually made up of enterprising young men who come together around a particular criminal opportunity. They exploit that opportunity and then drift apart.

This is also not to say that the individual crimes of these loosely arranged, opportunistic groups can not at times be organized—sometimes even highly organized—but rather that they are not the same as organized crime (Finckenauer and Waring, 1996). The committing of a single crime can sometimes involve considerable planning and implementation of the resulting plan by a number of individuals fulfilling very specifically defined roles and carrying out specific functions relative to that crime. Such would be an example of a crime that is organized. The sense of *organized crime,* however, goes beyond this.

It is not just the crime with which we should be concerned, nor even the organization of the crime, but also the organization of those committing the crime. In a similar vein, Russian criminologist Azalia Dolgova has pointed out the distinction between ongoing criminal organizations, with their economic and political connections, and the simple organization of a particular crime or crimes (Dolgova, 1997). The former, she says, are not created in individual cases for purposes of committing individual crimes, whereas the latter are.

"Real" organized crime groups possess criminal sophistication, structure, self-identification with the group, and reputation. They are characterized not by undertaking particular criminal activities but rather by the monopoly control of criminal enterprises—by their ability to dominate the criminal underworld. They possess the capacity to use violence, and a reputation for violence, that facilitates this monopoly control. They also have the resources and political connections to corrupt the legal and political systems at the highest levels. Indeed, there are such criminal organizations in Moscow and in Russia, as there are elsewhere in the world, but there are certainly not thousands of them as some have claimed. With respect to their criminal ventures, the issue of interest to us is whether any of the organizations that can accurately be said to be organized crime are engaged in human trafficking.

Why do these distinctions matter? What is wrong with calling something organized crime (or more particularly mafia) when it is neither? First, from a research perspective (simply trying to describe, understand, and explain the phenomenon of interest), if organized crime is so loosely or ambiguously defined as to encompass practically any crimes committed by, say, three or more persons, then it is a meaningless concept. Without a clear and focused definition of what the phenomenon is, description, explanation, and understanding are impossible. It then follows that mapping trends and measuring the impact of countermeasures will also be impossible. Even mounting countermeasures becomes problematical under circumstances of ignorance and misperception.

Martens (1998) has pointed out a further complication from the promiscuous application of the label *organized crime*. "Bad reputation," he says, is a valuable asset that permits criminals access to criminal markets that would, absent this reputation, be closed to them. Victims or potential victims who believe they are confronted by some omnipotent force called organized crime (or more especially mafia) are more fearful, more likely to succumb, and less likely to go to the police than would otherwise be true. Thus, he says, "law enforcement must not facilitate this perception, and in fact enhance the value of a bad reputation when it is undeserved" (Martens, 1998: 3). Feeding the stereotype of a Russian Mafia, according to this view, can actually increase criminals' chances of successfully victimizing others.

With respect to organized crime control policy, relatively amorphous and short-lived criminal groups (of the kind that are the norm) are not particularly vulnerable to the strategies and tactics designed to counter genuine organized crime. Use of such techniques as informants, undercover agents, and wiretapping, or (in the United States) of the RICO (Racketeer Influenced and Corrupt Organizations Act) statute, for example, assumes a degree of continuity both over time and over crimes. This continuity is not present in the simpler opportunistic crimes. The absence of hierarchical structure also makes infiltration difficult. Use of the standard organized crime fighting tools in a false belief that the enemy is the mafia will be ineffective, inefficient, and costly—not only in dollar terms but in human terms as well. At the same time, it should be recognized that true organized crime is not vulnerable to the usual techniques used against street crime because the ringleaders—the bosses—of sophisticated criminal organizations are insulated from direct association with the actual crimes and because these organizations have economic and political clout. For all these reasons, knowing who is the real enemy is important.

There have been numerous accounts of thousands of organized criminal groups operating in Russia in recent years. In 1995, for example, the Russian Ministry of Internal Affairs reported that 8,222 "organized criminal rings" had been uncovered by law enforcement agencies (Dolgova, unpublished). These rings were said to have some 32,000 members—meaning the average group had to be relatively small (approximately 4 persons). It is difficult, however, to interpret just how "8,000 organized criminal groups" should be understood in this context. This is because, as in most other countries including the United States, there is no clear definition of organized crime or organized crime group in Russian law. An offense (any offense) can be said to have been "committed by an organized group, if it has been committed by a stable group of persons who had previously united to commit one or more offenses" (Nikiforov, unpublished). Such groups can and do include, for example, several youths stealing from street stalls or committing any of a number of other crimes in concert. This rather broad definition probably accounts for the fact that nearly 40 percent of all persons convicted in Russia in 1995 were said to be members of organized criminal groups.

In Russia, the elites of the criminal organizations operate internationally as well as domestically. Their overseas operations extend into Austria, Britain, Turkey, Jordan, the Netherlands, the former Yugoslavia, Poland, Hungary, Germany, Italy, Israel, Canada, China, Japan, Afghanistan, and the United States. One of their main international criminal activities is money laundering and other banking-related schemes. In addition to these financial crimes, their major transnational activity most often includes some kind of trafficking—of stolen cars, drugs, arms, and so on.

Just as with the reported numbers of organized criminal groups, the estimates of the number of criminal organizations from the former Soviet Union engaged in these transnational activities vary enormously. For example, Dunn (1996) concluded that there are really only 6 groups in Moscow and 30 in the whole of Russia that wield the kind of power and have the extensive overseas operations that enable them to monopolize the criminal world and to infiltrate Russian business and government. On the other hand, according to a recent report on Russian Organized Crime, the FBI estimates that there are 200 to 300 such groups. The Russian Ministry of the Interior (MVD), using the same information as Dolgova, reported that there are more than 8,000. And at the upper end of the scale, at least in numbers of individual participants, the 1994 United Nations World Ministerial Conference on Organized Transnational Crime reported that there were 3 million individuals in 5,700 criminal groups operating in Russia (Center for Strategic and International Studies, 1997).

Despite their wide disagreement on the numbers involved, there is some agreement that the multiple criminal enterprises of Russian organized crime include crimes that are part of the traditional bailiwick of organized crime. These include drug smuggling, prostitution, counterfeiting, and extortion. They also include, however, many criminal ventures that are more typical of the white-collar crime variety, for example, financial swindles, illegal oil deals, and illegal exportation of raw materials. Of all these crimes, prostitution is most closely tied to the human trafficking issue.

Organized Crime and Human Trafficking

There are a number of possible ways that organized crime could be connected to human trafficking (Schmid and Savona, 1995: 28–31). For instance, organized crime figures might induce people to leave their homes, usually with false promises of employment. Promised jobs as models, dancers, tourist guides, or waitresses, for example, are one way that trafficked women are duped and then forced into prostitution. People who have decided to seek their fortune in another country might knowingly or unknowingly get involved with an organized trafficker who is part of a migrants trafficking network. Or the collection of the debt owed the traffickers might be turned over to organized crime, which then threatens the migrant and his or her family or forces them into prostitution or drug selling or other crime in order to pay off this debt.

With the possible exception of debt collection—and even that is not an open and shut case—it seems very reasonable that criminals not associated with organized crime, and indeed persons not otherwise involved in crime, could also become engaged in trafficking activities. Persons who decide to make money from human trafficking do not have to be members of organized crime to deceive women with false employment possibilities or even to organize a trafficking ring. Because the state of knowledge at present is so spotty, as we will see, there is much room for interpretation, and there are many gray areas. Such circumstances are often ripe for myth making and stereotyping. But from the relatively little that is now known, human trafficking does seem to fall more into the "crime that is organized" category than it does into true organized crime. The range of types of organizations involved is quite broad, with smugglers being everything from individual operators to members of possibly sophisticated international smuggling rings (Winer, 1997).

Two recent cases illustrate the organized (but not organized crime) nature of human trafficking. In the first case, which is the largest U.S. case of its kind, U.S. officials arrested twenty-one of thirty-one suspected smugglers named in indictments stating that they were operators of three international immigrant smuggling cartels (*Dallas Morning News,* November 21, 1998). The three ringleaders were natives of India. They were charged with transporting more than seven thousand immigrants from the Indian subcontinent to the United States for a profit of some $150 million. Their organization included transit routes through Moscow to countries in South and Central America. They had safe houses, forged documents, and transportation systems with both small boats and planes. Although INS commissioner Doris Meissner called them a "well-organized, well-financed international criminal network," there were no indications that the persons indicted were members of organized crime or that they had any connections to organized crime.

In the second case, a Thai woman was arrested in Karachi, Pakistan, for being the "matriarch of a Bangkok-based syndicate involved in the smuggling of sex workers, mainly Chinese, to North America and Europe" (Dawn News Service, Karachi, November 23, 1998). Again there is evidence that this was an organized operation. But apart from some local agents in China, the principals of the "syndicate" were the Thai woman and her Laotian partner. As with the previous case, no connections to organized crime were reported.

Salt and Stein (1997) conceptualized the organized nature of human trafficking and, using some of the limited empirical data now available, proposed a theoretical model illustrating how it works. Their model supports the idea that this is a crime that is organized. What they call the "migration business" is a "system of institutionalized networks with complex profit and loss accounts, including a set of institutions, agents and individuals, each of which stands to make a commercial gain" (468). This system is maintained by the performance of a variety of tasks: planning the smuggling operations, gathering information, financing, and certain specific technical and operational tasks (477). These tasks can be carried out by either larger or smaller trafficking organizations; but most important, they can be carried out by organizations engaged in no other forms of criminal activity. For example, Salt and Stein describe trafficking from Albania to Italy as typically involving mom-and-pop operations. These mom-and-pop trafficking rings "employ about a dozen people, including a driver in charge of getting the boat over and back, one or two crew members acting as enforcers during the voyage, and various others in charge of rounding up customers, collecting money, transporting passengers to secret departure points and acting as look-outs" (476). Describing this same sort of Albania to Italy trafficking, the International Organization for Migration said that there is usually a direct relationship between the women being trafficked and their traffickers. "Interviews suggest that traffickers are often young criminals, attracted by the possibility of earning easy money even at the cost of profiting from girls/women that were friends, school mates or neighbors in their home town or village" (1996, in *Trends in Organized Crime*, 1998: 33). The traffickers in these latter types of cases include relatives, friends, or boyfriends.

With respect to trafficking in children for child prostitution, the same sort of situation seems to prevail—namely, that a wide variety of organizational patterns are found. "The intermediary [who links demand and supply] can be an agent who buys children in rural villages and transports them to the towns or cities where they are turned over to brothel owners (who can be either individual entrepreneurs or members of criminal groups)" (ibid., 7).

Is the situation the same in Russia? There is indeed some anecdotal evidence that this same sort of mom-and-pop (or brother-and-brother) system operates. For example, the *Russian Magazine* described an interview with a man running a prostitution ring in Moscow. "I took a group of 'volunteers' to work as waitresses, strippers and dancers," he said. "I made fake papers. We had sort of a family business. My brother made visas and passports. . . . I never dragged anyone by force. They knew perfectly well what lay ahead—maybe not completely, but that was their problem. Once the plane landed, I dealt with them as I pleased" (ibid., 42).

It appears that human traffickers can range all the way from being enterprising individuals not previously or otherwise involved in crime, to individual criminals (not of the organized variety), to mixed groups of these types of individuals, to families, to local criminal groups, to networks made up of both criminals and noncriminals, to sophisticated organized groups operating nationally and internationally. True organized crime may play a role in some of these operations. As previously indicated, they may become debt collectors. Or, they may demand a "mob tax" to permit trafficking in their territory. What seems clear, however, is that viewing all the possible arrangements as being the same—and labeling them all as organized crime or worse, mafia—is both incorrect and unwise, from both a research and a policy perspective.

The Russian Connection to Human Trafficking and Prostitution

The specific question for us is whether what would be regarded as genuine Russian organized crime is participating in human trafficking and its derivative prostitution. We should state at the outset that the evidence of involvement by organized crime in general and Russian organized crime in particular in human trafficking is quite limited.

Let us start with the possibilities. There appear to be four possible ways in which Russian participation in trafficking might come about. For one of these types, however (trafficking in children), so little information is available that we cannot say anything about it. Trafficking in children was outlawed in Russian law only in 1995, and just four offenses were reported during that year. We will, therefore, focus on the other three.

Smuggling of Migrants from Other Countries

It is reported that on any one day there are thousands (200,000–300,000 est.) of illegal Asians (mostly Chinese), Africans, Afghans, Kurds, Somalis, and Iraqis in Moscow awaiting trans-shipment to Western Europe and the United States. Moscow is a central distribution point for these migrants (Ulrich, 1994: 7; 1997: 122). Some Russians collaborate in this smuggling with traffickers from other countries, for example, from China. It is not clear, however, just who these Russians are and with what criminal organizations they might be affiliated, if any. The Chinese in Russia often operate their Moscow pipeline themselves, whereas in other cases Russians operate as middlemen in the various transnational networks. As Salt and Stein show in their model, trafficking needs middlemen, and it would make sense to have middlemen who know the Moscow scene. Further, it would seem that the easy money and the relatively low risks entailed in human trafficking might attract local criminal elements as well as others looking for a fast buck.

Illegal immigrants need high-quality paperwork (documentation, visas, airline tickets, and so on) in order to cover their immigration. These documents are often highly sophisticated and of high quality—and the higher the quality, the greater is the cost. According to the International Organization for Migration, "the illicit trade in fraudulent documents feeds from organized migrant trafficking. Stealing, forging and altering travel documents and work and residence permits has become a major criminal activity as the ability to migrate largely depends on possessing the necessary documents" (1996: 1–2). These are all specialties of the Russians. With their long experience of circumventing Soviet bureaucracy, they are highly skilled in producing the necessary documentation. I was told by the INS that much of the problem of illegal immigrants in Moscow had to do with documentation, with "the paper." The U.S.

State Department cannot keep up with the volume of requests emanating from Moscow—from all sources—for permissions to enter the United States.

A 1994 United Nations report addressed this problem of false documentation: "Blank, unissued passports are stolen from passport-issuing authorities around the world. Issued passports are stolen from tourists and travel agencies, and corrupt officials provide passports to smuggling rings" (United Nations, 1994: 3). This has been said to be a problem in Moscow.

Given the complex planning and coordination on an international scale that would be necessary to operate a large network carrying out these tasks, such trafficking operations would certainly seem to qualify as an example of a crime that is organized.

Smuggling Illegals from the Former USSR

A second type of trafficking involving Russians is of persons from the countries of the former Soviet Union who simply want to establish legal residence in Europe, Israel, or the United States. Israel has reported an increase in the use of forged documents both to acquire immigrant rights and to carry out crimes. According to Israeli authorities, the subject of documentation and the issuance of immigrant visas and other permits are said to be so lax in Moscow that they cry out to be misused. There is said to be literally an industry operating out of Moscow producing false documents certifying Jewishness.

In the United States, the INS told me in 1996 that there were increasing indications of Russian involvement in bringing illegal aliens into the United States (mostly by air and many through Seattle, Washington). As of that time, however, the numbers caught had been rather small; for example, twenty-seven illegals from the former USSR were processed by the INS in 1992–93 and thirty-six in 1995–96. There were reports that female illegals from the former USSR had been put to work as prostitutes, bar girls, and go-go dancers and in peep shows in the United States and, in one known instance of women from Estonia, as nannies. But there were no criminal cases involving such activities. The situation in Israel has been said to be similar, where women are put to work in massage parlors, for example. Males were likewise said to be exploited, often as drug couriers and even small-time extortionists. In all these cases, the persons trafficked were forced to pay back the costs incurred in bringing them into the country. Here we see examples of both people being induced to leave home under false promises and migrants being forced into crime to pay their debt.

Prostitution has historically been one of the illegal services operated as a criminal enterprise by traditional organized crime in the West. Human trafficking through and from Russia has especially been linked to prostitution, as Russian women who are illegal migrants have become a source of providers of this illegal service. Prostitution may have become one of the main criminal exports from Russia to the rest of the world. "Organized prostitution by post-Soviet criminals has become an export commodity to foreign countries mainly since 1990. It has reached epidemic proportions as post-Soviet and East European prostitution rings develop in far-flung areas of the globe. Russian, Polish and Ukrainian women, for example, have been turning up in many of the countries of Eastern Europe, Germany, Austria, the former Yugoslavia, Israel, Greece, the United States, China, Turkey, Belgium, the Netherlands, Finland, Sweden, Italy, South Africa, Thailand, Hong Kong, Korea and Cyprus" (Ulrich, 1996: 36).

Prostitution from Russia figures into the issue of human trafficking in a number of ways. For example, in 1995 Greek authorities arrested a number of Greek policemen who were masterminding foreign call-girl trafficking rings in Greece. Scores of Russian and Eastern European women were enticed to come to Greece with promises of wealth and a better life. Once they arrived, their passports were confiscated and sold to nightclub owners. The women were turned into virtual prisoners and forced to prostitute themselves. More recently, it was reported that Greece had become a "European Union foothold for prostitution rings with links throughout the former Soviet bloc" (Murphy, 1998: 22:56). All the arrests in these cases so far have been Greeks, and thus possible Russian organized crime involvement remains an unknown.

Galeotti (1995) reported that German authorities had identified 10,000 women from Eastern and central Europe and the former Soviet Union working as prostitutes there—many of them under duress. Likewise in Israel, it was estimated that as of 1995 approximately 2,500 Russian prostitutes, and a variety of other criminals, had been smuggled in. In the case of the prostitutes, some were said to have come willingly whereas others were coerced.

The number one form of visa fraud involving Russians in the United States is said to be the establishment of false companies that are then used as a basis for inviting "co-workers" into the country. According to the U.S. Immigration and Naturalization Service, in the most common practice, Russians pay "firms" to "transfer" them to the United States. In a related scheme, bogus companies established in the United States sell "business invitations" to migrants in Russia. Once in the United States, these companies may help the migrant regularize his or her status.

In each of these possible types of Russian participation in human trafficking, the smuggling of people might simply be another moneymaking venture for those entrepreneurs who are able and willing to engage in such trafficking, as well as for some professional criminal types. It could be just another example of the crimes of deception at which the Russians are so good. After all, smuggling people might be simply of a kind with smuggling consumer goods, raw materials, and vehicles, in each of which some of the same persons could be involved. If the Russian traffickers are indeed affiliated with organized crime, they might use the money they get from would-be migrants in other criminal ventures. In this way trafficking could be a sideline form of investment.

Smuggling Criminals

The third form of human trafficking involves exporting known criminals—prostitutes, hit men, and so on. In these cases the refugee status is used as a cover for criminal activity. The INS told me in 1996 that people they regarded as leaders in Russian organized crime were "piggybacking" onto legal migrants to insert criminals into the United States. Some of these criminals were reported to be assassins and others fugitives from justice in Russia who had been sent out of the country to "cool off."

Whither the Russian Mafia?

Given these possibilities, what concrete links might be established between this illegal trafficking and the Russian Mafia? Before we turn to the evidence, let us first look at some of the claims that are being made—keeping in mind that we started off by alleging that there might be a Russian Mafia–hyping phenomenon in all of this. Are there allegations that Russian organized crime and specifically the Russian Mafia are in this human trafficking business? Yes indeed there are!

Let us look at just a few examples. The first two come from the media. An article entitled "Slavic Women in Demand in Sex Slave Markets" appeared on the Web site of the Office of International Criminal Justice at the University of Illinois at Chicago. Along with poverty and social disintegration, wrote Tim Stone (1998: 1–2), the "aggressive tactics of Russian organized crime have led to Slavic sexual slaves surpassing all other nationalities." Ukrainian and Russian women are said to be earning criminal gangs "upwards of $500 to $1,000 each." "Predatory Russian organized groups lure women into slavery," and "the Russian Mafia utilizes front companies" to facilitate this enslavement. Stone tells us that Moscow-based Russian crime gangs control international slavery routes, often through cooperative ventures with the Japanese Yakuza, the Italian Mafia, and other organized crime groups. But beyond some very general citations of various authorities, the article offers no hard evidence to support any of these claims.

An earlier article that appeared in the *New York Times* for January 11, 1998, described the human trafficking somewhat less dramatically than the Stone piece but concluded similarly. "Centered in Moscow and the Ukrainian capital, Kiev, the networks trafficking women run east to Japan and Thailand, where thousands of young Slavic women now work against their will as prostitutes, and west to the Adriatic Coast and beyond. The routes are controlled by Russian crime gangs based in Moscow" (Specter, 1998: 1). A UN official based in Vienna was cited as a source for the article. But interestingly, this official was reported as saying that despite his belief that tens of thousands of women were "certainly" sold into prostitution each year, "he was uncomfortable with statistics since nobody involved has any reason to tell the truth" (3).

Some of the most serious investigation of this issue has been done by the advocacy organization Global Survival Network. And it has made perhaps the strongest argument that it is Russian organized crime that is organizing the trafficking in women from the former Soviet Union. After a lengthy undercover investigation, the organization concluded: "Trafficking in Russia and throughout the world is organized by criminal groups. . . . Even in instances where they are not directly responsible for trafficking women overseas, Russian criminal groups provide a 'krisha' ('roof'), or security and protection, for the operations, and . . . they have incorporated the traffic of women as an increasingly profitable part of their activities inside and outside the country" (Global Survival Network, 1997: 34). But in reaching this conclusion, the Global Survival Network (GSN) seemed to lump together all the thousands of criminal groups identified by the Russian authorities into what they called "mafiya." They also concluded that "mafiya involvement in trafficking amounts to providing 'protection' to sex businesses," that is, the *krisha* concept. For many legitimate businesses in the former Soviet Union, and most particularly in Moscow, having a *krisha* is deemed necessary to their survival. A variety of individuals and groups, including criminal groups and former members of the security establishment, are in the business of providing insurance against trouble with criminals. That these businesses would perhaps include criminal enterprises in general, and human trafficking specifically, is certainly plausible. But without in any way detracting from the importance of the valuable contribution that the GSN has made in its ground-breaking research on the problem of trafficking in women for prostitution, concrete conclusions about a Russian Mafia connection seem at this point to be unwarranted and at best hypothetical.

Recalling the admonition to avoid helping criminals and criminal groups be bigger and tougher than they are, let us first deal with the label *mafia*. Unless one adopts only the most vague and all-encompassing definition of what a mafia is (the one commonly used by the media and the general public), the more than eight thousand criminal groups identified by the Russian Ministry of Internal Affairs are not a mafia or mafias. If a mafia is everything, it is nothing. Preferable, it seems to me, is the carefully delineated definition of mafia set forth by Gambetta (1993), which says that the core business of a mafia is supplying protection. Under this definition, mafias have a quasi-governmental role, and it is this that distinguishes them from simple criminals and criminal entrepreneurs and even from other forms of organized crime. Traditional mafiosi (in the Sicilian sense) are men of honor and respect. They ensure trust and credibility in transactions. As indicated, some Russian criminal groups, although it is unclear just how many, do indeed have the mafialike characteristic of being in this kind of protection business. And they may be providing protection (albeit extortionate)—as a *krisha*—to groups that are trafficking in women and children. But the only evidence for this so far is very limited and strictly anecdotal.

This lack of evidence is at the core of our problem in being able to understand and explain how much of human trafficking is controlled by organized crime. According to a series of reports by the International Organization for Migration, the organization that most closely follows developments in this area, there is a profound absence of data and information about this problem. IOM says that trafficking in women is a considerably underreported offense throughout Europe, but it nevertheless concludes that it is a "numerically small problem" (IOM, 1995: 11). In part because laws are not enforced, there have been few arrests and only a handful of prosecutions and convictions. Even in instances in which there have been arrests and convictions, trafficking in women for prostitution and prostitution in general may not be distinguished. For example, in the data of the Russian MVD for 1995, 1,756 cases of "keeping dens and promoting prostitution" were reported as organized criminal activities. Besides the fact that this seems to be a relatively small number, it does not distinguish between prostitution of the traditional domestic kind and possible cases of trafficking-related prostitution. This same lack of distinction is made between legal and illegal entry of women who may subsequently engage in prostitution.

As pointed out previously, trafficking may be carried out by individual persons as well as by organizations. Unless arrests are made and convictions ensue, the only source of information with respect to who the traffickers are is the women. But in some cases they refuse to testify because they fear legal repercussions or are personally afraid. In almost all cases, they do not know if there is a criminal organization running their trafficking. They do not know who and how many persons might be involved in such organization. "Women usually know about only part of the trafficking network, and often only come into contact with one person" (IOM, 1995: 29). In a report on trafficking and prostitution from central and Eastern Europe, the IOM concluded: "If trafficked women and their advocates are correct in their estimates, the number of known victims represents only the tip of the iceberg. Hardly any statistics are available on the extent of trafficking in women, partly because it is an illegal activity and, hence, difficult to assess, and partly because those agencies which might compile statistics do not regard the practice as important enough to warrant collecting data. Trafficking in women receives considerable media publicity, not so much because of concern for the welfare of victims, but because journalists know that stories about sex and prostitution attract attention" (1995: 33).

Salt and Stein (1997) made the point about lack of data over and over. It is "not yet clear," they said, how the migration business is organized and subdivided because statistics are not generally available (469). "It is uncertain how large a business trafficking has become, how much money it generates, and how many people it employs" (472). They, too, pointed out that the victims of trafficking—who have been almost our only sources of knowledge—often have little useful information because they know about only a minute part of the whole trafficking enterprise (478).

In my interviews with representatives of the Immigration and Naturalization Service (perhaps the U.S. agency most closely associated with the human trafficking problem), the view expressed was that there was organized smuggling involving Russians. But on the question of whether it was organized crime, the answer was "We don't know!" The INS conclusion was that the Russians were not then (1996) entrenched in trafficking activities but that their potential for becoming so was certainly great.

Conclusions

The absence of hard and reliable information leaves this subject open to speculation, to relying upon anecdotal information, and obviously to media sensationalism with respect both to the sex angle and to the Russian Mafia connection. Unfortunately, this can result in poorly informed and misdirected policies.

Ironically, in one sense it might make law enforcement easier if human trafficking were controlled by true organized crime. The targets for investigation and prosecution would at least be much clearer, and the effort could be more focused. It might also mean that law enforcement success against one area of criminal activity would spin off into other criminal ventures controlled by the same organizations. Thus, successful prosecution of a money-laundering scheme could also bring down a human trafficking scheme as well.

On the other hand, an absence of Russian organized crime control of trafficking would mean that the persons involved are in all likelihood less criminally sophisticated, not so well connected politically, and perhaps not as well organized. Mom-and-pop operators, although more numerous, are also more likely to be deterred by serious threats of being caught, prosecuted, and punished. In order for the latter to occur, of course, the threat must be credible.

Portraying human trafficking as almost exclusively linked with organized crime and mafia is also self-defeating in another way. The ultimate solution to the human trafficking problem will not come from law enforcement alone. There must be effective global migration policies that close off the opportunity for exploitation and victimization by criminal elements. But as with many of the business enterprises of organized crime, the ultimate foundation for profits from illicit goods and services is the customers for these goods and services. In this particular case those customers are the consumers and the buyers in the sex industry. It is those customers who make human trafficking profitable, and it is here that attention should be focused. Rationalizing commercial sexual exploitation as being caused by and controlled by the Russian Mafia furnishes a convenient scapegoat and allows the others who are responsible, including the supposedly respectable businessmen who avail themselves of the sexual services offered, to escape blame. Success in combating this problem will only come from a clear assessment of just what the problem is and who is involved.

This is clearly an area that requires much more attention and investigation. Such investigation must, however, avoid the sensationalism and hyperbole associated with a mythical Russian Mafia. Such simplistic explanations ignore the multilayered and complex nature of the trafficking problem. At the same time, attributing trafficking to the Russian Mafia inflates the reputations of two-bit traffickers so as to enhance their criminal success. Neither of these is a desirable outcome.

There have been a number of developments in the past decade with respect to the human trafficking phenomenon as it involves Russia and Russians. Two major global developments were the adoption in 2000 of the UN Convention on Transnational Crime and its Protocol to Prevent, Suppress and Punish Trafficking in Persons, especially Women and Children and, in the same year, the passage of the U.S. Trafficking Victims Protection Act (TVPA). Each of these brought a much more detailed country-by-country focus on the nature and magnitude of human trafficking. That more detailed focus has enabled us to see more specifically just what the Russian situation is. For example, one UN report, *Trafficking in Persons: Global Patterns* (April 2006), indicated that the Commonwealth of Independent States (CIS) was an important origin region for trafficking victims. The four highest ranked CIS countries in terms of numbers of trafficking victims were Belarus, Moldova, Ukraine, and Russia, and Western Europe and North America were the main destinations.

Similarly, the U.S. State Department has reported in its Trafficking in Persons Reports, required by the TVPA, that over the past seven years Russia has been a major source, transit, and destination country for men, women, and children being trafficked for various purposes. Specifically, Russia has been said to be a significant source of women being trafficked to over fifty countries for commercial sexual exploitation. Internal trafficking is also a problem in Russia, where women are trafficked from rural areas to urban centers for commercial sexual exploitation and men are trafficked to feed the maritime, construction, and agricultural industries. Corruption, which usually accompanies trafficking, is a very serious problem in Russia. Corrupt police officers and border guards reportedly accept bribes to facilitate or protect trafficking.

Trafficking in persons was specifically outlawed in Russia under legislation passed in 2003, but prosecution has been limited and slow. For example, there were only 17 cases of trafficking in persons prosecuted in 2004, a number that grew to just 112 in 2007. Since these numbers are considered to be only the tip of the iceberg, it is difficult to conclude much from them.

The questions of who the traffickers are and what the role of organized crime in trafficking is remain just that, questions. From the criminal cases made so far, there is evidence that trafficking indeed requires organization, but not necessarily true organized crime of the Mafia variety. Illustrative of both the varied nature of the trafficking networks and the corruption of law enforcement is the March 2009 case of 13 individuals charged with the sex trafficking of some 130 women from Russia and other CIS countries to Europe and the Middle East. The reputed head of the criminal network turned out to be a senior Russian intelligence official (www.russiatoday.com/Top_News/2009–03–31; accessed January 4, 2009).

REFERENCES

Amir, Menachem. 1996. "Organized Crime in Israel." *Transnational Organized Crime* 2 (4): 21–39.
Center for Strategic and International Studies—Global Organized Crime Project. 1997. *Russian Organized Crime.* Washington, D.C.: Center for Strategic and International Studies.
Dolgova, Azalia. 1997. "Organized Crime in Russia." Moscow, Russia: Unpublished.
Dunaeva, Victoria. 1997. "Selling Souls: Russia's Oldest Profession Takes a Grim Turn onto the International Market." *Russian Magazine* (Los Angeles) (October): 36–39. Reprinted in *Trends in Organized Crime* 3 (4) (1998): 40–43.
Dunn, Guy. 1996. "Major Mafia Gangs in Russia." *Transnational Organized Crime* 2(2–3): 63–87.
Finckenauer, James O., and Elin Waring. 1996. "Russian Émigré Crime in the United States: Organized Crime or Crime That Is Organized?" *Transnational Organized Crime,* 2/2/3 (Summer/Autumn): 139–55.
———. 1998. *Russian Mafia in America: Immigration, Culture, and Crime,* Boston: Northeastern University Press.
Galeotti, Mark. 1995. "Cross-Border Crime in the Former Soviet Union." *Boundary and Territory Briefing* (Durham, UK) 1(5).
Gambetta, Diego. 1993. *The Sicilian Mafia.* Cambridge: Harvard University Press.
Global Survival Network. 1997. "Crime and Servitude: An Expose of the Traffic in Women for Prostitution from the Newly Independent States," http://www.globalsurvival.net/femaletrade/9711russia.html, March 26.
International Organization for Migration (IOM). 1995. "Trafficking and Prostitution: The Growing Exploitation of Migrant Women from Central And Eastern Europe" (May).
———. 1996. "Organized Crime Moves into Migrant Trafficking." *Trafficking in Migrants* (Geneva, Switzerland), no. 11 (June): 1–2.

———. 1996. "Trafficking in Women to Italy for Sexual Exploitation." Migration Information Program, Budapest, Hungary (June). Reprinted in *Trends in Organized Crime* 3 (Summer 1998): 32–35.

LaGesse, David, and Ed Timms. 1998. "Immigrant-Smuggling Rings Broken Up, Authorities Say: Dallas-Based Cartels Accused of Moving 7,000 Workers in 3 Years." *Dallas Morning News,* November 21.

Maltz, Michael D. 1990. *Measuring the Effectiveness of Organized Crime Control Efforts.* Chicago: Office of International Criminal Justice.

Martens, Frederick T. 1998. "The 'Russian Mafia': Reinventing The 'Cold War' or a Social Reality." Paper presented to the Canadian Intelligence Officers' Symposium, Ottawa, Canada, September 30.

Murphy, Brian. 1998. "Prostitution Scandal Stuns Greece." Associated Press Office (Athens, Greece), November 19, 22:56.

Nikiforov, Alexander S. "What Shall We Have to Do with Organized Crime?" Unpublished.

Robinson, Laurie Nicole. 1998. "The Globalization of Female Child Prostitution." http://www.law.indiana.edu/glsj/vol5/no1/robinson.html, November 2.

Rosner, Lydia S. 1995. "The Sexy Russian Mafia." *Criminal Organizations* 10 (1): 29.

Rutland, Peter, and Natasha Kogan. 1998. "The Russian Mafia: Between Hype and Reality." http://www.ijt.cz/transitions/thrusmaf.html, November 5.

Salt, John, and Jeremy Stein. 1997. "Migration as a Business: The Case of Trafficking." *International Migration* 35 (4): 467–91.

Schmid, A. P., with E. U. Savona. 1995. *Migration and Crime: A Framework for Discussion.* Milan: International Scientific and Professional Advisory Council of the United Nations Crime Prevention and Criminal Justice Programme.

Siddiqui, Tahir. 1998. "Arrested Thai Woman Turns Out to Be Woman Trafficker." Dawn News Service, November 23.

Specter, Michael. 1998. "Traffickers' New Cargo: Naive Slavic Women." *New York Times,* January 11, A1.

Stone, Tim. "Slavic Women in Demand in Sex Slave Markets." 1998. *C & J International,* Office of International Criminal Justice, University of Illinois at Chicago, May, pp. 1–6.

Ulrich, C. J. 1994. "The Price of Freedom." Conflict Studies 275, Research Institute for the Study of Conflict and Terrorism, London (October), pp. 1–30.

———. 1996. "The New Red Terror: International Dimensions of Post-Soviet Organized Crime." *Low Intensity Conflict and Law Enforcement* 5 (1): 29–44.

———. 1997. "Transnational Organized Crime and Law Enforcement Cooperation in the Baltic States." *Transnational Organized Crime* 3 (2): 111–30.

United Nations. 1994. "Measures to Combat Alien-Smuggling." Report of the Secretary-General. August 30. Pp. 1–23.

Williams, Phil. 1998. "Overview." *Trends in Organized Crime* 3 (4): 3–9.

Winer, Jonathan M. 1997. "Alien Smuggling: Elements of the Problem and the U.S. Response." *Transnational Organized Crime* 3 (1): 50–58.

CHAPTER THIRTEEN

Migrant Smuggling and Threats to Social Order in Japan

H. Richard Friman

During the mid-1990s, Japanese debates over immigration turned to the threat posed by Chinese migrants—primarily male unskilled workers—and the smuggling networks facilitating their illegal entry into the country. Government and media reports attributed the rise in migrant smuggling to the shifting interests of foreign organized crime groups, especially the "Snakehead" syndicate rumored to be directed by Hong Kong's 14K triad. Police and immigration officials argued that Snakehead's targeting of Japan reflected two displacement effects, the first stemming from the U.S. crackdown on illegal Chinese immigration in the aftermath of the *Golden Venture* incident and the second from the reversion of Hong Kong to the People's Republic of China. As smuggling incidents surged in early 1997, the Maritime Safety Agency (MSA) noted further that the diversion of its resources to deal with a major oil spill had opened a unique window of opportunity for smugglers to expand their operations into Japan (*Asahi Evening News*, February 13, October 5, 1997; "Inside Story," 1997; *Mainichi Daily News*, February 7, 1997; National Police Agency, 1997).

Reports of the Snakehead threat, however, were not limited to migrant smuggling. Police officials noted that the new wave of migration was responsible for a crime spree threatening public safety and social order. Annual *White Papers on Police* released by the National Police Agency illustrated the Chinese propensity toward criminal behavior with statistics and graphical presentations positing that Chinese in Japan were responsible for more than 40 percent of crime by foreigners but constituted less than 13–16 percent of the foreign visitor population. To explain this behavior, police officials stressed the expansion of the membership of 14K affiliates in Japan but stopped short of arguing that this criminal propensity was necessarily inherent to all Chinese. A more common claim was that the combination of Japan's slowing economy and especially the debt burdens incurred by the new migrants had forced many into a life of crime. Japanese officials argued that to prevent a disruption to migrant trafficking operations, the Snakehead syndicate had facilitated the trafficking shift to Japan by offering its services at a discount. The migrant would rely on borrowed funds or pay a partial fee with the remainder to be paid by relatives in China or by the migrant after securing employment in Japan. The funds in the case of the latter mode of repayment would be routed back to China through what police identified as an extensive underground money-laundering network (*Asahi Evening News*, March 30, 1997; *Daily Yomiuri*, March 1, 1997; *International Herald Tribune*, March 4, 1997; *Japan Times*, March 13, 1998).

The Japanese concerns over migrant smuggling reflected a kernel of truth. Smuggling incidents had increased since the late 1980s, as had criminal offenses by Chinese. However, several pieces were missing from the prominent explanations of the extent and nature of the problem. One set of missing pieces appeared in the inconsistent, official conceptualization of migrant smuggling networks and the misleading public presentation of criminal statistics. The second set of missing pieces included Japan's history of labor brokering with China and the ramifications of a transition taking place in the structure and operations of Japanese organized crime.

I argue that these omissions reflect a broader pattern of state agents constructing foreigners as threats to social order. Though often referred to as a newcomer to immigration, Japan has a long history of arguments prominently linking migrants and crime in policy debates over immigration and crime control. These arguments have appeared during periods of severe dislocation such as the anti-Korean riots in the aftermath of the 1923 Tokyo earthquake and the incidents of gang warfare between Japanese and *sankokujin* (literally, "three country people," referring to Korean, Taiwanese, Chinese) over black markets during the early years of the American occupation (Aldous, 1997; Morris-Suzuki,

1998: 105). Arguments linking foreigners and crime resurfaced in the late 1980s in the context of increased migration and especially with the collapse of the bubble economy.

In this chapter I explore arguments linking foreigners and crime in the context of emerging concerns over the Snakehead threat of the mid-1990s. To do so, the chapter's first section addresses the question of the extent of migrant smuggling and Chinese crime rates in Japan. The second section turns to the issues of labor demand and organized crime missing from the prominent discussions of migrant smuggling. The third section explores the construction of the Snakehead as a threat to social order in Japan.

Snakeheads and Chinese Crime

Even a brief overview of agency reports, official statements, and media analyses of the Snakehead threat during the 1990s reveals inconsistencies in the conceptualization of the smuggling networks linking China and Japan. For example, the networks are often discussed as being directed by either a single organization or multiple organizations, while Japanese are members, allies, or victims of Snakehead operations. In contrast, the most prominent statistics on the criminal propensity of illegal Chinese migrants suffer from the selective presentation of Japanese crime data.

Snakeheads

In the aftermath of the *Golden Venture* incident, Chinese migrant smuggling began to attract extensive international attention, especially the role of Taiwanese "snakeheads" in facilitating the movement of migrants from China's Fujian Province abroad (Zhang and Gaylord, 1996: 5–8; Myers, 1997: 97–104). The term as applied to smuggling networks sought to capture the "image of slithering from point to point along clandestine routes" (Chin, 1997: 190). The expansion of the Taiwanese smuggling industry drew upon established drug transit routes and existing migrant smuggling networks that had facilitated the earlier, smaller-scale movement of Fujian Chinese to the United Sates and elsewhere (Myers, 1997: 105–6). Rather than a single network, snakehead groups were operating at multiple levels of the illegal migration process—local, national, international, and host country. Moreover, snakehead groups varied extensively in size and formal organizational structure (Zhang and Gaylord, 1996: 6–11; see also Zhang, 2007).

In contrast, the Japanese discussion of the Snakehead threat lacked this sense of nuanced complexity. All too often, enforcement agencies, and in turn the media, referred to migrant smugglers as members of a single, foreign organization. For example, according to Shirakawa Katsuhiko, the chairman of the National Public Safety Commission, Snakehead was "a Hong Kong based criminal syndicate which deals in illegal immigrants" (*Daily Yomiuri*, March 5, 1997). Similarly, National Police Agency (NPA) officials in reports and testimony before the Japanese Diet tended to refer to the "Hong Kong criminal syndicate Snakehead" in the singular, though occasionally acknowledging that the term referred more broadly to Chinese brokers that facilitate the smuggling process (e.g., *Asahi Evening News*, October 5, 1997; *Daily Yomiuri*, January 21, 1997; *Mainichi Daily News*, February 3, 1997). Immigration officials operating under the Ministry of Justice and MSA officials revealed a similar pattern.

References to the participation of Japanese in migrant smuggling operations also were inconsistent. By the mid-1990s enforcement authorities began to acknowledge the role of Japanese organized crime (*boryokudan,* or more commonly *yakuza*) in migrant smuggling cases. But authorities continued to posit that the guiding force in such operations remained Chinese. Perhaps the best example of this pattern was the August 1997 revelation of an international smuggling network linking China, Hong Kong, Cambodia, Europe (France, Italy), the United States, and Japan. The number of Japanese arrested in the case led to reports noting the Cambodian-based operation of the "Snakehead crime group, which is predominantly Chinese" and "directed by a Chinese leader" in which Japanese nationals were used to smuggle Chinese into the United States and Europe by passing them off as relatives. The following month, the police turned to investigating the syndicate for its role in the rash of illegal entries of Chinese into Japan (e.g., *Mainichi Daily News*, August 5, September 10, 1997).

Japanese concerns over the Snakehead threat initially focused on the smuggling of groups of Chinese migrants by boat into the country. As seen in Table 13.1, interdictions of group smuggling increased in 1992 and surged in the mid-1990s. Although seen as a cause for alarm, the numbers of Chinese apprehended even in the peak years of interdiction still fell short of Japan's prior experience with a brief wave of migrant smuggling in the latter half of 1989. International resettlement deliberations in mid-1989 over the fate of Indochinese refugees had the unintended effect of encouraging new waves of "boat people." Refugees who had fled Vietnam in the 1970s for Hong Kong and had been resettled in rural southern Chinese turned in 1989 to smuggling networks to seek resettlement in Hong Kong and Japan, claiming status as political refugees fleeing directly from Vietnam. In the latter half of 1989 Japanese authorities tallied thirty-seven separate incidents of interdiction at sea and boat landings of 3,497 persons claiming to be political refugees fleeing Vietnam. Charges of a Fujian connection and manipulation of refugee status by the boat people helped to fuel a tightening of Japanese immigration policy in 1989, and as part of the crackdown on group smuggling authorities subsequently designated and deported 82 percent of the arrivals as economic migrants (Komai, 1995: 177–86; Herbert, 1996: 126–27; Friman 2002).

Discourse over the group smuggling that emerged during the 1990s posited a new challenge from the Snakehead network. Yet the multiple networks at play revealed a greater complexity. Chinese unable to afford fees and commissions of high-end brokers for legitimate or altered visas and other travel documents turned to smuggling networks dedicated to clandestinely moving migrants across borders. Bangtu Mo (1997, 1998) traces multiple paths used by smugglers to move migrants from Fujian to Japan. During the early 1990s, one path combined boats from Fujian to Hong Kong and/or Taiwan, cargo ships to Ishigaki Island, air travel to Okinawa, and air travel with false documents to Tokyo and Osaka blending into the stream of Taiwanese tourist traffic. Rural Chinese unable to afford this route turned to networks offering more direct and risky passage from Fujian to Japan. Cargo ships and fishing vessels would offload migrants into smaller boats that would then land them along deserted areas of the Japanese coast or near smaller ports. As botched landings in the early 1990s increased the awareness of Japanese authorities of this path, interdictions began to increase. By 1998, as Japanese authorities were focusing their efforts on fishing boats and isolated coastal areas, they soon discovered that smuggling networks had adopted a new tack of using container and cargo ships to move large groups of migrants directly into the major ports of Tokyo and Yokohama. As authorities shifted focus to container ships, smugglers diversified further, combining new transshipment routes including movement through Russian ports with large- and small-scale smuggling by sea (see discussion in Friman, 2002).

The Japanese focus on group smuggling contributed to a decline in the practice. Table 13.1 illustrates the decrease in smuggling incidents following the peak in 1998. By 2005, total apprehensions linked to group smuggling incidents had dropped to pre-1992 levels. During the late 1990s, the scale of group

Table 13.1 Group Smuggling Incidents and Apprehensions,
Total and Chinese, 1990–2006

Year	Incidents	Total Apprehensions	Chinese	CA/T
1990	1	18	18	100.0
1991	4	89	89	100.0
1992	14	396	383	96.7
1993	7	335	329	98.2
1994	13	467	360	77.1
1995	13	324	151	46.6
1996	29	679	542	79.8
1997	73	1,360	1,209	88.9
1998	64	1,023	824	80.5
1999	44	770	701	91.0
2000	21	103	80	77.7
2001	43	419	349	83.3
2002	25	170	168	98.8
2003	26	139	108	77.7
2004	16	44	28	63.6
2005	11	26	21	80.8
2006	10	28	18	64.3

Source: National Police Agency (1999: 10; 2002: 293; 2007: sec. 1: 33);
Immigration Bureau (2006a: 47–49).
   Note: CA/T = Chinese apprehensions as percentage of total.

smuggling had prompted the Japanese government to engage in discussions
with Chinese officials over possible responses including the use of collective
deportations. From 2000 to 2003, the Japanese government conducted nine
such deportations, returning a total of 825 Chinese to the mainland. By 2004,
however, the "small number of collective stowaway cases" had led the Japanese government to discontinue the practice (National Police Agency, 2000:
94; Immigration Bureau, 2005c: 65; Immigration Bureau 2008a: 43).

   Although group smuggling incidents had dramatically ebbed, Table 13.2
reveals that illegal entries continued to increase through the mid-2000s. Chinese migrants constituted the largest group of those identified, accounting for
42.8 percent at the peak of Japanese government deportation for such entries
in 2005 (Immigration Bureau 2008a: 33). Table 13.3 suggests that the path of
choice for Chinese illegal entry also began to shift during this period. Chinese
migrants continued to seek illegal entry by sea into Japan. However, they constituted a steadily declining percentage of migrants choosing this path, from
79.4 percent of illegal entrants in 1997 to 59.6 percent in 2007. In contrast,

Table 13.2 Deportations for Illegal Entry and Landing, Total and Chinese, 1997–2007

Year	Total Entries	CE	CE/T	Total Landings	CL	CL/T
1997	7,117	3,045	42.8	776	—	—
1998	7,472	2,718	36.4	719	256	35.6
1999	9,337	3,511	37.6	831	344	41.4
2000	9,186	2,580	28.1	748	394	52.7
2001	8,952	3,032	33.9	826	489	59.2
2002	8,388	3,041	36.3	789	408	51.7
2003	9,251	4,077	44.1	777	390	50.2
2004	11,217	4,588	40.9	992	432	43.6
2005	11,586	4,960	42.8	690	374	54.2
2006	10,441	3,999	38.3	506	231	45.7
2007	7,454	2,410	32.3	342	137	40.1

Source: Immigration Bureau (2000: fig. 10; 2003: 52–56; 2005c: 50–52; 2008a: 33–34; 2008b: sec. 1: 33–35); Japan Immigration Association (2001: 77–78; 2002: 44–45, 66–68).

Notes: Illegal entry refers to entering Japan's territory without a valid passport or visa. Illegal landing refers to landing without permission from an immigration inspector (Immigration Bureau 2006a: 47, 49). CE = Chinese entries; CE/T = Chinese entries as percentage of total; CL = Chinese landings; CL/T = Chinese landings as percentage of total.

Table 13.3 Deportations by Path of Illegal Entry, Total and Chinese, 1997–2007

Year	Entry by Air			Entry by Sea		
	Total	Chinese	C/TA	Total	Chinese	C/TS
1997	4,382	874	20.0	2,735	2,171	79.4
1998	4,916	886	18.0	2,556	1,832	71.7
1999	6,281	1,220	19.4	3,056	2,291	75.0
2000	6,828	1,190	17.4	2,358	1,390	60.0
2001	6,299	1,405	22.3	2,653	1,627	61.3
2002	6,201	1,636	26.4	2,187	1,405	64.2
2003	6,694	1,317	19.7	2,557	1,760	68.8
2004	7,848	2,295	29.2	3,369	2,293	68.1
2005	8,065	2,570	31.9	3,521	2,390	67.9
2006	7,549	2,088	27.7	2,892	1,911	66.1
2007	5,448	1,215	22.3	2,006	1,195	59.6

Source: Immigration Bureau (2005c: 5–52; 2008a: 33–34; 2008b: 35); Japan Immigration Association (2001: 77–78; 2002: 44–45, 67–68).

Note: C/TA = Chinese entries as a percentage of the total entries by air; C/TS = Chinese entries as a percentage of the total entries by sea.

Chinese migrants began to account for an increasing portion of those seeking illegal entry by air, increasing from 20.0 percent of those deported for such entry in 1997 to a peak of 31.9 percent in 2005. Chinese migrants also constituted the single largest group of those deported for illegal landing—landing without the permission of an immigration inspector. Table 13.2 illustrates that the number of Chinese deported for illegal landing peaked in 2001, with Chinese migrants constituting 52.9 percent of those deported.

By the mid-2000s immigration officials increasingly pointed to the growing challenge of smuggling networks using document fraud to facilitate illegal entry (Immigration Bureau, 2005a: chart 2). Smuggling networks offered migrants stolen and fraudulent documents, ranging from Japanese and Taiwanese passports, identity cards, and visas to Chinese government certificates of kinship and Japanese family registration records used to prove "war orphan" status (Friman, 2002: 21–23). By 2007, snakehead smuggling networks appeared to have combined document fraud and "low cost aviation" to leave the days of smuggling by sea behind, as Japan began to emerge more as a transshipment point for migrant smuggling into the United States or the European Union than as a preferred final destination (e.g., Lintner, 2007).

Despite multiple paths into Japan and the potential pool of Chinese migrants, the numbers of Chinese illegally entering the country appear small relative to smuggling patterns faced by other advanced industrial democracies discussed in this volume. During the mid-1990s, Japanese immigration officials posited that interdiction efforts targeted at group smuggling were accounting for roughly 10 percent of illegal entries into the country. At peak, this would have raised the prospect of over twelve thousand Chinese smuggled in large groups into Japan. References to this percentage became a recurrent theme during discussions over further immigration controls in the spring of 1997, despite the absence of what would have been the readily observable presence of such a population surge (e.g., *Asahi Evening News*, October 5, 1997).

Chinese migrants legally entering the country—under tourist, trainee, student, and other categories—and overstaying their visas were a larger source of illegal presence in Japan. The estimated annual number of Chinese overstayers increased from 17,535 in 1991 to a peak of 39,738 persons in 1994. By the end of the decade, the estimates of Chinese overstayers had fallen to 34,800. The estimated number of overstayers from Taiwan, which potentially included Chinese working with smuggling networks as discussed above, increased from 5,241 in 1991 to 9,437 during the same period. However the combined Chinese and Taiwanese figures still paled in comparison with the peak of 298,646 total overstayers mid-decade and the larger estimated presence of Koreans and Filipinos (Tsuda and Cornelius, 2004: 442–43). From 2000 to 2008, annual estimates of Chinese overstayers continued to fall, from a peak of 33,522 in 2004 to 25,057 in 2008. The number of Taiwanese overstayers steadily decreased to 6,031. Japanese government estimates of the total numbers of overstayers declined from 251,697 in January 2000 to 149,785 persons in January 2008. Chinese surpassed Filipino migrants as the second-largest group of overstayers during this period—a shift reinforced by declining Filipino migration under stricter entertainment visa provisions introduced by Japan in response to international pressure to curtail human trafficking (Immigration Bureau, 2008a: 30).

Overstay remains the largest category of deportations for violation of Japan's Immigration Control Act, overlapping extensively with cases of illegal work. In 2003, Chinese migrants surpassed Koreans for the top spot in deportations for illegal work violations as well as in deportations for overstay and overall violations of the Immigration Control Act (Immigration Bureau, 2006a: 46, 58). In contrast to overstay estimates, figures on deportation procedures reflect patterns of Japanese enforcement and thus may not be the most accurate representation of actual patterns of illegal work. More important, although overstay figures suggest a linkage to smuggling networks, the multifaceted nature of Japanese labor markets and the role of individual companies of various sizes, native and foreign labor brokers, and organized crime groups make a direct connection difficult.

Crime by Chinese

During early 1997, in the midst of the surge in migrant smuggling incidents of Chinese and fears of a Chinese crime wave, the chief of the Investigation Bureau of the NPA, Higuchi Tateshi, observed that "Japanese society is completely unprepared for these people" (WuDunn, 1997). However, part of the difficulty in preparation lies in the tendency of enforcement agencies and, in turn, the Japanese media to overstate the criminal propensity of foreigners. In the mid-1990s, reports of crime by Chinese began to replace the high-profile stories of unemployed Iranians waylaying young, diet-obsessed Japanese schoolgirls to sell them methamphetamine (e.g., *Daily Yomiuri*, May 21, 1996; Friman, 1996: 974–75; *Mainichi Daily News*, November 3, 1996; Schreiber, 1997: 83–84). As Sugita Kazuhiro, head of the NPA's Security Bureau, noted in early 1997, "Crimes by Chinese syndicates have had a serious impact on Japan's security. It is imperative to arrest would-be illegal immigrants" ("National Police Agency and Maritime Safety Agency Hold Discussion," 1997). The director general of the MSA, Muto Kabun, argued further that "it is true that [illegal Chinese migrants] have brought narcotics into the nation or forged pachinko pre-paid cards, jeopardizing peace and order in Japan" ("National Police Agency to Dispatch Officials," 1997).

The most common statement by government officials, pundits, and the media was that Chinese committed more than 40 percent of crimes by foreigners but constituted only 16 percent of foreigners in Japan. The statement often glossed over the distinction between legal foreign visitors, illegal foreign visitors, and total numbers of foreigners, including permanent foreign resident Koreans and Chinese living in Japan (Mori, 1997: 136; Sassen, 1998: 65). The still rarer observation was to place these figures in the broader context of total crime statistics of the time, in which "only about one percent of all crimes in Japan are committed by non-Japanese" (*Daily Yomiuri*, February 27, 1997; "Inside Story of 'Chinese Mafia,'" 1997; WuDunn, 1997, quote).

Statistics on crime by foreigners can be shaped by a number of factors beyond the scope of this chapter, including potential bias in enforcement patterns, the nature of crime reporting by victims, and discretionary steps by street-level enforcement agents (Herbert, 1996; see also Friman, 1996). Other practices that can overstate crime patterns are the tendency of the police to arrest and rearrest a single individual for multiple crimes and to compare the foreign visitor population (overwhelmingly male and in prime working age) to the full Japanese population (male, female, and elderly) (e.g., National Police Agency, 1997: 113–14). These caveats aside, the presentation of criminal statistics plays an essential role in shaping public and governmental concerns over migrant smuggling. More important, this presentation has overstated the Snakehead threat.

Japanese criminal statistics are divided into two broad categories: penal code violations and special law violations. Penal code offenses include felonies, violent offenses, and larceny; special law offenses include issues such as drug crimes, prostitution, and immigration regulations. Penal law data have played the central role in the broader debate over crime by foreigners, though references to specific categories of special law violations such as drug crimes also garner attention. The 40 percent figure of crimes by visiting Chinese reflects penal code violations, though media reports during the 1990s often glossed over this distinction (e.g., *Japan Times*, October 18, 1997). Statistics published in the annual *White Paper on Police* and repeated in the media also are presented in a compartmentalized manner. Separate sections on crimes by foreigners do not compare their offenses with the total number of penal and special law violations. More important, the published statistics in the white papers on specific types of penal or special law offenses make no distinction according to legality of immigration status. In contrast, since the mid-2000s, the English-language overview *Crimes in Japan,* edited by the Police Policy Research Center and available on the National Police Agency Web site, has offered brief discussions of arrests by visa status (e.g., National Police Academy, 2006: 24; Police Policy Research Center, 2008: 37).

The statistics presented in Table 13.4 illustrate arrests for penal code violations, broken down by total arrests and arrests of visiting foreigners and visiting Chinese. Chinese have been the leading foreign violators of Japan's penal code, followed by Koreans (North and South) and a shifting mix of other groups including Iranians, Filipinos, Americans, Peruvians, Vietnamese, Brazilians, and Russians. For Japanese enforcement officials, the upturn in the raw numbers and percentage of Chinese violations beginning in 1993 (see Table 13.4) and the increase in migrant smuggling incidents (see Table 13.1) supported the linkage between illegal migrants and crime. However, the figures behind such a linkage are problematic. The category of Chinese migrants in Table 13.1, for example, refers to persons from the People's Republic. The category of Chinese offenders in Table 13.4, in contrast, has been inconsistent in its inclusion of nonmainland Chinese. Moreover, the figures in Table 13.4 reveal nothing as to whether these Chinese violators, regardless of specific area of origin, were legal foreign visitors, visa overstayers, or members of groups of smuggled into Japan. During the 1990s, all Chinese crime became Snakehead related in the public discourse.

Table 13.4 reveals nothing about the specific types of penal code violations committed by the Chinese. To make more specific claims, enforcement agencies and the media have selectively turned to reporting categories of offenses such as robbery and burglary, stressing the relative propensity of foreigners to commit crimes in groups, and high-profile incidents of violent offenses. During the 1990s, enforcement officials argued that the primary crimes committed by Chinese were larceny offenses in support of the view that Chinese migrants illegally in Japan were turning to crime to meet financial obligations to their Snakehead smugglers. As argued a decade later by the National Police Academy Policy (2006: 25), Chinese migrants "remained the highest percentage of offenders," accounting for 36.9 percent of robbery offenses by visiting foreigners and 65.7 percent of burglary offenses. Yet without direct comparisons of Chinese offenses with total offenses for specific penal code violations, these figures reveal little of the challenge posed. For example, Table 13.5 combines

Table 13.4   Penal Code Violations: Total Arrests and Arrests of Visiting
Foreigners and Chinese, 1990–2007

Year	Total Arrests	Visiting Foreigners		Chinese		
		Total	VF/TA	Total	C/VF	C/TA
1990	293,992	2,978	1.0	1,288	43.3	0.4
1991	296,158	4,813	1.6	1,732	36.0	0.6
1992	284,908	5,961	2.1	1,933	32.4	0.7
1993	297,725	7,276	2.4	2,668	36.7	0.9
1994	307,963	6,989	2.3	2,942	42.1	1.0
1995	293,252	6,527	2.2	2,919	44.7	1.0
1996	295,584	6,026	2.0	2,661	44.2	0.9
1997	313,573	5,435	1.7	2,320	42.7	0.7
1998	324,263	5,382	1.7	2,281	42.4	0.7
1999	315,355	5,963	1.9	2,721	45.6	0.9
2000	309,649	6,329	2.0	3,038	48.0	1.0
2001	325,292	7,168	2.2	3,232	45.1	1.0
2002	347,558	7,690	2.2	3,632	47.2	1.1
2003	379,602	8,725	2.3	4,554	52.2	1.2
2004	389,027	8,898	2.3	4,408	49.5	1.1
2005	386,955	8,505	2.2	3,742	44.0	1.0
2006	384,250	8,148	2.1	3,452	42.4	1.0
2007	365,577	7,528	2.1	2,899	38.5	1.0

Source: National Police Agency (1994: app. table 3-5; 1996: table 8-2, app. table 3-5; 1998b: table 9-2; 2002: 19, 288, 361; 2005: 538–39; 2006: table 3-13, app. table 2-6; 2007: sec. 1: 17; 2008: sec. 1: 2); National Police Academy (2006: 24).

   Note: VF/TA = visiting foreigners as a percentage of total arrests; C/VF = Chinese as a percentage of visiting foreigners; C/TA = Chinese as a percentage of total arrests.

statistics from data typically presented separately to reveal the relatively low proportion of visiting foreigners and specifically visiting Chinese arrested for selected penal code offenses in 1997 and 2007. Although Chinese remain a prominent component of the category of offenses by visiting foreigners, when viewed in the context of total arrests in Japan, Chinese migrants have consistently accounted for roughly 1 percent of the country's felonies and larcenies. The figures for violent offenses are lower while arrests for intellectual offenses are slightly higher.

   The second piece of the argument during the 1990s on the relative criminal propensity of Chinese among foreign visitors also is suspect. In addition to conflating all Chinese into one nationality category, estimates of the visiting foreigner population tend to be calculated from official figures on those legally

Table 13.5 Arrests for Selected Penal Code Offenses: Total Arrests, Arrests of Visiting Foreigners, Chinese, 1997, 2007

	Total	Visiting Foreigners		Chinese		
		Total	VF/T	Total	C/VF	C/T
Felonies						
1997	6,663	213	3.2	66	31.0	1.0
2007	5,923	259	4.4	79	30.5	1.3
Violent offenses						
1997	40,432	313	1.0	64	20.5	0.02
2007	54,163	961	1.8	243	25.3	0.05
Larceny						
1997	175,632	3,155	1.8	1,447	45.9	1.0
2007	180,446	3,755	2.1	1,526	40.6	1.0
Intellectual offenses						
1997	11,639	305	2.6	147	48.2	1.3
2007	15,264	536	3.5	265	49.4	1.7

Source: National Police Agency (1998a: 1; 2008: sec. 1: 17); Police Policy Research Center (2008: 53).
Notes: The category of felonies includes murder, robbery, arson, rape; violent offenses include assault and bodily injury; larceny includes burglary and nonburglary theft and vehicle theft; intellectual offenses include fraud, embezzlement, and counterfeiting. VF/T = visiting foreigners as a percentage of the total; C/VF = Chinese as a percentage of visiting foreigners; C/T = Chinese as a percentage of the total.

in Japan as collected under Japan's alien registration law. These figures do not include illegal entrants such as Chinese brought in through migrant smuggling operations. As a result, the foreign visitor population and the Chinese percentage of this population are understated in official figures. In contrast, the relative criminality of foreigners is overstated by including those foreigners who by virtue of their illegal entry are not captured in official immigration statistics but are arrested for penal code violations.

Clearly, there are Chinese migrants that are in Japan illegally, and some of them engage in criminal activity beyond that linked to path of entry and immigration status. At times this activity also has been heinous, ranging from the violence of Chinese organized crime groups operating in entertainment districts such as the Kabukicho area in Tokyo to high-profile murder cases (Friman, 1999; *Japan Times*, September 21, 2003; *Japan Today*, October 2, 2003; Kaplan and Dubro 2003: 273–76). However, arguments drawing on such incidents and selective crime statistics to posit a broader Chinese threat to social order do not offer an accurate portrayal of either migrant smuggling or crime.

Sources of the Snakehead Threat

Efforts to explain migration dynamics commonly explore an array of possible push and pull effects. The discussion of migrant smuggling in Japan has emphasized the push effects of economic and political uncertainty in China and the presence of organized smuggling networks controlled by Chinese organized crime. To a lesser extent these discussions also have addressed the pull effects of relative Japanese economic prosperity, lax security, and domestic Chinese affiliates of the Snakehead network. However, other pull effects such as Japan's demand for low-skilled labor and the growing interest of Japanese organized crime in the financial gains from migrant smuggling have attracted less attention.

Labor Demand and Paths of Access

Although Japan's demand for unskilled labor has been a major theme in the broader discussions of immigration, the ramifications of this demand for migrant smuggling remain underexplored. Scholarship on Japanese demand patterns commonly points to needs generated by the construction, manufacturing, and service sectors. These dynamics have combined with declining Japanese birthrates, a limiting socioeconomic structure regarding women and elderly in the workplace, labor market inefficiencies shaping employment practices in the service sector, and a general aversion of younger Japanese to unskilled, labor-intensive jobs (e.g., Shimada, 1994; Tsuda and Cornelius, 2004). Though faced with rising demand, employers lacked the legal framework for recruiting unskilled labor through the front door of Japanese immigration regulations. In brief, the import of unskilled workers was prohibited. As a result, employers turned to a number of side and back doors or indirectly explored these options by working through layers of subcontractor cutouts.

Access patterns for unskilled foreign workers into Japan have varied by country of origin. Through the early 1990s, migrants from countries such as Bangladesh, Pakistan, and Iran could draw on labor brokers at home and in Japan to take advantage of visa-exemption accords negotiated during the 1970s. These migrants would gain access into Japan as tourists but would engage in illegal work and overstay their visas (Mori, 1997). Lacking the option of exploiting similar visa-exemption accords, mainland Chinese migrants sought access to Japan through paths such as admission to Japanese language and vocational schools (e.g., Friman, 1996: 969; Herbert, 1996: 107–16; Mori, 1997: 22;

Friman 2002). Japanese regulations on such schools—and the outside work prohibitions on students attending them—had eased during the mid-1980s as part of the Nakasone administration's pledge to educate 100,000 students by the year 2000. New mainland Chinese entrants surged through this side door into the Japanese labor market. The mainland students were typically from Fujian Province, mid- to late twenties in age, and 50 to 60 percent male. Their numbers increased from 113 new Chinese students in 1982 to 7,178 in 1987, and 28,256 by 1988, the last figure constituting roughly 74 percent of all entrants through this category into Japan (Herbert, 1996).

In response to growing evidence of language schools serving primarily as side doors into the unskilled labor market, however, Japanese authorities slowly began to impose new regulations. These steps included new visa provisions in 1989 requiring proof of a financial guarantor and new restrictions in 1990 reducing the maximum allowable outside work by students to twenty hours per week. Seeking to offset these changes, brokerage agencies emerged in China and Japan offering potential students fraudulent documents of financial support and proof of acceptance from a Japanese language school. However, even tighter regulations through the mid-1990s and the ebb and flow of post-Tiananmen emigration provisions decreased the accessibility of the student path into Japan. By 1989, new Chinese students entering Japan had dropped to 9,142, roughly half of the total number of entrants. In 1992, new Chinese students increased to 16,265 out of a total of 27,000 students. By 1996, however, these numbers had fallen dramatically as only 2,567 new Chinese students, roughly 30 percent of the total foreign students, entered Japan on the precollege student visa (Herbert, 1996: 107–16).

The concurrent decline in entries by Chinese into Japan through student visas and the rise of migration through smuggling incidents suggested that the latter emerged, in part, as a replacement path into the Japanese labor market. Given economic conditions in Japan, this argument of a pull effect initially appears unconvincing. The collapse of the bubble economy and Japan's economic recession of the mid-1990s adversely affected employment opportunities, especially for illegal labor (Mori, 1997: 74, 76–77). In addition, illegal workers were displaced by the 1990 Immigration Act's provisions for side-door access by *nikkeijin,* unskilled, primarily Latin American labor of Japanese descent (e.g., Shimada, 1994; Mori, 1997: 10; Sassen, 1998: 60–62).

However, though well short of full employment conditions, demand for unskilled Chinese workers still existed in Japan. As larger firms turned to meeting labor needs through the *nikkeijin,* medium and especially smaller firms essentially were priced out of the legal unskilled labor market. Migrants from Asia offered such firms both a cheaper alternative to the *nikkeijin* and a labor force better able—than Iranians, for example—to pass cursory inspections by immigration authorities (Mori, 1997: 63–65, 112). Opportunities for Chinese workers also arose in the context of the post–Kobe earthquake reconstruction projects and the extensive work required for the Nagano Winter Olympics. Contractors interviewed in Nagano in early 1998, for example, noted that they did not want to use Chinese illegally in the country but had "no choice" given the labor needs. The source of the Chinese, according to media reports, appeared to be linked with snakehead smuggling networks. The Nagano incident also revealed, however, that although opportunities for Chinese illegally in the country exist they could be fleeting. Following the completion of the Olympic construction projects in 1997 and through 1998, police and immigration officials waged a large-scale crackdown on migrants in the Nagano area designated Operation White Snow (*Japan Times,* February 4, 1998; *Mainichi Daily News,* January 25, 1998).

Despite the ebb and flow of immigration crackdowns, multiple side doors into labor markets continue to exist for Chinese migration. For example, the number of new entrants into Japan on precollege visas began to recover during the mid-1990s. In 2003, precollege entrants increased to over 27,362 persons, only to drop to 15,027 with a renewed crackdown on illegal migration in 2004. Mainland Chinese constituted the single largest source of the increase as well as the fall. In 2003, new precollege entrants from China had increased to 19,337 persons only to drop dramatically to 5,705 in 2004. (Friman, 2002: 17; Immigration Bureau, 2006a: 7, 18). The number of entrants began to recover in 2005 to 8,938 and increased in 2006 to 9,543 before leveling off at 8,987 in 2007 (Immigration Bureau, 2008a: 12). Company trainee visas also have emerged as an alternative path for Chinese migrants seeking side-door access to Japan's labor market (e.g., Brasor, 2007). Following a steady increase during the 1980s to under 4,000 new entrants annually, the numbers expanded extensively during the 1990s. By the end of the decade the number of Chinese trainees had increased to over 22,000 persons, a figure greater than that from the next five largest source countries combined (Mori, 1997: 117; Friman, 2002: 17–19). New entrants under the trainee program continued to increase during the 2000s. In 2005, Japan accepted over 83,319 new entrants, of which 55,156 were from China (Immigration Bureau, 2006a: 7, 16). During 2007,

Japan accepted 96,807 entrants, of which 68,188 were from China (Immigration Bureau, 2008a: 10).

The Yakuza and Migrant Smuggling

During the 1990s Japanese authorities increasingly acknowledged the growing role of the *yakuza* in alien smuggling as part of a larger trend toward linkages between foreign and domestic organized crime groups. Police arrest reports and subsequent media stories noted instances of the *yakuza* affiliation of Japanese arrested in conjunction with migrant smuggling incidents. These reports revealed the participation of members of minor organized crime groups as well as affiliates of the major syndicates such as the Yamaguchi-gumi (*Daily Yomiuri*, June 15, 1997; *Japan Times*, February 7, 1997; National Police Agency, 1997). The most common explanation for why the *yakuza* might be participating in the migrant trade was economic. The collapse of the bubble economy adversely affected illicit operations as well as organized crime's incursion into the stock and real estate markets often termed the expansion of the economic, or *keizai yakuza* (Kaplan and Dubro, 2003: 175–204). Less attention in the public debate was focused on the longer history of organized crime's participation in labor brokering and its increased reliance on brokering as an unintended impact of legislation seeking to curtail organized crime.

For all the images of corporate networks, intensive education, and lifetime employment that dominate the public perception of Japan, unskilled labor has remained an essential part of the Japanese economy. Major Japanese cities all contain day laborer settlements with long histories, such as Kotobuki in Yokohama, Kamagasaki in Osaka, and Sanya in Tokyo. Labor brokers with ties to state employment offices or illegal, private networks link unskilled day laborers with construction and other jobs (Komai, 1995: 142–43; Fowler, 1996: 35–40; Stevens, 1997: 22, 26, 28). The *yakuza* have played an integral role in the construction industry as well as the day laborer areas, brokering labor supplies, running protection, drug, and gambling operations, and serving as a check on freelance crime. In some areas, the *yakuza* also have served as a check, implicitly state supported, on union organizing among day labors. In others, the *yakuza* have been less successful, with union conflicts erupting into full-scale violence (Fowler, 1996: 20–25).

By the mid-1980s, *yakuza* brokering of labor was still focused primarily on Japanese workers. Even as illegal foreign workers began to settle in and around the day laborer areas, Ministry of Justice figures estimated that only 14 percent of foreigners were being brokered by the *yakuza* (Herbert, 1996: 64, 79–84). The reason for the limited involvement was primarily based on cost considerations relative to other sources of income. For example, Wolfgang Herbert (1996: 65) notes a 1989 interview with a Yamaguchi-gumi lawyer who observed that "recruiting male migrant workers and acting as agent for them is not seen as being lucrative enough to warrant large-scale *yakuza* involvement." The one exception to this pattern of involvement with foreigners was with female migrants and a shift earlier in the decade in the entertainment/sex industry. During the 1970s, the *yakuza* played an integral role in facilitating the sex tourism business from Japan into East and Southeast Asia. By the early 1980s, faced with growing protest in the host countries, the *yakuza* shifted focus toward smuggling and trafficking women from the Philippines, Thailand, and other countries into the lucrative Japanese sex industry (e.g., Herbert, 1996: 28–29; Sellek, 1996: 159–75; Kaplan and Dubro, 2003: 233–43).

By the mid-1990s, however, the *yakuza* interest in male migrant labor had changed. According to Raisuke Miyawaki (1997), a former NPA official in charge of organized crime operations, the *yakuza* began to shift activities into a number of new areas with the collapse of the bubble economy, including "smuggling illegal aliens into the country." One sign of the competitive shift into migrant smuggling, according to police analysts, was that contending *yakuza* groups were even accepting smaller profit percentages from their Chinese counterparts. They were settling for 20 percent rather than a 50 percent share, which had distinguished earlier efforts at *yakuza* participation (e.g., *Daily Yomiuri*, January 21, 1997; *Japan Times*, February 7, 1997; see also Kaplan and Dubro, 2003: 273–74). Yet the reasons for the shift were not solely tied to changing economic circumstances.

The Anti–Organized Crime Law of 1992 increased the means by which Japanese authorities were able to interfere in the activities of organized crime groups, including protection rackets and gang-owned or operated establishments (Kaplan, 1996; Friman 1999; Hill, 2003). Subject to increased monitoring and declining revenues, membership in the *yakuza* began to fall. Organized crime groups turned to consolidation efforts to stem their losses, and violent conflicts erupted between and within syndicates over possible dissolution of affiliates, protecting established revenue sources, and capturing new areas of expansion.

By August 1997, these tensions had erupted into gangland-style slayings and broader gang warfare in cities including Kobe, Osaka, and Tokyo (e.g., *Asahi Evening News*, September 3, 1997; *Daily Yomiuri*, August 29, 1997; *Mainichi Daily News*, August 30, 1997). The wave of retaliatory shootings and firebombings prompted police crackdowns and the accelerated introduction of new anti-gang legislation that included measures to increase police powers under the Japanese criminal code, further adding to pressure on the *yakuza* (e.g., *Japan Times*, October 1, 1997; *Mainichi Daily News*, September 9, 1997; Hill, 2003: 137–76, 237–38). In this context, Japanese organized crime groups moved further underground. Some groups increased their willingness to subcontract higher-profile operations—such as street-level drug trafficking—to foreigners (Friman, 2004). More important, syndicates and lower-level affiliates turned their efforts to expanding less traditional sources of revenue, including cooperation with migrant smuggling networks (e.g., *Japan Times*, February 7, 1997).

The Construction of the Snakehead Threat

The selective presentation of smuggling and crime data and the relative absence of discussions of the impact of Japanese labor demand and government anticrime campaigns lead to the question of why these pieces have been missing from the discussion of the threat posed by migrant smuggling. The remainder of the chapter turns to the enforcement agencies that have played a central role in defining this issue, offering the primary information as to the extent of migrant smuggling, its ramifications, and its sources. One possible explanation for the absence of a more nuanced exploration of migrant smuggling lies in the simple, narrow self-interest of state enforcement agencies in Japan's postbubble economy. A second, broader explanation lies in constructed norms concerning the sources of social order in Japan and the place of enforcement agencies in defending that order.

Self-Interest

As argued by Masao Miyamoto (1994: 79–80), conflict over scarce economic resources and influence during the 1990s was extensive between and within the Japanese ministries. To obtain leverage, bureaucrats provide information to the media, knowing full well the media's reliance on the ministries for access to information and the media's tendency to oversell issues or threats to the public to enhance readership. The information can be leaked or provided through official reports written for public distribution. As the information from official sources generates "public concern" (demonstrated in the media headlines and reports and subsequent public reaction), the ministry, bureau, or section can point to this concern as justification for greater financial and staff resources (see Van Wolferen, 1993: 130, 305).

With the collapse of the bubble economy, Japanese ministries soon faced extensive economic pressures. In addition to falling revenue allocations from the Ministry of Finance, ministries were confronted with external as well as internal demands for reorganization as a means to decrease financial and staff requirements. That Japanese enforcement agencies in this context turned to stressing the criminal threats posed by the late 1980s wave of immigration has not gone unnoticed. Herbert (1996: 175) argues that "for the agencies of control themselves and for the framers of criminal policy, the postulation of rising crime rates [by foreigners] serves to legitimize demands for more financial resources and staff in the sector 'internal security.'" Such arguments, raised in the context of public concern with the threat of crime by foreigners, have been successful in generating support from the Ministry of Finance. This support has facilitated the expansion of the enforcement bureaucracy with staff allocations, new departments, new task forces, and crime-fighting equipment and training (e.g., author interviews with enforcement officials, 1995; National Police Agency, 1999: 13; *Daily Yomiuri*, July 16, August 27, 2001; *Asahi Shimbun*, August 27, 2003).

The narrow self-interest of enforcement agencies helps to explain the construction of the issue of migrant smuggling. The picture of a single Snakehead organization, directed by Chinese affiliated with the infamous crime groups, smuggling crime-prone Chinese migrants into Japan is threatening. The picture is clearly more threatening than if enforcement agencies posed the existence of multiple smuggling networks, migrants illegally in Japan but who are not prone to engage in additional criminal behavior, the culpability of Japanese employers, and the unintended results of anti–organized crime legislation on the *yakuza*. Moreover, the enforcement bureaucracy has benefited from the Snakehead threat. MSA, immigration, and national and prefectural police officials have obtained support for new personnel, task forces and operations, foreign travel, and enhanced criminal penalties to respond to the threat of alien smuggling and related crime (e.g., *Daily Yomiuri*, February 26, 1997, March 5, 1997, January 27, 1998; *Japan Times*, September 15, 2001, September 23, 2003, December 3, 2005; Immigration Bureau, 2005a: pt. III, sec. 2).

Homogeneity Myths and Social Order

To attribute the absence of the more nuanced conceptualization of Chinese migrant smuggling and its sources to the narrow self-interest of enforcement agencies for increased resources, however, would be misleading. Scholarship on Japan as well as interviews of national- and prefectural-level police officials over the past several years on questions of foreigners and crime suggest a more complex process at work. In his analysis of Japanese security issues, Peter Katzenstein (1996: 19, 22) argues for a focus on the "politically contested," constitutive norms that "express actor identities" and help to "define . . . and thus shape behavior." Perhaps the most pervasive constitutive norm in Japan is that of collective identity, conceptualized as Japan as a homogeneous country with the primary sources of its domestic social order deriving from this homogeneity (Yoshino, 1992).

Clearly, though less diverse than other advanced industrial democracies, Japan is not homogeneous, nor has it ever really been. The homogeneity myth, stridently promoted in the late 1800s and early 1900s, has recast, discounted, or simply ignored portions of Japan's history. These portions include the migrations that shaped the country's origins and the forced migration of Koreans and Chinese earlier in the century. They also include the postwar compromises that shaped the rise of a permanent foreign resident population and, in turn, the impact of the most recent waves of immigration of the 1980s and 1990s (e.g., Smith, 1995: 181–207; Hingwan, 1996: 52–53; Morris-Suzuki, 1998: 79–109). However, despite growing local efforts at greater integration of immigrants into Japanese society, the constitutive norm of Japan as a homogeneous country—especially the belief that this collective identity facilitates social order—is institutionalized and still carries weight.

This is particularly the case within the more conservative state agencies that constitute Japan's enforcement bureaucracy. For enforcement officials, immigration, especially the uncontrolled nature of illegal migration, poses a threat to the country's homogeneity and, in turn, the heart of Japan's social order. As observed by one immigration official, Yamanaka Masanori, illegal migrants "come to Japan through the black market, ignoring the system of immigration control, so this problem shakes the very foundation of the Japanese government" (WuDunn, 1997; also see Herbert, 1996). The Japanese police have always had difficulty in dealing with the country's minority populations. By the mid-1990s these difficulties had increased with new languages and the wider cultural diversity of the immigrant population. Where the police would often seek to hold immigration officials accountable for the access of illegal workers through violations of the country's visa system, the rise in migrant smuggling incidents bypassed the immigration control process entirely and posed additional challenges and responsibilities for the police. The prominence in these incidents of mainland Chinese, who were already a source of concern for the police and the *yakuza* alike in major cities such as Tokyo, added to the problem (e.g., Friman, 1999).

In short, operating under the linkage between homogeneity and social order, Japanese enforcement officials have perceived illegal migration by Chinese as a disproportionate criminal threat. They view the very dynamic of migrant smuggling as driven more by external than internal dynamics and more by organized Chinese gangs than by a varied array of smuggling networks. In addition, enforcement officials have used this interpretation to seek acknowledgment of the migrant smuggling threat from the broader public and to obtain support for a more active response. By the 2000s, their efforts were magnified as politicians at multiple levels, ranging from Tokyo governor Ishihara Shintaro to Prime Minister Koizumi Junichiro, turned to the threat of crime by foreigners as an electoral and public policy issue (e.g., Debito, 2002; *Japan Times*, October 7, 2003; *Japan Today*, September 20, 2003). In this context, Immigration Bureau officials in cooperation with the Tokyo Metropolitan Police Department and the Tokyo metropolitan government turned to a new enforcement effort in December 2003 aimed at halving the number of illegal migrants in Tokyo in five years (*Japan Today*, December 30, 2003; Tsuda and Cornelius, 2004: 470–71). By 2004, the focus on reducing the number of migrants illegally in Japan was a centerpiece of a broader amendment of the Immigration Control and Refugee Recognition Act (Kashiwazaki and Akaha 2006). Arguments positing illegal migration and foreign crime as threats to social order also have been used to justify subsequent amendments in 2005 and 2006, increasing penalties and tightening controls on illegal entry of foreigners. These arguments have been interwoven with other justifications noting the need to bring Japan into compliance with international treaties such as the United Nations Transnational Organized Crime Convention's protocols on migrant smuggling and human trafficking, and to address the challenge of regional and global terrorism (Immigration Bureau, 2005b; *Japan Today*, June 14, 2005; Immigration Bureau, 2006b).

Although institutionalized in the enforcement bureaucracy, the homogeneity myth, along with its linkage to social order, is not without its critics. A growing backlash to crime-by-foreigner arguments and restrictive immigration policies has emerged in Japan from an array of societal groups and in the writings of former national and metropolitan government officials (e.g., see Shipper, 2005; Kubo, 2006; Debito, 2007; Sakanaka 2007; Yamamoto, 2007). Despite these shifts, arguments posing illegal migration and foreign crime as threats to Japan's social order remain powerful.

Economic downturns and rising unemployment stemming from the global financial crisis reaffirmed these concerns. Faced with the prospect of a growing pool of displaced foreigners and the resulting social dislocation, the Japanese government in April 2009 began to offer financial incentives to unemployed Brazilian and Peruvian *nikkeijin* willing to leave the country and never return (*Japan Times*, April 2, 2009). While legal immigrants were offered financial subsidies, illegal immigrants were met with the prospect of greater sanctions. In early March 2009, the Immigration Bureau and ruling Liberal Democratic Party introduced legislative measures into the Japanese Diet calling for greater centralization of immigration control under the Ministry of Justice replacing the role of municipalities in conducting alien registration. The purpose of this shift, as argued by its proponents, was the need to better identify and punish overstaying foreigners. In July, with provisions including a new national residency card system, a centralized personal information database for foreigners, and financial and other penalties for noncompliance, the legislation was passed by the Diet (*Japan Times*, June 26, June 27, July 9, 2009).

Conclusion

During the bubble economy of the 1980s, Japan implicitly tolerated and relied on back-door migration by male, unskilled workers. Immigration reforms in 1990 reaffirmed the country's formal opposition to such paths but introduced a series of partially regulated side doors into the labor market that allowed access by unskilled workers. By the mid-1990s, however, migrant smuggling, especially from China, had added a new dynamic to the Japanese immigration debate. Japanese enforcement authorities posited the rise of the Snakehead threat and Chinese migrants as central to the foreign crime wave threatening Japan.

This chapter has argued that while migrant smuggling and foreign crime do take place, both threats have been oversold by Japanese enforcement authorities, echoed by the media, and increasingly utilized by politicians seeking electoral support. Through the selective use of statistical data, authorities have overstated the extent and nature of migrant smuggling as well as the relative criminal propensity of Chinese migrants. Authorities also have downplayed the impact of pull effects of Japanese labor demand and the diversification of the *yakuza* in the face of anti–organized crime measures. Their reasons for doing so reflect a combination of narrow self-interest in the context of fiscal pressures on the Japanese bureaucracy and the broader belief that illegal migration poses a threat to Japan's collective identity and the all-important, and related, linkage between homogeneity and social order.

NOTE

I thank the Social Science Research Council and the Japan-U.S. Friendship Commission (Fulbright program) for their earlier financial support of the original larger project on which this revised chapter is based, and Ekuni Tomoyuki for his research assistance.

REFERENCES

Aldous, Christopher. 1997. *The Police in Occupation Japan: Control, Corruption, and Resistance to Reform.* London: Routledge.
Brasor, Philip. 2007. "Immigrant Workers in Japan Caught in a Racket." *Japan Focus,* July 8. www.japanfocus.org/-Philip-Brasor/2464.Chin, Ko-lin. 1997. "Safe House or Hell House? Experiences of Newly Arrived Undocumented Chinese." In *Human Smuggling: Chinese Migrant Trafficking and the Challenge to America's Immigration Tradition,* edited by Paul J. Smith, 169–95. Washington, D.C.: Center for Strategic and International Studies.
Debito, Arudou. 2002. "The Zeit Geist: Published Figures are Half the Story, Foreigner Crime Stats Cover up a Real Cop-Out." *Japan Times,* October 4.
———. 2007. "*Gaijin Hanzai* Magazine and Hate Speech in Japan: The Newfound Power of Japan's International Residents," *Japan Focus,* March 19. www.japanfocus.org/products/details/2386.
Fowler, Edward. 1996. *San'ya Blues: Laboring Life in Contemporary Tokyo.* Ithaca, N.Y.: Cornell University Press.
Friman, H. Richard. 1996. "Gaijinhanzai: Immigrants and Drugs in Contemporary Japan." *Asian Survey* 36 (10): 964–77.
———. 1999. "Obstructing Markets: Organized Crime and Drug Control in Japan." In *The Illicit Global Economy and State Power,* edited by H. Richard Friman and Peter Andreas, 173–97. Boulder, Colo.: Rowman and Littlefield.
———. 2002. "Evading the Divine Wind through the Side Door: The Transformation of

Chinese Migration to Japan." In *Globalizing Chinese Migration: Trends in Europe and Asia,* edited by Pal Nyri and Igor Saveliev, 9–34. Burlington, Vt.: Ashgate.

———. 2004. "The Great Escape? Globalization, Immigrant Entrepreneurship and the Criminal Economy." *Review of International Political Economy* 11 (1): 98–131.

Herbert, Wolfgang. 1996. *Foreign Workers and Law Enforcement in Japan.* London: Kegan Paul International.

Hill, Peter B. E. 2003. *The Japanese Mafia: Yakuza, Law and the State.* Oxford: Oxford University Press.

Hingwan, Kathiane. 1996. "Identity, Otherness, and Migrant Labor in Japan." In *Case Studies on Human Rights in Japan,* edited by Roger Goodman and Ian Neary, 51–75. Surrey, England: Japan Library.

Immigration Bureau, Ministry of Justice. 2000. *Basic Plan for Immigration Control.* 2nd ed. Provisional Translation. www.moj.go.jp/ENGLISH/information/bpic2nd.html.

———. 2003. *Immigration Control in Recent Years (Nyukan meguro kinen no jyoko [Shutsun-yukokokanri]).* www.moj.go.jp/NYUKAN/NYUHAKU/index.html. (Japanese)

———. 2005a. *Basic Plan for Immigration Control.* 3rd ed. Provisional Translation. www .moj.go.jp/ENGLISH/information/bpic3rd.html.

———. 2005b. *The Immigration Control and Refugee Recognition Act, FY2005 Amendment.* www.immi-moj.go.jp/keiziban/happyou/H17nanmin.pdf (accessed October 28, 2007).

———. 2005c. *Immigration Control Report 2005: Part 1: Immigration Control in Recent Years.* www.moj.go.jp/content/000007269.pdf.

———. 2006a. *Immigration Control in Recent Years: Part 1: Immigration Control in Recent Years.* www.moj.go.jp/content/000007280.pdf.

———. 2006b. Law for Partial Amendment of the Immigration Control and Refugee Recognition Act (Law No. 43 of May 24, 2006). Enacted at the 164th Diet Session. www.immi-moj.go.jp/english/keiziban/happyou/law43_20060524.pdf.

———. 2008a. *Immigration Control Report: Part 1: Immigration Control in Recent Years.* www.moj.go.jp/content/000007316.pdf.

———. 2008b. *Immigration Control White Paper (Nyukan hakusho hesei 20 nenban [Shutsu-nyukokukanri]).* www.moj.go.jp/NYUKAN/nyukan78.html. (Japanese)

"Inside Story of 'Chinese Mafia' Operating in Japan—Frightening Infiltration." 1997. *Sentaku,* U.S. Embassy, Office of Translation Services.

Japan Immigration Association. 1995. *1994 Statistics on Immigration Control.* Tokyo: Japan Immigration Association.

———. 2001. *Statistics on Immigration Control, 2000.* Tokyo: Japan Immigration Association.

———. 2002. *Statistics on Immigration Control, 2001.* Tokyo: Japan Immigration Association.

Kaplan, David. 1996. "Yakuza Laughing All the Way from the Bank." *Asahi Evening News,* February 14.

Kaplan, David E., and Alec Dubro. 2003. *Yakuza: Japan's Criminal Underworld.* Berkeley: University of California Press.

Kashiwazaki, Chikako, and Tsuneo Akaha. 2006. "Japanese Immigration Policy: Responding to Conflicting Pressures." Migration Policy Institute, Migration Information Source. November.

Katzenstein, Peter J. 1996. *Cultural Norms and National Security: Police and Military in Postwar Japan.* Ithaca, N.Y: Cornell University Press.

Komai, Hiroshi. 1995. *Migrant Workers in Japan.* Translated by Jen Wilkinson. London: Kegan Paul International.

Kubo, Hiroshi. 2006. *Is Public Safety Really Deteriorating?* [*Chian wa honto ni akka shite iru noka*]. Tokyo: Kojinsha.

Lintner, Bertil. 2007. "A How to Guide for Fleeing China." *Asia Times,* April 19.

Masao, Miyamoto. 1994. *Straitjacket Society: An Insider's Irreverent View of Bureaucratic Japan.* Tokyo: Kodansha International.

Miyawaki, Raisuke. 1997. "Underworld Protected by Discriminatory Administrative Practices: Wage All-Out War against Organized Crime!" *Ronza* (August), U.S. Embassy, Office of Translation Services, October.

Mo, Bangfu. 1997. "Jato to Kyuzyosuru Mitsukosha" (Snakehead and rapid increase in smuggled persons). *Chuo Koron* 5:52–59.

———. 1998. "The Rise of the Chinese Mafia in Japan." *Japan Echo* 25 (1): 44–47.

Mori, Hiromi. 1997. *Immigration Policy and Foreign Workers in Japan.* New York: St. Martin's.

Morris-Suzuki, Tessa. 1998. *Re-inventing Japan: Time, Space, Nation.* Armonk, N.Y.: M. E. Sharpe.

Myers, Willard H., III. 1997. "Of Qinshu, Guanxi, and Shetou: The Dynamic Elements of Chinese Irregular Population Movement." In *Human Smuggling: Chinese Migrant Trafficking and the Challenge to America's Immigration Tradition,* edited by Paul J. Smith, 93–133. Washington, D.C.: Center for Strategic and International Studies.

National Police Academy. 2006. *Crimes in Japan 2005.* Tokyo: Alumni Association for National Police Academy.

National Police Agency. 1994. *White Paper on Police [Keisatsu Hakusho, Heisei 6].* www .npa.go.jp/hakusyo/h06/h06index.html. (Japanese)

———. 1996. *White Paper on Police [Keisatsu Hakusho, Heisei 8].* www.npa.go.jp/hakusyo/ h08/h08index.html. (Japanese)

———. 1997. *White Paper on Police 1996 (Excerpt).* Tokyo: Japan Times.

———. 1998a. *Criminal Statistics in 1997 [Hanzai Tokei, Heisei 9].* Tokyo: National Police Agency.

———. 1998b. *White Paper on Police [Keisatsu Hakusho, Heisei 10].* www.npa.go.jp/hakusyo/ h10/h10index.html. (Japanese)

———. 1999. *White Paper on Police 1999 (Excerpt).* Tokyo: Police Association.

———. 2000. *White Paper on Police 2000 (Excerpt).* Tokyo: Japan Times.

———. 2002. *White Paper on Police [Keisatsu Hakusho, Heisei 14].* www.npa.go.jp/hakusyo/ h14/h14index.html. (Japanese)

———. 2005. *Crime Statistics, 2004 [Hanzai Tokei, Heisei 16].* www.npa.go.jp/toukei/ keiji25/H16_27.pdf. (Japanese)

———. 2006. *White Paper on Police [Keisatsu Hakusho, Heisei 18].* www.npa.go.jp/hakusyo/ h18/honbun/index.html. (Japanese)

———. 2007. *The Arrest Situation of Crime by Visiting Foreigners, Heisei 18 [Rainichi Gaikokujin Hanzai no Kenkyo Jyokyo].* www.npa.go.jp/sosikihanzai/kokusaisousa/kokusai2/ contents.htm. (Japanese)

———. 2008. *The Arrest Situation of Crime by Visiting Foreigners, Heisei 19 [Rainichi Gaikokujin Hanzai no Kenkyo Jyokyo].* www.npa.go.jp/sosikihanzai/kokusaisousa/kokusai4/ contents.htm. (Japanese)

"National Police Agency and Maritime Safety Agency Hold Discussion to Fortify Smuggling Controls." 1997. Excerpted from *Nihon Keizai Shimbun,* March 5, U.S. Embassy, Office of Translation Services.

"National Police Agency to Dispatch Officials in Effort to Cope with Increasing Mass Smuggling." 1997. Excerpted from *Mainichi Shimbun*, March 5, U.S. Embassy, Office of Translation Services.

Police Policy Research Center, National Police Academy. 2008. *Crimes in Japan in 2007.* Tokyo: Alumni Association for National Police Academy. www.npa.go.jp/english/seisaku5/20081008.pdf.

Sakanaka, Hidenori. 2007. "The Future of Japan's Immigration Policy: A Battle Diary," *Japan Focus*, April 9. www.japanfocus.org/products/details/2396.

Sassen, Saskia. 1998. *Globalization and Its Discontents.* New York: New Press.

Schreiber, Mark. 1997. "Juvenile Crime in the 1990s." *Japan Quarterly* 44 (April–June): 78–88.

Sellek, Yoko. 1996. "Female Migrant Workers in Japan: Working for the Yen." *Japan Forum* 8 (2): 159–75.

Shimada, Haruo. 1994. *Japan's Guest Workers: Issues and Public Policies.* Tokyo: University of Tokyo Press.

Shipper, Apichai W. 2005. "Criminals or Victims? The Politics of Illegal Foreigners in Japan." *Journal of Japanese Studies* 31 (2): 299–327.

Smith, Herman W. 1995. *The Myth of Japanese Homogeneity: Social-Ecological Diversity in Education and Socialization.* Commack, N.Y.: Nova Science Publishers.

Smith, Paul J. 1997. "Chinese Migrant Trafficking: A Global Challenge." In *Human Smuggling: Chinese Migrant Trafficking and the Challenge to America's Immigration Tradition*, edited by Paul J. Smith, 1–22. Washington, D.C.: Center for Strategic and International Studies.

Stevens, Carolyn S. 1997. *On the Margins of Japanese Society: Volunteers and the Welfare of the Urban Underclass.* London: Routledge.

Tsuda, Takeyuki, and Wayne A. Cornelius. 2004. "Japan: Government Policy, Immigrant Reality." In *Controlling Immigration: A Global Perspective*, edited by Wayne Cornelius et al., 439–76. Stanford: Stanford University Press.

Van Wolferen, Karel. 1993. *The Enigma of Japanese Power.* Tokyo: Charles E. Tuttle.

WuDunn, Sheryl. 1997. "Japan Worries about a Crime Trend: Crime by Chinese." *New York Times*, March 12. www.nytimes.com/1997/03/12/world/japan-worries-about-a-trend-crime-by-chinese.html?scp=5&sq=japan%20crime&st=cse.

Yamamoto, Ryoko. 2007. "Migrant-Support NGOs and the Challenge to the Discourse on Foreign Criminality in Japan." *Japan Focus*, September 15. www.japanfocus.org/products/details/2521.

Yoshino, Kosaku. 1992. *Cultural Nationalism in Contemporary Japan: A Sociological Inquiry.* London: Routledge.

Zhang, Sheldon X. 2007. *Smuggling and Trafficking in Human Beings: All Roads Lead to America.* Westport, Conn.: Praeger Publishers.

Zhang, Sheldon X., and Mark S. Gaylord. 1996. "Bound for the Golden Mountain: The Social Organization of Chinese Alien Smuggling." *Crime, Law, and Social Change* 25: 1–16.

The Law at a Crossroads

The Construction of Migrant Women Trafficked into Prostitution

Nora V. Demleitner

In the late 1970s and throughout the 1980s, news reports proliferated about women and girls forced into prostitution in some Asian countries, which were heralded as tourist paradises for men from highly industrialized nations. While the accounts of abuse and torture that followed the abduction, seduction, or outright sale of young women into prostitution were shocking, for those who did not visit those countries, they were merely tales of faraway atrocities.

Globalization and increasing migration have dramatically expanded the location of women and (female) children who are being forced to prostitute themselves. The one-way street has been opened to two-way traffic: Men from wealthy countries go abroad for sexual "adventures"; women from poorer states migrate to the men's home states. Today these women and girls can be found in Tel Aviv, Berlin, Amsterdam, Milan, New York City, and rural Florida.[1] As human trafficking and forced prostitution have moved into our midst, they have also moved onto the political agenda of the Western, industrialized world.[2]

Human trafficking has been characterized as extremely violent, of "industrial scale" (U.N. Commission on Human Rights, 1995: 1), and involving huge profit margins. Since organized criminal groups are alleged to dominate trafficking, it has been portrayed as a security threat to Western countries, akin to drugs and weapons smuggling (Anderson et al., 1995: 156–67).[3]

Human trafficking and forced prostitution could be approached in multiple ways: as a moral issue, a public order problem, a labor question, a human rights problem, a migration issue, or a matter of (organized) crime (Wijers and Lap-Chew, 1997: 157–78). Because of the ways in which trafficking has been depicted in Western Europe, North America, and Australia, most of the focus has been on the migration and organized crime components of trafficking.

The emphasis on trafficking as a migration problem has also led to the criminalization of trafficking victims who generally violate prostitution and immigration laws. Despite their traumatic victimization, these persons tend to receive only very limited, if any, assistance from the governmental authorities in the countries in which they were forced to work as prostitutes and in their home countries. Neither regular admonitions by United Nations agencies (U.N. Commission on Human Rights, 1995: 2, 4) nor accusations by women's organizations have changed this approach. However, with the increasing entry of women from central and Eastern Europe into Western Europe and the United States, the dual abuse that these women suffer at the hands of traffickers and governments has been more highly publicized.[4] Moreover, it has become clear that the immediate deportation of trafficking victims because they are undocumented migrants generally thwarts the successful prosecution of the traffickers.

Much of the reluctance to help trafficked women effectively can be ascribed to the social ambivalence that surrounds their construction as prostitutes and as undocumented migrants. Often unreflected and stereotyped images of the women have driven the application of laws and the implementation of policies that have characterized them as offenders rather than victims.[5] Only powerful images, such as the forced prostitution of very young girls or brutal forms of physical abuse amounting to torture, have succeeded in overcoming the negative attitude toward prostitutes and "illegal" migrants, which is reflected in the reluctant passage and enforcement of antitrafficking laws. Although compelling depictions of victimhood may be able to counteract the negative constructions of the women, they also carry with them dangers as they construe women generally as helpless and in need of rescuing.[6] Since many migrant women do not fit this image, they are unlikely to benefit from a framework that aids only the "typical" victim. Therefore, the depiction of trafficking victims as victims may not provide substantial assistance to most of the women.

Rather than attempting to replace the current construction of trafficked women with that of "victims," we must question the image of the prostitute and the "illegal alien" that drives the implementation of current law and the further use and abuse of trafficked women by the state.[7]

The Legal Construction of "Illegal" Migrants
Trafficking "Illegal" Migrants

In recent years, highly industrialized countries in Europe, North America, and Asia have increasingly restricted legal, long-term immigration. Although certain highly skilled immigrants and close family members, primarily spouses and minor children, of citizens will still be admitted, almost all others are excluded from legal migration.

For many foreigners even short-term visas, which include entry permits for tourists, seasonal workers, fiancé(e)s, and, in some countries, models and dancers, are difficult to obtain. The demand for these visas far exceeds the supply; and many of these visas are, explicitly or implicitly, reserved for the educated and affluent. Because of sexual inequality around the world, which results in men as a group being better educated and wealthier than women as a group, men are the more likely beneficiaries of long- and short-term entry permits that allow them to work legally or at least put them in the position to earn higher wages than in their home countries, even in illegal employment.

However, many women in the less industrialized and less developed world also frequently desire to migrate to improve their own and their family's economic situation, especially in light of high unemployment or the availability of only low-paying jobs at home. The media portrayal of Western economies and the accounts of other migrants promise higher-paying employment and a better life abroad. Often the women's home governments support migration to decrease unemployment and population pressures and to increase foreign remittances and the wealth of their people. Some countries have not even shrunk from promoting sex work for women.[8]

Not surprisingly, the contraction of legal immigration in the Western world combined with global economic inequality has caused an upsurge in illegal or undocumented migration. Potential migrants may be willing to attempt illegal border crossings; procure visas illegitimately, such as through marriage fraud; or stay on even after the expiration of a short-term visa. Such a combination of legal and illegal methods is typical for entry into Western countries (International Organization for Migration [IOM] and International Centre for Migration Policy Development, 1999: 72).

While in decades past illegal migration tended to be an individual matter, with the increasing fortification of borders by Western countries, organized groups have begun to assist migrants in crossing international borders, gaining short-term entry visas, and even finding (fraudulent) spouses (Wijers, 1998: 72). However, these services do not come cheap, and the migrants and their families often become deeply indebted to traffickers. Traffickers then use that debt to pressure these migrants. For female migrants that has meant forced labor in sweatshops or forced prostitution.

Even though much has been written about undocumented migration, the number of migrants, whether trafficked or entering on their own or with the help of smugglers, is subject to conjecture. The media, governments, and nongovernmental organizations publicize increasingly higher figures (Campani, 1998: 231–32). The U.S. Department of State has spoken of fifty thousand women trafficked into the United States every year (U.S. House of Representatives, 1999). Precise data, however, are difficult to collect because of the clandestine nature of all undocumented migration and the impossibility of determining how many of these migrants will move on to third states or return to their home countries. Moreover, definitional questions and uncertainties pose a substantial difficulty in accurately assessing the number of individuals trafficked. Frequently, all undocumented migrants, whether smuggled or trafficked, are considered together.[9]

Data on trafficked migrants no longer focus exclusively on their number but have shifted to the amount of money organized criminal groups make from human trafficking. This reconfiguration further commodifies human beings and equates them with other trafficked goods, such as drugs, rather than treating them as individuals. Moreover, such a change in focus does not solve the definitional problems inherent in the term *trafficking*.

Despite its frequent use in popular and academic discourse, the meaning of the term *trafficking* is ambiguous. Three primary meanings are distinguishable. To many the term is synonymous with *illegal entry*. The European Union's definition of trafficking, on the other hand, ties entry into a member state to sexual exploitation or abuse, with sexual exploitation connoting forced prostitution (Council of the European Union, 1997). The link between trafficking and forced prostitution severs the connection between women who are forced to work in the sex industry, women who are trafficked into forced labor generally

(Bindman, 1998: 65), and men who are trafficked. The issue of whether trafficking for sexual exploitation and other slaverylike employment should be treated separately has been fiercely contested and has caused a rift in the anti-trafficking community. The United Nations General Assembly depicts trafficking more broadly as connecting the "illicit and clandestine movement of persons across national or international borders" to sexual or economic oppression and exploitation, which can take the form of "forced domestic labour, false marriages, clandestine employment and false adoption" (Chuang, 1998: 87).[10] One of the most comprehensive definitions suggested construes trafficking as "consist[ing] of all acts involved in: within or across borders; whether for financial or other gain or not; and in which material deception, coercion, force, direct or indirect threats, abuse of authority, fraud, or fraudulent non-disclosure is used; for the purpose of placing a person forcibly, against her/his will or without her/his consent; in exploitative, abusive or servile situations, such as forced prostitution, sweatshop labor, domestic servitude or other abusive forms of labor or family relationships, whether for pay or not" (Stewart, 1998: 16).

All these definitions attempt to focus attention on the illegality of the traffickers' actions rather than the migrants'. They also highlight particularly the subjugation and abuse of the person trafficked and may lead states to protect the victims of this practice (Chuang, 1998: 88).

However, so far Western countries have deemed illegal migration, with or without the help of traffickers, a menace to their economic and social well-being and their territorial integrity. Ultimately, they have considered illegal migrants and traffickers threats to their national security (Vernez, n.d.: 1, 8).

The Portrayal of Undocumented Migrants as Criminals

Although many migrants, and especially those who are undocumented, become the victims of crime, including forced labor and forced prostitution, in the countries of destination, generally undocumented migrants are portrayed as *lawbreakers* (Demleitner, 1997: 43; Pickup, 1998: 47). That label, however, deprives them of the compassion and empathy that generally extends to crime victims.

Many of the offenses ascribed to undocumented migrants pertain to violations of the immigration laws, such as staying in the country without legal permission, evading an official border crossing, and obtaining fraudulent documents; other offenses grow out of the experience of illegal migration, such as the use of fraudulent work permits and the violation of tax laws.[11] Additional violations arise out of the often desperate situation in which undocumented migrants find themselves on their travels or upon arrival at their destination. However, the public portrayal of migrants as criminals is much less differentiated. Frequently, all noncitizens are aggregated and treated as potential offenders without regard to their personal situation or the type of law violated (Demleitner, 1997: 43–44). This perception is often reinforced by law enforcement activities against traffickers that lead to the indiscriminate arrest of traffickers and trafficked persons alike. Like the citizenry, however, migrants encompass law violators, victims, victims/lawbreakers, and those who do not fall into any of the above categories.

The situation is most complex, morally and legally, when the lawbreaker becomes a victim. Smugglers—as well as immigration officials and police in transit countries or countries of destination—exploit and abuse many of the migrants who enter without documents. In addition to all the risks that their male compatriots shoulder, female migrants face threats to their bodily integrity because of the ever present, added risk of sexual abuse by the smugglers, male migrants, and even police and immigration officials. Others find themselves either outrightly forced into prostitution or horribly abused and degraded as sex workers, or both. Even if they are victimized, however, these undocumented migrants continue to be classified as criminals because of their immigration status and attendant offenses they may have committed.

Female Migrants and Sexual Abuse

Historically most migrants were men who were later joined by their spouses, but increasingly women migrate on their own rather than in response to familial or spousal migration. Many view emigration as the sole avenue to find any or more lucrative employment or a more attractive marriage partner. Often it is the economic and familial structure in their home countries that prompts women to leave to provide a better life for themselves and their families. High female unemployment, a negative economic outlook, and the economic and social oppression of women cause many of them to depart their home countries in search of a better future.

While some of these women succeed in finding lucrative and fulfilling employment or an attractive marriage partner abroad, many are less lucky. Most of them end up crossing international borders either without documentation or with fraudulent papers. For an appropriate fee, traffickers facilitate both the illegal border crossing and the provision of fraudulent entry documents.

However, since women are generally less able than men to procure the amount of money demanded by the smugglers, they are frequently forced to tie their destiny to the smugglers in a form of debt bondage that requires them to work for the smuggling organization until they have paid off their debt. The labor demanded may take the form of sweatshop employment or of forced sex work.

Although there is no generally recognized legal definition of *forced prostitution,* for the purpose of this chapter it will refer to women or girls who are compelled to engage in sexual acts with strangers in exchange for commodities with the compulsion emanating from either physical violence and abuse, threats to their lives or bodily integrity or those of their families, emotional and physical coercion based on their indebtedness to the smugglers and procurers, and/or their presence in a foreign country without legal status and any support network. This definition ties forced prostitution to trafficking into a geographical area, including a foreign country, in which the women have no connections, do not speak the language, have no legal status, or are not permitted to work.

Like the number of undocumented migrants as a whole, the number of women forced into prostitution is undetermined and possibly indeterminate. Not only is it difficult to classify women as being "forced" or "voluntarily" working in prostitution, but, as prostitution is largely concealed, it is also difficult to obtain any reliable data on the practice.[12]

Despite the recent discovery of trafficking groups that forced young Mexican, Thai, and Korean women into prostitution, not much attention has been paid to forced prostitution in the United States. Israel, on the other hand, appears to deny the existence of forced prostitution even though a number of Russian women have charged that they were forced into prostitution upon arrival in Israel. In Germany the forced prostitution of women from central and Eastern Europe and the former Soviet republics has triggered almost hysterical commentary, especially since trafficking has been tied to the Russian Mafia.

Many media reports focus on the very small number of women who were forcibly abducted from their home country, transported to Western Europe, and there forced into prostitution. Although these cases do occur, they constitute the least likely scenario of sexual slavery (Schroeder, 1995: 236–37). Nevertheless, they are frequently used as paradigmatic cases of forced prostitution because these women represent the innocent, the "true" victim, a victim who did not choose to migrate illegally, let alone prostitute herself. While technically these women were illegally in the country in which they were abused, neither the police nor the public view them as illegal migrants but rather—and correctly so—as the victims of kidnappers. The stories that surround this group of women are reminiscent of the newspaper accounts published at the turn of the century in the United States about the abduction of innocent women— either recent immigrants or women from small towns and rural areas—who were taken to American cities for prostitution (James, 1977b: 11). At that time it was assumed that both groups of women would want to be repatriated—to their city or country of origin.

The more likely scenario of how migrant women are forced into prostitution involves those women who want to migrate to an economically more prosperous country and leave their home country voluntarily. However, these women do not form a cohesive group. Some of them will neither know nor suspect that they will be forced into prostitution. Often traffickers promise them legal immigration status and legitimate employment as domestic workers or in the service industry; sometimes they promise marriage. Some women may suspect or assume that the traffickers expect them to engage in prostitution to pay off their debt; others may have planned to migrate to work as prostitutes. While some women may have already worked as prostitutes in their home countries, others may envision that they could engage in that activity long enough to pay off the smugglers. Whatever their situation, none of these women agreed to the inhumane, forced, and oppressive circumstances in which they would find themselves once abroad. Nevertheless, legally all of them are undocumented migrants who entered or stayed in a country without legal permission. And, "in most countries . . . state policy on trafficking in women derives from policy on aliens" (Rayanakorn, 1995: 15).

The women may be tried for immigration violations and ultimately be deported to their countries of origin, often at their own expense. Traffickers, pimps, and brothel owners use the legal situation to their advantage. To immobilize their victims psychologically and prevent their escape, frequently they threaten the women with deportation. Since deportation implies risks to the women's families because of the still existing smuggling debt, public humiliation, and ostracization owing to disclosure of the woman's activity, and possibly further victimization, this threat is highly effective.

Even though policymakers and legislators know of the legal vulnerability of trafficking victims, almost no country has made serious attempts to change its immigration laws to protect women in forced prostitution. Their reluctance to act may be due to three reasons. First, they fear that granting any special benefit to forced prostitutes may either increase the number of women who seek to be categorized as such or may allow smuggling networks to exploit such a legal change to their advantage. While both effects may seem unlikely, the despair of some migrants may know no boundaries, and the ingenuity of the traffickers knows none either.

Second, in their struggle against illegal migration, most Western countries seem to be more concerned about closing potential loopholes and stopping illegal migrants than disturbed by the victimization and sacrifices their policies cause.[13] Therefore, any exception to the anti-immigration policy may be viewed as weakness or as an invitation to further undocumented migration.

Third, because of the legal construction of prostitutes, trafficking victims, even though forced into prostitution, may not be sympathetic enough as victims to bring about legal change. Ultimately, the law would have to protect persons who fall into two groups that are not generally held in high regard— undocumented migrants and prostitutes. Therefore, the women's dual status as (illegal) migrants and prostitutes may exacerbate the lack of interest in their fate.

The Legal Construction of "Prostitutes"

Gender stereotypes have long supported the existence of (female) prostitution. Since men's need for sex is deemed biologically based and therefore uncontrollable, many men around the world have been socialized to expect sexual access to women (James, 1977a: 39).[14]

Prostitution has been characterized as "the oldest profession," but in Western countries it has been tied to immorality, and especially the immorality of women. Courts in the United States have characterized prostitutes as "fallen women," whereas they have described their customers as respectable members of the community (Haft, 1977: 24). The early research on prostitution focused exclusively on the women involved in the exchange and attempted to discover their motivations. In addition, studies of forced prostitution in Western countries so far have provided little to no insight into the customers of women who are forced into prostitution. However, the customers could be potentially important in alerting authorities to the existence of forced prostitution (Altink, 1995: 51–52).

Legally prostitution is being approached in one of three ways: legalization, decriminalization, or criminalization.[15] In the United States prostitution and attendant activities, such as solicitation, are outlawed in all states, with the exception of Nevada. Not surprisingly, such a prohibitionist legal regime is reflected in the immigration laws, which allow for the exclusion of suspected prostitutes at the border and the deportation of noncitizens for engaging in prostitution.

The official criminalization of prostitution does not necessarily reflect on whom the burden of enforcement proceedings will fall. While prostitutes, their customers, and their procurers are subject to criminal penalties, recently localized drives against (male) customers notwithstanding, enforcement efforts have traditionally focused on the (female) prostitutes. The women, particularly those working on the streets, are easily identified, powerless, and therefore most likely to become police targets (James and Withers, 1977: xiv). Frequently, women will be charged with prostitution offenses even if it is suspected that they were forced into prostitution (Rosenberg, 1998).

In other countries, such as Germany, prostitution is governmentally regulated, even though procuring and pimping are criminalized. Decriminalization allows the police to stay in close contact with registered prostitutes and use them as informal informants. Even in countries that regulate prostitution, in general only citizens or long-time permanent residents are permitted to work as prostitutes.[16] Moral opprobrium continues to attach to the work of prostitutes, who are considered a "necessary evil." The moral requirements for migrants tend to be higher than those for the "native" women, a small group of whom are permitted to "service" men. Any female migrant who is perceived as intending to engage in prostitution will be excluded at the border; those convicted of a prostitution-related offense will be removed.

The Netherlands has recently taken an additional step and fully legalized prostitution. Prostitution is considered a form of work (Sterk-Elifson and Campbell, 1993: 196; Gillan, 1999).[17] The Dutch government views the right to self-determination as so broad that it permits every individual to choose freely how to use her body, even if she decides to prostitute herself. With this legal change, the government also hopes to combat forced prostitution more effectively. However, it is unlikely that the Dutch government will provide work visas to non-EU citizens who would like to work as prostitutes in the Netherlands.

Because of the Dutch legalization policy, since 1994, European Union documents explicitly distinguish between *prostitution* and *forced prostitution*. The latter term refers to the situation of women who are compelled to prostitute themselves either because of physical violence or duress, or who were lured into prostitution through misrepresentations. Generally, these women are non-EU nationals who hail from the former USSR, Eastern Europe, and Asia.

The distinction between *voluntary* and *forced* prostitution has angered women's organizations that argue for the abolition of all prostitution because its practice denigrates and humiliates all women. On the international scene the most vocal and best known of these organizations is the Coalition against Trafficking in Women (CATW), spearheaded by Kathleen Barry. Together with the International Abolitionist Federation and a few other groups, the CATW charges that the distinction between forced and voluntary prostitution fails to recognize that all prostitution is forced in some way (Edwards, 1997: 72–74; Murray, 1998: 52–53). It also claims that the increasing legitimation of prostitution in Europe in the 1980s was responsible for the rise in trafficking (Raymond and CATW, 1995).

The debate surrounding the treatment of prostitution has caused rifts between antitrafficking organizations and between feminists in the north and the south (Seabrook, 1996: 144). Despite what appeared to be successes of the CATW's position in the 1980s, the distinction between forced and voluntary prostitution remains dominant because it falls within the liberal legal tradition that has traditionally distinguished between actions that are forced because of social circumstances, on the one hand, and duress, on the other. While it is not the function of this chapter to map a position on the question whether all prostitution is forced, the existing legal framework and the prevailing public attitude toward prostitution will color a country's legal and political approach to forced prostitution. As much as the advocates in the struggle against forced prostitution have attempted to leave the question of prostitution generally unresolved, this avoidance strategy has caused conceptual confusion and prevented the development of a consistent antitrafficking program (Reanda, 1991: 226).

Independent of the legal framework, women who work as prostitutes are identified with their work: they *are* prostitutes, a fact that remains unchanged even after they leave prostitution. When women are forced into prostitution through the threats, coercion, or abuse of others, they can also expect to be defined by their past (or present) status. Not surprisingly, enforcement of antitrafficking laws is often absent or low because of the attitude of law enforcement and the judiciary with respect to sex workers (Skrobanek, Boonpakdee, and Jantateero, 1997: 97–98; Heine-Wiedenmann, 1992: 123–27). When the laws are enforced, their impact often falls on the women rather than the traffickers, replicating enforcement patterns against prostitution generally.

The Impact of Legal Constructions: "Solutions" That Are None

Since the turn of the century, the international community has labeled the trafficking of women and forced prostitution as abuses of the most grievous type (Demleitner, 1994: 167–79). Means to combat these practices encompassed punitive measures—severe penalties for procurers and pimps—and prevention, rescue, and rehabilitation of the victims of the white slave traffic (Berkovitch, 1999: 41).

Today trafficking and forced prostitution are labeled human rights violations. They are outlawed explicitly in a number of international treaties and conventions (Demleitner, 1994: 172–78), including the Convention on the Elimination of All Forms of Discrimination against Women (Toepfer and Wells, 1994).[18] Signatory states obligate themselves to take all measures to combat trafficking and the exploitation of prostitution. This includes devising effective penalties for traffickers and procurers, rehabilitating and training former prostitutes, but also attacking what are perceived as the root causes of prostitution, including "underdevelopment, poverty, drug abuse, illiteracy, and lack of training, education and employment opportunities" (U.N. Centre for Human Rights, 1994: 13–14). Over time different emphases have been set in the international arena in combating trafficking (Reanda, 1991: 211, 219), and with them have changed the strategies, the commitment of resources, and the view of the participants (Fitzpatrick, 1994: 537).

Startling, however, is the apparent overall lack of political will in the receiving and sending countries to protect the victimized women. Although international cooperation with respect to most criminal activity is still sorely inadequate, the women's status as undocumented migrants and as prostitutes may exacerbate the lack of interest and collaboration in the detection of networks that traffic women and force them to prostitute themselves. The depiction of the women forced into prostitution and their ambiguous legal position as offenders and victims have made it difficult for countries to develop a coherent policy of enforcement against the traffickers and of protection and support for the women. Tied inexorably to trafficking, forced prostitution has become primarily an immigration problem. Governments seem to assume that to deter undocumented migration, no migrant, however abused, should be able to benefit from her illegal entry or stay but rather must be deported. This holds particularly true for migrants who appear of dubious morality. The ambivalence displayed toward the victimized women often makes it difficult, if not impossible, to convict the traffickers and procurers.

One of the crucial problems in the enforcement of antitrafficking laws is the lack of a coherent definition for *forced* prostitution. This definitional problem is partly due to the ambivalence about prostitution in many societies and even the feminist community (Murray, 1998: 52–53). While advocates of the position that only forced prostitution, defined as prostitution under conditions of physical and emotional abuse, is a human rights violation shape the current antitrafficking agenda, countries have found it difficult to define *force* in domestic antitrafficking legislation comprehensively and accurately.[19] It is striking, however, that although frequently traffickers and brothel owners could be indicted for a whole host of criminal activities, including debt bondage, kidnapping, or extortion, such prosecutions appear rare (Wijers and Lap-Chew, 1997: 152).

Many of the potential receiving countries have worked on preventing the arrival of trafficked women in their territory. These proposals are designed to shelter the women from exploitation and abuse, but they also serve to dissuade women from migrating.[20] Most of these preventive measures center around publicity campaigns warning the women of the dangers of sexual and other abuse should they cross the border (Pickup, 1998: 48).

More distressingly, although often hailed as a panacea, these campaigns are problematic (Wijers and Lap-Chew, 1997: 169). They are designed to create a fear of leaving one's country and help immobilize women in their current position. They also create a dutylike obligation on women to abstain from certain behavior that is characterized as highrisk.[21] Ironically, some of the educational materials used have had an effect contrary to that envisioned as they portray the possibility of riches to be found in prostitution in the West. Additionally, women from Eastern European countries tend to be little concerned about the morality of being engaged in illegal activities because of their experiences under Communism, when everyone seemed to do something illegal (Altink, 1995: 159–60).

Some of the legal changes the potential host countries have made have proven counterproductive, especially since "often, 'trafficking' is used by states to initiate and justify restrictive policies" (Doezema, 1998: 45). Canada, for example, grants visas to dancers and models, which tends to mean strippers who are at high risk of being forced into prostitution (Godfrey, 1998b). Since anti-trafficking and feminist groups have strongly criticized these visa categories, to prevent exploitation, Canada has begun to require that women coming as exotic dancers be professional strippers (Godfrey, 1998a) and has dramatically limited the number of women admitted into the country under this visa category (Heinzl, 1999). However, in response, trafficking organizations have apparently encouraged women to enter Canada claiming refugee status and then forced them to work as strippers and prostitutes (Godfrey, 1999). Therefore, de jure or de facto bans on immigration that appear attractive for protective purposes may lead to increased rather than decreased exploitation.[22] It may be more effective to schedule follow-up visits for those visa recipients who are likely to be victimized.[23] However, when Belgium required a number of protective measures for women who entered under "artist" visas, the issuance of such visas in Belgium stopped. This measure probably caused traffickers to bring women into Belgium illegally or obtain "artist" visas for other countries that did not have such a protective framework (IOM, 1995: 20).

Protective measures are problematic not only because of the reaction of traffickers but also because of the measures' paternalistic nature, which causes women to be further disadvantaged. For example, abolishing the visa categories for dancers would further limit women's opportunities for legal migration and drive yet more of them into the arms of traffickers. In addition, it reinforces already existing value judgments about the work women do as strippers and models. Finally, governments may feel that entry restrictions absolve them of responsibility for persons trafficked into their states (Caldwell, Galster, and Steinzor, 1997).

Another example is visa requirements for citizens of countries from which women seem disproportionately involved in forced prostitution. For example, Germany introduced a visa requirement for citizens of the Philippines and Thailand, as entrants from those countries were disproportionately women (Lipka, 1989: 132–33). The result of such requirements is not the end of forced prostitution. Traffickers will either bring women into the country illegally or with fraudulent documents, or shift to trafficking women from countries without a visa requirement. Both occurred in Germany. The former dramatically increased the cost for Filipinas and Thai women, which increased their debt and dependence on the traffickers. At the same time, the number of women from central and Eastern Europe who are forced into prostitution in Germany has risen dramatically (Streiber, 1998: 5). Another consequence of such a governmental response is the stigmatization of all women hailing from certain countries as potential prostitutes or undocumented migrants ("Russian Envoy," 1999; Braun, 1989: 294).[24] Therefore, any measures further hindering women's entry must be carefully weighed against their disadvantages, as they pertain to potential migrants and women as a whole.

Practically, situations of forced prostitution are difficult to uncover. Forced prostitution generally comes to the attention of either immigration officials or those investigating sexual offenses. Sometimes, trafficking networks are discovered through proactive policing in the form of undercover work. However, police often find trafficking groups difficult to infiltrate because they are run either by extended families or by ethnically homogeneous gangs. Occasionally one or more of the trafficked women are able to flee the subhuman conditions under which they are forced to labor. Such escapes are less likely to occur or to be successful if the women are psychologically coerced and under the impression that their abusers will retaliate against them or their families. The women will also not attempt to flee if threatened with deportation or if they are afraid of the police, often because of experiences with corrupt and abusive police in their home countries. Alternatively, in countries in which prostitution is regulated or legalized, registered prostitutes may tip off the police, often because they resent competition. Such tips are less likely if the trafficked women's "customers" are drawn exclusively from a group of men that does not patronize registered prostitutes.[25] Finally, customers may inform the police once the prostitutes confide in them.

Discovery guarantees the women no protection. As in rape cases, the burden of proof for women forced to work as prostitutes seems often reversed. Unless they can demonstrate their lack of consent to prostitute themselves, law enforcement officials appear to assume that they worked as prostitutes in their home countries or knew what was expected of them in the receiving country. The only woman who will be able to escape moral doubt is the one who was snatched off the streets by criminals, drugged, taken across an international border, raped, and then chained to a bed or at least severely beaten to engage in sex for money, paid to her captors.

Often the media focus on the fate of teen girls, frequently emphasizing their virginity, who were kidnapped and sold into prostitution (Murray, 1998: 55; Doezema, 1998: 43). Alternatively, they report on conditions amounting to torture and possibly culminating in the death of one of the women.[26] Presumably such stark portrayals of abuse will allay any doubt as to the forced nature of the women's involvement in prostitution. They could never have chosen such abuse.

This picture of captive and underaged migrants not only dominates media reports but is also prevalent in depictions of forced prostitution by human rights organizations. This focus resembles the emphasis of the turn-of-the-century crusaders who fought the white slave traffic. They created the image of "helpless innocent young women being 'ruined,' transported, and sold by traffickers to brothels in other countries" (Berkovitch, 1999: 38). This depiction created national and international backing for the anti–white slave trafficking movement and galvanized women and men alike (ibid.).[27] The goal of such portrayals is to engender public sympathy for the victims and remove any potential stigma from the victimized women. The result of such a strategy, however, may be less benign. Once it becomes obvious that only a small number of women have been victimized in such egregious manner (Campani, 1998: 256), interest in and sympathy for all other women forced to work as prostitutes might evaporate, leaving them with less protection. Another problematic aspect of this discourse is the depiction of women as powerless, helpless, and pure.[28] The legal process may tend to declare any woman not fitting this childlike image—and most victims of unscrupulous traffickers will not conform to this model—as unworthy of support and protection.[29]

Much more common than the tortured and abducted victim is the woman willing to be smuggled across an international border, either knowing or suspecting that her stay and employment may be illegal but not expecting to work as a prostitute. Most of the women trafficked and forced into prostitution have shown courage and initiative in attempting to change their situation through migration (Wijers, 1998: 70). Many are assertive, well-educated, independent, self-possessed, and strong women. When forced into prostitution, many of the women suffer some physical abuse, but more prevalent is serious emotional coercion based on their illegal status and debt to the traffickers. This situation creates a dilemma for law enforcement because the women intentionally broke the laws of their country.[30] Once classified as "illegal" migrants rather than as victims, the women will be deported and possibly even penalized. The prosecution of the traffickers will most likely depend on the amount of harm the woman has suffered, especially in terms of physical abuse.

Another group of women found in forced prostitution consists of those who were either willing to engage in prostitution abroad or at least knew that this was likely. The authorities of the receiving countries view this subset of women not only as "illegal" migrants but also as of dubious morality and therefore undesirable. Even though a number of countries, including Germany, have passed legislation that treats all women forced into prostitution alike independent of whether they had worked as prostitutes in their home countries, in reality police, prosecutors, and courts continue to discriminate against these women throughout the criminal justice process. Moreover, for women who plan on continuing to work as prostitutes after having been liberated from a forced situation, "compassion turns into indifference or outright hostility" (Wijers, 1998: 77).

Often the last group of women dictates the approach law enforcement officials take to all migrant women who are sexually abused and forced into prostitution abroad. Akin to the attitude frequently displayed toward (date) rape victims, police and prosecution often doubt that the women were forced into prostitution. Rather, they view the migrants as complicit in the trafficking and prostitution, especially when the women do not show any signs of physical abuse. As is the case with other sex offenses, often the victim is blamed because she "should" have known what was going to happen or because she "should" have acted differently. This attitude fails to appreciate that these women reacted to the economic and social situation in their home countries in the only way possible.

Even though the women's fate may evoke empathy, especially if the abuse they endured was severe, their primary portrayal as illegal immigrants and "loose" women rather than victims of violent crime supports demands for their removal (Wijers, 1998: 72). Therefore, the legal "solution" currently offered to these trafficked women is deportation to their home countries. Some of the women choose deportation so that the traffickers do not assume that they cooperated with law enforcement officials. Others want to return home as quickly as possible and not relive the abuse they endured. However, even women who do not want to return to their home countries because they fear for their lives are being deported.

In some cases women willing to testify against the ringleaders of the trafficking and forced prostitution ring were deported prior to trial. Some of these prosecutions were dismissed because the main witnesses could not be re-called to testify in court.[31] While ostensibly the lack of cooperation between law enforcement and immigration authorities causes such prosecutorial failure, the inability to convict the traffickers might be indicative of the primary construction of forced prostitutes as illegal migrants and the hierarchy of goals in Western countries. The removal of undocumented migrants is of primary importance, independent of their situation. The receiving country is not seen as sharing any blame in their victimization, even though it was unable to prevent their victimization in its territory.

Deportation implies not only return to the conditions the women attempted to leave in the first place but often also intimidation and threats by the smuggling operation either because the women owe the traffickers money for the failed trip or because they testified or are perceived to have provided information against the procurers. Upon their return home, many of the women can also be expected to be shunned by their families and friends for being deported or, if their prior experience becomes known, being prostitutes.

To prevent the women from continuing to work as prostitutes in their home countries and presumably from attempting to return to the country to which they had wanted to migrate, some Western European countries have now begun to offer "rehabilitation" programs to victimized women, ranging from vocational training to psychological counseling. The choice of the term *rehabilitation* is telling.[32] How many *victims* generally need to be rehabilitated?

Legal and logistical hurdles to the successful prosecution of traffickers may be overcome more successfully if the will existed to protect the victims. However, the current legal treatment of migrant women who are forced to prostitute themselves serves to stigmatize them as double outcasts. Largely the legal and social construction of the female victims drives the lax enforcement of existing laws against forced prostitution. In many respects the way in which trafficked women are being treated is comparable to the treatment of victims of gang-related attacks in the United States. Police and courts tend to view them either as having contributed to the crime or as criminals when they belong to another gang (U.S. Department of Justice, 1996: 14–15).

Forced prostitution is caused in part by current migration laws, reinforced by gender inequalities, and supported by the precarious legal position of the victims. Because of the current restrictive immigration climate and the continued oppression of women around the globe, we can expect to witness the growth of trafficking networks and an increase in the exploitative situations in which migrants, and especially women, find themselves. Therefore, it is crucial to reevaluate the portrayal of the victims and to grant them more effective protection.

Recommendations

Respect and Protection

Currently, discussions about female migration and prostitution are often grounded in unsupported and even dubious claims. Fragmented and anecdotal stories drive the discourse. Quantitative empirical analysis and data are missing (Streiber, 1998: 22). The absence of hard data can be ascribed to the secretiveness of the activity, the lack of reporting by the victims of forced prostitution, and the still low priority trafficking seems to have for many law enforcement agencies, despite statements to the contrary (IOM, 1995: 7). Divergent claims with respect to the magnitude of trafficking and forced prostitution may also be due to the differing definitions of the phenomenon.

Resolution of numerical claims may help chart a more effective course in the protection of victims. Should the number of women forced into prostitution be smaller than expected, the receiving countries may be more willing to grant them protection within their territory. Should the number be larger than projected, the focus is likely to shift further to preventive strategies and repatriation. Whatever the ultimate goals, the debates surrounding victim protection must be grounded in better empirical knowledge about the scope of the problem.

Anthropological and sociological studies exist that document dramatic differences between trafficked women, but often a "one size fits all" model drives prescriptions to assist the victims. However, "even today the practice of prostitution pertains more specifically to certain groups of immigrant women and certain countries" (Campani, 1998: 231). Is this a function of divergent social settings in the sending countries, their economic development, or rather different male-female relationships? How may women differ overall by nationality in terms of the pressure exerted upon them to work as prostitutes?[33] What conditions await the women in their home countries upon repatriation? Answers to these questions must be ascertained to allow for precisely targeted legal solutions.

Some policy and legal responses should, however, apply to all women forced to work in prostitution. First, the women should not be incarcerated based on their violation of criminal laws or their status as undocumented migrants (Heine-Wiedenmann and Ackermann, 1992: 340). Both situations, however, occur frequently and indicate the preeminence of concerns about illegal migration over compassion. Second, victims of forced prostitution should not be subject to penal sanctions or be deported.[34] To prevent deportations, closer cooperation is required between immigration services on the one hand and the police and prosecutors who develop the case against the traffickers on the other.

The prevention of negative consequences, however, is insufficient. The victimized women should also be granted protection and assistance, and that not only in exchange for their assistance in law enforcement efforts against their abusers.[35] To create effectively targeted programs and help empower the women forced into prostitution, such support programs should be developed in conjunction with trafficking victims rather than designed solely by government officials and feminist organizations (Skrobanek, Boonpakdee, and Janta-teero, 1997: 18). Currently, two bills are pending in the United States Congress that would allow specifically for the temporary (and permanent) protection of victims of human trafficking.[36] Ultimately, we must empower these women by presenting them with realistic options for their future, including permission to stay and repatriation, which they may choose depending on their personal goals and situation. Should humanitarian and gender-based considerations not suffice in structuring a comprehensive strategic package, practical law enforcement reasons also counsel to pursue such a path. Otherwise the state will not act much differently than the traffickers and "us[e] women as witnesses for combatting organized crime in [its] interest . . . without allowing them the corresponding protection" (Wijers, 1998: 77).

The Netherlands and Belgium were the first countries to grant trafficked women who would testify against their abusers a temporary right to stay while the case went to trial. Although the two countries have been praised for their progressive program, this presents a very limited approach (Rayanakorn, 1995: 21–22) in which the state uses the victims for its own purposes. The United States also has a visa category that allows trafficking victims to stay while assisting in the investigation and prosecution of the traffickers.[37]

The moral and legal ambiguities created by the women's status as former prostitutes, albeit forced, and as illegal migrants often make the women reluctant to cooperate in criminal proceedings against their abusers, even though they would like to see them punished. If they do not participate in the prosecution out of fear for their lives and those of family members or because they were treated as accomplices rather than victims, chances are that the accused will go free.

Police and prosecutors mistrust the women's testimony. If the women succeed in convincing law enforcement authorities of their credibility, defense attorneys will attack their testimony as untrustworthy because of their prior work as prostitutes. To escape criminal actions against themselves, the women must often enter into "deals" with the prosecution that the traffickers' lawyers may use in court to allege bias.

Most distressingly, the host countries generally do not grant the women long-term financial and physical protection. Therefore, the women should be provided with the legal tools to demand compensation from the traffickers. The United States allows for civil causes of actions against violent offenders whose actions were motivated by gender. Therefore, trafficking victims and women forced into prostitution may be able to recover compensatory and punitive damages from their victimizers.[38] Other countries provide similar opportunities for compensation.

Some women may require permanent protection from their victimizers, but others will only need to be sheltered prior to and during the trial. Temporary isolation from the prostitution milieu will prevent the victimizers from influencing the women's testimony (Reinhardt, n.d.: 6). As temporary relocation is more cost-effective and decreases the administrative burden on law enforcement, it should be made available whenever necessary. In the United States similar programs have been put in place to protect the victims and witnesses in gang prosecutions (U.S. Department of Justice, 1996).

Women whose lives would be threatened even after the trial should be able to benefit from permanent witness protection programs. Most of the European countries at this point do not have a witness protection program comparable to the U.S. federal witness protection program,[39] but they have developed relocation programs that entail the changing of the identity of witnesses. In light of their high cost and logistical burden, permanent witness protection efforts can be expected only infrequently (Reinhardt, n.d.: 6). So far, trafficking victims have often been unlikely to benefit from full-fledged protection programs because their knowledge of the trafficking and procuring operation, while helpful, will generally not justify the expense of their protection. However, there is limited judicial precedent in the United States for forcing the offenders who necessitated the relocation to pay for the witness protection program.[40] To increase protection and distribute the cost of witness protection, a regional rather than national approach might be desirable in certain parts of the world.[41]

Those women assisting the prosecution whose lives would be endangered by the traffickers in their home country must be provided with long-term guarantees of security. However, most schemes currently under consideration or in place are administratively burdensome, dependent on the goodwill of prosecutors, and do not guarantee permanent residence. The United States holds out the promise of permanent legal residence as a reward for witnesses assisting their new home country in its crime-fighting function.[42] The European Parliament has called for the grant of permanent residency status to victims of trafficking (Chuang, 1998: 102). Short-term visa status often proves of little avail to the women. Many prefer to be deported so as to avoid giving the traffickers the impression that they assisted law enforcement agencies (IOM and International Centre for Migration Policy Development, 1999: 77).

The Netherlands permits the grant of permanent residency to trafficking victims on humanitarian grounds. Despite its legal availability, this benefit is rarely granted (IOM, 1995: 25). An alternative approach may be to encourage trafficking victims to petition for asylum based on their fear of persecution upon their return home. Their persecution would be based on membership in the group of former forced prostitutes. If their home government is unable to protect them from potential violent attacks by the traffickers, the women should be granted asylum. Moreover, women who would be ostracized and socially stigmatized because of their previous status should also be able to benefit from such a regime. While the potential for abusing such benefits exists, it is unlikely, in part because of the biases of police and prosecutors, in part because the requirements for such status remain high (Altink, 1995: 47).

Mere protection of the women's physical lives is insufficient. The victims of forced prostitution should be provided with "support services," not "rehabilitative" measures.[43] The Netherlands provides a partial model for this approach. Among the support services offered there is counselling, akin to the type generally provided for victims of sexual violence. Whether skills training is appropriate and advisable should depend on the individual victim and her plans for the future.[44] Should she contemplate returning to her home country, potential skills training should primarily include the victim's interests and abilities but also take into account the economic situation in her home country. Such support measures can be funded in different ways, including out of restitution payments ordered against convicted traffickers or out of a general victims' fund.

Not all women will want to stay in the receiving states. Those who choose to return to their home country should be given free transportation (Murray, 1998: 64). Support programs should also be continued there. Counseling and shelters may be of particular importance (Pickup, 1998: 48). For any of these measures, it is important that the trafficked woman be allowed to make an informed decision whether to participate. The focus on the victim's needs and desires will lead to her empowerment and explicitly recognizes her as an independent individual rather than stigmatizing her as a victim for whom others will make decisions (agisra, 1990: 11).

Although the protection of individual victims is important, more comprehensive approaches are necessary to control trafficking and provide its victims with realistic survival chances.

Creating Opportunities

In the concern about individual trafficking victims, Western countries should remember that their victimization does not occur in a social and political vacuum. Rather, national and global structures of power and privilege cause and aggravate this type of abuse. Among those structures are not only gender-based domination in the sending and receiving states but also economic power relationships between north and south and between East and West. Therefore, the concern about human trafficking and forced prostitution may be largely symptomatic of global and domestic economic disparity and gender inequality.[45] Frequently, Western economic policies, in the guise of free trade and market liberalism, have exacerbated poverty and unemployment in the developing world (Seabrook, 1996: 134). Even developmental aid has contributed to a further deterioration in the position of women (Braun, 1989: 296). A growing consumer culture, combined with traditional assumptions about gender relationships, has led to the breakup of families, which in turn appears to fuel much of the trafficking (Campani, 1998: 259n. 15). As governments in the developing world have grown dependent on the remittances of migrants, they have done little to protect intending migrants from abuse. Therefore, the international economic framework, also in light of gender considerations,[46] must be reconsidered to prevent women and men from being forced to migrate to better their lives. While some of the underlying problems have been recognized and acknowledged and international organizations have suggested remedies, in Western countries these considerations seem to have taken a backseat compared with the emphases on criminalization and prosecution of traffickers and the repatriation of their victims.

As long as a global imbalance exists between wealthy and poor states and the media glamorize life in highly industrialized countries, legal and undocumented migration will continue. However, in recent years wealthy nations have increasingly closed their borders to migrants even though their governments' economic policies have frequently fostered migration pressures (Martin, 1999: 834). Because of the global distribution of power and education, women who have traditionally received fewer market skills have been disproportionately deprived of the legal opportunity to move. However, the developed world also appears to demand an increasing number of low-paid workers in the domestic sector and in the services industry, including sex work. Traditionally, these positions have been available to women (Chant, 1992: 198). In light of their limited options and the demand for their services in Western countries, women may act rationally in crossing international borders with the help of traffickers, even though they realize that they may have to or could be coerced to work in prostitution, at least for a limited period of time. Therefore, long-term strategies that attack these types of inequalities must be actively pursued rather than paid mere lip service.

Forced prostitution could not exist without customers. We must learn more about the clients of trafficked women who work in prostitution. While much of the discussion seems to be on targeting them to decrease the demand for prostitution—an approach grounded in abolitionist ideals—practically it might be more useful to co-opt potential customers so that they will report potential trafficking situations to law enforcement authorities. Therefore, the criminalization of clients would prove counterproductive if the goal is to protect trafficked women.

The current portrayal of victims, however, may prevent us from acknowledging a disconcerting truth. Although applied to the English debate about prostitution and white slavery in the last century, the critique of the portrayal of victims as sexually innocent and passive who were violated by evil individuals may hold equally true today. "Had they allowed themselves to see that many young girls engaged in prostitution not as passive, sexually innocent victims but because their choices were so limited, the reformers would have been forced to recognize that the causes of juvenile prostitution were to be found in an exploitative economic structure" (Gorham, 1978: 355). In the long run only a fundamental change in global economic inequities and an opening of Western countries to migration will undermine the power of traffickers and prevent the victimization of women.

Conclusion

The construction of women forced into prostitution as illegal migrants and as immoral has informed and prevented effective policy making and law enforcement against the traffickers. The portrayal of trafficking victims has also hampered the provision of legal protection and assistance to them. The receiving countries must break the negative imagery and tackle the stereotyped framework underlying their legal approaches to trafficking and forced prostitution. Should this not occur, it will become blatantly obvious that Western concerns about forced prostitution are instrumental, tied to illegal migration rather than the exploitation of human beings. Humanitarian considerations and the empowerment of women, however, should drive the prevention of trafficking and forced prostitution and the protection of its victims.

NOTES

A special note of gratitude extends to Rey Koslowski and David Kyle, the two editors of this volume, to Hans-Jörg Albrecht, Deborah Anker, Christopher McCrudden, Michael D. Smith, and Michael Tonry. Sincere thanks go the *Polizeipräsident* for Middle Franconia, Dr. Max von der Grün, and his staff in the sex crimes unit. My lengthy discussions with them have shed light on forced prostitution, human trafficking, and the treatment of prostitution in Germany.

1. In recent years a few traffickers have been prosecuted in the United States, among them the members of a family who forced twenty Mexican women and underage girls to work as prostitutes in rural Florida (Wilson, 1998).

2. Examples are the creation of the Working Group on Trafficking in Women and Children within the U.S. Department of Justice in 1998 and the various European Union antitrafficking initiatives.

3. European Union action plans to combat trafficking have highlighted the connection between organized crime and human trafficking. Nevertheless, some commentators have argued that Western countries' perceptions of threats to their national security emanating from organized criminal groups in central Europe and the Newly Independent States (NIS) that focus on "drugs, illegal immigration, prostitution and forms of protection, car ringing" are exaggerated (Hebenton and Spencer, 1998: 30).

4. Whether this is a result of the increasing number of women trafficked into prostitution in Western Europe and the United States or because of latent racism in favor of white women is debatable.

5. This is not only true for the host countries but also for the sending states. In the Philippines the portrayal of "Filipina migrant entertainers [as] the Other[,] the prostitute[,] the willing victim . . . and the heroine" has driven policies regulating their condition (Tyner, 1996: 77).

6. The race and ethnicity of the women may also affect these constructs and engender yet more discrimination against them (Murray, 1998: 58–60). This holds particularly true for Asian women.

7. This chapter addresses the trafficking of *women* and does not deal with the issue of underaged *girls* who are forced into prostitution. International conventions and national laws treat children substantially differently than adults.

8. The suggestions of Russian politicians to export Russian women for sex work and to turn Russia into a sex tourist paradise, made possible by the "service" of Russian women, are only shocking because of their frankness. More traditional has been the practice of politicians in some Asian states to market their countries as tourist paradises, with the special attraction of prostitution (agisra, 1990: 15), and to use prostitution as a tool for economic development in this way.

9. The Human Rights Caucus has put together a fact sheet discussing succinctly the differences between trafficking and smuggling (Human Rights Caucus, n.d.).

10. Wijers and Lap-Chew describe various definitions of *trafficking* in national laws (1997: 149–51). The divergent legal definitions demonstrate the difficulty in assessing accurately the scope of trafficking and forced prostitution.

11. The proposed draft for a supplemental instrument to the as of yet uncompleted United Nations Convention against Transnational Organized Crime would exempt the persons trafficked from criminal liability and punishment "on account of such trafficking and transport" (U.N. General Assembly, 1999).

12. An example of the uncertain scope of forced prostitution is drawn from a newsmagazine article: "A conservative estimate by Jonas Widgren, of the International Centre for Migration Policy Development in Vienna, reckons that 400,000 people are smuggled into the European Union each year; others suggest that is simply the number of girls brought into the EU and forced into prostitution" ("A Single Market in Crime," 1999).

13. Another example of this phenomenon is the increasing number of deaths from heatstroke, hypothermia, and drowning along the U.S.-Mexican border.

14. Although male prostitutes have been the topic of media reports and movies, they constitute only a small percentage of all prostitutes, and even they tend to serve primarily men.

15. Frequently, other terms are used to describe the same tripartite division. Among them are *abolitionist, regulationist,* and *prohibitionist* (Reanda, 1991: 203). An overview of prostitution legislation in select countries is provided in *Prostitution: An International Handbook on Trends, Problems, and Policies* (Davis, 1993).

16. In the member states of the European Union (EU) that condone prostitution, at least unofficially citizens of other EU countries may also work as prostitutes.

17. Were prostitution universally classified as a form of legal employment, the International Labor Organization's (ILO) International Convention on the Protection of the Rights of All Migrant Workers and Members of Their Families would cover all prostitutes, whether working legally or without documentation. This convention, which includes a reporting requirement and an optional complaint mechanism, would provide women trafficked into prostitution with an international forum to publicize their exploitation and a legal basis for compensation claims. The ILO already considers child prostitution to fall under the forced labor conventions that cover children.

18. Even within the human rights framework, international and regional documents

have set different priorities in their antitrafficking strategies, depending on whether they view forced prostitution primarily as discrimination, as a violation of the principles of equality, or as a deprivation of human dignity (Fitzpatrick, 1994: 556).

19. An example is the German antitrafficking provisions that have been frequently criticized by legal scholars because of their ambiguity and the difficulties in application that result (Kelker, 1993; Heine-Wiedenmann, 1992: 126–30).

20. In that respect these campaigns pursue the same purpose as the attempts at urging country girls to stay in their hometowns around the turn of the century when it was feared that they would be forced into prostitution in the cities (Connelly, 1980: 122).

21. In the domestic context, David Garland has classified such publicity campaigns as part of a responsibilization strategy designed to achieve private action to prevent the occurrence of crime (Garland, 1996: 452–53).

22. The U.S. Commission on Immigration Reform has proposed a ban on immigration to Saipan for "foreign contract workers engaged in exploitative occupations" (U.S. Commission on Immigration Reform, 1997: 21), which includes employment that may lead to sexual abuse.

23. This is not a novel idea. The League of Nations proposed in the 1920s that "governments should exercise supervision over the employment of girls in theaters and music halls, in order to secure that no attempt should be made to induce them to lead immoral lives" (Berkovitch, 1999: 78). However, my proposal is not motivated by a belief in the frailty of women but rather by an understanding of the greater likelihood of victimization of men and women who live in a country with whose language, customs, and legal framework they are unfamiliar.

24. A similar fate may befall men. When men from certain countries are disproportionately identified as traffickers, all men from these states are subject to stigmatization as criminals and traffickers ("Russian Envoy," 1999).

25. Not much information exists about the customers of women forced into prostitution, but there is some indication that in Germany young, male asylum applicants, who could not otherwise afford a prostitute, may frequent these women, especially when the traffickers bring them to the men's living quarters. In the United States migrant farmworkers were the primary customers of the Mexican women forced into prostitution in rural Florida.

26. Concerns about the trafficking victims do not motivate such reporting. Rather, the combination of sex, prostitution, and crime increases the audience (Dreixler, 1998: 203).

27. As Eileen Scully indicates in her work (this volume, Chapter 3), that description of white slaves at the turn of the century was incorrect.

28. The characterization of trafficked women as "products" akin to illegal narcotics or arms also fortifies the impression of women as goods rather than as free-willed human beings.

29. Women who do not fit the victim image become easily categorized as offenders (Henderson, 1998: 586).

30. If the migrant was forced to work in prostitution, a duress defense is available to charges of violating antiprostitution laws.

31. Currently, most countries expect the women who returned home, either voluntarily or involuntarily, to cover transportation costs to the trial subject to later reimburse-

ment. This makes it virtually impossible even for willing witnesses to testify against their abusers.

32. In the late 1800s, the Progressive Party offered "'Christian rehabilitation'" to women who had fallen into "white slavery" (James, 1977b: 11).

33. Studies in Italy have shown that women's nationality is related to differences in age and levels of education. The latter affect the living and working conditions of the women (Campani, 1998: 249–50). A recent IOM study also found some illuminating differences between trafficked women by nationality. Distinctions that may allow for the creation of a targeted legal response pertained, for example, to the way in which the women were recruited and how they entered the country in which they were forced to work in prostitution (IOM, 1995: 14–18).

34. A group of human rights organizations has developed *Human Rights Standards for the Treatment of Trafficked Persons* (Human Rights Caucus, 1999). They include a list of strategies designed to protect trafficked persons, including a temporary stay of deportation and no criminal prosecution for activities connected to them having been trafficked.

35. International working groups in this area and the European Parliament (EP) have made similar recommendations (European Parliament, 1996).

36. The bills are S. 600 (106th Cong., 1st sess.), entitled "International Trafficking of Women and Children Victim Protection Act of 1999," introduced by Senator Paul Wellstone, and H.R. 3244 (106th Cong., 1st sess.), entitled "Trafficking Victims Protection Act of 1999," introduced by Representative Christopher Smith.

37. The recently introduced "International Trafficking of Women and Children Victim Protection Act of 1999," S. 600, proposes to grant every trafficking victim a stay of up to three months in the United States unless the individual has an asylum petition pending or is involved in civil or criminal litigation, in which cases he or she would be permitted to stay until the proceedings are completed. The bill would also require that trafficking victims not be incarcerated and that they be granted any protection needed.

38. 42 U.S.C. § 13981 (1999). The women forced to prostitute themselves in southern Florida won restitution orders against the members of the family who trafficked them (Smith, 1999).

39. 18 U.S.C. § 3521 (1999). The program has not been designed to protect "innocent" witnesses but rather those who can provide inside information on criminal organizations.

Italy and Sweden have protection programs similar to but less comprehensive than the U.S. program. Germany also makes the protection of endangered witnesses possible through changing their identity but does not provide an explicit legal basis for such a procedure (Soiné and Soukup, 1994).

40. In *United States v. Malpeso*, 126 F.3d 92 (2nd Cir. 1997), the appellate court affirmed a district court's decision ordering the defendant to pay restitution to the FBI for relocating the victim and his family. Similar arguments have also been made in Germany (Reinhardt, n.d.: 7).

41. Cooperation of this type might be especially likely within the European Union, which has already approved plans to protect witnesses in the fight against organized crime. The government of Trinidad and Tobago has suggested a regional plan for the Caribbean (Zagaris, 1996).

42. The antitrafficking bills pending in the U.S. Congress also promise permanent residency.

43. This language is taken from recommendation No. 19 issued by the Committee on the Elimination of Discrimination against Women, which suggests that states provide support services to victims of violence (U N. Centre for Human Rights, 1994: 31).

44. Trafficking victims from Eastern Europe and the former Soviet Union are generally more highly educated than women from Southeast Asia (Shelley, 1999: 1). Therefore, their education and support needs will be different from those of women who did not complete secondary schooling.

45. A similar concern had been voiced during the white slave era (Daly, 1988: 173).

46. In many countries, the unemployment rate for women is a multiple of that for men (IOM and International Centre for Migration Policy Development, 1999: 68).

REFERENCES

agisra. 1990. *Frauenhandel und Prostitutionstourismus.* München: Trickster Verlag.

Altink, Sietske. 1995. *Stolen Lives: Trading Women into Sex and Slavery.* London: Scarlet Press.

Anderson, Malcolm, Monica den Boer, Peter Cullen, William Gilmore, Charles Raab, and Neil Walker. 1995. *Policing the European Union.* Oxford: Clarendon Press.

Berkovitch, Nitza. 1999. *From Motherhood to Citizenship: Women's Rights and International Organizations.* Baltimore: Johns Hopkins University Press.

Bindman, Jo. 1998. "An International Perspective on Slavery in the Sex Industry." In *Global Sex Workers: Rights, Resistance, and Redefinition,* edited by K. Kempadoo and J. Doezema, 65–68. New York: Routledge.

Braun, Eva. 1989. "Zur politischen Dimension von Frauenhandel." In *Frauenhandel in Deutschland,* edited by Tübinger Projektgruppe Frauenhandel, 286–97. Bonn: Verlag J. H. W. Dietz Nachf.

Caldwell, Gillian, Steven Galster, and Nadia Steinzor. 1997. *Crime and Servitude: An Exposé of the Traffic in Women for Prostitution from the Newly Independent States.* Washington, D.C.: Global Survival Network.

Campani, Giovanna. 1998. "Trafficking for Sexual Exploitation and the Sex Business in the New Context of International Migration: The Case of Italy." *South European Society and Politics* 3:230–61.

Chant, Sylvia. 1992. "Conclusion: Towards a Framework for the Analysis of Gender-Selective Migration." In *Gender and Migration in Developing Countries,* edited by S. Chant, 197–206. London: Belhaven Press.

Chuang, Janie. 1998. "Redirecting the Debate over Trafficking in Women: Definitions, Paradigms, and Contexts." *Harvard Human Rights Journal* 11:65–107.

Connelly, Mark Thomas. 1980. *The Response to Prostitution in the Progressive Era.* Chapel Hill: University of North Carolina Press.

Council of the European Union. 1997. *Joint Action to Combat Trafficking in Human Beings and Sexual Exploitation of Children.* Joint Action 97/154/JHA, February 24.

Daly, Kathleen. 1988. "The Social Control of Sexuality: A Case Study of the Criminalization of Prostitution in the Progressive Era." In *Research in Law, Deviance, and Social Control*, edited by S. Spitzer and A. Scull, 9:171–206. Greenwich, Conn.: JAI Press.

Davis, Nanette J., ed. 1993. *Prostitution: An International Handbook on Trends, Problems, and Policies*. Westport, Conn.: Greenwood Press.

Demleitner, Nora V. 1994. "Forced Prostitution: Naming an International Offense." *Fordham International Law Journal* 18:163–97.

———. 1997. "The Fallacy of Social 'Citizenship,' or the Threat of Exclusion." *Georgetown Immigration Law Journal* 12:35–74.

Doezema, Jo. 1998. "Forced to Choose: Beyond the Voluntary v. Forced Prostitution Dichotomy." In *Global Sex Workers: Rights, Resistance, and Redefinition*, edited by K. Kempadoo and J. Doezema, 34–50. New York: Routledge.

Dreixler, Markus. 1998. *Der Mensch als Ware*. Frankfurt am Main: Peter Lang.

Edwards, Susan. 1997. "The Legal Regulation of Prostitution—a Human Rights Issue." In *Rethinking Prostitution*, edited by G. Scambler and A. Scambler, 57–82. London: Routledge.

European Parliament. 1996. "Resolution on Trafficking in Human Beings." A4–0326/95. In *Official Journal of the European Communities* No. C 32/88–93 February 5.

Fitzpatrick, Joan. 1994. "The Use of International Human Rights Norms to Combat Violence against Women." In *Human Rights of Women: National and International Perspectives*, edited by R. Cook, 532–71. Philadelphia: University of Pennsylvania Press.

Garland, David. 1996. "The Limits of the Sovereign State." *British Journal of Criminology* 36:445–71.

Gillan, Audrey. 1999. "Dutch Make Oldest Profession Just a Job." *Guardian*, October 30.

Godfrey, Tom. 1998a. "Blitz on Foreign Strippers: Feds Require Interview before Arrival." *Toronto Sun*, June 24.

———. 1998b. "Woman Was Sex Slave." *Toronto Sun*, July 16.

———. 1999. "Strip Their Rights: Peelers Claim Refugee Status." *Toronto Sun*, July 22.

Gorham, Deborah. 1978. "The 'Maiden Tribute of Modern Babylon' Re-examined: Child Prostitution and the Idea of Childhood in Late-Victorian England." *Victorian Studies* 21:353–69.

Haft, Marilyn G. 1977. "Legal Arguments: Prostitution Laws and the Constitution." In *The Politics of Prostitution*, 2d ed., edited by J. James, J. Withers, M. Haft, S. Theiss, and M. Owen, 20–36. Seattle: Social Research Associates.

Hebenton, Bill, and Jon Spencer. 1998. "Law Enforcement in Societies in Transition." *European Journal of Crime, Criminal Law, and Criminal Justice* 6:29–40.

Heine-Wiedenmann, Dagmar. 1992. "Konstruktion und Management von Menschenhandels-Fällen." *Monatszeitschrift für Kriminologie und Strafrechtsreform* 75 (2/3): 121–30.

Heine-Wiedenmann, Dagmar, and Lea Ackermann. 1992. *Umfeld und Ausmass des Menschenhandels mit ausländischen Mädchen und Frauen*. Stuttgart: Kohlhammer.

Heinzl, Mark. 1999. "Canada's Government Gets Skimpy with Work Visas for Exotic Dancers." *Wall Street Journal*, April 5.

Henderson, Lynne. 1998. "Co-Opting Compassion: The Federal Victim's Rights Amendment." *St. Thomas Law Review* 10:579–606.

Human Rights Caucus. N.d. *Clarification: Trafficking and Smuggling*. www. hrlawgroup.org/site/programs/traffic/No3.htm

————. 1999. *Recommendations and Commentary on the Draft Protocol to Prevent, Suppress, and Punish Trafficking in Persons, Especially Women and Children, Supplementing the United Nations Convention Against Transnational Organized Crime.* www.hrlawgroup.org/site/programs/traffic/No3.htm

International Labor Organization. 1990. *International Convention on the Protection of the Rights of All Migrant Workers and Members of Their Families,* adopted by General Assembly Resolution 45/158, December 18.

International Organization for Migration. 1995. *Trafficking and Prostitution: The Growing Exploitation of Migrant Women from Central and Eastern Europe.* Geneva: International Organization for Migration.

International Organization for Migration and International Centre for Migration Policy Development. 1999. *Migration in Central and Eastern Europe—1999 Review.* Geneva: International Organization for Migration.

James, Jennifer. 1977a. "Answers to the 20 Questions Most Frequently Asked about Prostitution." In *The Politics of Prostitution,* 2d ed., edited by J. James, J. Withers, M. Haft, S. Theiss, and M. Owen, 37–63. Seattle: Social Research Associates.

————. 1977b. "The History of Prostitution Laws." In *The Politics of Prostitution,* 2d ed., edited by J. James, J. Withers, M. Haft, S. Theiss, and M. Owen, 9–19. Seattle: Social Research Associates.

James, Jennifer, and Jean Withers. 1977. "Introduction." In *The Politics of Prostitution,* 2d ed., edited by J. James, J. Withers, M. Haft, S. Theiss, and M. Owen, xiii–xviii. Seattle: Social Research Associates.

Kelker, Brigitte. 1993. "Die Situation von Prostituierten im Strafrecht und ein freiheitliches Rechtsverständnis-Betrachtung der Situation nach dem 26. Strafrechtsänderungsgesetz." *Kritische Vierteljahresschrift für Gesetzgebung und Rechtswissenschaft* 76 (3): 289–312.

Lipka, Susanne. 1989. *Das käufliche Glück in Südostasien: Heiratshandel und Sextourismus,* 3d ed. Münster: Verlag Westfälisches Dampfboot.

Martin, Michael T. 1999. "'Fortress Europe' and Third World Immigration in the Post–Cold War Global Context." *Third World Quarterly* 20:821–37.

Murray, Alison. 1998. "Debt-Bondage and Trafficking: Don't Believe the Hype." In *Global Sex Workers: Rights, Resistance, and Redefinition,* edited by K. Kempadoo and J. Doezema, 51–64. New York: Routledge.

Pickup, Francine. 1998. "More Words but No Action?: Forced Migration and Trafficking of Women." In *Gender and Migration,* edited by C. Sweetman, 44–51. Oxford: Oxfam.

Rayanakorn, Kobkul. 1995. *Special Study on Laws Relating to Prostitution and Traffic in Women.* Bangkok: Research and Action Project on Traffic in Women.

Raymond, Janice G., and Coalition Against Trafficking in Women. 1995. *Report to the Special Rapporteur on Violence against Women.* www.uri.edu/artsci/ wms/hughes/catw

Reanda, Laura. 1991. "Prostitution as a Human Rights Question: Problems and Prospects of United Nations Actions." *Human Rights Quarterly* 13:202–28.

Reinhardt, Andreas J. n.d. "Frauenhandel-eine moderne Form des Slavenhandels (Teil 2)." *MFDP* 265:4–8.

Rosenberg, Amy S. 1998. "13 Women Arraigned in Prostitution Case." *Philadelphia Inquirer,* October 9.

"Russian Envoy on Immigrants, Peace Process, Iranian Arms." 1999. *Yedi'ot Aharonot* (Tel Aviv), March 1.

Schroeder, Friedrich-Christian. 1995. "Irrwege aktionistischer Gesetzgebung-das 26. StÄG (Menschenhandel)." *Juristenzeitung* 5:231–38.

Seabrook, Jeremy. 1996. *Travels in the Skin Trade: Tourism and the Sex Industry.* London: Pluto Press.

Shelley, Louise. 1999. "Human Trafficking: Defining the Problem." *Organized Crime Watch—Russia* 1 (2): 1–2.

"A Single Market in Crime." 1999. *Economist.* http://www.economist.com/editorial/free forall/current/sa3284.html (visited October 16, 1999).

Skrobanek, Siriporn, Nataya Boonpakdee, and Chutima Jantateero. 1997. *The Traffic in Women: Human Realities of the International Sex Trade.* London: Zed Books.

Smith, Stephanie. 1999. "Women Smuggled into U.S., Forced into Prostitution Try to Recoup $1M." In *Palm Beach Daily Business Review,* April 8.

Soiné, Michael, and Otmar Soukup. 1994. "'Identitätsänderung,' Anfertigung und Verwendung von 'Tarnpapieren.'" *Zeitschrift für Rechtspolitik* 12:466–70.

Sterk-Elifson, Claire, and Carole A. Campbell. 1993. "The Netherlands." In *Prostitution: An International Handbook on Trends, Problems, and Policies,* edited by N. Davis, 191–206. Westport, Conn.: Greenwood Press.

Stewart, Alison N. 1998. "Report from the Roundtable on the Meaning of 'Trafficking in Persons': A Human Rights Perspective." *Women's Rights Law Reporter* 20:11–19.

Streiber, Petra. 1998. *Internationaler Frauenhandel.* Berlin: Freie Universität Berlin.

Toepfer, Susan Jeanne, and Bryan Stuart Wells. 1994. "The Worldwide Market for Sex: A Review of International and Regional Legal Prohibitions Regarding Trafficking in Women." *Michigan Journal of Gender and Law* 2:83–128.

Tyner, James A. 1996. "Constructions of Filipina Migrant Entertainers." *Gender, Place, and Culture* 3:77–93.

U.N. Centre for Human Rights. 1994. *Fact Sheet No. 22—Discrimination against Women: The Convention and the Committee.* Geneva: U.N. Centre for Human Rights.

U.N. Commission on Human Rights, Subcommission on Prevention of Discrimination and Protection of Minorities. 1995. *Report of the Working Group on Contemporary Forms of Slavery on its twentieth session. Draft programme of action on the traffic in persons and the exploitation of the prostitution of others.* E/CN.4/Sub.2/1995/28/Add.1, June 13.

U.N. General Assembly, Ad Hoc Committee on the Elaboration of a Convention against Transnational Organized Crime (First Session—Vienna, January 19–29, 1999). 1999. *Draft Elements for an International Legal Instrument against Illegal Trafficking and Transport of Migrants (Proposal Submitted by Austria and Italy).* A/AC.254/4/Add.1, December 15.

U.S. Commission on Immigration Reform. 1997. *Immigration and the CNMI.* Washington, D.C.: GPO.

U.S. Department of Justice, Office of Justice Programs, Office for Victims of Crime. 1996. *Victims of Gang Violence: A New Frontier in Victim Services.* Washington, D.C.: U.S. Department of Justice.

U.S. House of Representatives, Subcommittee on International Operations and Human Rights. 1999. *Hearing on "Trafficking of Women and Children in the International Sex Trade."* Testimony of Theresa Loar, Director, President's Interagency Council on Women and Senior Coordinator for International Women's Issues, U.S. Department of State, September 14.

Vernez, Georges. n.d. "National Security and Migration: How Strong the Link?" Manuscript in author's possession.

Wijers, Marjan. 1998. "Women, Labor, and Migration: The Position of Trafficked Women and Strategies for Support." In *Global Sex Workers: Rights, Resistance, and Redefinition,* edited by K. Kempadoo and J. Doezema, 60–78. New York: Routledge.

Wijers, Marjan, and Lin Lap-Chew. 1997. *Trafficking in Women: Forced Labour and Slavery-Like Practices in Marriage, Domestic Labour, and Prostitution.* Anraad: Foundation Against Trafficking in Women and Global Alliance Against Traffic in Women.

Wilson, Catherine. 1998. "20 Women Forced into Prostitution." Associated Press, April 24.

Zagaris, Bruce. 1996. "Trinidad Government Leads Witness Protection Initiative." *International Enforcement Law Reporter* 12:266–68.

Contributors

Peter Andreas is a professor of political science and international studies at Brown University in Providence, Rhode Island. He is the author, coauthor, and coeditor of eight books, including *Policing the Globe: Criminalization and Crime Control in International Relations* (2006) and *Sex, Drugs, and Body Counts: The Politics of Numbers in Global Crime and Conflict* (2010). Forthcoming with Oxford University Press is his book on the politics of smuggling in America, tentatively titled "Smuggler Nation: Illicit Trade and the Making of America."

Ko-Lin Chin is a professor in the School of Criminal Justice at Rutgers University. He has written several books on Chinese organized crime, gangs, and drug trade, including *Smuggled Chinese: Clandestine Immigration to the United States* (1999) and *Heijin: Organized Crime, Business, and Politics in Taiwan* (2003). Dr. Chin is currently writing a book about drug trade in the Wa region of the Golden Triangle and conducting a study on the cross-border drug trafficking along the China-Burma border.

John Dale is an assistant professor of sociology at George Mason University in Fairfax, Virginia. His forthcoming book *Free Burma: Transnational Legal Action and Corporate Accountability* argues that bringing a transnationalist perspective of justice to the national legal systems is a fundamental dynamic of globalization that can aid individuals "from below" with resources to defend and advance human rights. He currently serves as chair of the Global Division of the Society for the Study of Social Problems.

Nora V. Demleitner is a dean and professor of law at Hofstra University School of Law in Long Island, New York. Dean Demleitner has coauthored several publications on issues of criminal law and justice, including *Replacing Incarceration: The Need for Dramatic Change* (2009) and *Terms of Imprisonment: Treating the Noncitizen Offender Equally* (2009). She is currently an editor of the *Federal*

Sentencing Reporter and serves on the executive editorial board of the *American Journal of Comparative Law.*

James O. Finckenauer is a professor in the School of Criminal Justice at Rutgers University in New Brunswick, New Jersey. His is the author of *Mafia and Organized Crime: A Beginner's Guide* (2007). He is currently researching transnational organized crime and sex trafficking, cultural deviance, and the culture of lawfulness in Russia.

H. Richard Friman is a professor of political science and director of the Center for Transnational Justice at Marquette University in Milwaukee, Wisconsin. His recent books include *Crime and the Global Economy* (2007) and *Challenges and Paths to Global Justice* (2007). His current research focuses on the intersection of the legal and illegal global economies, politics of migration and crime, and the illicit global economy.

Barak Kalir is a postdoctoral researcher at the Amsterdam Institute for Social Research at the University of Amsterdam. His current publications include *Finding Jesus in the Holy Land and Taking Him Back Home to China* (2009) and "The Conversion of Chinese Migrant Workers to Evangelical Christianity in the Jewish State" (working paper series, 2009). He currently coordinates the research program Illegal but Licit: Transnational Flows and Permissive Polities in Asia at University of Amsterdam.

Khalid Koser is an associate dean, head of the New Issues in Security Programme, and director of the New Issues in Security Course (NISC) at the Geneva Centre for Security Policy. His recent publication *International Migration: A Very Short Introduction* (2008) focuses on the global phenomenon of human migration, both illegal and legal, and the ways in which migration is linked with other global concerns such as development, human rights, and poverty. He currently serves as the coeditor of the *Journal of Refugee Studies* and on the editorial board of *Ethnic and Racial Studies, Forced Migration Review,* and *Global Governance.*

Rey Koslowski is an associate professor of political science and public policy at the University at Albany. He is the author of *Global Mobility and the Quest for an Internatonal Migration Regime* (2008) and *Towards an International Regime for Mobility and Security* (2006). His current research project, "Global Mobility Regimes," explores the economic, political, and security dimensions of global human mobility, which includes international migration and short-term international travel.

David Kyle is an associate professor of sociology at University of California, Davis, and the executive director of the Gifford Center for Population Studies (UCD). He is the author of *Transnational Peasants: Migrations, Networks, and Ethnicity in Andean Ecuador* (2000), which developed the concept of "migration merchants" and their role in a wider migration industry. His current book project is entitled "Human Traffic: Imagining Mobility in Unsettling Times."

Zai Liang is a professor of sociology at the University of New York in Albany. His work has been recognized by awards such as the Dorothy Swaine Thomas Award (Population Association of America). His recent publications include *Frontiers in Demographic Research* (under contract with People's University of China Press) and *Internal Migration in China in the Reform Era: Patterns, Policies, and Challenges* (2007). His current research projects focus on internal migration in China and international migration from China to the United States.

Kamal Sadiq is a professor of political science at University of California, Irvine. He is the author of *Paper Citizens: How Illegal Immigrants Acquire Citizenship in Developing Countries* (2010). His current research focuses on illegal immigration, citizenship, and the concept of "documentary citizenship."

Eileen P. Scully is a professor at Bennington College and senior online instructor at Norwich University. She is the author of *Bargaining with the State from Afar: American Citizenship in Treaty Port China* (2001). In 2005, she was awarded the Eugene Ascher Distinguished Teaching Prize, given annually by the American Historical Association.

David Spener is an associate professor of sociology and anthropology at Trinity University in San Antonio, Texas. His most recent book is *Clandestine Crossings: Migrants and Coyotes on the Texas-Mexico Border* (2009). He currently coordinates the Languages Across the Curriculum Program at Trinity University.

Eric Tagliacozzo is an associate professor of history at Cornell University. His most recent publication is *Secret Trades, Porous Borders: Smuggling and States along a Southeast Asian Frontier, 1865–1915* (2005). He received the competitive Smithsonian/CAORC Grant for research in Yemen and Southeast Asia in 2006.

Wenzhen Ye received a Ph.D. in sociology from the University of Utah and conducted postdoctoral work at Princeton University. He is a professor of economics at Xiamen University, China. His main research areas are demography of China and the Asian American population.

Index

military: and borders, 24, 34, 154, 167, 178;
of Myanmar, 45–47; and prostitution, 112,
113, 115, 121, 123, 126–27; Taiwanese,
220
mining, 88, 90, 93, 109, 114
Mogadishu, Somalia, 262
Mohawk Indians, 9
Moldova, 277
money-laundering, 37, 63, 127, 310, 321
moneylenders, 41–42, 51. *See also* debt
morality, 2, 24–25, 35–36, 116, 120, 360
Morona Santiago, Ecuador, 40
Moscow, 7, 314
Mukden, China, 123
Mumbai, India, 244
Myanmar. *See* Burma
Myanmar Holdings Company Ltd., 46

Nairobi, Kenya, 114
National Anti-Smuggling Program, 143
National League for Democracy, 46
Native Americans, 114, 222
Nepal, 3, 238, 244, 277
Netherlands, 20, 92, 93, 115, 262, 268; and
prostitution, 361, 371, 373
Netherlands Indies, 89, 100
New Delhi, India, 110
New Guinea, 95, 99, 100
New Mexico, 146, 147
New York, 20, 216, 352; Chinatown, 205, 208,
218, 220, 222, 223–24, 225; and Chinese
smugglers, 189, 192; and Ecuadorians,
40–41; enforcers in, 65; and garment and
sex workers, 54; labor market in, 205;
restaurants and garment factories in, 221;
Russian organized crime in, 63–64
New Zealand, 210
Nias, Indonesia, 95
Nicaragua, 69
9/11 attacks, 12, 68, 69, 153–54, 162, 249
9/11 Commission, 12
Nogales, Arizona, 145, 147
North Africans, 6, 115
North America, 54, 76, 80, 113, 262, 263
North American Free Trade Agreement, 139
North Borneo, 94, 97–98

Oasis Program, 177–78, 180n8
Obama administration, 79
Okinawa, Japan, 329
Operation Blockade, 146, 163
Operation Disruption, 151
Operation Gatekeeper, 146, 147
Operation Global Reach, 69
Operation Hold-the-Line, 146, 147
Operation Rio Grande, 147, 163, 167
Operation Safeguard, 147
Operation Sea Dragon, 192–93
Operation Seek and Keep, 9
Opium War, 113, 209
Organization for Security and Cooperation in
Europe (OSCE), 70
Osaka, Japan, 329, 341, 343

Pacific islands, 110
Pacific Northwest, 112
Pakistan, 20, 234, 235, 237, 244, 245, 247–50
Pakistani Federal Investigation Agency, 237
Palembang, Indonesia, 100
Palestine, 122, 126
Palestinians, 277, 284
Panama, 69, 126, 187, 198
Pasir, Borneo, 98
passports, 5, 42, 235, 237, 244–45, 249. *See also*
documents
Pegatan, Borneo, 98
Penang, Malaysia, 91
Persian Gulf states, 244, 246
Peru, 69, 187
Peruvians, 335
Peshawar, Pakistan, 244
Philippines, 3, 110, 208, 277, 288; and
prostitution, 126, 342, 365, 376n5
Phoenix, Arizona, 148
Pingtan, China, 212, 219
Poland, 115, 126
Pontianak, Indonesia, 100
prostitution, 3, 7, 65, 118, 161, 352–76; and
abolitionists vs. regulationists, 118, 128; after
World War II, 126–28; and autonomy, 111;
and bribery, 243–44; and Brussels and Madrid
conferences, 120, 121; and central and
Eastern Europeans, 112; and children, 5, 66,